Organized Secularism in the United States

Religion and Its Others

Studies in Religion, Nonreligion, and Secularity

Edited by
Stacey Gutkowski, Lois Lee, and Johannes Quack

Volume 6

Organized Secularism in the United States

New Directions in Research

Edited by
Ryan T. Cragun, Christel Manning
and Lori L. Fazzino

DE GRUYTER

This work is licensed under a Creative Commons Attribution-NonCommercial-No-Derivatives 4.0 License. For details go to https://creativecommons.org/licenses/by-nc-nd/4.0/.

ISBN 978-3-11-064403-6
e-ISBN (PDF) 978-3-11-045865-7
e-ISBN (EPUB) 978-3-11-044195-6
ISSN 2330-6262

This volume is text- and page-identical with the hardback published in 2017.

Library of Congress Cataloging-in-Publication Data
A CIP catalog record for this book has been applied for at the Library of Congress.

Bibliographic information published by the Deutsche Nationalbibliothek
The Deutsche Nationalbibliothek lists this publication in the Deutsche Nationalbibliografie; detailed bibliographic data are available on the Internet at http://dnb.dnb.de.

© 2019 Ryan T. Cragun, Christel Manning and Lori L. Fazzino, published by Walter de Gruyter GmbH, Berlin/Boston
The book is published with open access at www.degruyter.com.

Printing and binding: CPI books GmbH, Leck
♾ Printed on acid-free paper
Printed in Germany

www.degruyter.com

Phil Zuckerman
Preface

On Nov. 19–20, 2014, forty-five scholars, from nine different countries, gathered at Pitzer College in Claremont, California, for the third International Conference of the Nonreligion and Secularity Research Network (NSRN). The theme of the conference was "Explaining Nonreligion and Secularity in the U.S. and Beyond," and the scope of the papers presented was impressively broad: from Lori Beaman's keynote address on church-state battles in Quebec, to Catherine Caldwell-Harris's talk on low levels of religiosity among college students in Turkey, and from Penny Edgell's look at anti-atheist sentiment in the United States, to Kevin Lenehan's analysis of secularization in Australia – various aspects of nonreligion and secularity were explored, both theoretically and empirically, and from a multiplicity of disciplinary lenses.

But one topic at the conference definitely stood out: collective, organized nonreligion and secularism. Amidst the historical narratives, political analyses, sociological data, psychological models, and meta typologizing, there was a clear prominence of papers at the conference that looked at how and why nonreligious, anti-religious, and/or secular people – of varying shades and hues – come together collectively. The common concerns underlying these papers were along the following lines of inquiry: what social movements and communal institutions are secular or nonreligious individuals coming together to create in order to serve their social, communal, and/or political needs and interests? And just what exactly are those needs and interests? How are they being met?

Given the deep interest in organized secularism that was evident at the conference – and given the recent growth of social movements created by and for nonreligious people – it was clear to meeting participants Christel Manning, Ryan Cragun, and Lori Fazzino that a book bringing together and publishing those papers presented at the conference addressing these issues within the study of secularity, secularism, and nonreligion would be timely.

Hence, this volume.

Organized Secularism in the United States brings together thirteen papers looking at different aspects and angles of collective secularity. It is a welcome addition to the burgeoning field of secular/nonreligious studies, an interdisciplinary endeavor which seeks to understand the lives, worldviews, beliefs, opinions, values, challenges, and activities of nonreligious people. The scholarly focus of secular/nonreligious studies is placed upon the meanings, forms, relevance, and impact of political secularism, philosophical skepticism, and personal and cultural secularity – and all of these matters, in one manifestation or another, and in varying degrees – are delved into in the chapters ahead.

Since Barry Kosmin established the Institute for the Study of Secularism in Society and Culture at Trinity College in 2005, and Lois Lee and Stephen Bullivant founded the Nonreligion and Secularity Research Network in 2008 while at Cambridge University and Oxford University respectively, scholarly attention to the secular/nonreligious has been blossoming. Significant developments include the following: in 2011, the open-access, peer-reviewed academic journal *Secularism and Nonreligion* was launched; also in 2011, a Secular Studies department was established at Pitzer College; in 2012, the Anthropology Department of the London School of Economics launched a "Programme for the Study of Religion and Non-Religion;" also in 2012, New York University Press launched a Secular Studies book series and Palgrave Macmillan launched a book series on "Histories of the Sacred and the Secular, 1700–2000;" in 2014, De Gruyter launched a book series on "Religion and Its Others: Studies in Religion, Nonreligion, and Secularity" (of which this volume is a part); in 2016, the University of Miami endowed a chair in the study of atheism and secularism.

Subsequent to the NSRN conference of 2014 at Pitzer College, from which this book springs, an abundance of academic conferences have been held with a focus on the secular, including: "Approaching Nonreligion: Conceptual, methodical, and empirical approaches in a new research field" (2016) at the University of Zürich, Switzerland; "The End of Religion?" (2016) at the University of San Diego; "Secularisms and the Formations of Religion in Asia: Pluralism, Globalization, and Modernities" (2016) at Queen's University, Belfast; "Varieties of Secular Society" (2015) at the Institut Francais de Londres, United Kingdom; "Secularism and Religion in Modern Europe" (2015) at the Escuela Espanola de Historia y Arqueologia, Italy; "Women's Religious Agency: Negotiating Secularism and Multiculturalism in Everyday Life" (2015) at Uppsala University, Sweden; "Old Religion and New Spirituality: Continuity and Changes in the Background of Secularization" (2015) at the University of Tartu, Estonia.

In sum, the academic study of secularity, secularism, and non-religion is currently in full swing, and this volume both reflects and bolsters this burgeoning scholarly enterprise.

Table of Contents

Ryan Cragun & Christel Manning
Introduction —— 1

Charles Louis Richter
"I Know It When I See It:" Humanism, Secularism, and Religious Taxonomy —— 13

Michael Rectenwald
Mid-Nineteenth-Century Secularism as Modern Secularity —— 31

Lori L. Fazzino and Ryan T. Cragun
"Splitters!": Lessons from Monty Python for Secular Organizations in the US —— 57

John R. Shook
Recognizing and Categorizing the Secular: Polysecularity and Agendas of Polysecularism —— 87

Amanda Schutz
Organizational Variation in the American Nonreligious Community —— 113

Aislinn Addington
Building Bridges in the Shadows of Steeples: Atheist Community and Identity Online —— 135

Jesse M. Smith
Communal Secularity: Congregational Work at the Sunday Assembly —— 151

Jacqui Frost
Rejecting Rejection Identities: Negotiating Positive Non-religiosity at the Sunday Assembly —— 171

Joseph Langston, Joseph Hammer, Ryan Cragun & Mary Ellen Sikes
Inside The Minds and Movement of America's Nonbelievers: Organizational Functions, (Non)Participation, and Attitudes Toward Religion —— 191

Björn Mastiaux
A Typology of Organized Atheists and Secularists in Germany and the United States —— 221

Dusty Hoesly
Your Wedding, Your Way: Personalized, Nonreligious Weddings through the Universal Life Church —— 253

Nicholas J. MacMurray & Lori L. Fazzino
Doing Death Without Deity: Constructing Nonreligious Tools at the End of Life —— 279

Barry Kosmin
Old Questions and New Issues for Organized Secularism in the United States —— 301

Index —— 319

Ryan Cragun & Christel Manning
Introduction

What would happen to a high school senior deep in the bible belt of the United States if they told their high school administrators that they would contact the American Civil Liberties Union (ACLU) if the school had a prayer at his high school graduation? This isn't a hypothetical scenario – it happened in 2011. Damon Fowler, a senior at Bastrop High School in Louisiana, informed the superintendent of the school district that he knew school-sponsored prayer was illegal and that he would contact the ACLU if the school went ahead with a planned, school-sponsored prayer at the graduation ceremony. Damon's threat was leaked to the public. What followed were death threats from community members and fellow students, weeks of harassment, and eventually his parents disowning him and kicking him out of their home.

One more thing happened, which is why we recount this story at the beginning of this book on organized secularism: the secular community came together to support Damon. As his story made its way into the local, national, and eventually international press, nonreligious[1] and/or secular individuals made offers of a place to stay, protection, and transportation, and a college fund was set up for Damon since his parents had cut him off financially. Various secular organizations explicitly offered Damon help. The Freedom From Religion Foundation gave him a $1,000 college scholarship and other organizations volunteered to help him legally.

Damon's story should be surprising in a country that prides itself as a melting pot of races, ethnicities, cultures, and religions. Yet, it is also a not entirely uncommon scenario in the United States, where atheists' morality is esteemed at about the same level as is rapists' (Gervais, Shariff, and Norenzayan 2011) and only about 50% of Americans would vote for an atheist for President (Edgell, Gerteis, and Hartmann 2006). Damon's story also serves to highlight several important characteristics of the organized, secular community in the US. First, perhaps to the surprise of many Americans, there actually is an organized secular community in the US. While the numbers are still quite small (see below) relative to the total proportion of the US population that is nonreligious, those involved in the community are not insignificant. Second, the response of the organized secular community to Damon's situation also illustrates that organized secular-

---

[1] Many people use the terms non-religious and secular interchangeably, but scholars continue to debate their precise meaning.

ism in the US is often reactive. Many of the formal organizations exist specifically because they are reacting to the privileging of religion in American culture and the law (Blumenfeld, Joshi, and Fairchild 2008; Schlosser 2003). Likewise, many of these organizations spring into action precisely when religious privilege moves from the abstract or implicit into the concrete and blatant, undermining the rights of secular individuals. Third, secular organizations in the US share a common goal: to normalize nonreligiosity. In other words, the aim of many of these organizations is to make it so people who are not religious, whether they are atheists,[2] agnostics,[3] or those who are unaffiliated with any religion, can live ordinary lives without fear of unequal and discriminatory treatment. While in many ways Damon Fowler's story is a tragedy – a failure of public schools to follow the law and protect minorities and a tragic failure of parental support – his story also helps delineate the characteristics of organized secularism.

Before we go much further, we should be clear in what we mean by "organized secularism." The term "secular" originated to distinguish the things of this world (e.g., work, food, sex) from religious things (e.g., prayer, heaven, god). Secular can most simply be defined as "not religious" (though how we determine what is religious and what isn't remains a matter of debate). "Secularism," in its primary meaning, is a theory, philosophy, or ideology that distinguishes the secular from other (usually religious) phenomena.[4] In its most common use, secularism refers to a political philosophy that there should be a separation between religions and government (Berlinerblau 2013). The logic behind such a separation is that, when government and religion are intertwined, typically there is favoritism toward certain religions and therefore implicit or explicit discrimination against other religions and those with no religion. Secularism can and does manifest itself in many ways around the world, from French laïcité (Bowen 2013), to Turkey's unique restrictions on Islam despite being a predominantly Muslim country (Hurd 2013), to the supposed "wall of separation" that exists in the US (Smith 2013). Regardless of the particular manifestation of secularism, the idea remains that the safest way to manage religiously pluralistic populations is with a government that is separate and distinct from religion.

Secularism in the sense described above is a neutral term. Over time, however, partly in reaction to cultural and/or state resistance to such neutrality, sec-

---

[2] By "atheist" we mean those who do not have a belief in a god.
[3] By "agnostic" we mean those who do not believe there is any way to gain knowledge about a god.
[4] See the Oxford Dictionary of Atheism for more detailed discussion of these and related definitions.

ularism has acquired a second, more ideological meaning: not just the separation of religious and non-religious phenomena, but the celebration and promotion of the secular as a worldview or value system that is the functional equivalent of religion. Secularism, then, is what nonreligious people believe and practice. Just as religion comes in a variety of different flavors such as Christianity, Hinduism, or Islam, there are different kinds of secularism including Humanism, Atheism, and Freethinkers. And just as religious people tend to see their particular worldview as the truth, or at least the most sensible way to live, so do secular people. The difference is that secularism, at least in the United States, is a minority worldview. It is secularism in this second sense that is of interest in this volume.

By combining "secularism" with "organized," we are making explicit reference to the many ways that individuals have come together around one common interest – their shared desire to celebrate that they are not religious and find ways to normalize their nonreligiosity. Specific aims of secular organizations may vary (see Chapter 7, Schutz), as some bring secular individuals together to socialize and others gather for educational purposes or for political action. But all secular organizations in the US have at least one shared goal: the normalizing of nonreligion in the US (Cragun 2015b). Thus, by "organized secularism" we are referring to groups of people who have some sense of togetherness and are organized around their shared desire to be openly and safely secular in the US. All of the chapters in this volume relate to organized secularism in this sense, though how individual authors define secularism varies slightly and is explained in those chapters.

As just noted, organized secularism takes many forms – from regular meetings in bars to discuss philosophy to secular parenting groups and charitable organizations. While Damon Fowler's story illustrates how organized secular groups in the US can come together, there is another side to organized secularism in the US. Many of the now prominent, national secular organizations have been around for decades, and their relationships with other prominent secular organizations have not always been amicable (see Chapter 4, Fazzino and Cragun). There is a long and somewhat sordid history of infighting, competing over donors, splintering, and tension among these organizations (see Chapter 3, Rechtenwald). Perhaps still the most well-known leader of a secular organization in the US – at least among a certain generation of Americans – was Madalyn Murray O'Hair, who for a period in the 1980s was billed as "the most hated woman in America" (O'Hair and O'Hair 1991). O'Hair gained fame (and notoriety) for her involvement in a court case, *Murray vs. Curlett* (later combined with *Abington School District v. Schempp*), which banned school official led Bible reading in public schools. O'Hair later created several organizations to fight for the rights of atheists and other nonreligious Americans. O'Hair literally disappeared from the organized secularism movement when she was abducted by an employee, along with one of her sons and a granddaughter, extorted for money she had raised through her secular organizations, and then murdered along with her son and granddaughter (LeBeau 2003). Yet her legacy lives on in the secular organization she founded, American Atheists, which is widely known as the secular organization that places prominent billboards espousing secular values around Christmas, among other provocative actions. Several chapters in this volume (Chapter 2, Richter; Chapter 3, Rectenwald, and Chapter 4, Fazzino and Cragun) provide detailed information on the tensions that have existed among secular organizations since the term "secular" was first coined in the mid 19th century.

The goal of this volume is to address a lacuna in the scholarly study of organized secularism. While organized secularism in its various forms is close to 200 years old, to date there is very little social scientific research on the topic, though there is a growing body of historical research (Hecht 2004; Jacoby 2005; Royle 1980; Warren 1966). The aim of this volume is to expand early efforts to theorize the discussion of organized secularism (see Campbell 1971), from organizational theory to social movement and social identity theory, as well as to present fresh empirical data. We hope the various chapters in this volume further our understanding of this growing and important movement.

Organized secularism has gained more visibility in recent years, but it is difficult to put actual numbers on its growth. While surveys show the nonreligious population has grown significantly in the last two decades (Pew Forum on Religion 2014), many secular individuals do not join organizations (see Chapter 9, Langston et al.). To date, there is no nationally representative survey with a large enough sample of nonreligious individuals that has asked whether such individuals are part of a secular organization. The closest thing there may be to this is a question asked by the Pew Forum on Religion in a 2012 survey which asked survey participants how important it is for them to belong to a community of people who share their beliefs and values; 49% of the nonreligious said it was very important (Pew Forum on Religion 2012). If we overlay that number onto the nonreligious population in the US (which was the population of interest in that Pew survey), that would correspond to about 32 million adult Americans who would be interested in being part of a secular organization. If we limit the potentially interested population to just atheists in the US,[5] the corresponding number would be about 4 million atheist Americans who consider it very impor-

---

[5] Roughly 3% of adult Americans are atheists based on the 2014 General Social Survey (Smith, Marsden, and Kim 2012).

tant to belong to a community of people who share their beliefs and values. Based on interviews with leaders of the most prominent secular organizations in the US,[6] the actual number of members of these organizations or subscribers to their various magazines totals somewhere in the range of 50,000 to 100,000 individuals. These disparate numbers are not all that surprising when you think about them from a social movements perspective. All social movements have varied constituencies. There are core members[7] – those who are actively involved in the day-to-day activities of the various social movement organizations. Then there are the members who support the movement – often financially, but potentially in other ways – and are involved when they can be. There is also a sympathetic public – individuals who would support the movement but are either not aware of it, too busy with other things, or simply free-riding (i.e., getting the benefits from the social movement without doing any of the work). Finally, there is the unsympathetic public, or those who actually oppose the aims of the movement. For organized secularism in the US, the core leaders likely number in the hundreds, the members number in the tens of thousands, and the sympathetic public number in the tens of millions. However, the unsympathetic public numbers in the hundreds of millions. Organized secularism may be growing, but there is still a proverbial mountain to climb.

While organized secularism is a global phenomenon, we necessarily had to limit the scope of this volume. As a result, almost all of the chapters focus on the US. There are two exceptions. A chapter that compares the US and Germany (Chapter 6, Mastiaux), and a chapter that discusses the organizational dynamics in England at the time the terms "secular" and "secularism" were coined (see Chapter 3, Rectenwald) which has significant implications for later developments in the US. The decision to focus on the American context resulted from several factors. On the surface, there is the practical reason that the idea for this book grew out of an international conference held in California in 2014 and various papers about organized secularism in America that were presented there. But there's a more important theoretical reason, which was reflected in that choice of venue for the conference, and that is a perception of change in the American context. The US has long been seen as atypical in its relatively high levels of religiosity compared to other wealthy, industrialized societies, especially those in Europe. The recent dramatic increase in those claiming no reli-

---

6 See Chapter 4 for more information on the study that serves as the basis for this estimate.
7 Some of these individuals refer to themselves as "professional atheists," though not all do.

gion (often dubbed the "Nones"),[8] from between 4 and 7 percent of the US population in the mid 20th century to around 25 percent today, represents a dramatic shift from the past. While not all individuals who decline to affiliate with religion are secular and, among those who are, not all of them affiliate with secular organizations, they constitute a large and growing audience and pool of potential members for secular organizations. This means organized secularism in the US faces a very different environment than it did in the past, which is worth studying.

Limiting our focus to the US also has a methodological benefit. It enables a multi-perspective, multi-dimensional analysis of organized secularism in one particular geographical setting, which deepens our understanding and enables a richer comparative framework in the future. By focusing on the US, we don't mean to suggest that the secular movement is more highly organized in the US or that what is happening with organized secularism is more important in the US than in any other part of the world. To the contrary, there is a lot that organized secularism in the US can learn from other countries (Cragun 2015a), and there is a great deal that scholars have learned from the study of organized secularism elsewhere (e.g., see Engelke 2012, 2014; Lee 2015; Kosmin & Keysar 2007; Mumford 2014; Quack 2011; Wohlrab-Sahr 2012, 2015). We strongly encourage more research on organized secularism in other countries around the world.

This volume is organized into three sections. The first is primarily historical and theoretical. The aim is to provide some background both on the history of organized secularism but also on the terminology that is often used when describing those who would consider themselves part of the organized secular movement. The chapters in the second section offer fresh empirical data about a variety of secular organizations with an aim to better understand what they do, how they function, and what their aims are. The final section provides some insight into what secular and nonreligious individuals need and how organized secularism can help fulfill those needs. In a sense, the last section is pointing out that becoming nonreligious does require some reconfiguring of one's life. How does one manage important life transitions, like marriage and death, without the trappings of religion? Obviously it is possible, but more can

---

[8] A growing number of publications refer to the nonreligious as "nones." This label comes from a response to a survey item that asks people, "What is your religion, if any"? One of the options was "none." Those who chose this option were labeled as "nones." In line with suggestions in various publications on the nonreligious, we generally refrain from using the term "none" as it implicitly suggests that these individuals are lacking something (see Cragun and Hammer, 2011; Lee, 2012).

be done by secular organizations to provide secular alternatives to religious rituals for those individuals who want them.

The first chapter, by **Charles Richter,** takes readers on a trip through history, illustrating that definitions of terms like "secular" and "humanist" are complicated. They are complicated by the time period, the context, and, in particular, by who is using the term, as all people bring biases and agendas into discussions surrounding these topics. Questions raised in this chapter are further illuminated in the following chapter, by **Michael Rectenwald,** which describes the origins of the terms "secular" and "secularism" in mid 19th century England by George Jacob Holyoake. His chapter goes on to illustrate that, shortly after the terms were coined, debate over what they should mean arose, and – foreshadowing much of the history of organized secularism – what followed was divisions, tensions, and splits within the fledgling secular movement. The history Rectenwald describes, as well as that in the chapter by **Lori Fazzino and Ryan Cragun,** makes it clear that organized secularism is, like most social movements, contentious, with significant internal divisions. As Fazzino and Cragun point out, internal division can be but often is not a definitively negative characteristic of a social movement, as conflict has the propitious effect of making room for people of varied perspectives within a movement. This is true even if conflict may, in some sense, distract the focus of the movement from the change it wants to instead focus on what it wants to change.

The final chapter in this section, by **John Shook,** questions the way in which scholarship has conceptualized organized secularism in the past. Shook shows how previous research in secular studies has often allowed itself to be defined by theology and religion. In contrast, Shook argues that the secular predates that which is religious, supercedes it, and that those studying it (whatever "it" is) should set out their own agenda separate from religious studies, the study of religion, and theology. As Shook argues, the domain of the secular should not be contingent upon its "otherness" from religion, but rather can and should be a self-chosen collection of topics that secular scholars and scholars of secularism choose to include within this area of inquiry. To do otherwise is to continue to allow religion to control the study of that which religion should not control. Shook also illustrates that predetermined secular categories may not represent reality, and that those studying the secular need to be careful that they do not reify the realities they have created. By recognizing that the secular is not contingent upon the religious, Shook is then able to develop the ideas of 'polysecularity' and 'polysecularism', which reflect the many ways people, organizations, and nations can be secular and the varied interests and agendas that may be espoused by secularism, respectively. Shook is not the first to suggest there is variety within secularism (see, for example, the Diversity of Non-religion Project, http://www.nonreligion.net/or the Multiple Secularities Project, http://www.multiple-secularities.de/), but the terms he coins offer a fresh way to frame the idea that what is secular is not singular; it is many.

The next section offers much needed new empirical data illustrating the variety of contemporary forms of organized secularism, how they build group identity and structure, and the activities in which they engage. **Amanda Schutz**'s chapter looks inside the growing diversity of organizations that exist within the larger movement. While earlier research often depicted atheists who attend atheist groups as old, crotchety, white men (see Hunsberger 2006), Schutz's chapter illustrates that the nonreligious are far more diverse than that stereotype. Drawing on organizational theory, Schutz shows that nonreligious individuals are increasingly aware of and accepting of the fact that secular people are diverse and have varied needs. Some want to get together with other nonreligious people to have fun, while others are more interested in education or volunteering. As the number of nonreligious people grows in the US, it seems likely, based on Schutz's research, that the variety of secular organizations in any given location will continue to grow to meet the demands and interests of the nonreligious.

A number of previous studies have noted the importance of the internet for atheist and secular activism. **Aislinn Addington**'s chapter adds to this growing body of research by describing in detail how atheist identity construction, finding support for often newly adopted and marginalized secular identities, and secular organizing all rely upon the internet, at least for a sizable proportion of atheists.

A relative newcomer to organized secularism, the Sunday Assembly (SA) garnered significant media attention when it launched in 2013. **Jesse Smith**'s chapter describes the origins of the SA and argues that these "atheist churches" function to shape secular identities (at the individual and communal level), to demarcate boundaries between the secular and the religious, and to create secular communities. Of particular interest is how Smith draws connections between the structure, rituals, and functions of religious congregations and their corresponding manifestations in Assemblies.

Jacqui Frost's chapter provides a different perspective on SA, focusing on its role in helping individuals forge a secular identity. SA is attractive to many secular Americans who want to move beyond rejecting religion and build a "positive" secular community. Yet, as Frost shows, there are inherent tensions in this quest that can be difficult to reconcile. SA's explicit goal is to be "radically inclusive" while simultaneously drawing boundaries that keep spiritual and supernatural rhetoric out of the assembly. SA also engages in selective appropriation of the institutional form of "church" that eschews the hierarchy and dogma found in a religious church while attempting to replicate its ritualized, emotionally engaged communality.

The final section shifts the focus to the personal and social needs of nonreligious individuals who join these organizations. The chapter by **Joseph Langston, Joseph Hammer,** and **Ryan Cragun** provides some valuable quantitative data on the question of why some nonreligious and secular individuals belong to secular, humanist, atheist, or freethought groups and others do not. Langston et al. find that a number of factors influence membership in organized secularism, from age and sex to general opinions on what the movement should be doing. However, one of the more important findings is that there are many nonreligious and secular individuals who would be involved in organized secularism if there were groups in their local area, suggesting that there is unmet demand for organized secularism.

Bjorn Mastiaux's chapter explores the motives of individuals who do affiliate with secular organizations. Drawing on qualitative data from affiliates in Germany and the United States, he analyzes both their primary motives (e.g., the need for belonging or the desire for political change) and their dominant behavioral patterns (e.g., self oriented or other oriented), resulting in a typology of eight ideal types of organized atheists.

Religion has long offered the cultural toolkit for individuals and families to celebrate life passages such as marriage, childbirth, or death. These religious structures are so dominant in American society that even nonreligious people will often use them, either by default or because of cultural pressure. In some societies, such as Denmark, the national Church is a fairly successful provider of such resources for nonreligious individuals (Zuckerman 2008). Yet research shows that, in the US, organized religious structures often do not adequately meet the needs of and may sometimes even cause harm to nonreligious people (c.f. Smith-Stoner 2007). In recent years the nonreligious are increasingly looking to create their own symbols and meaning systems that authentically reflect their secular value systems and secular organizations can help them do that. **Dusty Hoesly**'s chapter explores how secular couples use the Universal Life Church (ULC) to create nonreligious wedding ceremonies. Yet ULC's status as a secular organization is ambiguous. Though it's teachings and practices appear to be secular, it identifies as a religious organization, albeit for entirely pragmatic reasons: US law favors religious organizations when it comes to recognizing marriages. This suggests that the rights of secular organizations in the US may still lag behind those of some of their European counterparts. The chapter by **Nick MacMurry** and **Lori Fazzino** examines how secular individuals understand death and dying and the resources they draw on to help them manage that process. The final chapter of the book, by **Barry Kosmin**, offers some concluding reflections on the issues raised in the volume and outlines an agenda for future research.

Collectively, the chapters in this volume offer a variety of insights and theoretical perspectives that can help those of us interested in organized secularism to understand more about the roots of the movement, how it currently functions, and what the future will bring for organized secularism in the US. While there are still a number of challenges for this small but growing movement to overcome, that the movement has grown to the point that it warrants serious scholarly attention suggests that organized secularism in the US has come of age.

Bibliography

Berlinerblau, Jacques. 2013. *How to Be Secular: A Call to Arms for Religious Freedom*. Reprint edition. Boston: Mariner Books.
Blumenfeld, Warren J., Khyati Y. Joshi, and Ellen E. Fairchild, eds. 2008. *Investigating Christian Privilege and Religious Oppression in the United States*. Rotterdam: Sense Publishers.
Bowen, John R. 2013. "The Indeterminacy of Laïcité: Secularism and the State in France." Pp. 163–80 in *Contesting Secularism: Comparative Perspectives*, edited by A. Berg-Sørensen. Surrey, England: Ashgate.
Burchardt, Monica, Wohlrab-Sahr, Monika, and Matthias Middell, eds. *Multiple Secularities Beyond the West: Religion and Modernity in the Global Age*. Boston and Berlin: De Gruyter, 2015.
Campbell, Colin. 2013 (1971). Towards a Sociology of Irreligion (Alcuin Academics).
Cragun, Ryan T. 2015a. *How to Defeat Religion in 10 Easy Steps: A Toolkit for Secular Activists*. Durham, North Carolina: Pitchstone Publishing.
Cragun, Ryan T. 2015b. "Time to Name a Movement?" *NSRN blog*. Retrieved May 1, 2015 (http://blog.nsrn.net/2015/05/01/time-to-name-a-movement/).
Cragun, Ryan T. and Joseph H. Hammer. 2011. "'One Person's Apostate Is Another Person's Convert': Reflections on Pro-Religion Hegemony in the Sociology of Religion." *Humanity & Society* 35(February/May):149–75.
Edgell, Penny, Joseph Gerteis, and Douglas Hartmann. 2006. "Atheists As 'Other': Moral Boundaries and Cultural Membership in American Society." *American Sociological Review* 71:211–34.
Engelke, Matthew. 2012. "An Ethnography of the British Humanist Association." ESRC End of Award Report.
Engelke, Matthew. 2014. "Christianity and the Anthropology of Secular Humanism." *Current Anthropology Supplement*, Vol. 55, pp. S292-S301.
Gervais, Will M., Azim F. Shariff, and Ara Norenzayan. 2011. "Do You Believe in Atheists? Distrust Is Central to Anti-Atheist Prejudice." *Journal of Personality and Social Psychology* 101(6):1189–1206.

Hecht, Jennifer Michael. 2004. *Doubt: A History: The Great Doubters and Their Legacy of Innovation from Socrates and Jesus to Thomas Jefferson and Emily Dickinson*. Reprint. HarperSanFrancisco.

Hunsberger, Bruce. 2006. *Atheists: A Groundbreaking Study of America's Nonbelievers*. Amherst, N.Y: Prometheus Books.

Hurd, Elizabeth Shakman. 2013. "Contested Secularism in Turkey and Iran." Pp. 181–206 in *Contesting Secularism: Comparative Perspectives*, edited by A. Berg-Sørensen. Surrey, England: Ashgate.

Jacoby, Susan. 2005. *Freethinkers: A History of American Secularism*. New York: Holt Paperbacks.

LeBeau, Bryan F. 2003. *The Atheist Madalyn Murray O'Hair*. New York: New York University Press.

Lee, Lois. 2012. "Research Note: Talking about a Revolution: Terminology for the New Field of Non-Religion Studies." *Journal of Contemporary Religion* 27(1):129–39.

Lee, Lois. 2015. *Recognizing the Non-religious, Reimagining the Secular*. Oxford University Press.

Lee, Lois, and Stephen Bullivant, eds. 2016. *Oxford Dictionary of Atheism*. Oxford University Press.

Kosmin, Barry, and Ariela Keysar. 2007. Secularity and Secularism: Contemporary International Perspectives. Hartford, ISSSC.

Mumford, Lorna. 2014. "Living Non-religious Identity in London." Pp. 153–170 in *Atheist Identities: Spaces and Social Contexts*, edited by Lori G. Beaman and Steven Tomlins. New York, New York: Springer

O'Hair, Madalyn Murray and Madalyn Murray O'Hair. 1991. *Why I Am an Atheist; Including, A History of Materialism*. Austin, Tex.: American Atheist Press.

Pew Forum on Religion. 2012. *"Nones" on the Rise: One-in-Five Adults Have No Religious Affiliation*. Washington, D.C.: The Pew Forum on Religion & Public Life. Retrieved June 3, 2013 (http://www.pewforum.org/Unaffiliated/nones-on-the-rise.aspx).

Quack, Johannes. 2012. Disenchanting India: Organized Rationalism and Criticism of Religion in India. New York: Oxford University Press.

Royle, Edward. 1980. *Radicals, Secularists and Republicans: Popular Freethought in Britain, 1866–1915*. Manchester: Totowa, N.J: Manchester University Press.

Schlosser, Lewis Z. 2003. "Christian Privilege: Breaking a Sacred Taboo." *Journal of Multicultural Counseling and Development* 31(1):44–51.

Smith-Stoner, M. "End-of-life preferences for atheists." *Journal of Palliative Medicine* 10(4):923–928.

Smith, Rogers M. 2013. "Secularism, Constitutionalism and the Rise of Christian Conservatives in the US." Pp. 113–36 in *Contesting Secularism: Comparative Perspectives*, edited by A. Berg-Sørensen. Surrey, England: Ashgate.

Smith, Tom W., Peter Marsden, and Jibum Kim. 2012. *General Social Survey*. Chicago, IL: National Opinion Research Center.

Warren, Sidney. 1966. *American Freethought, 1860–1914*. Gordian Press, Inc.

Wohlrab Sahr, Monika, and Marian Burchardt. 2012. "Multiple Secularities: Toward a Cultural Sociology of Secular Modernities." *Comparative Sociology*. Vol. 11 Issue 6, 875–909.

Zuckerman, Phil. 2008. *Society without God*. New York University Press.

Charles Louis Richter
"I Know It When I See It:" Humanism, Secularism, and Religious Taxonomy

1 Introduction

When Supreme Court Justice Potter Stewart defined "hard-core pornography" in 1964's *Jacobellis v. Ohio* with the phrase "I know it when I see it," he may as well have been talking about religion (378 US 197 (1964)). Anyone who has taken or taught a religion course in the Humanities or Social Science disciplines is likely familiar with the conceptual difficulties in defining "religion" (or "a religion," for that matter). While it often feels like a simple matter to recognize religion when one sees it, it is just as often a challenge to justify that identification. A room of students struggling to come up with the perfect definition of religion—not too broad, not too limiting, not dependent on essentialist claims, etc.—is an illuminating classroom activity. The fact is, though, that most people have not taken such a course, let alone taught one, and public discourse on religion rarely recognizes the ambiguity of religion as a discursive category. Indeed, many people do not see the project of defining religion as problematic at all. They simply know it when they see it.

For most Americans, "religion" and "church," when used as descriptive terms, retain Christian connotations of structure, belief, practice, and community. These connotations are retained when they attempt to describe quasi-religious or non-religious philosophies or movements in terms of religion. The construction in the public consciousness of "secular humanism" as a political bogeyman and threat to American religion demonstrates this propensity to use Christian forms. By examining how people outside the academic study of religion have wrestled with the relation of various forms of irreligion – especially secular humanism – to religion, we can see how the idea of secular humanism is conceptually disruptive by illuminating normative pitfalls in colloquial definitions of religion.

Ironically, Justice Stewart's legal reasoning could be held at least partially responsible for secularism being thought of as a religion. His claim, "I know it when I see it," with its colloquial, common-sense language, has been a popular and oft-cited phrase in both federal court decisions and everyday speech. Although in later cases he did attempt to further define pornography, Stewart ultimately settled on the "I know it when I see it" standard as the best solution when attempting to define the undefinable (Gewirtz 1996, 1027). Earlier in his tenure on the Supreme Court, Stewart had used a similar yardstick when it came to religion. In his lone dissent to *School District of Abington Township v. Schempp* (1963), he described the majority's decision to ban Bible readings in public schools "not as the realization of state neutrality, but rather as the establishment of a religion of secularism" (374 US 203 (1963)). Stewart did not attempt to define religion, but he knew it when he saw what he called "government support of the beliefs of those who think that religious exercises should be conducted only in private." While Stewart did not elaborate further on what he meant by "religion of secularism" beyond the claims made in the oral arguments, he most likely did not imagine secularism to be a religion in the same sense that he would consider Christianity or Buddhism to be. Rather, it was a rhetorical flourish countering the charge that Bible reading in schools violated the Establishment Clause. This particular turn of phrase happened to fit in neatly with a longstanding tradition of attempting to delegitimize the idea of secularism by framing it as an anti-religious religion, subject to the Establishment Clause, and contrary to American ideals.

2 Defining Religion and nonreligion

Scholars of religion have to acknowledge that no matter how much they might balk at it, in some circumstances, a working definition of religion is necessary. As Talal Asad reminded the academy in a 2014 interview on the twentieth anniversary of his book *Genealogies of Religion:*

> To define "religion" is (...) in a sense to try and grasp an ungraspable totality. And yet I nowhere say that these definitions are abstract propositions. I stress that definitions of religion are embedded in dialogs, activities, relationships, and institutions that are lovingly or casually maintained—or betrayed or simply abandoned. They are passionately fought over and pronounced upon by the authoritative law of the state. (Martin and Asad 2014, 12–13).

When the courts are called upon to rule on matters of religious exercise or establishment, they need to be able to inform their decisions with a reasonable definition of religion. Likewise, when courts must deal with organized irreligion, they need to be able to speak meaningfully about their relations to religion in order to apply First Amendment protections equally. Historically in the United States, humanism has been among the thorniest of these beasts. There is much confusion about what exactly it is: is it, following the framers of the original *Humanist Manifesto* of 1933, a new religion to replace the old (Kurtz 1973, 8)? Is it, following Paul Kurtz, an expression of values and a method of inquiry

(Kurtz 1983, 8)? Is it, as a federal judge recently decided, simply a religion for the purposes of the establishment clause (*American Humanist Assoc. v. Bureau of Prisons, et al.*, 3:14-CV-00565-HZ (2015))? Representatives of the American Humanist Association today would have different ideas of what the term connotes from, for example, Jesse Helms and Francis Schaeffer in 1979. Complicating matters is the problem of terminology: particularly when employed to attack irreligion, the terms "humanism," "secularism," and "secular humanism," have been used interchangeably to describe a wide range of irreligious practice and thought (see the Introduction of this volume for a discussion of some of these terms). A historical perspective on how Americans have dealt with nonreligion that looks something like religion since the 1920s can help to make sense of the confusion surrounding the use of humanism. Writers of catalogues of religions, activists, and legislators and judges have all tried to nail down this slippery concept, and in doing so have illuminated their own prejudices as to what does and does not constitute a religion.

3 Cataloguing nonreligion

The twentieth century, with its increases in globalization, in religious pluralism, and in proliferation of new religions, saw the creation of a market for books that attempted to make sense of the diverse religious landscape. These catalogues of religions, adhering to no academic rigor, comprise a particularly interesting genre, especially those volumes that focus on religions the author sees as cults, heresies, or otherwise unorthodox. They bring to mind Tomoko Masuzawa's observation that "the modern discourse on religion and religions was from the very beginning (...) a discourse of secularization; at the same time, it was clearly a discourse of othering" (Masuzawa 2005, 20). Masuzawa has shown how the language of religious studies developed in conjunction with European colonialism, reading the cultural practices of non-European peoples through the lens of Protestant Christianity. Further, Tracy Fessenden has discussed the "unmarked" nature of Christianity in discourse on religions, especially in the United States, which often implicitly conflates "Christian" and "religious" (Fessenden 2007, 4). Indeed, both the discourse of secularization and the discourse of othering are at play in these catalogues of religions. The catalogues treated religion as a category with identifiable traits held in common; in this view, a taxonomy of religions can easily be derived by identifying not only the genealogies of religion, but also how religions fulfill particular traits. Even (or especially) when written from an explicitly sectarian viewpoint, the catalogues evaluated movements, organizations, or institutions as religious insofar as they could fulfill the same criteria as the so-called world religions, most particularly Christian traditions. The writers of these catalogues were conscious of religious pluralism, and they understood that their own religion was not the only option in the spiritual marketplace. It is this recognition of secularism and pluralism that prompted some of these authors to embark on their projects in the first place; many of the catalogues are polemic in their condemnation of "alternative" religions. This deliberate othering of minority religions served to validate the author's favored tradition, but also, in the case of humanism, secularism, or even agnosticism and atheism, to apply the conceptual frameworks of religion onto non-religious phenomena. These catalogues were the product of both an environment of rampant religious pluralism as well as the discomfort such a fertile field for new religious movements provoked among the dominant traditions. Complicating matters further was the ever-changing international flow of ideas and ideologies; although the Cold War with its threat of godless Soviet Communism is the emblematic period of moral panic over atheism, Americans consistently associated nonreligion with the foreign bogeyman of the day, whether that was anarchism, fascism, or socialism (Richter 2015).

In 1928, Charles Ferguson, the former religion editor for Doubleday, Doarn, and Company, published *The Confusion of Tongues: A Review of Modern 'Isms'*, also printed under the title *The New Books of Revelations*. In its pages, he detailed more than twenty so-called cults ranging from New Thought and Mormonism to the Dukhobors to Kukluxism. Ferguson had been inspired in this project by the increase in new religious movements since the World War. "America has always been the sanctuary of amazing cults," he said, but recently they had been claiming all of the growth in a rich field of religious sentiment (Ferguson 1929, 4). These "isms"— an enormously popular term of the time for any religious, political, or social movement out of the mainstream—were gaining so many adherents due to what he called democracy's disintegrating influences on orthodox faiths. Ferguson saw the "true temper" of the American people displayed in these new movements:

> We find the genuinely religious type of mind, not in the orthodox churches, but rather in the cults; the willingness to break with home and old alignments signalizes the true faith in the spiritual mirage. The cults stand for creative religion in the hands of the people. We shall not know America until we know the religions that America has made and created (Ferguson 1929, 9).

"Cults" represented to Ferguson the enterprising spirit of the nation and according to him, there was "no more evangelical cult in modern times than the American Association for the Advancement of Atheism" (Ferguson 1929, 13).

The American Association for the Advancement of Atheism (4A, hereafter) was the first serious atheist organization in the United States, and in the 1920s inspired a short-lived burst of college atheist clubs. For a few years, its president and co-founder Charles Lee Smith gained notoriety through media stunts designed to shock religious Americans. They held a "Blamegiving" service in 1931 to replace Thanksgiving, and Smith enjoyed an extended blasphemy trial in 1928 courtesy of the state of Arkansas – the last successful conviction for blasphemy in the United States (Schmidt 2011, 219). The 4A and its affiliated groups were very successful at getting attention, but never actually had significant numbers[1]. Ferguson took them very seriously, however, and saw them as "the most clear-cut example of how a religion gets formed, what it does, and how it operates" (Ferguson 1929, 427). He examined the 4A's materials and saw in their structure a familiar form: that of a religion. The 4A professed its own five "fundamentals" to match those of the Fundamentalists: Materialism, Sensationalism, Evolution, the Existence of Evil, and Hedonism. "It is as though the apostles of the 4A had gone carefully through the catalogue of theology and set down the opposite of every conventional doctrine," Ferguson wondered (Ferguson 1929, 431). And certainly that is what Smith had done in a conscious act of satire, which speaks to a familiar or colloquial way of defining religion: both Smith and Ferguson saw religion as understandable if it could fit into a neat grid with boxes for such criteria as "holy book," "nature of the universe," "core beliefs," or "hierarchy." Smith's stated intent was not to establish 4A as a new religion, but rather the eventual elimination of all religions. But Ferguson argued that the organization was indeed a religion for three reasons.

First, he considered the very act of Smith's inversion of every aspect of fundamentalism to be religion-formation in its essence. Regardless of Smith's intentions, he had assembled a religion from its components. Second, Ferguson believed that the 4A's "solemn denial of God" produced for its adherents the same "psychic kick" that affirming God did in believers (Ferguson 1929, 432). If religion was in part an embodied phenomenon, then there was no difference between 4A and the religious fundamentalism it mocked. Rather, it offered a new, yet familiar, avenue by which to access religious experience. Finally, there was the social program of the 4A, including a campaign to remove "In God We Trust" from coins, to eliminate the military chaplaincy, and eventually to eliminate religion worldwide. Dismissing the likelihood of these plans actually

---

[1] It is unclear how many members the 4A had at its height, but there is no evidence that their actual membership was more than a few thousand, even though their literature frequently claimed millions of atheists in America.

bearing fruit, Ferguson stressed that there was "a vast gulf between the irreligious and the Atheistic" (Ferguson 1929, 435). Someone who simply professed no religion was, for him, not religious, while those who loudly proclaim their lack of religion are, ironically, participating in the religion of Atheism as established by the 4A.

A decade later, in 1938, Jan Karel Van Baalen published *The Chaos of Cults*, which, like its predecessor, would go on to multiple editions and printings over the following years. Writing just before World War II, Van Baalen was concerned with the growth of non-Christian religions in the United States, and what he believed to be the lack of teaching of orthodox Christianity. In a new edition of his text published in 1944, he worried that religious "isms" would lead to political "isms," eventually producing an American Hitler (Van Baalen [1938] 1944, 11). One of the most insidious of these cults, he maintained, was modernism, especially in what he called its humanist form.[2] Van Baalen saw modernism as essentially humanist, and thus open to an easy slide away from even nominal Christianity. What most alarmed him was how humanist hymns – that is, modernist hymns that focused on social issues – could be quickly modified to apply to any other religion, nationalism, or other ism. William George Tarrant's hymn "My Master Was a Worker" was particularly problematic for him; aside from its themes of labor and shared burden, the titular "My Master" could be replaced by any person or concept of three syllables or less, such as "Old Bismarck was a worker," "Our Lincoln was a worker," or even "Mohammed was a worker" (Van Baalen 1944, 216–17). In this way, Van Baalen feared, modernist hymns quietly promoted worship of man rather than of God. Humanism disguised as modernist theology, he believed, was eating away at Christianity from the inside.

By the 1960s, Humanism, atheism, and other non-religious worldviews were finding prominence in both the courts and the public eye (see Fazzino and Cragun, this volume). Richard R. Mathison's *Faiths, Cults, and Sects of America: From Atheism to Zen* catalogued a variety of irreligious expressions along with other new religious movements and interlopers on the American religious scene. While Mathison suspected many of his cults of simply seeking a quick buck, he saw humanism as offering an honest if empty appeal to the leftist intellectual. Although he dismissed the idea that the "quasi-religious" movement of humanism could be "called a religion in the formal sense" without providing any reasoning for this judgment, he saw its appeal to the extreme left in its "be-

---

[2] Since the 1920s, Fundamentalists defined themselves largely in opposition to theological modernism, a term that for them included the higher criticism of the Bible. In popular usage, "modernism" often encompassed all Christian denominations that were not strictly Fundamentalist. See Marsden, *Fundamentalism and American Culture*.

lief in man's moral obligation to use his intellectual and moral endowments in such a way that man everywhere can 'develop to his fullest capacity'" (Mathison 1960, 22–23). In stark contrast, he presented an account of an American Association for the Advancement of Atheism meeting, in which a dour group meets on a Saturday night to hear a speaker coldly rail against God, the Bible, and superstition until the allotted time is up:

> The speaker has finished. The notebooks are closed. The ritual has been completed. There is neither joy nor laughter as the grim cultists sip tea and discuss the virtues of the lecture. Next Saturday night they will meet again. Another speaker will give a lecture much like the one tonight. Meanwhile, the unhappy rebels will study the Scriptures to justify their empty creed. It is, after all, a Holy Cause – even if each of them is alone in eternity (Mathison 1962, 122).

The fact that the 4A had been virtually disbanded for decades mattered little when it came to its value as anti-atheist propaganda. The organization's very existence in the 1920s and 1930s left a lasting impression in the imaginations of those concerned about the creeping threat of secularization. Surviving copies of 4A pamphlets popped up well into the 1960s as evidence of the secular threat to Christian America. In 1964, for example, WSB-TV in Atlanta cited the 4A platform in a news broadcast discussing the latest exploits of Madalyn Murray O'Hair and her organization American Atheists.[3] The irony of this conflation was that American Atheists has been immeasurably more successful than the 4A in its impact on the legal status of atheism.

4 Nonreligion and the Law

In 1961, the year after Mathison's book was published, the Supreme Court produced one of its most quoted footnotes regarding humanism in the case *Torcaso v. Watkins*. The case itself held that the states as well as the federal government could require no religious test for public office. But for those interested in the religious status of humanism, footnote eleven was the important part of the decision: "Among religions in this country which do not teach what would generally be considered a belief in the existence of God are Buddhism, Taoism, Ethical Culture, Secular Humanism and others" (367 US 488 (1961)). The fact that a footnote has no legal power of precedent could not stop legions of Americans from

---

[3] WSB-TV (Television station: Atlanta), Mr. Birch Warns of the Evils of Atheism, March 13, 1964, http://dlg.galileo.usg.edu/news/id:wsbn46298.

believing that the Supreme Court had ruled that secular humanism was a religion. *Torcaso*, along with *Engel v. Vitale* the next year, led even US Senators to this conclusion, as when Senator Herman Talmadge of Georgia argued during Senate discussion of *Engel* on August 25, 1962 that "the Supreme Court had set up atheism as a new religion." Absalom Robertson, the Senator from Virginia and father of Pat Robertson, agreed: "Atheism is a religion. It is a religion that denies god. Buddhism is a religion. Mohammedism[4] is a religion. Shintoism is a religion. There are many religions. Of course atheism is a religion. The Unitarians do not believe in the Trinity. They have a religion."[5] Robertson's impromptu Senate floor discourse on the nature of religion is illuminating in its recapitulation of the evolution of scholarly thought on what makes a religion. He recognized that Christianity no longer had sole claim to the status of "religion" in the West – that belief in the Trinity could not be the defining criterion for a religion in a pluralistic world – and listed a handful of what were considered "world religions" at the time. Articulating a theory of religion in this way has often been an effective method of displaying a limited acceptance for religious pluralism without recognizing the complexities in the modern religious landscape. The landmark Supreme Court rulings regarding religion in the 1960s made nonreligion and secularism hot button political issues to be seized upon by groups such as the Heritage Foundation and the Moral Majority. The Heritage Foundation fired one of the foundational salvos in a 1976 pamphlet by Onalee McGraw: "Secular Humanism and the Schools: The Issue Whose Time Has Come." In this tract, which school reformers mailed out to school districts and parents by the thousands, McGraw argued that "humanistic education" had replaced traditional teaching in America's public school system. The fifth grade humanities program, "Man: A Course of Study" (MACOS), exemplified this trend in curriculum. McGraw used the words of Peter Dow, one of its developers, to condemn MACOS as challenging "the notion that there are 'eternal truths' (e.g., the Ten Commandments) that must be passed down from generation to generation" (McGraw 1976, 5). This challenge to essential truth lies at the heart of the fears of secular humanism and irreligion in general – the concern that if transcendent sources of morality are removed, people will have no reason not to act on their every base impulse.

In 1978, two lawyers provided comprehensive legal argument that the religion of secular humanism had been established in the public schools of the United States. John W. Whitehead, later the founder of the Rutherford Institute,

---

4 I.e., Islam.
5 Senator Robertson, *Congressional Record*, 108 (August 25, 1962): S 13, 17590.

and John Conlan, who had just lost a re-election bid for a third term in the US House of Representatives, published a long paper in the Texas Tech Law Review in which they laid out the history of the Supreme Court's changing definitions of religion to reflect an increasingly secularized culture, leading to, in their view, a de facto establishment of Secular Humanism in violation of *Abington Township v. Schempp*, in which the Supreme Court had ruled that "the state may not establish a 'religion of secularism' in the sense of affirmatively opposing or showing hostility to religion, thus 'preferring those who believe in no religion over those who do believe'" (Whitehead & Conlan 1963, 1). Whitehead and Conlan interpreted an absence of explicitly Christian textbooks as "affirmatively opposing or showing hostility to religion." Further, they interpreted the court's phrase "religion of secularism" literally, imagining that it was a plain description of an analogue to theistic religions, rather than a metaphor for overreaction by the state:

> "Secularism" is nontheistic and "humanism" is secular because it excludes the basic tenets of theism. Therefore, Secular Humanism is nontheistic. However, while Secular Humanism is nontheistic, it is religious because it directs itself toward religious beliefs and practices, that are in active opposition to traditional theism. Humanism is a doctrine centered solely on human interests or values. Therefore, humanism deifies Man collectively and individually, whereas theism worships God (Whitehead & Conlan 1963, 30).

For their historical context, Whitehead and Conlan relied almost exclusively on Rousas John Rushdoony, the father of modern Christian Reconstructionism, and this comes out in their repeated dismay that the foundations of law had moved away from theistic absolutes and toward sociological relativism. Citing Rushdoony fourteen times in their paper, they adopted his position that all law is "inescapably religious," and thus "a fundamental and necessary premise in any and every study of law must be, *first*, a recognition of this religious nature of law" (Rushdoony and North 1973, 4). Therefore, Whitehead and Conlan imagined a clash between religions – Christianity was not merely being edged out of the government in favor of religious neutrality, but rather being replaced by a rival religion that denied any transcendent source of morality. This position allowed them to use the Establishment clause as a wedge, arguing for the expulsion from the governmental sphere of anything that could be interpreted as constituting the religion of secular humanism. Dozens of law review articles cited this paper, with many continuing the argument to return American jurisprudence to Christian underpinnings and disestablish secular humanism (e.g. Eigner 1986; Melnick 1981; Schmid 1989).

The Whitehead and Conlan paper also became a foundational document for many culture warriors of the late seventies and eighties. Homer Duncan quoted extensively from it in his book *Secular Humanism: The Most Dangerous Religion in America*, which featured an introduction by Jesse Helms. Duncan again relied on a fill-in-the blanks format to define "religion," identifying secular humanism's "adherents...central doctrine...rosary...and...last rites" as evidence that it fit neatly into the category of religion (Duncan 1979, 15). Duncan had a great deal of evidence from early humanists to support his claims, but conflated the desires of humanists like Charles Francis Potter and John Dewey to instill the values of a new humanist religion via the public schools with the realities of modern schooling. Like many critics of humanism, Duncan frequently used the two *Humanist Manifestos* as damning evidence, but never mentioned the changes from 1933 to 1973 in the authors' approach to humanism as a religion. The second *Manifesto* no longer proposed the creation of a new religion or described humanism as a religious movement; instead, it explicitly disclaimed the articulation of "a new credo" (Kurtz 1973, 13). According to Duncan, secular humanism was dangerous because its goal was to destroy Christianity; because it was inherently deceptive; and because it was propagated through public schooling (from kindergarten through university), the media, the courts, and government agencies (Duncan 1979, 18). The prime example of the insidiousness possessed by humanism was in Madalyn Murray O'Hair's success, as "one atheistic woman" to convince the Supreme Court to end school prayer in *Abington School District v. Schempp*, which Duncan believed would have been impossible if the courts had not been "strongly biased by Humanism" (Duncan 1979, 102). Duncan also relied on an idea that would be familiar to viewers of Bill O'Reilly today: the notion that Christianity is more than just a religion, and thus not subject to the same restrictions of the establishment clause as mere "religions" like secular humanism would be.[6] This line of argument interprets the Establishment Clause of the First Amendment as only prohibiting the establishment of any particular Christian denomination; it absolutely rejects the idea that the clause even considers non-Christian religions or nonreligion. Duncan read the Constitution as the blueprint for a Christian nation and could not imagine it standing in the way of a Christian state. But according to Duncan, Christianity no longer held its traditional role in America. He argued that *Schempp* "not only violated the right of free exercise of religion for all Americans; it also established a national religion in the United States – the religion of secular humanism" (Duncan 1979, vi), In an appendix to his book, Duncan listed the most prominent organizations promoting humanism; in addition to the usual suspects such as

---

6 On the November 28, 2012, episode of *The O'Reilly Factor* with guest David Silverman, president of American Atheists, O'Reilly argued, "Christianity is not a religion; it is a philosophy," and thus acceptable for the government to promote.

American Atheists and the American Humanist Association, the "most powerful and effective means for promoting Humanism" was the United States Government itself (Duncan 1979, 121).

Duncan's position on the status of secular humanism became for a brief time the law, when in 1987, Judge William Brevard Hand of the United States District Court in Alabama ruled that not only was secular humanism a religion, it had in fact already been established in the public schools, and thus he ordered forty-four suspect textbooks removed from use in Alabama schools in the middle of the school year. Although the decision would be quickly overturned by the 11th Circuit, the Center for Judicial Studies published Judge Hand's decision with an introduction by Richard John Neuhaus, who expected that most of its readers would agree that secular humanism was a religion under either a substantive or functional definition of religion (in Hand 1987, vi).[7] Testimony in the case indeed brought out numerous definitions, ranging from Tillich's "ultimate concern" to a meandering version of Durkheim's definition. Judge Hand found the most expansive definitions of religion helpful to his cause, in particular that of Dr. James Kennedy, who acknowledged that the commonplace first approach to defining religion – that it involves belief in God – does not include the various non-theistic religions of the world, and thus a capacious definition like Tillich's would be most useful (Hand 1987, 30). This stance allowed Judge Hand the leeway he needed to consider secular humanism, for all its nebulous nature, to be a religion for the purposes of the Establishment Clause. For the second half of his argument, that it had already been established in the nation's public schools, he compiled an exhaustive list of quotations from textbooks used in Alabama, categorizing them as examples of "Anti-theistic Teaching," "Subjective and Personal Values Without an External Standard of Right and Wrong," "Hedonistic, Pleasure, Need-Satisfaction Motivation," and "Anti-Parental, Anti-Family Values" (Hand 1987, 71–96). Not one of the allegedly anti-theistic quotations Judge Hand selected contained any directly negative language about religion or God. Instead, he objected to them because of their *lack* of religious language. One textbook included the statement: "Even though you are a special, one-of-a-kind human being, you share certain basic needs with all people. These needs are physical, emotional, mental, and social," which Judge Hand deemed an anti-theistic teaching on the basis that it did not acknowledge religious or spiritual basic needs (Hand 1987, 71). The rest of his examples were no more damning. One of

---

[7] Substantive (or essentialist) definitions of religion define the phenomenon in terms of what Peter Berger has called its "meaning-complexes," while functional definitions describe what it does in its relationships to other human systems. See Berger (1974).

the key points in the case was John Dewey's goal in the thirties of replacing a watered down established Christianity with a religion of humanism (Kurtz 1973, 8). Because Dewey and the other signatories of the 1933 Humanist Manifesto had agreed to this religious language, Judge Hand had all the evidence he needed to rule secular humanism as a religion, and the public schools, inspired as they were by Dewey's reforms, as their humanist churches.

The argument that secular humanism was an established religion carried weight even in Congress. While still a US representative from Arizona, Conlan introduced two amendments to a 1976 education appropriations bill in order to prevent public schools from falling into secular error. The first of these dealt specifically with "Man: A Course of Study," and was heavily influenced by Onalee McGraw's pamphlet for the Heritage Society. To section 302 (g) of H.R. 12835, the General Education Provisions Act, Conlan added the following amendment: "No grants, contract, or support are authorized under this or any other Act for any purpose in connection with the *Man: A Course of Study* (MACOS) curriculum program or materials, or in connection with the high school sequel to MACOS, *Exploring Human Nature*."[8] Conlan argued that MACOS was "a subtle but sophisticated attack on Judaic-Christian values." The curriculum used examples from many world cultures, some of which seemed to have value systems alien to American Christianity. For example, one unit described certain Netsilik Inuit practices such as wife-stealing and euthanasia as necessary for the Netsilik to survive in the far north of Canada. Conlan and others interpreted the curriculum as asserting a moral equivalency between all value systems, from which he inferred an endorsement of absolute moral relativism. Conlan entered into the record numerous statements from concerned parents, teachers, and conservative activists who raised objections to the content and agenda of the curriculum. Parents in the Wallkill school district in New York protested to their Board of Education that the proposed implementation of MACOS was based on "Humanism... a system of belief which teaches that man is all there is and that there is no God."[9] Although a social studies teacher took pains to explain that humanism and the humanities had nothing to do with belief or unbelief in God, neither the Wallkill parents nor Conlan were buying it. The controversy over MACOS in Wallkill led to the ousting of an incumbent school board member in favor of Donald W. Richter, an outspoken opponent of the new curriculum. The

---

[8] Representative Conlan, speaking on H.R. 12835, on May 11, 1976, 94th Cong., 2nd sess., *Congressional Record*, 122 pt. 11:13419.

[9] "Wallkill Humanism Course Protested," *Newburgh Evening News* (New York), May 1, 1976, entered by Representative Conlan, speaking on H.R. 12835, on May 11, 1976, 94th Cong., 2nd sess., *Congressional Record*, 122 pt. 11:13424.

local victory was ammunition for Conlan to use in getting his amendment attached to the House bill, which passed comfortably.

Conlan's second amendment of the day prohibited "grants, contract, or support ... for any educational program ... involving any aspect of secular humanism unless there is also a fair and equal teaching of the world and life view of Judaic-Christian principles set forth in the Old and New Testaments."[10] On a second reading, the provision to include the "fair and equal teaching" of Biblical principles was stripped out, although Conlan's argument hinged on secular humanism's supposed declaration that there is no God. Again relying on Hugo Black's footnote in *Torcaso v. Watkins*, the Congressman defined secular humanism as a religion for the purposes of the law and Constitution. He complained that teachers "advocating a secular humanist view" consistently excluded religious moral perspectives from their lessons, constituting a de facto establishment of the religion of secular humanism rather than harmless "scientific neutralism." To Conlan, the idea that ethics could be anything other than absolute was an inherently religious belief. Citing *Abington v. Schempp*, he reminded Congress that the Supreme Court had ruled that the government could not establish a "religion of secularism." Following Onalee McGraw's logic, Conlan saw any discussion of ethics divorced from explicitly Christian sources as necessarily, in the words of the Court's ruling, "affirmatively opposing or showing hostility to religion." His impassioned arguments notwithstanding, Conlan saw his second amendment that day rejected without even a recorded vote. The entire bill would go on to rejection by the Senate, so his MACOS amendment never gained force of law either.

Senator Orrin Hatch of Utah succeeded in banning federal education funding for "secular humanist" curriculum in one of his amendments to the Education for Economic Security Act in 1984, although what that actually meant, no one was quite sure. Without any grandstanding about the evils of secularism on the Senate floor, he simply inserted a prohibition against grants for magnet schools going toward "courses of instruction the substance of which is secular humanism."[11] With strong bipartisan sponsorship from leaders of both conservative Republicans and liberal democrats, no debate over the provision ensued, and the amendment became part of the education spending law. Indeed, no real understanding of the meaning of the phrase "secular humanism" was

---

10 Representative Conlan, speaking on H.R. 12851, on May 11, 1976, 94th Cong., 2nd sess., *Congressional Record*, 122 pt. 11:13427.
11 Amendment 3162 to Education for Economic Security Act, Title V, Sec. 509, on June 6, 1984, 98th Cong., 2nd sess, *Congressional Record*, 130 pt 11:15027. In the United States, "magnet schools" are public schools that provide specialized curriculum and draw students from beyond typical geographic boundaries.

agreed upon or even discussed at that time. For Senator Daniel Patrick Moynihan of New York, another sponsor of the bill, the Hatch amendment was simply a minor concession to secure 75 million dollars for magnet schools in desegregating districts—the "price [he] had to pay to get school desegregation money."[12] Asked what secular humanism meant, Moynihan said, "I have no idea what secular humanism is. No one knows." Although he admitted that he might have pushed the issue harder, and that he would be "more aware" if the issue were to come up again, he maintained that "there is much less here than meets the eye." Hatch acknowledged that he was essentially testing the waters for further legislative action against secular humanism. He described his motivation as being "tired of seeing the dumbing down of textbooks and schools to ignore all reference to religion and patriotic values," but also said that he "personally didn't feel very strongly about secular humanism." Hatch recognized that secular humanism, regardless of its nebulous meaning to Americans, could be used as a wedge to maintain a level of commitment to the idea of America as a Christian nation. Conlan had made the mistake of overstating the threat of secular humanism at a time when it had not yet become a watchword for a politically active religious right. Twelve years later, after the Moral Majority and other conservative Christian organizations had succeeded in imbuing the phrase with a host of negative associations, Hatch had no trouble in passing his prohibition.

The federal Department of Education's response to the Hatch amendment was to push the responsibility for defining secular humanism to the local school districts, effectively enabling parents to decide that a given curriculum has secular humanist elements and is therefore vulnerable to challenge. Even though the legislation and the Education Department rule only applied to particular earmarked funds for magnet schools, for those primed with an antipathy toward irreligion, the prohibition easily read as blanket federal disapproval of secular humanism. A legal aid to Hatch confirmed this aim of the amendment: "It has put the federal government on record saying that federal funds should not be spent on propagandizing an atheistic philosophy to our kids. If Mr. Lear doesn't like it, tough noogies."[13]

Norman Lear certainly did not like the government taking steps against humanism of any kind, although he considered the idea of an organized secular humanism, a right-wing hoax.[14] The television producer and founder of advoca-

---

[12] "Of 'Secular Humanism' And Its Slide Into Law," *New York Times*, February 22, 1985, A16.
[13] Felicity Barringer, "Department Proposes Rule to Curb Teaching of 'Secular Humanism': Controversial Term Remains Undefined," *Washington Post*, January 10, 1985, A19.
[14] Judy Mann, "What's Secular Humanism?" *Washington Post*, January 30, 1985, B3.

cy group People for the American Way had just published an exchange of letters with Ronald Reagan over what he saw as the President's "endorsement of the so-called Christian Nation movement."[15] In these letters, a remarkably candid Reagan explained a number of key positions regarding his interpretation of the relationship between religion, the state, and culture. Lear presented Reagan with a selection of quotations from televangelists and senior White House staffers who advocated for what Lear described as a "Christian nation" movement. His evidence included Pat Robertson claiming, "the minute you turn the [Constitution] into the hands of non-Christian people and atheistic people they can use it to destroy the very foundation of our society. And that's what's been happening." He also cited Reagan's own liaison for religious affairs, Carolyn Sundseth, who had called for "all saved Christians" to pray that her fellow White House staffers "get saved or get out" of government. Reagan suggested that these and other sentiments were not in fact indicative of an aggressive Christian nationalism, but rather defensive reactions to remarks derogatory of religion made in the *Humanist*, the magazine of the American Humanist Society. Describing statements published by a magazine with only a few thousand subscribers as a threat worthy of panicked action on the part of religious Americans as a whole was characteristic not only of Reagan's approach to irreligion, but also of the broader conservative Christian movement of the eighties.

5 "I Know It When I See It" Revisited

Today, amid the latest iteration of the "New Atheism" (a term that has emerged several times since the beginning of the twentieth century; see Fazzino and Cragun, this volume, for more on New Atheism), the visibility of atheists, agnostics, humanists, secularists, the nonreligious, and the non-affiliated has reached unparalleled levels. And yet the "I know it when I see it" approach to defining religion is still in ubiquitous use.

Perhaps the best recent example is found in reactions to the Sunday Assembly, a "godless congregation" founded in 2013 by British comedians Sanderson Jones and Pippa Evans, which consciously uses organizational models derived from Christianity, but divested of revealed doctrine or deity (see Smith's and Frost's chapters, this volume). The idea of a church-like community that uses a congregational model, but without theistic belief is not new; the Sunday Assembly has its precursors in the Ethical Societies, the 4A, Unitarian Universal-

---

15 "A Debate on Religion Freedom," *Harper's*, October 1984, 15.

ism, and even Madalyn Murray O'Hair's American Atheist Church, all of which used the form of churches without incorporating belief in a god.[16] None of the early organizations had the benefit of the Internet; the Sunday Assembly has leveraged online communities to seed local communities very effectively. The first meetings of the initial Sunday Assembly group in London got some media attention, but it was when the founders announced a world tour to seed new congregations in November of 2013 that the organization got widespread attention as an "atheist megachurch," in the words of salon.com reporter Katie Engelhart (Engelhart 2013). As other media outlets took notice, including a widely republished Associated Press piece, they also picked up on this language, regardless of the fact that the founders intentionally avoided calling their movement either an atheist organization or a church. The "megachurch" label is also a misnomer – all the Sunday Assembly attendees worldwide might fit into one good-sized American mega-church.

And yet the "atheist church" label sticks because, again, we know it when we see it. Observers of the Sunday Assembly see a group with a set of beliefs about humanity and the world, a familiar form of celebration, a peculiar form of reverence, and a community built on local congregations linked in a global body. It fits into the grid. So the Sunday Assembly, like secular humanism, is a disruptive element; it seems to fit the category of religion, but there is cognitive dissonance preventing it from fitting too neatly. Here is something we can learn from colloquial approaches to defining religion: a disruptive element like secular humanism betrays the observer's biases and shows how tightly intertwined religion is with politics and culture. The interpretation of secular ways of knowing as inherently and necessarily anti-religious or anti-theistic also shows the normative quality of both religiosity and Christianity in American culture. Sometimes it is not politically expedient to call it as one sees it, and in this, the study of nonreligion can help us better understand religion.

---

[16] Secularist organizations have also claimed religious status under the law to gain equal footing with religious organizations. See the American Humanist Association's religious tax exemption (Fazzino and Cragun, this volume) and the Universal Life Church's authority to perform marriages (Hoesly, this volume) for examples.

Bibliography

Duncan, Homer. 1979. *Secular Humanism: The Most Dangerous Religion in America*. Lubbock, Tex.: Christian Focus on Government.

Eigner, Linda. 1986. "Secular Humanism: A Blight on the Establishment Clause." *Loyola University of Chicago Law Journal* 18: 1245.

Engelhart, Katie. 2013. "Atheism Starts Its Megachurch: Is It a Religion Now?," Salon, September 22. http://www.salon.com/2013/09/22/atheism_starts_its_megachurch_is_it_a_religion_now/.

Ferguson, Charles W. 1929. *The New Books of Revelations : the Inside Story of America's Astounding Religious Cults*. Garden City, N.Y.: Doubleday, Doran, & Co.

Fessenden, Tracy. 2007. *Culture and Redemption Religion, the Secular, and American Literature*. Princeton, N.J.: Princeton University Press.

Gewirtz, Paul. 1996. "On 'I Know It When I See It'." *The Yale Law Journal* 105 (4): 1023–47. doi:10.2307/797245.

Hand, W. Brevard, Douglas T Smith, Mobile County (Ala.), and Board of School Commissioners. 1987. *American Education on Trial: Is Secular Humanism a Religion?: the Opinion of Judge W. Brevard Hand in the Alabama Textbook Case*. Cumberland, Va.: Center for Judicial Studies.

Kurtz, Paul. 1973. *Humanist Manifestos, I and II*. Buffalo: Prometheus Books.

Kurtz, Paul. 1983. *In Defense of Secular Humanism*. Buffalo, N.Y.: Prometheus Books.

Martin, Craig, and Talal Asad. 2014. "Genealogies of Religion, Twenty Years On: An Interview with Talal Asad." *Bulletin for the Study of Religion* 43 (1): 12–17.

Masuzawa, Tomoko. 2005. *The Invention of World Religions, or, How European Universalism Was Preserved in the Language of Pluralism*. Chicago: University of Chicago Press.

Mathison, Richard R. 1960. *Faiths, Cults, and Sects of America: From Atheism to Zen*. Indianapolis: Bobbs-Merrill.

McGraw, Onalee. 1976. *Secular Humanism and the Schools: The Issue Whose Time Has Come*. [Washington]: [Heritage Foundation].

Melnick, Robert Russell. 1981. "Secularism in the Law: The Religion of Secular Humanism." *Ohio Northern University Law Review* 8: 329.

Richter, Charles. 2015. "'A Deeply-Felt Religious Faith, and I Don't Care What It Is': American Anti-Atheism as Nativism" in Rectenwald, Michael, Rochelle Almeida, and George Levine, eds. 2015. *Global Secularisms in a Post-Secular Age*. Berlin: De Gruyter.

Rushdoony, Rousas John, and Gary North. 1973. *The Institutes of Biblical Law*. [United States]: Presbyterian and Reformed Pub. Co.

Schmid, Peter D. 1988. "Religion, Secular Humanism and the First Amendment." *Southern Illinois University Law Journal* 13: 357.

Schmidt, Leigh Eric. 2011. "A Society of Damned Souls: Atheism and Irreligion in the 1920s." *Perspectives in Religious Studies* 38 (2): 215–26.

Van Baalen, Jan Karel. 1938. *The Chaos of Cults; a Study of Present-day Isms*. Grand Rapids, Mich.: Eerdmans Pub. Co.

Whitehead, John W., and John Conlan. 1978. "Establishment of the Religion of Secular Humanism and Its First Amendment Implications, The." *Texas Tech Law Review* 10: 66.

Michael Rectenwald
Mid-Nineteenth-Century Secularism as Modern Secularity

1 Introduction

In the early 1850s, a new philosophical, social, and political movement evolved from the Freethought tradition of Thomas Paine, Richard Carlile, Robert Owen, and the radical periodical press. The movement was called "Secularism."[1] Its founder was George Jacob Holyoake (1817–1906) (Grugel 1976, 2–3).[2] Holyoake was a former apprentice whitesmith turned Owenite social missionary, "moral force" Chartist, and radical editor and publisher. Given his early exposure to Owenism and Chartism,[3] Holyoake had become a Freethinker. With his involvement in Freethought publishing, he became a moral convert to atheism. However, his experiences with virulent proponents of atheism or infidelity and the hostile reactions to them on the part of the state, church, and press induced him to develop in 1851–1852 the new creed and movement he called Secularism.

In retrospect, Holyoake claimed that the words "Secular," "Secularist," and "Secularism" were used for the first time in his periodical *The Reasoner* (founded in 1846), from 1851 through 1852, "as a general test of principles of conduct apart from spiritual considerations," to describe "a new way of thinking," and to define "a movement" based on that thinking, respectively (Holyoake 1896a,

---

[1] The foundational texts of Secularism include Holyoake (1854) and Holyoake (1870).
[2] In addition to Grugel's biography, for biographical sketches of Holyoake, see Royle (1974, esp. at 3–6, 72–74, and 312); and McCabe (1908).
[3] Chartism was a working-class movement that emerged in 1836 and was most active between 1838 and 1848. The aim of the Chartists was to gain political rights and influence for the working classes. Chartism got its name from the formal petition, or People's Charter, that listed the six main aims of the movement. These were: 1) a vote for all men over twenty-one, 2) the secret ballot, 3) no property qualification to become an MP, 4) payment for MPs, 5) electoral districts of equal size, 6) annual elections for Parliament.

The movement presented three petitions to Parliament – in 1839, 1842 and 1848 – but each of these was rejected. The last great Chartist petition was collected in 1848 and represented, it was claimed, six million signatories. The Chartists planned to deliver the petition to Parliament, after a peaceful mass meeting on Kennington Common in London. The government sent 8,000 soldiers, but only 20,000 Chartists turned up on a cold rainy day. The demonstration was deemed a failure, and the rejection of this final petition marked the end of Chartism. Many excellent works on Chartism have been published, including Chase (2007) and Royle (1996).

45–49). In using these new derivatives, he redefined in positive terms what had been an epithet for the meaner concerns of worldly life or the designation of a lesser state of religiosity within the western Christian imaginary. His bold claims for the original mobilization of the terms are corroborated by the Oxford English Dictionary. Never before Holyoake's mobilization had "secular" been used as an adjective to describe a set of principles or "secularism" as a noun to positively delineate principles of morality and epistemology, or as a movement to carry them forth.

Like Thomas H. Huxley's later agnosticism, Holyoake's Secularism deemed that whatever could not be "tested by the experience of this life" should simply be of no concern to the science practitioner, progressive thinker, moralist, or politician. The "Secularist" was one who restricted efforts to "that province of human duty which belongs to this life" (*Reasoner* 1852, 12: 34). But, as in Huxley's agnosticism, atheism was not a prerequisite for Secularism. Secularism represented "unknowingness without denial" (Holyoake 1896a, 36–37). Holyoake did warn against the affirmation of deity and a future life, given that reliance on them might "betray us from the use of this world" to the detriment of "progress" and amelioration, but belief in the supernatural was regarded as a matter of speculation or opinion to which one was entitled, unless such beliefs precluded positive knowledge or action.

It is important to distinguish Holyoake's brand of Secularism from that of his eventual rival for the leadership of the Secularist movement, Charles Bradlaugh. Unlike Bradlaugh, for Holyoake the goal of Freethought under Secularism was no longer first and foremost the elimination of religious ideology from the public sphere. While Bradlaugh maintained that the primary task of Secularism was to destroy theism – otherwise the latter would impede the progress of the new secular order – Holyoake envisioned Secularism as superseding or superintending both theism *and* atheism – from the standpoint of a new scientific, educative, and moral system. Holyoake insisted that a new, secular moral and epistemological system could be constructed alongside, or above, the old religious one.[4]

Mid-century Secularism thus represents an important stage of nineteenth-century Freethought – an intervention between the earlier infidelity of Richard Carlile and "Bradlaugh's rather crude anti-clericism and love of Bible-bashing" (Lightman 1989, 287–88). While he inherited much from the earlier infidelity of Carlile and Owen, Holyoake offered an epistemology and morality independent of Christianity, yet supposedly no longer at war with it. By the term "secular,"

---

4 Colin Campbell (1971, 54) referred to these two approaches as the "substitutionist" (Holyoake) and "eliminationist" (Bradlaugh) camps.

Holyoake did not mean the mere absence or negation of religion or belief, but rather a substantive category in its own right. Holyoake imagined and fostered the co-existence of secular and religious elements subsisting under a common umbrella.

In this essay, I examine the development of Secularism as a movement and creed, but also connect it to modern notions of the secular and secularity. I begin by briefly sketching Holyoake's periodical and pamphleteering career in the 1840s, distinguishing it from that of another prominent freethinker, Charles Southwell, and showing how Holyoake eventually developed Secularism as a moral program – to escape the stigma of infidelity, but more importantly to move Freethought toward a positive declaration of principles as opposed to the mere negation of theism. I treat Holyoake's Secularism in terms of class conciliation between artisan-based Freethinkers and middle-class skeptics, literary radicals, and liberal theists. I continue by outlining the principles of Secularism as sketched by Holyoake in several formats and across four decades, which also amounts to a brief word history of the associated term. I then distinguish Holyoake's branch of Secularism from that led by Bradlaugh, especially on the questions of atheism and sexual policy. I conclude with further remarks regarding the significance of mid-century Secularism as a historic moment inaugurating modern secularity.

2 From Infidelity to Moral Philosophy

A series of freethought periodicals from whence Secularism emerged began as working-class productions aimed at working-class readers and others with interests in the condition of the working classes. By the early 1850s, the policies of Secularism changed that exclusive basis. In 1841, the former Owenite Social Missionary, Charles Southwell – with Maltus Questell Ryall, "an accomplished iconoclast, fiery, original, and, what rarely accompanies those qualities, gentlemanly," and William Chilton, a radical publisher and "absolute atheist" – founded in Bristol, England, a periodical that its editors claimed was "the only exclusively ATHEISTICAL print that has appeared in any age or country," entitled *The Oracle of Reason, or Philosophy Vindicated* (*Oracle* 1842, 1: ii).[5]

Charles Southwell might, with important exceptions, be thought of as the Ludwig Feuerbach of British infidelity in the early 1840s, at least as Karl Marx

---

5 Holyoake (1892, Vol. 1, 142) described Chilton as "a cogent, solid writer, ready for any risk, and the only absolute atheist I have ever known."

and Friedrich Engels characterized the latter in *The German Ideology* (1845).⁶ In this work, contemporaneous with the founding of *The Reasoner* (founded in 1846), Marx and Engels argued that the Young Hegelian Feuerbach was merely substituting one kind of *consciousness* for another, "to produce a correct consciousness about an existing fact; whereas for the real communist it is a question of overthrowing the existing state of things" (Marx and Engels 1988, 65). Marx and Engels wrote:

> The Young Hegelians consider conceptions, thoughts, ideas, in fact all the products of consciousness, to which they attribute an independent existence, as the real chains of men [...] it is evident that the Young Hegelians have to fight only against these illusions of consciousness. Since, according to their fantasy, the relationships of men, all their doings, their chains and their limitations are products of their consciousness, the Young Hegelians logically put to men the moral postulate of exchanging their present consciousness for human, critical or egoistic consciousness, and thus of removing their limitations (Marx and Engels 1988, 36).

An atheist martyr, the criticism cannot be applied to Charles Southwell without qualifications. His writing constituted a political act with material and political consequences. However, the end he hoped to effect was in fact a revolution in ideas, which would, he thought, eventuate a change in material circumstances – precisely what Marx critiqued in Feuerbach (*Oracle* 1841, 1: 1).

My aim is not to engage in an extended comparison of English infidelity and post-Hegelian German philosophy, but rather to underscore the irony of Southwell's abstraction of atheistic materialism from its socio-historical context in order to contrast it with the direction Freethought was soon to take under Holyoake. In warring strictly on the level that Marx referred to as ideological, seeing religious ideas as the real "chains of men," Southwell insinuated that atheism was a purely intellectual affair, the proclamation of a truth that has arisen at different times in places, including ancient Greece, but that has been continually thwarted by priests of all ages (*Oracle* 1841, 1: 28).

Soon growing impatient with the lack of response to his philosophical disquisitions (*Oracle* 1841, 1: 2–4, 19–21, 27–9, 35–7),⁷ however, Southwell opened the fourth number of *The Oracle* with a caustic and belligerent article entitled

---

6 The differences were many, such as the fact that Southwell was an artisan-class radical, not a university-educated philosopher trained in German philosophy. But Robertson (1930, Vol. 1, 75) compares the atheism in *The Oracle* to positions developed by Feuerbach. For biographical sketches of Southwell, see Royle (1974, 69–73); and Robertson (1930, Vol. 1, 73).

7 As Charles Southwell and William Carpenter noted (1842, 2–7), several of these articles ("Is There A God?") were also cited in the indictment as counts of blasphemy.

"The Jew Book." Here, he took aim at sacred text, which proved more dangerous and thus more effective for his purposes:

> That revolting odious Jew production, called BIBLE, has been for ages the idol of all sorts of blockheads, the glory of knaves, and the disgust of wise men. It is a history of lust, sodomies, wholesale slaughtering, and horrible depravity, that the vilest parts of all other histories, collected into one monstrous book, could scarcely parallel! Priests tell us that this concentration of abominations was written by a god; all the world believe priests, or they would rather have thought it the outpouring of some devil! (*Oracle* 1841, 1: 25).

On the date of its publication, Southwell was arrested for blasphemy and taken to Bristol Jail.[8] His trial became a *cause celebre* in the liberal press (Southwell and Carpenter 1842, iii-iv). His self-defense was unsuccessful, however, and on January 15, 1842, he was fined 100 pounds and sentenced to a year's imprisonment (Southwell and Carpenter 1842, 102).

With Southwell incarcerated and unable to manage the publication, George Jacob Holyoake became the editor of *The Oracle*. Under Holyoake's editorship, a change in rhetoric and tone was immediately evident. Holyoake would not change *The Oracle*'s purpose – to "deal out Atheism as freely as ever Christianity was dealt out to the people" (*Oracle* 1841, 1: 1) – but he refrained from such odiously provocative and offensive language as Southwell's "The Jew Book" (*Oracle* 1842, 1: 67). Eschewing incendiary rhetoric, Holyoake sought sympathy for atheism on the basis of the conditions of poor workers and the failure of the Christian state to remedy them. Conditioned by personal loss from material want and its connection to religious observation, Holyoake had been predisposed to lose his faith in divine providence. For instance, Holyoake's daughter died while he served a sentence for blasphemy in Cheltenham Jail in 1841–42. His continual exposure to worldly want and suffering eventually spelled the end of whatever faith he may have had.

When Southwell declined to resume editorship of *The Oracle* upon his release from Bristol Jail, Holyoake and company decided to fold the publication. But a new periodical, *The Movement And Anti-Persecution Gazette*, was founded on December 16, 1843, allegedly to continue the mission of *The Oracle* and to report the activities of the Anti-Persecution Union.[9] Central to *The Movement* was

---

[8] He remained there for seventeen days until an offer of bail was finally accepted.
[9] The Anti-Persecution Union was formed primarily in response to the imprisonment for blasphemous libel of Charles Southwell and grew out of the "Committee for the Protection of Mr. Southwell." Subscriptions for the Union and its establishment were announced in *The Oracle*

its departure for freethinking journalism. Not only did the editors maintain the tonal and rhetorical moderation characteristic of *The Oracle* after Southwell was removed but also *The Movement* launched the "third stage" of Freethought. As Holyoake saw it, the first two stages, free inquiry and open criticism of theology, were essential, but not constructive. The third stage, however, involved the development of morality: "to ascertain what rules human reason may supply for the independent conduct of life" (Holyoake 1896a, 34). The difference in emphasis marked what Holyoake later referred to as the "positive" side of Freethought, which would not simply destroy theism, but replace its morality with another, superintending system. With this, Holyoake echoed Auguste Comte, who held that "nothing is destroyed until it has been replaced" (Holyoake 1896a, 34).[10]

3 The Upward Mobility of Freethought

The successor *to The Movement, The Reasoner* was founded in 1846 by Holyoake with the fifty pounds he won for his five entries into the Manchester Unity of Oddfellows contest for the best new lectures, to be read to graduates into the Oddfellowship (Holyoake 1892, Vol. 1, 204–8). The publication became the central propagandist instrument for Freethought. By the time he began the new weekly, Holyoake was a leading freethinker. In *The Reasoner*, Holyoake was not only interested in distancing himself from the old infidel rhetoric but he also had another kind of Freethought movement in mind. While maintaining his right to the profession of atheism, he came to advocate the accommodation of other than atheistic views within a broader movement. Unbelievers, deists, monists, utilitarians, and liberal theists might all cooperate, provided that together they promoted a morality, politics, economics, and science of worldly improvement. While a seemingly contradictory position that alienated and angered some within the Freethought community, it represented the differentiation of a religious public sphere, within which belief and unbelief coexisted by means of an overarching secularity. Secularism marked a new stage in secularity itself, evincing a recognition that religious belief was unlikely to disappear.

After publishing *The Reasoner*, Holyoake soon became involved with George Henry Lewes and Thornton Hunt and connected with middle-class literary and political radicals, and budding scientific naturalists. They met in a group called

---

(1842, 1: 72). Maltus Q. Ryall was its first secretary; Holyoake became its secretary by 1843; see *Movement* (1843, 1: 5–7).
10 See also George Holyoake and Charles Bradlaugh (1870, iv).

a "Confidential Combination." Francis W. Newman, whose book *The Soul, its Sorrows and Aspirations* (1849) greatly impressed Holyoake, was among those who, including Hunt and the pantheist William Maccall, encouraged the formation of such a club (Royle 1974, 158). William Ashurst bankrolled *The Reasoner* and under the pseudonym "Edward Search," suggested the words "secular" and "secularist" to describe Holyoake's new branch of Freethought. Holyoake responded in the same issue of *The Reasoner* by calling the new movement "Secularism." The connections initiated the cross-pollination of working- and middle-class Freethought that resulted in the development of Secularism proper. Adherents included W.H. Ashurst, Francis Newman, Thornton Hunt, George Henry Lewes, Harriet Martineau, Herbert Spencer, Louis Blanc, and others. (McCabe 1908, Vol. 1, 145; Royle 1974, 154–55; Blaszak 1988, 17; and Ashton 2008, 8–9). A few of these heterodox thinkers would even contribute articles to *The Reasoner*.

Many from this same circle of London writers also met at 142 Strand, the home and publishing house of John Chapman, the publisher of *The Westminster Review*, the organ of philosophical radicalism (Ashton 2008, 8–9).[11] Contributors to the periodical included Lewes, Marian Evans (formerly Mary Ann Evans and soon to adopt the penname of George Eliot), Herbert Spencer, Harriet Martineau, Charles Bray, George Combe, and, by 1853, Thomas Huxley. Many of the *Westminster* writers showed an interest in the writings of Auguste Comte "and in his platform for social improvement through a progressive elaboration of the sciences" (White 2003, 70). Marian Evans reviewed for the *Westminster* Robert William MacKay's *The Progress of the Intellect* (1850), a work of Comtean orientation (*Westminster Review* 1850, 54: 353–68). Holyoake came to know Comte's ideas through his association with Lewes and Evans, as well through Harriet Martineau, who was then preparing her translation of his *Positive Philosophy*. Holyoake's contact with Comtean ideas was essential for the step that he was contemplating – to take Freethought in a new direction (Royle 1974, 156). Like Comte, Holyoake believed that religion had to be either substituted with or superintended by a "positive" creed rather than being simply negated by atheism. Martineau approvingly noticed the new direction that Holyoake was taking Freethought:

> The adoption of the term Secularism is justified by its including a large number of persons who are not Atheists, and uniting them for action which has Secularism for its object, and not Atheism... [I]f by the adoption of a new term, a vast amount of impediment from prej-

---

[11] Another, overlapping circle centered on W. J. Fox and the Unitarian South Place Chapel. See Barbara Taylor (1993, 60–74).

udice is got rid of, the use of the term Secularism is found advantageous (Martineau 1853, *Boston Liberator*, quoted in *The Reasoner* 1854, 16.1: 5).¹²

In 1853, *The Westminster Review* ran an article that included a discussion of Secularism, stressing that with Secularism, Freethought had "now abandoned the disproof of deity, contenting itself with the assertion that nothing could be known on the subject" (*Westminster Review* 1853, 60: 129). In 1862, the *Westminster* claimed, as evidence of the failure of Christian orthodoxy, that Secularism had become the belief system of the silent majority of the working classes, whatever the number of those who subscribed to its periodicals or associated with its official organizational structures (*Westminster Review* 1862, 77: 60–97). Here, the author echoed the earlier remarks about Secularism by Horace Mann in his Introduction to the 1851 census on religious worship (1854, 93), albeit with fewer histrionics.

By the early 1850s, the cross-pollination between the middle- and working-class Freethought movements was well underway. Holyoake's reviews and notices of the works of Francis Newman, Lewes, Martineau and others in *The Reasoner*, together with his work at the *Leader* and the notices of his Secularism in the *Westminster*, completed a two-way circuit of exchange.

4 The principles and word history of secularism

Within two decades of its inception by George Jacob Holyoake in 1851–1852, although Holyoake was widely recognized as Secularism movement's founder and first leader, Secularism had come to be identified with the much more charismatic and bombastic speaker, Charles Bradlaugh, and the National Secular Society (NSS), of which Bradlaugh was the first president at its founding in 1866. Previous to the founding of the NSS, Secularism had been a loose federation of local branches headed by Holyoake. By the late 1860s, Holyoake had ceded, somewhat unwittingly, his former centrality in the movement. Further, he no longer maintained exclusive control of the term Secularism, which he had coined to represent the movement.¹³ Secularism, both the movement and the word, had slipped from Holyoake's grasp for several reasons. First, Holyoake alienated staunch

---

12 The quote circulated widely and was found as far afield as the *Scripture Reader's Journal* (1856: 363–64).
13 Holyoake's inability to hold sway over his neologism may be seen as parallel to Huxley's later difficulty with "agnosticism", which Huxley had coined in 1869 to represent his own creed in the context of the Metaphysical Society.

freethinking atheists, who essentially refused his construal of Secularism, while they nevertheless operated under the rubric and remained important advocates for the movement. Confidence in Holyoake's leadership was undermined as his disputed business practices, aversion to centralized organization, and comparably measured rhetorical approach were criticized and challenged (Grugel 1976, 54–55). The founding of the secularist *National Reformer* in 1860, with Bradlaugh as co-editor, along with the establishment of the NSS in 1866 with Bradlaugh as president, did much to officially reduce Holyoake's prominence within Secularism. Further, the Knowlton affair of 1877 (discussed below) calcified the rift between the Holyoake and Bradlaugh camps, evoking the censure of the latter by the former.[14] Yet this disapprobation was a consequence of the significant media attention paid to Bradlaugh and Annie Besant on the occasion of their trial for obscenity, which further associated Secularism with Bradlaugh. Bradlaugh's election to the House of Commons for Northampton in 1880 and his eventual seating in 1886 augmented his renown (Crosby 1997, 177–78).

After the critical early years, Holyoake intervened on the behalf of Secularism on many occasions, for example to write the *Principles of Secularism Briefly Explained* in 1859, to pen *The Principles of Secularism* in 1870, to debate Bradlaugh in March of 1870, and with Charles Watts (Sr.), G. W. Foote and others, to (unsuccessfully) challenge the presidency of the NSS in the wake of the Knowlton affair (Holyoake 1859; Holyoake 1870; and Holyoake and Bradlaugh 1870). Despite these efforts, Secularism was often regarded in the terms provided by the older infidelity, as reintroduced by Bradlaugh. That is, it was understood as the equivalent of atheism. Yet, as I show elsewhere (Rectenwald 2013, 46.2: 231–254; Rectenwald 2016, 107–134), it was to Holyoake and his version of Secularism that the scientific naturalists looked for a respectable and useful example of Freethought as they named, developed, and promoted their cosmology.

Late in the century, Holyoake sought to reassert his priority where Secularism was concerned – to solidify his legacy as its founder, and, yet again, to insist upon its original principles. In 1896, in *English Secularism, A Confession of Belief*, he left a retrospective index of ten documents that he regarded as foundational for Secularism's inception and establishment (Holyoake 1896a, 45–49). Other than the first two articles, the Preface to *The Movement* and the lectures to the Manchester Order of Odd-fellows, the documents had been published in *The Reasoner*. Holyoake clearly demonstrated that *The Reasoner* had been at the center of the movement. He reminded readers that he wrote all of the foundational texts, other than those that were addressed to him: "These citations from my own

---

14 See *The Secular Review and Secularist* (1877, 1: 22–23, 65–66, 77, 78, 85–86, 93, 142, and 189).

writings are sufficient to show the origin and nature of Secularism" (Holyoake 1896a, 48–49). While an exclusive textual focus is by no means sufficient for understanding the cultural meaning and significance of Secularism, these texts nevertheless testify to the essential character of the Secularist creed as Holyoake saw it. Further, such a reading represents an exercise in "word history" or "historical semantics." As Gowan Dawson and Bernard Lightman point out, drawing on Thomas Dixon's *The Invention of Altruism* (2008), "the relation between words and concepts is never simply neutral, and the changing fortunes of a term have significant implications for the construction and communication of the ideas it might entail" (Dawson and Lightman 2013, 3; Dixon 2008). In the case of Secularism, the fate of the word involved its appropriation by others in the Freethought movement and especially the larger Secular camp headed by Bradlaugh. This appropriation had significant implications concerning the meaning and understanding of Secularism proper, and has impacted the meaning and significance of modern secularism in general. It has led to confusion such that modern secularism is understood primarily as the absence or negation of religion and belief.

The first principle of Holyoake's Secularism was materialism, as enunciated in *The Movement*: "Materialism will be advanced as the only sound basis of rational thought and practice" (*Movement* 1843, 1: 117), which "restricts itself to the known, to the present, and ... to realise the life that is" (*Reasoner* 1846, 1: i). The remaining points were made in *The Reasoner*, and included some of the first usages of the words "Secular" and "Secularism" as denoting and describing a new system of knowledge and morality. The twelfth volume of *The Reasoner* opened with an article entitled, "Truths to Teach," which undertook to "indicate some of the objects which this journal endeavors to explain and enforce." The first two points had been made in *The Oracle* and *The Movement*, and in earlier volumes of *The Reasoner*:

> 1. To teach that Churches, in affirming the existence of a Being independent of Nature, affirm what they do not know themselves – that they who say they have discovered Deity assume to have found what he has evidently chosen to conceal from men in this life by endowing them with finite powers ... – that whoever bids us depend upon the fruition of a future life may betray us from the use of this world.
> 2. To teach men to limit, therefore as a matter of truth and certainty, their affirmations to what they know – to restrict, as a matter of self-defence, their expectations to that which their experience warrants (*Reasoner* 1852, 12: 1).

In this article, later recognized as foundational to the incipient Secularism, one of *The Reasoner*'s stated aims was to set limits on knowledge claims. Such limits would involve the restriction of knowledge to "that which experience warrants."

Theology was deemed a "science of conjecture" in affirming what can only be believed without knowledge, given the "finite powers" of the human faculties. With these principles, Holyoake sought to remove Freethought from the field of conjecture, and to confine it, as stated in the second point, to matters of "certainty," or what could be known given our limited faculties. Under this principle, science was deemed the sole "Providence of Man," which could be relied upon as an insurance against "false dependencies" (Holyoake 1854, 5–6).

With this announcement of aims, *The Reasoner* did not make the denial of deity necessary for the would-be Secularist. Knowledge for the benefit of humanity was separated from conjecture, which had not proven its benefits in the realm of experience. *The Reasoner did* warn against the affirmation of deity and a future life, given that reliance on them might "betray us from the use of this world" to the detriment of "progress" and amelioration. However, it warned only that such conjecture should be left behind for the purposes of pursuing knowledge and improving material conditions. Likewise, belief was not a disqualification for the pursuit of knowledge or progress, only a possible obstacle. One's belief in the supernatural was a matter of speculation or opinion to which one was entitled, unless such belief precluded positive knowledge or action. This rhetorical and philosophical turn represented the cleanest break hitherto from the previous dogmatism of earlier Freethought considered as equivalent to atheism, while also marking the nascent Secularism as a precursor of agnosticism and scientific naturalism (Rectenwald 2013, 46.2: 234; Marsh 1998, 240). While Holyoake was inconsistent on this point and included atheism as the "negative aspect" of Secularism as late as 1854, he reiterated the distinction between Secularism and freethinking atheism often. For example, in March of 1858, he argued that:

> [t]o make Atheism the Shibboleth of the Secular party would be to make Secularism an atheistic sectarianism as narrow and exclusive as any Christian Sectarianism. The principles of Secularism are distinct both from Atheism and Theism, and there can be no honest, useful, wide, and liberal party without keeping this point well understood (*Reasoner* 1858, 23: 81).

He later suggested that Secularism considered both theism and atheism as "belonging to the debatable ground of speculation" with their "theories of the origin of nature." Secularism "neither asks nor gives any opinion upon them, confining itself to the entirely independent field of study – the order of the universe." Holyoake could note in hindsight that similarly, "Huxley's term agnosticism implies a different thing [than atheism] – unknowingness without denial," but "unknowingness without denial" was fundamental to Secularism from its inception. (Holyoake 1896a, 36–37).

With the third object of "Truths to Teach" – "to teach men to see that the sum of all knowledge and duty is secular – that it pertains to this world alone" (*Reasoner* 1852, 12: 1) – Holyoake could rightly claim to have been an innovator, if not a neologist; "this was the first time the word 'Secular' was applied as a general test of principles of conduct apart from spiritual considerations," Holyoake claimed (1896b, 51). The Secular principle was in effect an ontological demarcation stratagem, dividing the metaphysical, spiritual, or eternal from "this life" – the material, the worldly, or the temporal: "Secularity draws the line of demarcation between the things of time and the things of eternity" (*Reasoner* 1852, 12: 127). The "secular" for Holyoake designated the only domain where knowledge could be gained and effective action taken (*Reasoner* 1852, 12: 34). Like Karl Popper's later demarcation of science from pseudoscience and metaphysics in the *Logic of Scientific Discovery* (1959), Secularism deemed that whatever could not be "tested by the experience of this life" should simply be of no concern to the scientist, moralist, or politician. The "Secularist" was one who restricted efforts to "that province of human duty which belongs to this life" (*Reasoner* 1852, 12: 34). According to Holyoake (1896a, 47), this was the first time the word "Secularist" was used to denote an adherent to a "new way of thinking" – to represent one who avowed Secular principles. In fact, W. H. Ashurst, writing to *The Reasoner* under the pseudonym "Edward Search," first suggested the words "Secular" and "Secularist" to describe the new branch of Freethought that Holyoake was developing, and one who aligned with it. In the same article, Holyoake coined the term "Secularism" to describe "the work we have always had in hand" (*Reasoner* 1851, 11: 88).

Secularism was advanced not only as an epistemology but also as a morality and politics. With his fourth aim, Holyoake argued for the "independent origin" of morality. Rather than being based on religious doctrine, the source of morality was nature – "the real nature" of human beings – and its warrants were to be found in the consequences of actions, "natural sanctions of the most effective kind" (*Reasoner* 1852, 12: 1). Never a strict Benthamite, and harking back to the social environmentalism of Godwin and Owen, Holyoake based morality primarily on the purported goodness of human nature itself, and only secondarily, in conjunction with practical results. Without a basis of natural goodness, a secular system would be unable to warrant motives for right actions (Holyoake 1854, 6). Intelligence, an aspect of human nature developed by knowledge, was required in order to discriminate between good and deleterious effects. The results were evaluated by intelligence according to utilitarian ethics, which in turn resulted in moral knowledge that influenced future actions. Politics was simply morality writ large. Thus, a moral and political science was advanced, comprised of a guiding principle and a scientific method.

In its claims for a political science based on human nature, Secularism was similar to the Positivism of August Comte. However, Holyoake never suggested, as did Comte, that once discovering the social laws, human beings must subject themselves to those laws in an act of acquiescence, which has been seen as Positivism's conservative character. For Comte, the laws for conduct were not necessarily in human nature alone, but in a "social physics" based on human nature. Comte avowedly aimed at establishing a "social physics" in order to avert social and political chaos by positing a social lawfulness consistent with physical regularity.[15]

The fifth point urged the trust of nothing but "Reason" for the establishment of all knowledge. The concept of reason was, as usual, a very slippery one. Its meaning could really only be completely understood by reference to what it excluded – in all cases, religious and other metaphysical speculation. It was not primarily distinguished from imagination as in Romanticism, but rather from the unsubstantiated belief of theology. Reason was figured as the logical treatment of experience, relying on "nothing which does not come within the range of phenomenon, or common consciousness, or assumes the form of a law" (*Reasoner* 1852, 12: 130). The point was to derive knowledge by means of the intellectual processing of empirical data as opposed to accepting *a priori* convictions.

Free inquiry and discussion comprised the sixth aim. Only those statements withstanding the test of "universal free, fair and open discussion ... the highest test of vital truth ... can be trusted, " Holyoake argued (*Reasoner* 1852, 12: 1). "[O]nly that theory which is submitted to that ordeal is to be regarded, as only that which endures it can be trusted" (*Reasoner* 1852, 12: 130). In the requirement that all propositions stand the test of criticism and "testing," the sixth object resembles Popper's criterion for science – the subjection of statements to possible disqualification or falsification in an agnostic field of testing and discourse.

These principles represented the "positive aspect" of Secularism. At least until 1854 and possibly later, Holyoake wavered slightly on the dividing line between Secularism and earlier Freethought; Secularism's "negative side," which was to "protest against specific speculative error" (theism), was occasionally revived. The two sides sometimes remained together under Secularism as a "*double protest*" (1854, 5). However, the tendency of the Holyoake camp was to jettison the protest and to emphasize Secularism as a new kind or stage of Freethought – that is, to assert Secularism's limitation to the field of positive knowledge and

---

[15] In an introduction to her compilation of Comte's major works, Gertrude Lenzer (1975, xxxiii), described Comte's form of materialism as an "anticipatory conservatism."

to posit a substantive morality, as opposed to or exclusive of the negation of deity and theology.

5 Atheism, sex, and secularism

On 5 April 1877, as was widely reported in the press, Annie Besant and Charles Bradlaugh were arrested and charged with printing and publishing "a certain indecent, lewd, filthy, bawdy, and obscene book, called 'Fruits of Philosophy,' thereby contaminating, vitiating, and corrupting morals" (Mills, Stone, Wilson, and Bulwer 1878, 607). Besant and Bradlaugh would stand trial for the publication, a trial that would gain enormous publicity and bring significant, and for some, unwanted attention to the Secularist movement. For Besant and Bradlaugh, the Knowlton affair, as it came to be called, represented a test of a free press, as well as the defense of "a discussion of the most important social question which can influence a nation's welfare" (Knowlton, Bradlaugh, and Besant 1877, vi). This discussion involved the doctrine of population and the right of a free people to critically examine the issue of birth control. Although the trial ended in February 1878 in an acquittal on the grounds of a technicality exploited by Bradlaugh, the savvy former legal clerk, the trial put contraception onto the breakfast tables of the middle class and associated it with Secularism.

Dr. Charles Knowlton wrote and first published *Fruits of Philosophy, or the Private Companion of Young Married People* in 1832 in Massachusetts. The pamphlet was a neo-Malthusian pro-birth-control manual detailing the physiology of human sexuality and the means of couples for limiting the size of their families. In the "Philosophical Proem" introducing the text, Knowlton argued that the practice of sex was a physiological and moral necessity; he reasoned from Benthamite principles that any moderate expression of sexual passion that did not result in misery added a net pleasure to the world and thus was to be encouraged. Furthermore, the sexual instinct would not be curbed in the mass of humanity according to Malthusian abstentionism. Only practical measures to limit procreation – new methods of contraception – could solve the predicament resultant from the sexual instinct on the one hand and the tendency of population growth on the other (Knowlton, Bradlaugh, and Besant 1877, 9–11). Although the pamphlet was released anonymously, Knowlton was arrested, tried, and convicted of obscenity, serving three months of hard labor in East Cambridge jail.

Fruits of Philosophy was imported into Britain and published by the radical disciple of Richard Carlile, James Watson, who took over Carlile's publishing ventures while Carlile was in Dorchester jail. Watson also became Holyoake's publisher and in 1853 Holyoake bought Watson's stock and sold it under the Secularist banner. As noted by Bradlaugh and Besant in their chronicling of the Knowlton affair in the Publisher's Preface of their republication of the work, *Fruits of Philosophy* was listed in Holyoake's "Freethought Directory" in 1853 (Knowlton, Bradlaugh, and Besant 1877, iii). *The Reasoner* had sometimes listed the birth control pamphlet among the books sold by Holyoake's Fleet Street House for Watson (although Holyoake had never explicitly supported the publication).[16] *Fruits of Philosophy* was published for a time by Austin Holyoake, George Holyoake's brother, in conjunction with the *National Reformer*, and when Watson died, the plates for all of his publications, including *Fruits of Philosophy*, were purchased from Watson's widow by Charles Watts, who published the work until 23 December 1876 (Besant, 1885, 83).

As a publisher of *Fruits of Philosophy*, it was Watts who, in January 1877, was first charged with printing and publishing an obscene book. The legal attention attracted by the work was probably due to several factors, not the least of which included new drawings inserted by Watts, and his lowering of the price (Besant 1885, 31). But another factor was the passage in August 1857 of the Obscene Publications Act, which made a court's interpretation the new test for obscenity. According to the new Act, a publication could be deemed obscene if it demonstrated – as argued successfully by Lord Chief Justice, Sir Alexander Cockburn in 1868 in the celebrated case of Regina v. Hicklin – a "tendency ... to deprave and corrupt those whose minds are open to such immoral influences, and into whose hands a publication of this sort may fall" (Green and Karolides 2005, 232). Obscenity, that is, was now legally in the eye of the beholder, rather than based on something "objective" in the text itself. The law apparently emboldened prosecutors and facilitated arrests. Further, given this new definition of obscenity, the accused was effectively guilty until proven innocent (Dawson 2007, 116–61).

After his arrest, Watts met with Bradlaugh and Besant, who agreed to support him in his defense and to raise money for his trial. But upon further reflection, once out of Besant's and Bradlaugh's company, Watts decided not to defend the right to publish the book and to recant his not-guilty plea and enter a plea of guilty as charged. Upon his trial, Watts was fined 500 pounds and released (Besant 1885, 81). Besant and Bradlaugh not only immediately cut their business ties with Watts, who had been their publisher for the National Review and other works but also they decided to republish *Fruits of Philosophy* under the banner of their newly formed publishing partnership, the Freethought Publishing Com-

---

16 See, for example, the advertisement "Books on Free Inquiry" (*Reasoner* 1854, 17: 95 and 256).

pany (Besant 1885, 80). While they found much wanting in *Fruits of Philosophy*, the right of publication, they argued, was a matter of principle. Bradlaugh and Besant reasoned that if they failed to assert "The Right of Publication" of a book that was not obscene but was also a scientific text, then the Freethought movement would be damaged and the cause of a free press severely compromised (Besant 1885, 82).

Not everyone in the Secularist movement agreed with this decision to republish, least especially Holyoake, who (unsuccessfully) attempted to remove Bradlaugh and Besant from the Executive Committee of the National Secular Society (NSS) (Besant 1885, 133). In 1877, in the midst of the Knowlton affair, Holyoake was invited by Freethinkers to chair a committee charged with reviewing the rules of the NSS. The commission challenged the position of president itself, a position that Bradlaugh had held from the beginning of the organization. The failure to rid the NSS of the presidency and thus to unseat Bradlaugh led to the formation of the British Secular Union (BSU) in August 1877, a new organization of the Secular movement established in opposition to the Bradlaughian NSS and supported by the new periodical *The Secular Review* as its official publication (Royle 1980, 18).[17] This organization, I suggest, was the result of more than the Knowlton affair; it registered a long-standing alienation between Holyoake and Bradlaugh and their respective camps. But the secession of George Holyoake, Charles Watts, and other Secularists from the NSS, and their founding of the BSU in the wake of the Knowlton affair, solidified an already significant breach within the Secularist movement, one that now appeared to ossify around the issue of sexuality.

In his study of Darwin and respectability, Gowan Dawson devotes a chapter to obscenity legislation in connection with Darwinism, treating in some detail the relationship between the Darwinian scientific naturalists and the two branches of Freethought, which Michael Mason has referred to as the "anti-sensual progressive" (Holyoake) and the "pro-sensual" (Bradlaugh) Secularist camps (Dawson 2007, 116–61; Mason 1994). Dawson suggests that the primary division between the Secularist camps was predicated on differences over sexual policy and birth control. According to Dawson, Bradlaugh and Annie Besant's republication and legal defense in 1877–1878 of Knowlton's *Fruits of Philosophy* became the primary reason for the split between the Holyoake and Bradlaugh

---

[17] The final division of the Secularist camps as a result of the Knowlton affair is at quite odds with Laura Schwartz's assertion (2013, 200) that Holyoake "remained neutral on the question" of the republication and defense of the *Fruits of Philosophy*. In fact, Holyoake wrote specifically to disavow the text in the press and seceded from the NSS to form a new secular union, the British Secular Union (BSU) in the aftermath of the controversy.

camps. Birth control and sexual policy, Dawson argues, "were by far the most divisive issue[s] within the British Freethought movement in the nineteenth century" (Dawson 2007, 119).

In figuring sexual policy as the fault line dividing the two Secularist camps, Dawson overlooks the well-documented, fundamental division within Secularism. This division, as Royle points out, not only took hold between the major two camps of Secularism, but also within them (1980, 120). The primary split dated to the early 1850s and went to the definition of Secularism itself. Differences in sexual policy may be understood in large part in terms of this fundamental split. From the beginning of the movement and creed, Holyoake had differentiated Secularism from the older Freethought movement, shifting its emphasis from a "negative" to a "positive" orientation. Philosophically, this entailed what he and others sometimes called a "suspensive scepticism," which included not only denying atheism as a requisite commitment but also definitively disavowing any declarative assertion on the question of deity (Grant and Holyoake 1853, 56 and 200). As Holyoake argued (rather misleadingly) in the celebrated debate with the Reverend Brewin Grant in 1853, "[w]e have always held that the existence of Deity is "past finding out, and we have held that the time employed upon the investigation might be more profitably devoted to the study of humanity" (Grant and Holyoake 1853, 8). In terms of strategy, as we have seen, this position meant cooperation between unbelievers and believers; the invitation to join the Secularists extended not only to Christian Socialists such as Charles Kingsley and his ilk but also to liberal theists with reformist politics, such as Francis M. Newman and James Anthony Froude. In terms of principle, it meant that Holyoake's Secularism, as opposed to Bradlaugh's, was specifically not atheist.

Many leading Freethinkers rejected the construction that Holyoake had put on Freethought with his Secularism, as well as his aversion to centralized organization and purported failures in organization. These included, as we have seen, Charles Southwell; but the defectors also included Holyoake's brother Austin, Robert Cooper, and most importantly, Charles Bradlaugh.

With Bradlaugh's meteoric rise to prominence in the Secular field in the 1860s, the divide between the Secularist camps became more pronounced. In 1850, Holyoake had chaired a Freethought meeting and invited the young Bradlaugh, at the mere age of seventeen, to speak on "The Past, Present, and Future of Theology" (Courtney 1920, 105). By the late 1850s, Bradlaugh had found in the *Investigator* a vehicle for his trenchant atheism. In 1858, he had been elected president of the London Central Secularist Society, assuming the position Holyoake had held for nearly a decade. By 1860, he had become founder and co-editor of the *National Reformer.* Yet in an attempt to close the ranks of the Secularist body, in November 1861, Bradlaugh invited Holyoake to join the *National Reformer* as a special contributor. Holyoake accepted, and even signed a letter entitled, "One Paper and One Party," published in the periodical. Beginning in January 1862, he was responsible for curating three pages – either of his own writing, or from his associates. But in February, a correspondent to the paper complained of the paper's diversity of opinion and asked what the *National Reformer* definitively advocated regarding religion. Bradlaugh's answer effectively marked the end of Holyoake's involvement: "Editorially, the National Reformer, as to religious questions, is, and always has been, as far as we are concerned, the advocate of Atheism." The consequence was a fall-out between Bradlaugh and Holyoake that included a financial dispute, with Holyoake apparently demanding a year's salary, after having only served three months in his capacity as "chief contributor" (Bonner 1895, 128–30).

By 1870, the lines were even more severely drawn. In a debate between Holyoake and Bradlaugh (chaired by Holyoake's brother, Austin, by then an acolyte of Bradlaugh's), the topic was the place of atheism within Secularism. In effect, George Holyoake denied that Bradlaugh was a Secularist at all. Further, Bradlaugh admitted that, according to Holyoake's definition – a definition, he suggested, that the founder of the movement had a right to maintain – Holyoake was right that he should not be called a Secularist (Holyoake and Bradlaugh 1870, 10). Nevertheless, by then the President of the NSS, Bradlaugh asserted that Secularism necessarily amounted to atheism – "I hold that Atheism is the logical result to all who are able to think the matter out" – and that Holyoake's reasoning was simply flawed (Holyoake and Bradlaugh 1870, vii). Holyoake, for his part, remained as firm as ever that Secularism did not "include" atheism, but concomitantly, that it did not "exclude" atheists (Holyoake and Bradlaugh 1870, 19–20), a point which Bradlaugh considered illogical (Holyoake and Bradlaugh 1870, 11). Holyoake further suggested that making atheism a condition of Secularism was to delay the work of Secular improvement indefinitely, while atheism made its clean "sweep" of theological notions:

> Mr. Watts [then still a Bradlaugh supporter] goes on to state [in the *National Reformer*], "The province of Secularism is not only to enunciate positive principles, but also to break up old systems which have lost their vitality, and to refute theologies which have hitherto usurped judgment and reason." *Here is an immense sweep.* None of us will live to see the day when the man who has made it, will be able to give us the secular information which we are waiting to receive now (Holyoake and Bradlaugh 1870, 19, emphasis added).

Instead of advocating the undertaking of such "an immense sweep," Holyoake contended that Secularism should be established independently of theology as a creed having positive principles of its own, and that the work of secular improvement should be undertaken at once. He quoted a contributor to the *National Reformer* (again, his brother, Austin), who had asserted that it was "impossible to advocate Secular principles apart from Atheism ... There is no man or woman who is willing to listen to Secular views, knowing they are intended to set up a system entirely apart and devoid of all religion." George Holyoake did not spare his brother criticism:

> You set up Secular principles *for their own value*. Many persons are Secularists who can see religion even in this. *The provision is not to set up a thing "devoid of all religion," but to set up a thing distinct in itself*, and you have no more right to say it is set up apart from the religion, than the clergyman has a right to say, when you set up Secular knowledge apart from his creed, that you intend thereby to set it up *devoid* of religion or public piety (Holyoake and Bradlaugh 1870, 8–9).

We see here that by Secularism Holyoake meant a substantive doctrine, not the mere absence or negation of religion or religious belief. For this reason, it could (logically or otherwise) stand parallel to (or above) religious systems. Moreover, he was even willing to allow Secularism to be construed as a religion in its own right. This was a more acceptable option than including atheism as a necessary element of Secularism.

Furthermore, whenever the question of sexual policy was raised, the issue of atheism was never far removed. In the 1870 debate between Bradlaugh and Holyoake, for example, Holyoake had distinguished between what he called "positive" and "negative" atheism. While the former was "a proud, honest, intrepid, self-respecting attitude of the mind," "Negative Atheism" consisted of "mere ignorance, of insensibility, of lust, and gluttony, and drunkenness, of egotism or vanity" (Holyoake and Bradlaugh 1870, 47). With this distinction, which he registered seemingly out of the blue, Holyoake was in fact acknowledging a long-standing association of atheism with immorality, in particular with sexual profligacy and other sensual licentiousness. His definitions represented a not-so-subtle chastisement of the Bradlaugh camp for its neo-Malthusian advocacy in the *National Reformer* – its recommendations of preventive checks to procreation (birth control). Moreover, Holyoake also apparently commented on the position of his brother, Austin, whose own neo-Malthusian pamphlet, *Large or Small Families*, had appeared in 1870. While Bradlaugh denied knowledge of any such "Negative Atheism" or anyone who practiced it (Holyoake and Bradlaugh 1870, 56), given his well-known neo-Malthusianism, it must have been clear to those familiar with the contentious field of Secularism what Holyoake meant by the phrase "Negative Atheism."

In the Publisher's Preface to the 1877 edition of *Fruits of Philosophy*, the edition that led to the obscenity indictments brought against Bradlaugh and Annie

Besant, Bradlaugh and Besant charged Holyoake and company with hypocrisy, suggesting that he and Watson had sold and profited by the book for decades. If they had considered the book obscene all the while, then they had carelessly "thus scattered obscenity broadcast over the land" (Knowlton, Bradlaugh, and Besant 1877, iv). Likewise, why did they not stand behind the republication of the book? Holyoake's disapproval of the decision by Bradlaugh and Besant to republish and defend the book had been registered by the time they wrote their publisher's preface, given Holyoake's disavowals in the press (Royle 1980, 92). It was clear that Bradlaugh and Besant were already acutely aware of Holyoake's position.

Neo-Malthusian doctrine necessarily involved Secularists of the Holyoake camp in a moral quandary. Should birth control apply strictly to the moderation of family growth within the confines of marriage? If not, might it encourage sexual profligacy? Given his concern for Secularism's respectability, Holyoake had always recommended moral discipline and reservation. Although possibly having some sympathy for neo-Malthusian practices within marriage, having supported more liberal laws for divorce, and despite his contact with Hunt and Lewes, he had for decades effectively skirted the issues invoked by Freethought in connection with sexual policy.[18] Further, with roots in the communitarianism of Owenite socialism, the implications of Malthusian political economy had always been unpalatable. Thus, the Knowlton affair thrust him into a confrontation he would have rather avoided. The Knowlton affair had connected Secularism with neo-Malthusianism, potentially embarrassing Holyoake, and not only for the associations with immorality that he feared. Not only did neo-Malthusian doctrine, *per se*, conflict with his socialist predilections but also the problem of sexual conduct exposed theoretical and practical contradictions within his kind of Secularism; Holyoake's refusal to place primary importance on the elimination of Christian theology and morality, his insistence on suspending judgment regarding Christian values that supposedly did not conflict with secular progress – this abdication of normativity was impossible where sexual conduct was concerned. To be strictly consistent theoretically, a Utilitarian and neo-Malthusian moral code for sexuality would have signified widespread use of contraceptives and such extensive sexual activity as afforded a net pleasurable return for all concerned, regardless of the legal status of the partners. Yet Holyoake never advocated such a position. Certainly, as Michael Mason has observed, "[t]he exalted status of rationality in the advanced thought of the eighteenth cen-

---

18 The debates in *The Reasoner* in 1855 over George Drysdale's *The Elements of Social Science* (1854) reveal Holyoake's equivocation.

tury had a lasting influence on all radical and reforming creeds in the nineteenth," including Secularism (Mason 1994, 284–85). But, arguably, the utilitarianism of Holyoake's Secularism was buttressed by and dependent upon prevailing Christian values, what Mason refers to as "classic moralism," at least where human sexuality and social reproduction were concerned. Arguably, Holyoake's position on sexuality owed less to anti-sensualist rationalism inherited from the Enlightenment than it did to the observance of Christian-based propriety. As John Stuart Mill put it to Holyoake in a letter in 1848:

> [T]he root of my difference with you is that you appear to accept the present constitution of the family & the whole of the priestly morality founded on & connected with it – which morality in my opinion through[ly] deserves the epithets of "intolerant, slavish & selfish" (Mill, Mineka, Priestley, and Robson 1963, 741).

That is, Holyoake's Secularism had not established an entirely unalloyed social science in place of or independent of religious systems. Rather, in his attempt to erect a substantive creed alongside (or above), but not necessarily in contradiction to Christianity,[19] his Secularism had implicitly assumed standards for sexual conduct having little or nothing to do with its own stated principles. In terms of secularity, this meant that Holyoake's version of Secularism never entirely differentiated itself from the religious sphere.

6 Conclusion: Secularism versus the standard secularization thesis

Secularism, as Holyoake conceived it, opened up a space where working-class and genteel radicals, atheists, theists, and, anachronistically speaking, agnostics, could potentially cooperate for the material improvement of humanity, especially the working classes. But many Freethinkers, both those of his own generation and those to follow (see Richter and Shook, this volume), differed with Holyoake's conception of Secularism and either rejected it outright, or modified it for their own purposes. As I have suggested, the major division between the Holyoake and Bradlaugh camps was based primarily on the question of atheism, but also included differences over Malthusian political economy and a pro-birth

---

[19] Secularism did include the contradictory ambition of replacing religious belief and morality with secular values. This tension is explored in the epilogue of my book (Rectenwald 2016, 197–201).

control sexual policy derived from it. Sexual policy and atheism were not so easily disentangled; the mere mention of one often implied the other. Finally, sexual policy represented a contradiction within Holyoake's Secularism and, thus, illustrated the extent to which Holyoake had failed to establish a secular system as fully differentiated from the religious sphere.

Remarkably, the two different senses of Secularism that I have discussed, at least where the primary distinction is concerned, survive to this day in the forms and understandings of general modern secularism (and, so does confusion between them; see Langston et al. this volume). Under Bradlaugh's model, the mission of secularism is evacuative, the category of the secular is negative, and secularization is understood as progressive and teleological. Secularism amounts to a gradual, but eventual emptying of religion from the public (and in some cases, even the private) sphere. That is, Bradlaugh's Secularism amounted to a belief in what we now understand as the standard secularization thesis.[20] On the other hand, under Holyoake's model, Secularism is constructive, the category of the secular is positive and substantive, and secularization is understood as an increasingly developing, complex plurality of belief, unbelief, and suspension between the two, along with other creedal commitments. As we have seen, Holyoake represented Secularism as a pluralistic, inclusive, and contingently constructed combination of willing theists, unbelievers, and agnostics. He did this by positing improvement in this life as a common aim of believers and unbelievers, leaving metaphysical questions largely out of the question. In this, I argue, Holyoake tacitly acknowledged the unlikelihood that Enlightenment rationality, extended into the nineteenth century, would utterly eradicate religious belief. As he put it in the 1870 debate with Bradlaugh, the complete evacuation of religiosity would require such "an immense sweep" that to attempt it was tantamount to insanity and resulted in the gross negligence of pressing secular matters. Holyoake grasped a sense of secularity as involving recognition and cooperation between religion and its others, a vision of the public and political spheres not unlike that which Jürgen Habermas has recently described as "post-secular" (2008, 25.4: 17–29). Rather than (or even while) expecting its disappearance according to a model of secularization (or Secularism), that is, the secularist had best accommodate religious discourse within a public sphere notable for its uneven and forever incomplete secularization. In fact, secularization and Secularism represented just this incomplete and permanent unevenness.

---

20 David Nash (2004, 1: 302–25) suggests that such a *belief* is in fact common among contemporary sociologists and others who maintain the standard secularization thesis, regardless of empirical evidence and theoretical disputation to the contrary.

Once Freethought entered this positive phase, however – one of positing a substantive moral and epistemological value system, as opposed to merely antagonizing religious believers and negating theism – it could develop into a new, more inclusive, sophisticated creed and movement. Edward Royle (1974, 160–62) has suggested that this development should be understood in terms of a kind of limited ecumenism, as the transformation of a religious sect into a denomination. However, such an interpretation fails to grasp the secular as a category distinct from and yet necessarily related to and dependent upon the religious (see Shook, this volume). With Holyoake's Secularism, Freethought was not, or was no longer, an entirely religious movement *per se*. Instead, by virtue of a demarcation principle that removed from consideration Christianity's metaphysical convictions, the secular began a process of differentiation from within the religious sphere. With Secularism, Freethought no longer contended for metaphysical sovereignty precisely on the grounds of theology itself. Or to put it another way, with mid-century Secularism, some Freethinkers began to understand secularity differently. Rather than positing the category of the secular as the mere negation or absence of religion and belief, thus keeping it securely within the religious ambit, secularity (called Secularism by Holyoake and company) was understood and described as a distinct development, a new stage resulting in an overarching *condition* that embraced unbelief and belief, the secular and the religious, and not the negation of one by the other.

Laura Schwartz puts it thusly for the benefit of contemporary historiography:

> Once secularism is approached as a substantive rather than a negative category – as something more than simply an absence of religion – it becomes possible to see how religion may indeed play a role within a secular worldview without simply collapsing secularism into the wider category of religion (Schwartz 2013, 20).

Schwartz is of course speaking to *our* understanding of secularity, invoking Charles Taylor's rejection of and alternative to the standard secularization thesis – of secularization as continual "subtraction" (Taylor 2007) – and applying this new conception to the period. However, this understanding of secularity should not only guide our research but also should be recognized as precisely the conception that was dawning on Holyoake by the late-1840s, and what he consciously understood as developing with Secularism. This was in fact how Holyoake had envisaged Secularism proper at mid-century.

Bibliography

Periodicals

Boston Liberator
The Movement
Our Corner: A Monthly Magazine of Fiction, Poetry, Politics, Science, Art, Literature
The Republican
Scripture Reader's Journal
The Nineteenth Century: A Monthly Review
The Oracle of Reason, or Philosophy Vindicated
The Reasoner And Herald of Progress (Various subtitles hereafter)
The Secular Review and Secularist
The Westminster Review
Weekly Dispatch

Primary and Secondary Sources

Ashton, Rosemary. 2008. *142 Strand: A Radical Address in Victorian London*. London: Vintage.

Berger, Peter L. 1999. *The Desecularization of the World: Resurgent Religion and World Politics*. Washington, D.C.: Ethics and Public Policy Center.

Besant, Annie. 1885. "Autobiographical Sketches," *Our Corner: A Monthly Magazine of Fiction, Poetry, Politics, Science, Art, Literature* 5: 83.

Blaszak, Barbara J. 1988. *George Jacob Holyoake (1817–1906) and the Development of the British Cooperative Movement*. Lewiston, NY: The Edwin Mellen Press.

Bonner, Hypatia Bradlaugh and John M. Robertson. 1895. *Charles Bradlaugh: A Record of His Life and Work*. London: TF Unwin.

Bush, M. L. 1998. *What Is Love?: Richard Carlile's Philosophy of Sex*. London: Verso.

Campbell, Colin. 1871. *Toward A Sociology of Irreligion*. London: Macmillan.

Chase, Malcom. 2007. *Chartism: A New History*. Manchester and New York: Manchester University Press.

Courtney, Janet E. H. 1920. *Freethinkers of the Nineteenth Century*. New York: E.P. Dutton.

Crosby, Travis L. 1997. *The Two Mr. Gladstones: A Study in Psychology and History*. New Haven: Yale University Press.

Dawson, Gowan. 2007. *Darwin, Literature and Victorian Respectability*. Cambridge: Cambridge University Press.

Dawson, Gowan and Bernard V. Lightman. 2013. "Introduction." In *Victorian Scientific Naturalism: Community, Identity, Continuity*, edited by Gowan Dawson and Bernard V. Lightman, 1–23. Chicago: The University of Chicago Press.

Dixon, Thomas. 2008. *The Invention of Altruism: Making Moral Meanings in Victorian Britain*. Oxford: Oxford University Press.

Grant, Brewin and George Holyoake. 1853. *Christianity and Secularism: Report of a Public Discussion between Brewin Grant... and George Jacob Holyoake, Esq*. London: Ward.

Green, Jonathon and Nicholas J. Karolides. 2005. *Encyclopedia of Censorship*. New York: Facts on File.
Grugel, Lee. 1976. *George Jacob Holyoake: A Study in the Evolution of a Victorian Radical*. Philadelphia: Porcupine Press.
Habermas, Jürgen. 2008. "Notes on Post-Secular Society." *NPQ: New Perspectives Quarterly* 25.4: 17–29.
Holyoake, George Jacob. 1854. *Secularism, The Practical Philosophy of the People*. London: Holyoake & Co.
Holyoake, George Jacob. 1859. *Principles of Secularism Briefly Explained*. London: Holyoake & Co.
Holyoake, George Jacob. 1870. *The Principles of Secularism Illustrated*. London: Austin & Co.
Holyoake, George Jacob. 1892. *Sixty Years of an Agitator's Life*, 2 vols. London: T. F. Unwin.
Holyoake, George Jacob. 1896a. *English Secularism: A Confession of Belief*. Chicago: Open Court Pub. Co.
Holyoake, George Jacob. 1896b. *The Origin and Nature of Secularism; Showing that Where Freethought Commonly Ends Secularism Begins*. London: Watts.
Holyoake, George Jacob and Charles Bradlaugh. 1870. *Secularism, Scepticism, and Atheism: Verbatim Report of the Proceedings of a Two Nights" Public Debate between Messrs. G J. Holyoake & C. Bradlaugh: Held at the New Hall of Science ... London, on the Evenings of March 10 and 11, 1870*. London: Austin.
Huxley, Thomas H. February 1889. "Agnosticism." *The Nineteenth Century: A Monthly Review* 25.144: 169–94.
Huxley, Thomas H. March 1889. "Agnosticism: A Rejoinder." *The Nineteenth Century: A Monthly Review* 25.145: 481–504.
Huxley, Thomas H. June 1889. "Agnosticism and Christianity." *The Nineteenth Century: A Monthly Review* 25.148: 937–64.
Knowlton, Charles, Charles Bradlaugh, and Annie Besant. 1877. *Fruits of Philosophy: An Essay on the Population Question*. Rotterdam: v.d. Hoeven & Buys.
Lenzer, Gertrude. 1975. *Auguste Comte and Positivism: The Essential Writings*. New York: Harper & Row.
Lightman, Bernard. 1989. "Ideology, Evolution and Late-Victorian Agnostic Popularizers." In *History, Humanity and Evolution: Essays for John C. Greene*, edited by James Moore, 285–310. Cambridge: Cambridge University Press.
Lightman, Bernard. 2002. "Huxley and Scientific Agnosticism: the Strange History of a Failed Rhetorical Strategy." *British Journal for the History of Science* 35.3: 271–89.
Mann, Horace. 1854. *Census of Great Britain, 1851: Religious Worship in England and Wales*. London: G. Routledge.
Marsh, Josh. 1998. *Word Crimes: Blasphemy, Culture, and Literature in Nineteenth-Century England*. Chicago: University of Chicago Press.
Marx, Karl. 1998. *The German Ideology: Including Thesis on Feuerbach*. Amherst, N.Y.: Prometheus Books.
Mason, Michael. 1994. *The Making of Victorian Sexual Attitudes*. Oxford: Oxford University Press.
McCabe, Joseph. 1908. *Life and Letters of George Jacob Holyoake*, 2 vols. London: Watts & Co.

Mill, John Stuart, Francis E. Mineka, F. E. L. Priestley, and John M. Robson. 1963. *The Collected Works of John Stuart Mill. (f.e.l. Priestley [Subsequently] J.M. Robson, General Editor.) (Vol. 12, 13. the Earlier Letters of John Stuart Mill, 1812–1848. Edited by F.E. Mineka.)*, 33 vols. Toronto: University of Toronto Press; London: Routledge & Kegan Paul.

Mills, William, Arthur P. Stone, Arthur Wilson, and James Redfoord Bulwer. 1878. *The Law Reports*, Vol. 3. London: Printed for the Inc. Council of Law Reporting for England and Wales, by W. Clowes and Sons.

Nash, David. 2004. "Reconnecting Religion with Social and Cultural History: Secularization's Failure as a Master Narrative." *Cultural and Social History* 1: 302–25.

Owen, Robert Dale. 1875. *Moral Physiology, or, a Brief and Plain Treatise on the Population Question*. Boston: J. P. Mendum.

Popper, Karl. 1959. *The Logic of Scientific Discovery*. New York: Basic Books.

Rectenwald, Michael. 2013. "Secularism and the Cultures of Nineteenth-Century Scientific Naturalism." *British Journal for the History of Science* 46.2: 231–54.

Rectenwald, Michael. 2016. *Nineteenth-Century British Secularism: Science, Religion and Literature*. Basingstoke, Hampshire: Palgrave Macmillan.

Robertson, John M. 1930. *A History of Freethought in the Nineteenth Century*. New York: G P Putnam's Sons.

Royle, Edward. 1974. *Victorian Infidels: The Origins of the British Secularist Movement, 1791–1866*. Manchester: University of Manchester Press.

Royle, Edward. 1980. *Radicals, Secularists and Republicans: Popular Freethought in Britain, 1866–1915*. Manchester: University of Manchester Press.

Royle, Edward. 2014. *Chartism*. New York: Longman.

Schwartz, Laura. 2013. *Feminism: Secularism, Religion and Women's Emancipation, England 1830–1914*. Manchester, U.K.; New York: Manchester University Press.

Simpson, J. A., and E. S. C. Weiner. 1989. *The Oxford English Dictionary*. Oxford: Clarendon Press. Print.

Southwell, Charles and William Carpenter. 1842. *The Trial of Charles Southwell: (editor of "the Oracle of Reason") for Blasphemy, Before Sir Charles Wetherall [i. e. Wetherell] Recorder of the City of Bristol, January the 14th, 1842*. London: Hetherington.

Taylor, Barbara. 1993. *Eve and the New Jerusalem: Socialism and Feminism in the Nineteenth Century*. Cambridge, Mass.: Harvard University Press.

Taylor, Charles. 2007. *A Secular Age*. Cambridge: Belknap Press/Harvard University Press.

Warner, Michael J., Jonathan VanAntwerpen, and Craig J. Calhoun, eds. 2010. *Varieties of Secularism in a Secular Age*. Cambridge, Mass.: Harvard University Press.

White, Paul. 2003. *Thomas Huxley: Making the "Man of Science."* Cambridge: Cambridge University Press.

Lori L. Fazzino and Ryan T. Cragun
"Splitters!": Lessons from Monty Python for Secular Organizations in the US

Aside from a handful of books from secular authors like Susan Jacoby (2004, 2009) and David Niose (2012) and even fewer scholarly publications (Cady 2010; Blankholm 2014; LeDrew 2016; Turner 1986), little is known about the origins and evolution of American secularism or the factors that contributed to the proliferation of secularist organizations (though see Rectenwald, this volume, for the origins of secularism in the UK). In this chapter, we begin by recounting some of the history of organized secularism in the US, including some emphasis on the tensions and the splits that occurred.

We then turn our attention to two specific figures in the movement – Paul Kurtz (1929–2012) and Madalyn Murray O'Hair (1919–1995) – and argue that, while these individuals were obstinate, autocratic, and even over-bearing at times, they were arguably the very types of personalities that were necessary during the Cold War in the US to maintain a small, but vocal movement of stigmatized nonbelievers. We conclude by arguing that the divisions and the tensions have transformed organized secularism in the US into a de-centered, segmented, polycephalous movement (see Gerlach and Hines 1970). While the movement may be more diffuse than some think is in its best interest, we argue that there are potential advantages to such an arrangement.

1 Introduction

While we came to the study of organized secularism for different reasons – Fazzino worked for several secular social movement organizations (SMOs); Cragun was asked to speak at the conventions of some of the organizations – both of us were initially under the impression that the secular movement in the US was contentious and fractured. It was with this understanding – that there was significant conflict between the various social movement organizations (SMOs) – that the second author (Cragun) began a project to better understand the relationships between the various secular movement organizations in 2013. He teamed up with the first author (Fazzino) shortly after the project began. Cragun's initial conception – that there were tensions between the various secular movement organizations – is why this chapter derives its name from the dialogue in a scene from Monty Python's *The Life of Brian*. In the scene, the members of a revolutionary Jewish organization that opposed the Roman occupation of Israel, the People's Front of Judea (PFJ), are seated in an arena watching a gladiator battle while they discuss the aims of their social movement organization. During the conversation, the following ensues:

> *PFJ Leader: Listen, the only people we hate more than the Romans are the fucking Judean People's Front!*
> *PFJ Members [in unison]: Yeah, yeah!*
> *PFJ Member #1: And the Judean People's Popular Front.*
> *PFJ Members [in unison]: Oh yeah, yeah!*
> *PFJ Member #2: Splitters!*
> *PFJ Member #3: And the People's Front of Judea...*
> *PFJ Member #2: Splitters!*
> *PFJ Leader: What?*
> *PFJ Member #3: People's Front of Judea...SPLITTERS!*
> *PFJ Leader: We're the People's Front of Judea!*
> *PFJ Member #3: Oh. I thought we were the Popular Front...*
> *PFJ Leader: People's Front!*
> *PFJ Member #3: Whatever happened to the Popular Front?*
> *PFJ Leader: He's over there...*
> *PFJ [in unison]: SPLITTER!*

The takeaway from this scene is that social movement organizations can be schismatic. Competing logics of action can often generate factions that lead to in-fighting; likewise, differing visions for the movement often lead to splits and divisions (Gamson 1990; McAdam 1998). There is a great deal of truth to this for American secularism.

A later scene in the same movie depicts how competing social movement organizations can end up working at cross-purposes. In this scene, the People's Front of Judea and another revolutionary Jewish movement organization, Campaign for Free Galilee, both sneak into a Roman palace in the middle of the night and encounter each other. Once they realize they are there with the same end (to kidnap Pilate's wife and demand that the Romans leave as a ransom), a physical fight ensues between the members of the two organizations. The movie's main character, Brian (who is regularly mistaken for Jesus throughout the film), makes explicit the irony of the two groups fighting each other:

> *Brian: Brothers! Brothers! We should be struggling together.*
> *Fighting Revolutionaries: We are!*
> *Brian: We mustn't fight each other. Surely we should be united against the common enemy.*
> *Fighting Revolutionaries: The Judean People's Front?*
> *Brian: No! No! No! The Romans!*

In this scene, Brian tries to stop the fight, fails, and watches as all of his revolutionary comrades collapse in their struggle with each other. The implication at this point is quite obvious: social movement organizations are sometimes ineffective because they end up fighting each other rather than working together for a common cause. This tension was confirmed in some of the interviews we conducted for this project. In what seems like it could be a direct quote from *The Life of Brian*, Frank Zindler of American Atheists (AA) described in an interview a similar degree of tension between founder, Madalyn Murray O'Hair, and Anne Nicol Gaylor, co-founder of the Freedom From Religion Foundation:

> We saw Madalyn many times, and she would always have disparaging things to say about Ann Gaylor. I later found out the same thing was happening on the other side. Ann was really, really scathing about Madalyn. It really, you know, it sounds corny, but it breaks my heart to see this or to recall all this because I so firmly am of the opinion that the enemy is religion. It shouldn't be each other. It should be other people who have, at least nominally, committed to a life of reason, an evidence-based life. To see these divisions just depresses me.

In our interviews, we found other examples of this kind of tension. But we also quickly realized that the current situation for secular SMOs in the US is more complicated than just tension and conflict. We have two quotes from our interviews we want to use to help frame our argument in this chapter. One quote illustrates just how serious the conflict and tension was at times in the secular movement. The other quote shows that the movement has changed, the tension has eased, and there is now evidence that secular SMOs are working together.

Numerous scholars have argued that American secularism is fractured and is better understood as "disorganized secularism" than "organized secularism" (Baker and Smith 2015; Cimino and Smith 2014). There is certainly reason to believe this *was* the case during the 20th century. Tom Flynn, the editor of *Free Inquiry*, the freethought and humanist magazine published by the Council for Secular Humanism or CSH (now a subsidiary of Center for Inquiry or CFI), recounted an incident during an interview that illustrated the very frosty relationship that existed between the founder of CSH, Paul Kurtz, and Madalyn Murray O'Hair, the founder of another prominent secular movement organization, American Atheists (AA):

> This is going back into the late 80s or very early 90s when we were on the east side of Buffalo. For some years we had been maintaining a membership at AA so that we would receive AA's magazine. What we ordinarily did is we would have a different staff member send in a personal check, because if you thought Paul [Kurtz] was into the zero-sum game model, Madalyn Murray O'Hair was way out ahead of him. One year our then-executive director made a mistake and forgot to arrange for someone to send in a personal

check, and sent in a Council for Democratic and Secular Humanism[1] check, which came back, scrawled on it in magic marker with as large as you could fit this many words, in Madalyn Murray O'Hair's handwriting, "Fuck you, Paul Kurtz."

There is a lot worth noting in this short quote, but we will leave most of the analysis for below. In the early stages of movement building, as Tom Flynn notes, there was a sense that secular organizing was a "zero-sum game," meaning that any gains made by one organization detracted from the success of the other organizations. There was no collective identity to mobilize action toward a common goal. As a result, there was limited communication between the various secular movement organizations and a significant amount of competition over donors, nasty frame disputes,[2] and an overarching culture of organizational and interpersonal distrust. There was not, at that time, a sense that all of the secular organizations in the US were working together for some clear purpose (e.g., normalizing nonreligion in the US).

Contrast the incident described above by Tom Flynn with this account of the 2012 Reason Rally from David Silverman, the President of American Atheists:

> The biggest part of the Reason Rally, the biggest victory of the Reason Rally was getting all of us together in one place at one time, including the Freedom From Religion Foundation, with money, a common cause, behind a common leader, which in this case was me, but next time it won't be. But it was the first time that that had actually happened and it was huge! It was a massive success and the members loved it and the members told us loud and clear that they want more. So, when you're talking about unifying big groups, don't forget about the Reason Rally Coalition.

This quote suggests cooperation between the various secular SMOs. Cooperation does not mean that the leaders of the various secular SMOs are all now friends who regularly get together just to hang out. But it does indicate that the acerbic and caustic relationships that existed in the 20th century between the various secular SMOs have given way to detentes, more amicable relations, and a growing sense of unity in the secular movement in the US. While the 2012 Reason Rally was a fairly notable success with an estimated 25,000 nonreligious individuals in attendance, it was actually the result of decades of effort by various people and organizations to try to bring a greater sense of coherence to organized

---

[1] This was the original name of what is now the Council for Secular Humanism.
[2] "Frames" refer to the ways that social movement organizations explain their purpose and desired changes to their followers. Thus, "frame disputes" would be conflict between the various secular movement organizations in what their collective purpose was as secular movement organizations.

secularism in the US (see also the introduction in Cimino and Smith 2014 and LeDrew 2016). Towards the end of the chapter we proffer an explanation for how we got from "Splitters!" and "Fuck You, Paul Kurtz" to a co-sponsored Reason Rally and more amicable relations between the various secular SMOs.

2 Taking Organized Secularism Seriously

Colin Campbell ([1971] 2013) called for a sociology of irreligion over 40 years ago. But it was the emergence of public atheism (otherwise referred to as "New Atheism") in the early 21st century that finally put American secularism[3] on the radar of scholars across various social science and humanities disciplines. Philosophers and theologians wasted no time examining the ideological components of non-theistic worldviews. Political scientists and religious studies scholars followed suit, reevaluating the intertwining of religion, nonreligion, and politics in the public sphere. As for sociologists, our primary concern was with the implication of public atheism on broader trends of secularization. Eventually, studies of the nonreligious began diversifying as scholars from subfields like gender/sexualities (Brewster 2013; Foster et al. 2016; Linneman and Clendenen 2009; Miller 2013; Schnabel et al. 2016; Stinson and Goodman 2013), family (Manning 2015; Merino 2012; Zimmerman et al. 2015), deviance (Fazzino, Borer, and Abdel Haq 2014; Cimino and Smith 2007), and communications/media (Cimino and Smith 2011; Smith and Cimino 2012) conducted research, expanding what had been a nearly non-existent body of literature. There is still, however, much work to be done.

Nowhere is this more apparent than in the lack of research on the organized American Secularism Movement by social movement scholars.[4] There are those who utilize a movements lens to examine the contours of nonreligion in the US, however, they: (1) are often not movement scholars, (2) do so narrowly, focusing on just one ideological segment, rather than being inclusive to the much larger nonreligious constituency, and/or (3) use concepts like collective identity, collective action, and framing in their analysis, but do not explicitly apply the social movement label to their findings or treat different ideological sentiments as distinct but related movements (Cimino and Smith 2007;Cimino and Smith 2007;

---

3 When discussing secularism in this chapter, we are referring to intentional efforts to normalize nonreligion.
4 A handful of scholars have used a social movement lens to examine issues such as community, identity politics, collective action, organizational dynamics, and the strategies and goals of activism.

Guenther, Mulligan, and Papp 2013; Kettell 2014; McAnulla 2012; Schulzke 2013; Smith 2013).

This ambiguity – *Is it a movement? Is it not a movement?* – has been connected to characteristics, such as ideological diversity, movement infighting, competing strategies, tactics, and goals, and the lack of an agreed upon set of doctrines/beliefs that unify all nonbelievers (Cimino and Smith 2007). Although internal dissension and conflict are very common in contemporary American movements, schisms and splits in the secular movement are often understood as a sign of movement decline/demise (Gamson 1990). Such perspectives have an overly-narrow conception of effective structural dynamics and ignore how factionalism and splitting can be beneficial to movements. The seminal work of Gerlach and Hines (1970) examined the structure of a handful of American movements in the post 1960s era, including Pentecostalism, Black Power, and "Participatory Ecology" and found that the most common type of organizational structure was not centralized, bureaucratic, or amorphous, but rather movements that had a segmented (multiple diverse groups), polycentric (decentralized authority; multiple leaders/centers of leadership), and reticulate (form a loosely integrated network) structure. In other words, social movements are rarely single organizations with a clear vision and goal; social movements are messy.

It's not often that scholars try to pinpoint the exact moment when collective efforts become a legitimate social movement. Movement origins are often contested, making them difficult to trace. Because movement scholars are rarely historians, sociological approaches to social movements can sometimes yield a structurally essentialist view of movements, creating a biased perception that sees a diffuse and decentered structure as a *symptom* of dysfunction, rather than as an *outcome* of movement growth, change, and institutionalization. Contrary to the obituarist view of some scholars, we argue that ideological and organizational diversity does not make American secularism *dis*organized – it makes it dynamic. It makes it a movement!

In what follows, we identify key events, leaders, and dynamics that facilitated the evolution of a handful of very small nontheist and freethought organizations on the verge of collapsing into the segmented, polycentric, reticulate movement it is today.

3 Methods

This chapter is based in part on data derived from interviews with 15 past and present leaders of various secular SMOs in the US (see Table 1 below). The interviews, lasting between one to three hours, were conducted either via phone or in person by Cragun, recorded, and later transcribed by Fazzino. Because all of the individuals who participated are public individuals, the identities of our participants are not anonymous.

Table 1. Interviewees.

Participant	Organizational Affiliation	Position(s) Held	Term
Louis Altman	Society for Humanistic Judaism American Humanist Association	President Board Member	2006–2012 2009–2012
Dan Barker	Freedom From Religion Foundation	PR Director Co-President	1987–2004 2004–
August Brunsman	Secular Student Alliance	Founder & Executive Director	2000–2017
Bette Chambers	American Humanist Association	Board Member President Editor – *Free Mind*	1966–1972 1973–1979 1980–2002
Edd Doerr	American Humanist Association Americans United Council for Secular Humanism	President Vice-President Board Chair Staff Editor, *Church & State* Columnist, *Free Inquiry*	1995–2002 1985–1991 1960s–1982 1970–1982 late 2000–
Fred Edwords	American Humanist Association Camp Quest United Coalition of Reason	Executive Director Editor, *The Humanist* President National Director	1984–1999 1994–2006 2002–2005 2009–2015
Tom Flynn	Council for Secular Humanism	Editor, *Free Inquiry* Executive Director	2000– 2009–
Mel Lipman	American Humanist Association	Board Member President Nominating Committee	2000–2002 2003–2008 2009-
Amanda Metskas	Camp Quest	Board Member Executive Director	2004–2007 2008–
David Silverman	American Atheists Reason Rally 2012	President Executive Director	2010– 2012
Herb Silverman	Secular Coalition of America American Humanist Association	Founder & President Board Member	2003–2012; 2014 1999–2006; 2009–
Roy Speckhardt	American Humanist Association	Executive Director	2005–

Table 1. Interviewees. *(Continued)*

Participant	Organizational Affiliation	Position(s) Held	Term
Todd Stiefel	Stiefel Freethought Foundation	Founder & President	2009–
	Secular Coalition for America	Advisory Board	2009–
	American Humanist Association	Vice President	2011
	Secular Student Alliance	Advisory Board	2010–2015
	American Atheists	Advisory Board	2009–2015
	Openly Secular Coalition	Develop. Committee	2009–2010
	Reason Rally 2	Chair	2014–
		Advisor	2015
Michael Werner	American Humanist Association	President	1993–1994
Frank Zindler	American Atheists	Interim President	2008
		Editor, *American Atheist*	until 2011
		Board Member	

The chapter also draws on internal organizational records and previously published material. As we describe aspects of the history of the various groups, we have done our best to confirm what our informants shared with us by triangulating interview data with archival and textual data. We analyzed organizational materials, such as board meeting minutes, websites, news media, and biographical works. Where there are conflicting accounts of events, we have described events in a general way or noted the differing accounts. The aim of the project was not to develop a comprehensive history of the movement but rather to gain a better sense of the dynamics of organized American secularism in the 21 century.

4 A Brief History of Organized Secularism in the United States

While there are dozens of organizations that would fall under the umbrella of atheist, humanist, secularist, and freethought activism and advocacy, there are just a handful that are very large and particularly prominent in the US today: the American Humanist Association (AHA), American Atheists (AA), Freedom From Religion Foundation (FFRF), and Council for Secular Humanism (CSH). There are other notable organizations, like the American Ethical Union, Society for Humanistic Judaism, and the Atheist Alliance of America, among many others. While each of these other organizations is important in its own right, we focus primarily on the four largest organizations in this chapter.

4.1 American Humanist Association

The origins of modern humanism[5] in the US, which is now often referred to as "secular humanism," can be traced back to Britain circa 1915, when positivist Frederick James Gould wrote an article introducing a non-theistic conception of "humanism." A couple of years later, in 1917, at the Western Unitarian Conference, two Unitarian ministers – John H. Dietrich, who read Gould's article, and Curtis W. Reese – joined forces and began discussing and advocating religious humanism, an idea that gained some popularity amongst philosophers, liberal religionists, and freethinkers alike. One of the earliest efforts to organize humanism began at the University of Chicago in 1927 when a group of scholars and Unitarian theologians with a shared interest in humanism started an organization called the Humanist Fellowship.

The fellowship began publishing *The New Humanist* in 1928, the magazine in which the first iteration of the *Humanist Manifesto* would appear. The manifesto was to be a short and simple overview of how humanists understood the world. Edwin H. Wilson, also a Unitarian minister and the editor of *The New Humanist*, was one of the manifesto's lead authors, and the final document, endorsed by 34 of the leading intellectuals of the time, was published in the magazine in 1933 (Wilson 1995). The American Humanist Association was formally established in 1941 and took over publication of *The New Humanist*, the publication of which had lapsed, renaming it *The Humanist*. *The Humanist* remains the primary publication of the AHA up to today (2017).

At roughly the same time as the American Humanist Association was being organized, (i.e., in 1939), a group of ex-Quakers formed the Humanist Society of Friends in Southern California and adopted *Humanist Manifesto I* as their official doctrine. The Humanist Society of Friends became an adjunct of the American Humanist Association (AHA) in 1991, and contributed the foundation for Humanist Celebrant training that is now run by the recently (2003) renamed group, The Humanist Society, which continues as an adjunct to the AHA.[6] Celebrants are

---

[5] We refer to this as "modern humanism" rather than simply "humanism" here to distinguish it from other forms of "humanism," such as the version of humanism that developed during The Renaissance that encapsulated a vision for how to educate students in universities, which now serves as the root of the term "humanities" (Kraye 1996). This is a very different conception of the word "humanism" than how it is used in the secular movement in the US today in reference to a set of naturalistic – as opposed to supernaturalistic or religious – philosophical principles used to provide guidance for making moral decisions.

[6] As an interesting side note, the AHA maintained a religious tax exemption for years, in part because of the AHA's relationship with the Humanist Society of Friends and their training of Hu-

secular individuals trained to officiate during important life milestones, like marriages or funerals. They are, in a sense, a secular equivalent to clergy.

One of the first splinters that occurred out of the AHA came from one of its founders – Edwin H. Wilson. Wilson had developed a policy which was effectively an agreement between the Unitarian Church and the AHA that the AHA would not form organizations that were the functional equivalents of congregations. Wilson eventually relaxed his position on this and allowed a Los Angeles based chapter of the AHA to form, which resulted in Wilson being fired from the position of Executive Director of the AHA in 1962. He later founded an organization titled the Fellowship of Religious Humanists, which was later renamed as the HUUmanists, encapsulating the close relationship between Unitarian Universalists and Humanists. As of 2016, there are 61 local HUUmanists groups in the US.[7]

As it will become relevant shortly, it is worth noting that Paul Kurtz was hired by the AHA in 1968 to edit *The Humanist*. Kurtz was highly recommended by several well-known humanist philosophers in part because Kurtz had an important humanist pedigree, having studied philosophy under Sidney Hook (who studied under John Dewey) at Columbia University. Under Kurtz's leadership, subscriptions to *The Humanist* increased substantially, drawing greater interest in the AHA. Kurtz also founded Prometheus Press in 1969 and his first skeptical magazine, *Zetetic*, which eventually became *The Skeptical Inquirer*, during his tenure at the AHA (the first was independent of the AHA, while the second was not, but was made independent at the request of Kurtz). While the precise number of members of the AHA or subscribers to the organization's magazine are not known, according to Executive Director Roy Speckhardt, as of 2016 the AHA prints and distributes approximately 84,000 copies of *The Humanist* annually.

4.2 American Atheists

The second oldest national-level group is American Atheists, founded in 1963. Contemporary atheism in the U.S. can trace its history back before WWI to notable figures like Thomas Paine, Robert G. Ingersoll, known as "the Great Agnostic," sociologist W.E.B. DuBois, founder of the Harlem Renaissance, and Emma

---

manist Celebrants. They have since dropped the religious exemption and now have an educational tax exemption.

7 http://huumanists.org/local-groups/list.

Goldman, a Jewish anarchist who would later be deported. The first explicitly anti-religious example of organized American atheism was the American Association for the Advancement of Atheism (4 A), founded in 1925 by Charles Lee Smith (see also Richter, this volume). Contrary to the idea that public atheism in 21st century America is somehow new, Charles Lee Smith was a strident antitheist, among the earliest to publicly parody religion, and fought for removing "In God We Trust" from the currency and revoking the tax-exempt status afforded to religious institutions. Charles Lee Smith founded The American Association for the Advancement of Atheism, which took over publication of *The Truthseeker*, one of the oldest atheist magazines in the US (founded in 1878). The association outlived its founder and passed to James Hervey Johnson in the 1960s, along with *The Truthseeker*. Johnson's views and mismanagement drove membership in the organization down dramatically. It is unclear when the American Association for the Advancement of Atheism ended, but it did not outlive James Hervey Johnson. However, *The Truthseeker* has continued to be sporadically published, with a new run of the magazine beginning in 2014. There is a vestige of 4 A left, though it is indirect. James Hervey Johnson left a $14 million dollar estate when he died. His estate became the James Hervey Johnson Educational Charitable Trust, which is now used primarily to fund various secular movement activity.[8]

While 4 A was still extant when Madalyn Murray O'Hair gained prominence due to her legal battles over bible reading in public schools, O'Hair's organization quickly became more influential than 4 A. O'Hair noted in one of her biographies that she requested help from a variety of secular organizations during her lawsuit (including from 4 A), but found little support. She did join the AHA board of directors at one point, but her participation in the organization was short-lived, due largely to her brash personality and unapologetic rhetoric. She founded American Atheists in 1963 as an advocacy group for atheist civil liberties but also as a way to continue her advocacy work on behalf of atheists, providing her with the necessary funds and resources for such efforts. As noted above, O'Hair gained prominence in the US as a result of the *Abington School District v. Schempp* (a.k.a. *Murray v. Curlett*, 1963) Supreme Court case in which O'Hair and her older son, William Murray, filed suit against compulsory Bible reading and reciting prayers in public schools. The court found these religious activities to be unconstitutional, and as a result, school official led bible reading was no longer allowed in public schools (though, of course, student-led bible reading that is not compulsory is still allowed).

---

[8] More information can be found about the trust on its website: http://jamesherveyjohnson.com/trust.html.

American Atheists experienced a period of significant turmoil when O'Hair, along with her younger son, John Murray, and granddaughter Robin were abducted by a former employee, David Waters, and several accomplices in 1995. Robin was held separate from the other two while the abductors forced O'Hair and her son to empty various AA bank accounts. After the abductors had extracted as much money as they could, Madalyn, John, and Robin were killed and buried in a field in Texas. While they were still alive, but after they had disappeared, they were still in contact with various members of the AA board. O'Hair was unable to tell her staff why she had disappeared, but indicated they were on important business. For many AA insiders, that important business could have involved an important financial bequest that had been rumored to be coming to AA. As a result, despite concerns among AA board members, it took a significant amount of time (over a month) for the AA board to begin trying to put people into place to take on the day-to-day management of the organization as they believed Madalyn, John, and Robin would be returning from this "important business." Eventually, contact with Madalyn, John, and Robin was lost completely and rumors spread that they absconded with the money themselves. It wasn't until 2001 that their bodies were discovered, making it clear what had happened. While others have provided the details about this incident (LeBeau 2003; Seaman 2006), we note it here as it resulted in serious difficulties for AA moving forward. As Frank Zindler, an AA board member at the time and former interim President noted in an interview:

> Well, we figured we had probably lost about 60% of our membership after the disappearance. In fact, things were so horrible, I was running AA Press entirely out of my own pocket. Other members of the board who were moderately affluent were helping pay the salaries of the staff we still had working there. We had a printer still and had somebody working in the shipping and, you know, book selling…that sort of thing. But it was a gruesome road back up. I don't know if we ever fully recovered, but it's just been a very difficult time. We really took it on the chin. So you know, we have gradually come back.

Like the AHA, it is uncertain how many members the AA have nor the number of subscribers to the magazine, but from what we have been able to discern, AA is currently the smallest of the four organizations we are detailing in this chapter in terms of membership and magazine subscriptions.

4.3 Freedom From Religion Foundation

The largest national-level group in the US in terms of membership is the Freedom From Religion Foundation (FFRF), which was co-founded in 1976 by Anne Nicol

Gaylor, her daughter Annie Laurie Gaylor, and John Sontarck. Both Anne Nicol Gaylor and her daughter, Annie Laurie Gaylor, contributed to *The American Atheist* magazine, and along with John Sontarck, were on the masthead for a period of time until early 1978. Sontarck was also, at one time, the treasurer for O'Hair's trusteeship, the Society of Separationists.

Anne Nicol Gaylor was a high-profile feminist activist who focused on abortion and women's reproductive rights. Numerous accounts indicate that FFRF was founded as a response to the role of religion in hindering women's reproductive rights. FFRF was originally affiliated with O'Hair and American Atheists, but sometime between February 1978, when Annie Laurie Gaylor appeared on the cover of the *American Atheists* magazine, and April of that same year, there was a falling out between Anne Nicol Gaylor and Madalyn Murray O'Hair that resulted in a significant degree of animosity between these two women. It was after this schism that Anne Nicol Gaylor made FFRF a national secular organization in its own right. In our research we came across explanations for the split that included: accusations over mailing lists, anti-Semitic attitudes from O'Hair's youngest son, Jon Murray, Anne Nicol Gaylor's loyalty to the atheist cause, and O'Hair's misappropriation of organization donations. We have been unable to confirm any of these specific details. What we have been able to discern definitively is that a serious and contentious split occurred, and that the tension between the two organizations continued for decades.

FFRF is led today by Annie Laurie Gaylor and her husband, Dan Barker. FFRF has been very public about their membership growth, noting it in their publications and on their weekly radio show. As of 2016, they have just over 20,000 dues paying members. Membership has been spurred by a number of successful court cases the FFRF has fought on behalf of secular individuals as well as their willingness to help secular individuals when there are clear violations of the separation of church and state in the US.

4.4 Council for Secular Humanism

The Council for Secular Humanism (CSH) is another large, national-level organization that was founded in 1980 by Paul Kurtz. The CSH is part of a larger organization, Center for Inquiry (CFI), which was founded in 1991. CFI is the umbrella organization for CSH and a division devoted to skeptical inquiry, the Committee for Skeptical Inquiry (CSI, but formerly known as CSICOP, which Kurtz started while at the AHA, but spun off the AHA).

CSH is also the result of a split. Paul Kurtz worked for the AHA as the editor of the organization's magazine *The Humanist* from 1968 until 1978. While it is possible Paul Kurtz might remember things differently (he died before we began our interviews), we think we have been able to verify sufficiently what led to Kurtz's split from the AHA. Most accounts suggest that Paul Kurtz wanted to wrest control of *The Humanist* from the AHA, both editorially (something he largely already had) and financially. The board of the AHA was unwilling to agree to this arrangement and members of the board were already upset about his financial (mis)management of the magazine.[9] According to then AHA President, Bette Chambers, Kurtz was reticent to share financial information with the board, was misrepresenting the circulation numbers which could have resulted in legal problems for the AHA, and he was unwilling to allow AHA oversight of the finances of *The Humanist*. All of this came to a climax at a board meeting in July of 1978 just after taking a sabbatical from his editorial duties, during which Lloyd Morain was appointed acting editor.

What was *not* at issue were Kurtz's editorial skills; his tenure at the helm of *The Humanist* was widely applauded by the board of the AHA. What was at issue was financial transparency, which Kurtz likened to censorship. The minutes from the meeting suggest that Kurtz was to be given complete editorial and managerial control of *The Humanist*, but financial control would be overseen by a committee (one that included Kurtz, but also others). According to Bette Chambers, this was unacceptable to Kurtz. The minutes from the meeting do not include a record of votes, but Bette Chambers, who chaired the meeting (and Fred Edwords who has listened to the audio recording of the meeting), recalled that the motion to reinstate Kurtz as the Editor-in-Chief of *The Humanist* after the end of his sabbatical failed to pass. The first two votes were tied, but the vote swung against Kurtz on the third ballot. Paul Kurtz did not take the decision well. The tension over financial oversight of *The Humanist* between Kurtz and the AHA Board was what led Paul Kurtz to leave the AHA.

Splits can sometimes lead to the formation of new organizations when people take resources and reputation with them (Zald and McCarthy 1980), as appears to have occurred when Kurtz was ousted from the AHA. As Bette Chambers recalled, Kurtz quickly contacted their largest donor, Corliss Lamont, who was giving tens of thousands of dollars every year to the AHA and to *The Humanist*:

---

[9] While Kurtz was on sabbatical from his editorial duties at AHA in 1977–78, internal conflict erupted when then president Bette Chambers and acting Editor-in-Chief Lloyd Morain discovered irregularities having to do with unethical business transactions between Prometheus Books and the AHA under Kurtz's leadership and his true intentions for the magazine. These issues ultimately divided the AHA board into pro-Kurtz and anti-Kurtz factions.

So that in that instance [after the motion failed to pass] Kurtz was out. Then Kurtz sometime that day called Corliss Lamont and told him that he had been summarily dismissed as editor of *The Humanist* without a hearing. Lamont called me and asked me what in the hell went on. And of course I immediately corrected that point of view, I said Kurtz was there. He was there the entire meeting, he heard everything. He voted! ... I corrected this and told Lamont what happened and then in a matter of days within the first couple of weeks after this event, Kurtz wrote to the people that he knew as his major donors who gave money every year to support the magazine, and he told them he had been dismissed without a hearing. I think that the whole thing in terms of loss... Of course he sent out a few hundred statements like that, it got to the membership in general... I calculated – the next year I compared the membership data with one year later compared to what it had been in Oct 1978 – and I figured that the lying about what had actually had taken place had cost us about $240,000.

This event triggered extreme discontent (Kemper 2001), which Kurtz internalized and refused to let go, using these emotions as motivation to maintain rigid social boundaries (Lamont and Molnar 2002) between himself and the AHA from that point on. While there is no place that we know of where Kurtz explicitly stated his desire to "destroy the AHA" after he left the organization, numerous people told us that they had heard him indicate as much.

Following his split, Paul Kurtz built one of the largest, most well-funded secular, freethought, and skeptical organizations in organized secularism. Today, *Free Inquiry*, the magazine published by CSH, has the largest number of subscribers of the various secular magazines and the umbrella company, CFI, has one of the largest budgets of the four organizations we examine in this chapter.

5 Personality as Catalysts of Growth and Change in Social Movements

Paul Kurtz and Madalyn Murray O'Hair were two of the most notable leaders of the movement during the late 20 century. To date, we have seen no research describing their personalities, which we believe were remarkably similar. In this section of the chapter, we describe the personalities of Madalyn Murray O'Hair and Paul Kurtz and argue that their personalities: (1) were shaped by both their social context and the larger cultural context, (2) influenced their interactions with other movement actors, and (3) were not only at the core of the organizational splits discussed above, but also created an organizational culture which contributed to an attitudinal shift among a new cohort of secular activists with different political consciousness at the end of the 20 century (see Whittier 1997).

To discuss the personalities of Paul Kurtz and Madalyn Murray O'Hair, we turn to the impressions they left on others. Without the availability of direct data, such as personality test scores, we rely on how those personalities were interpreted by those who knew and worked with these people. While this method does not capture their personalities in full, it does provide pictures of their personalities, even if they are a bit fuzzy. We are interested in these personalities as we believe they inform the organizational splitting observed during that time period.

Paul Kurtz and Madalyn Murray O'Hair both possessed the authority and charisma to push boundaries and blaze new trails for organized secularism in the 20th century. This authority, however, came at the cost of harmonious interpersonal dynamics.

Paul Kurtz was something of a conundrum. Kurtz is widely recognized by many in organized secularism as the "Father of Secular Humanism."[10] He is remembered as brilliant, hardworking, and an instinctive empire-builder. His reputation as a charismatic visionary is widely recognized among those who knew him. Yet, at the same time, there was a part of Kurtz that wasn't pretty. Kurtz could be disingenuous, vengeful, petty, and manipulative. Some of our interviewees referred to this as Kurtz's "dark side."

Part of this "dark side" were Kurtz's autocratic tendencies. Paul Kurtz was rarely willing to compromise. When he found himself at odds with an executive board, he was willing to strike out anew, founding another organization that would allow him the control he demanded (as he did when he left the AHA in the 1970s and later when he left CFI). Though he claimed that his voluntary departure from CFI in 2009 was under duress, these claims along with many others are disputed. One of our interviewees, August Brunsman, had personal experience working under Kurtz, as he, along with several others, branched out of CFI's college campus initiative, CFI on Campus, to form the Secular Student Alliance. August described Kurtz's autocratic tendencies like this,

> "Paul's total approach to humanist organizing is that he wanted to own it, he wanted to be in charge and run it, and he just didn't trust anybody else to do anything worthwhile that [he] didn't control."

---

[10] Kurtz began to describe the Council for Secular and Democratic Humanism – later just the Council for Secular Humanism – as adhering to "secular humanism" in order to distinguish his new organization from the American Humanist Association. This was, in large part, a marketing ploy as it could then be suggested that the AHA was more favorable toward "religious humanism" (which, in fact, was true at the time), while Kurtz's new organization was not. While Kurtz did not coin the term "secular humanism" (see Richter's chapter, this volume), he did work hard to co-opt the term and embraced it as being descriptive of his organization's views.

Another illustration of Kurtz's "dark side" was his tendency to hold grudges. When Kurtz lost the vote at the AHA to be reinstated as the editor of The Humanist, he didn't forgive and forget or move on. This is not an uncommon practice among social movement leaders who seek to create symbolic hegemony in their respective movement (Zald and McCarthy 1980). Kurtz's actions also suggest that was his intention, which was confirmed by several of our interviewees. Here is what Bette Chambers recounted of the relationship between Kurtz and the AHA after the 1978 board meeting:

> Fred [Edwords] and I, at the time that Michael Werner was president of the AHA in, I think, early 1990s, Fred and I pressured him and the board to 'Get the hell out of dodge;' to move out of Amherst[11] and to someplace else. The harm that Kurtz was doing even then to the AHA never stopped. He had a coterie of sycophantic friends who were doing all sorts of peculiar things like jamming the locks on the office doors... I mean, you know childish tricks like that. Now Kurtz himself wasn't doing them, but these were... When I say sycophants they really were. You could hear them say they would follow Paul Kurtz to hell and back if they had to. And that always struck me as so strange, because if there is anything I know about Humanists they are not followers. If I run into one that's a follower of something I get very nervous because it just doesn't seem right.

From the information we have gathered, it appears that Paul Kurtz was an autocratic leader who wanted to have complete control over organized secularism. To this end, he actively worked to undermine the other secular SMOs, particularly the AHA. We also find it somewhat ironic that Kurtz, who was, professionally, an ethicist, had problems being and behaving ethically. Even so, people still maintained favorable opinions of Kurtz. He was a strategic visionary with an uncanny ability to rebound from organizational conflict with his reputation relatively unscathed. As the evidence above suggests, Kurtz had an over-bearing personality and others found it difficult to work with him. But it may be the case that precisely these types of characteristics were what was needed during that particular period in America's history, as we will discuss at greater length below.

Madelyn Murray O'Hair's reputation is even more contested than is Paul Kurtz's. Also considered quite difficult to work with, O'Hair was perceived as brash and vulgar. She was thought of as behaving highly inappropriately by the

---

11 At the same time that Kurtz was voted out as the editor of The Humanist, the AHA moved its headquarters from San Francisco to a building owned by Lloyd Morain, a wealthy benefactor of the AHA. The move to Amherst was in order to bring the AHA headquarters next to the publishing headquarters of The Humanist, which were located in Amherst where Paul Kurtz worked as a college professor. Kurtz and the AHA remained in the same building for a period of time even after Kurtz was voted out of the AHA.

standards of her day. She had a deep distrust of others and a justified paranoia cultivated by abuse from a hostile public and government officials as well as from a series of betrayals in her life. Her response to most threats, perceived or otherwise, was typically the same: "excommunication". The hardline she maintained meant that the splitting that occurred around her typically took the form of others being banished, or leaving of their own accord. One of our interviewees, Bette Chambers, who hosted O'Hair in her home, offered this description:

> Madalyn O'Hair...she was Madalyn Murray at the time...I still hold the view that atheism would've become popular in this country far sooner than it has even today, which isn't very much, but we wouldn't have had quite so much trouble relating to the public and explaining our position since she called herself the spokesperson for American atheism. I think that she set the movement back a whole generation. That's my opinion. She was an extremely unpleasant person and offended people right and left, primarily at private gatherings. But she was quite kind of popular on television, and she came across as a loudmouth. There was nothing intellectual about her. Not in my opinion. She was an atheist – period – because she detested religion, the churches. You don't find Humanists today who are so anti-mainstream religion. She was anti-all religion.

This sort of impression is contrasted by others who offered a more balanced opinion of her personality. According to Frank Zindler who, along with his wife, was very close to O'Hair:

> Madalyn was very, very warm and generous with us almost all of the time. However, she was a brutal diabetic and there would be times...I never could figure out whether it was high blood sugar or low blood sugar – it was totally impossible for me to ever figure this out, but there would be moments when she would just go off like a roman candle and she would shout and scream, 'You're excommunicated,' and she would fire off the most outrageous letters to people, uh, excommunicating them....

We do believe these quotes are illustrative of O'Hair's personality. However, it is important to keep in mind that the *perception* of O'Hair as brash, vulgar, and, at times, inappropriate was generated within the cultural milieu of the time. O'Hair's rise to fame started in the 1950s, and continued through the 1980s. This period is widely recognized to have been a time of significant change in cultural values toward women's roles in society (Brown 2012). However, women's position in society throughout this period remained (and to a large degree still remains) conflicted (Hochschild 1997). The rise of women's participation in the workforce starting in the late 1960s, spurred in part by the second wave of the feminist movement but also by economic necessity (Coontz 1992), began to shift cultural expectations for women. However, women still faced expectations about how they should behave; women were to be passive, soft, caring, and kind (Gerami and Lehnerer 2001).

It was in this cultural milieu that Madelyn Murray O'Hair's rise to prominence occurred. It is also in this cultural milieu that we must now consider how Madelyn Murray O'Hair's personality was perceived. O'Hair's persona and behaviors were, undoubtedly, counter to the normative expectations for women at the time when she gained prominence. But they were not all that different from what would be expected behavior for a man at that time. In other words, Madelyn Murray O'Hair is often judged harshly for her tough, brash, and aggressive demeanor, precisely because she was a woman. If O'Hair had been a man, it is highly unlikely that she would have received the same degree of acerbic criticism for her persona or behavior. We are not trying to challenge descriptions of Madelyn Murray O'Hair's personality. We are, however, arguing that criticisms of O'Hair's personality reflect a gendered double-standard.

From everything we've been able to gather, Paul Kurtz's personality was not all that different from Madalyn Murray O'Hair's. Kurtz was an autocrat and micro-manager who could also lose his temper and yell at his employees. Yet, we have been unable to find comparable criticisms of Kurtz's personality to those of Madalyn Murray O'Hair's. Certainly there are those who are critical of Paul Kurtz and his personality, and it was his leadership style that eventually led to his ouster at CFI.[12] Despite the similarities in personalities between Madalyn Murray O'Hair and Paul Kurtz, very few people describe Paul Kurtz as eminently disagreeable or caustic, like they do with O'Hair. This leads us to believe that a gendered double-standard has been applied to O'Hair.

In considering the personalities of these two leaders, several commonalities are apparent. First, and most glaring, both were self-aggrandizing megalomaniacs who acted as dictators over their respective organizations. Coupled with this dominance was a great strength. If creation is an act of will, then these individuals shared a strength of willpower. This appears to be the double-edged sword of the brand of leadership shared by O'Hair and Kurtz. While they possessed the authority and charisma to push boundaries and blaze new trails, this authority came at the cost of harmonious interpersonal dynamics. They demanded complete control of those with whom they worked. When these standards were not met, organizational splitting occurred.

---

12 Per our conversation with Tom Flynn, Paul Kurtz was not formally removed from his position at CFI but rather was marginalized in his position and lost a substantial amount of power as a result of several votes by the CFI board. After this occurred, Kurtz resigned his position and started a new organization, the Institute for Science and Human Values.

It is likely that the personality characteristics of O'Hair and Kurtz contributed to the organizational splits in the secular movement (CSH from AHA and FFRF from AA) we described above, though there were likely other factors involved. Interestingly, even though organizational fracturing was common to both O'Hair and Kurtz, their public reputations were quite different. Kurtz's reputation was and remains largely positive. Despite the difficulties in working with him, his work and many accomplishments are generally held in high regard. In essence, his "dark side" is largely overlooked. Yet, O'Hair, who was not all that different from Kurtz personality-wise, has been and continues to be criticized for her personality, which overshadows her organizational leadership. This is yet more evidence for a gendered double-standard being applied to these monumental figures in organized secularism.

Perhaps more important than why these splits occurred is that they occurred at all. Organizational schisms and the resulting fragmentation are rarely thought of as a positive for social movements. As intra-organizational schisms become inter-organizational schisms, communication among like-minded SMOs is limited. These sorts of factors might generally be thought of as impediments to movement success, as power becomes more diffuse and alliances and coalitions that might strengthen the movement are torn apart.

Historically, then, it might appear as though interpersonal dysfunction was a hallmark of secular organizing during this time and the splitting we have documented certainly seems to support this. However, it is our argument here that, while this may be the case, social movement theory reminds us that nearly anything can be a resource. In the case of Kurtz and O'Hair, it appears that perhaps difficult personalities and the resulting organizational splits which resulted from them were ultimately a resource of sorts for the movement, both at that time and later.

Finally, while these personality characteristics are not necessarily those we would associate with ideal leaders, we would be remiss not to consider the context in which these individuals developed. The trajectories of our lived experiences as well as the turning points to those trajectories are informed by the social structure we encounter, which is relative to time and place. In the case of these leaders, both physically went to war (i.e., they served in the military). Both faced power struggles from within their organizations as well as external threats. Both lived in a time when being openly secular was highly stigmatized, more so than today. O'Hair and Kurtz were at the helm of secular SMOs during a very difficult time in America's history: the Cold War. As others have documented (Cragun 2017), there were intentional efforts in the US during the Cold War to create a religious American identity that differed from the "godless communists" of the Soviet Union. As a result, being secular, humanist, atheist, or a freethinker during this time period was highly stigmatized. While we cannot say that O'Hair and Kurtz's personalities were "necessary" to maintain secular SMOs during this time period, it is likely the case that their strong personalities and their unwillingness to compromise helped them cope with the widespread stigma against nonreligion and irreligion that existed during their tenures. Thus, while their personalities were difficult and alienating to many, it is also arguably the case that O'Hair's and Kurtz's personalities were a resource for the secular movement in the US during one of its more challenging periods.

6 Unifying the Secular Movement

In this section we address the following question: *how did organized secularism get to where it is today – diffuse, de-centered, and somewhat unified?* The tensions with AHA/CSH and AA/FFRF mentioned above are where we begin to explore this question. Three splits, two of which (in 1978) were extremely contentious, instigated organizational growth but led to nearly three decades of animosity and minimal inter-movement contact. The result of these tensions was that there was limited coordination among the secular SMOs during this time period. Despite several decades of limited coordination, bitter and hurt feelings, and incivility between the various secular SMOs, organized secularism in the US today is far more collaborative and unified, even if there remain several national level organizations and thousands of local grassroots groups. How the movement transformed from significant internal turmoil to relative calm and cooperation will be the focus for the rest of this chapter.

As various informants told us, there has historically been more tension between the groups that split than between the others. After Paul Kurtz left the AHA, there was a significant amount of tension between Paul Kurtz's organization, CSH, and the AHA, with Kurtz even offering to co-opt the AHA at one point. Likewise, after Anne Nicole Gaylor left the AA, there was significant tension between those two organizations that has continued until just recently. Part of the tension has resulted from the original splits. But another part of the tension stems from the fact that the organizations that split remain the most similar in mission, membership, and motivation.

For instance, both the AHA and the CSH identify as "Humanist" organizations. The label "humanist" provides them a broader label that encapsulates the many ways of being secular or nonreligious, or potentially even religious.[13]

---

[13] One of Paul Kurtz's early criticisms of the AHA was that it was too religious in the sense that

Atheists, agnostics, freethinkers, brights, nonbelievers, antitheists, and others can all identify as humanist, but not all of them are, obviously, atheists. As a result, both AHA and CSH have broad appeal. Both have engaged in similar activities, working toward the advancement of science and for some progressive issues (like women's and sexual and gender minorities' rights). However, there is a bit more of a libertarian sentiment at CSH, perhaps stemming from Paul Kurtz's personal political views[14] than there is at the more progressive AHA.

Similarly, AA and FFRF have many things in common. While FFRF bills itself as a "freethought" organization, a term that has fairly old origins that suggest independence from organized religion, in much of its promotional material the organization identifies itself as an advocacy group for nonbelievers or atheists. AA, of course, is specifically geared toward advocacy for atheists. While FFRF has focused very heavily in recent years on litigation, AA has its own litigation division. Both, also, have run billboard and advertising campaigns and arguably have had greater appeal to atheists and nonbelievers who are a bit more strident in their views or more "eliminationist" in their approach toward religion (see Langston et al. chapter, this volume). Thus, some of the continued tension between these organizations stems from their similarity to each other. David Silverman commented about the similarities:

> Now, in a market segmentation issue, FFRF and AA are most closely competitive. Um, they, they're harder than AHA and CFI. They're not as hard as us, but they're closer than the others. So, we have a competitive aspect going on between us, um but at the same time, while Madalyn and Ellen Johnson were not very good at membership cultivation, they [FFRF] were, so they have far more members than we do, which is just great for them, but it also makes them care less about working with us. So, it's a tough thing because I'm just trying to do right for the movement and she's [Annie Laurie] still angry. I think she's getting

---

members of the AHA could be "religious humanists" or both religious and a humanist. It was Paul Kurtz's efforts in trying to differentiate his new organization from the AHA that resulted in the heightened use of the phrase "secular humanism." Prior to that point in the 1980s, humanism was not exclusively secular (and still, technically, is not). However, to simultaneously criticize the AHA, which still catered to and included religious humanists, and to distinguish his new organization from the AHA, Kurtz called his organization The Council for Democratic and Secular Humanism (or CODESH). "Democratic" was originally included in the label to distinguish Kurtz's new organization from the AHA as well, as the AHA was heavily influenced by very left-leaning individuals, some of whom identified as socialists (like Corliss Lamont). Given the degree of competition that existed between these groups, it is important to recognize just how influential branding was for the organizations.

14 One of our informants, Michael Werner, informed us that Paul Kurtz identified as a Republican.

past it. We just had a big, a legal symposium. And they went. They came. Annie Laurie came. Cold to me, but there.

As far as AA's relationship with the AHA and CSH, again we quote David Silverman:

> Oh, I like them very much. I have very good relationships with Ron [Lindsay from CFI] and Roy [Speckhardt from the AHA]. Um, I think we respect each other and like each other. I think we see each other as allies. I think we see each other as different market segments. I think there are people at AHA that don't like AA. There are some people on the board of AHA that don't like AA. And some see us as competitors because that's just where their mind goes. But for the most part, I think the relationship with us is as good as it can be or should be. I mean, if I have a question for Roy, I can just call him or email him and he'll come right back and give me an honest answer. Same with Ron. And if we disagree with each other, we can say it and we can do well. So I think the relationship between the three of us is positive and looks positive moving forward.

The market competition between groups was recognized in several interviews, with some informants going so far as to suggest that AHA and CSH really could and maybe even should merge, as should FFRF and AA. However, other informants disagreed and believed that the various organizations were different enough that they appealed to slightly different niches of the secular public. When asked about this, Roy Speckhardt said:

> I had talks with Ron Lindsey at CFI as recently as a couple of years ago about ways we could potentially bring the two organizations together and it didn't go that far [merging] as there were you know some things didn't work out for that. But we did come up with a couple of projects we can work on together. Who knows, down the road it might happen. I think the philosophical differences between our groups are pretty minor at this point. Still the memberships are a little different. You know a little more anti religious on one side, a little less on the other; a little more libertarian on their side, a little more socialist leaning on our side.

And when Roy Speckhardt was asked about the possibility of FFRF and AA combining into a single organization, Roy noted that such a unification is probably not in the movement's best interest:

> Well, it's tricky. Financially speaking it's not necessarily an advantage to merge organizations because most people in their annual giving... If you look at the 20,000 people who support us, they're people who say I'm going to give each of my member organizations my membership dues. That might be $50 a year and if there's one organization they give it $50. If there's ten, they give each of them $50 and that's $500 that goes out.

Roy Speckhardt, like many of our informants, no longer believed the various secular organizational movements were involved in a zero-sum game. To the contrary, there is variation among the constituents – they have different interests and different desires (as various chapters in this volume suggest; see chapters by Schutz, Smith, Frost, and Langston et al.). Additionally, while there is some competition among the organizations for donations, there is also evidence that the competition is both: (a) quite limited as big donors tend to have their preferred organizations as well, and (b) minimal because donors will often give more if they are giving to multiple organizations than if they are giving to just a single organization.

What the above suggests is that the dynamics of the secular movement in the US have changed. While there was, for decades, competition, fracturing, and even hatred among the various organization, today there is a growing sense of unity and common purpose. While there is still competition between the organizations, it is probably more accurate to characterize that competition as "friendly." Likewise, the implication of calling the movement "disorganized" misses the mark. A diffuse organization can be just as useful for a social movement or potentially even more effective than a centrally organized social movement. Polycephalous movements are also more likely to withstand controversies within the movement; problems within one of the constituent organizations will not destroy the entire movement. Thus, when scandals occur in the secular movement – and they certainly have occurred – the entire movement is not destroyed, as might be the case if there was just a single secular social movement organization.

The closer degree of coordination in organized secularism, as noted at the beginning of this chapter, is relatively recent. We believe a combination of factors coalesced in the early 2000s to change the dynamics of the movement. To begin with, a transition in leadership – from Kurtz and O'Hair to the current crop of leaders – took place. Many of the new leaders had observed the caustic personalities of prior leaders and intentionally chose not to follow that lead. The change in leadership was coupled with the rise of a common enemy – fundamentalist and conservative religion. Fundamentalism in the US has its origins in the early 20th century, and conservative religion has gained prominence in American politics prior to this point with the rise of the Religious Right and the Moral Majority in the late 20th century. However, the perceived threat of religious fundamentalism became particularly prominent as a result of the September 11th, 2001 attacks. The clear and present danger of fundamentalism to secularism combined with new leadership changed the environment of the secular movement. In what follows we attempt to describe this change in greater detail.

In 2000, Mel Lipman, an attorney and activist from Las Vegas, was nominated and elected to the national board of the American Humanist Association (AHA). In 2002, at the urging of a fellow board member, Lipman ran for the AHA presidency on a platform of bringing together all of the varied organizations who believed in doing good without a belief in a supernatural entity. His agenda was not to merge the organizations, but rather to work together towards common goals.

In 2003, Mel Lipman succeeded Edd Doer, who served 14 years as president of the AHA. On January 15, 2005, Mel Lipman convened the "Inauguration Summit" – an unprecedented meeting of secular elites with a history of frosty relationships from over 22 freethought groups to discuss how their respective organizations could work together for common interests, namely tackling the religious right in the upcoming November election. There was, however, one organization that missed the summit, the Council for Secular Humanism (CSH), allegedly due to scheduling conflicts.[15]

At the conclusion of the weekend the most promising impact was the commitment among those in attendance to remain in communication and to look for ways to collaborate. To this end, attendees were extended an invitation to join the Secular Coalition for America (SCA). Founded by Herb Silverman, a math professor who became a secular activist in the early 1990s, the SCA provided an opportunity for its member organizations to come together to cooperate in areas of mutual interest and to support the other organizations in their efforts to uphold separation between government and religion. SCA is a lobbying organization, but for Silverman, this was secondary to decreasing in-fighting and fostering a sense of community. He believed that through cooperation the nonreligious would be able to amplify their voice, increase visibility, change public opinion, and be as effective as possible in their lobbying efforts.

True to their skeptical nature, the largest national secular, humanist, atheist, and freethought organizations were hesitant to join SCA, until the AHA signed on in 2005. Between 2006 and 2008, American Atheists (AA), Society for Humanistic Judaism (SHJ), Freedom From Religion Foundation (FFRF), Military Association of Atheists and Freethinkers (MAAF), American Ethical Union (AEU), and Camp Quest (CQ) became members. As of 2016, SCA is comprised of 18 voting member organizations. According to AHA's current Executive Director, Roy Speckhardt, "The secular coalition, as it became more prominent, helped established groups get along better and get to know each other better." Prior to these efforts in the early 2000s, when leaders from different organizations came to-

---

15 http://americanhumanist.org/hnn/archives/?id=177&article=10.

gether, it was almost a given that fights would ensue. The 2005 Summit catalyzed a significant transformation in how the various organizations interacted with one another.

7 Conclusion

Today, there are several national, member-based secularist movement organizations and thousands of local grassroots organizations in existence. Contemporary social movements, especially in the Western world, are heterogeneous, ideologically diverse, and loosely integrated (Gerlach and Hines 1970). It's not uncommon for movements to have a decentralized, or "leaderless" authority structure, the very characteristic that Baker and Smith (2015) problematize for secular groups.

When looking historically at the development of secular organizing in the United States, it appears that difficult personalities and interpersonal conflict were a bit of a hallmark. The many splits that occurred imply a contentiousness within the movement. As discussed, these personalities did not develop within a vacuum. Some of the roughness of these personalities seems well-adapted for the trying times and numerous threats these leaders encountered. Still, for those who have joined the movement since this period of fragmentation, the splits and the personalities driving them may not be the fairy tale story of a unified effort towards a common goal one might hope to find. Even so, in the case of nonreligious organizing, it appears that dysfunctional personalities had functional outcomes. Oddly, the difficulty of working with O'Hair and Kurtz ultimately served as a resource for movement mobilization, as organizational splintering diversified and strengthened the movement.

When we view these events through a social movements lens, these contentious inter-movement politics lead to an important conclusion. Drawing on Gerlach and Hines's (1970) work, we see how the diversity of secular organizations creates a more diverse, or polycephalous, movement landscape, which is a strength of the movement, not a weakness. In a variety of ways, the fragmentation that occurred during the contentious 1970s and 1980s led to a variety of secular SMOs, which has allowed them to develop specialized niches with greater appeal to different segments of the secular public. This diversified the landscape of the movement, with various groups taking on different issues and developing along unique trajectories. This ultimately set the stage for the unification that did occur. As of 2016, it's unlikely you'll hear members of one secular SMO calling members of another, "Splitters!" Perhaps we can finally say that the various secular SMOs are, as Brian begged his Jewish brothers to do in *The Life of Brian*, "struggling together" against a common enemy.

Bibliography

Armstrong, Elizabeth A. 2002. *Forging Gay Identities: Organizing Sexuality in San Francisco, 1950–1994.* Chicago: University of Chicago Press.
Baker, Joseph O., and Buster G Smith. 2015. *American Secularism: Cultural Contours of Nonreligious Belief Systems.* New York: New York University Press.
Balser, Deborah. 1997. "The Impact of Environmental Factors on Factionalism and Schism in Social Movement Organizations." *Social Forces* 76: 199–228.
Blankholm, Joseph. 2014. "The Political Advantages of a Polysemous Secular." *Journal for the Scientific Study of Religion* 53(4): 775–790.
Brown, Callum G. 2012. *Religion and the Demographic Revolution: Women and Secularisation in Canada, Ireland, UK and USA since the 1960s.* Woodbridge: The Boydell Press.
Buechler, Steven M. 2000. *Social Movements in Advanced Capitalism: The Political Economy and Cultural Construction of Social Activism.* New York: Oxford University Press.
Cady, Daniel. 2010. "Freethinkers and Hell Raisers: The Brief History of American Atheism and Secularism." In *Atheism and Secularity, Issues, Concepts, and Definitions Vol.1*, edited by Phil Zuckerman, 229–250. Santa Barbara: Praeger.
Campbell, Colin. [1971] 2013. *Toward a Sociology of Irreligion.* London: Macmillan.
Cimino, Richard, and Christopher Smith. 2007. "Secular Humanism and Atheism Beyond Progressive Secularism." *Sociology of Religion* 68(4): 407–424.
Cimino, Richard, and Christopher Smith. 2014. *Atheist Awakening: Secular Activism & Community in America.* New York: Oxford University Press.
Coontz, Stephanie. 1992. *The Way We Never Were: American Families and the Nostalgia Trap.* New York, NY: BasicBooks.
Cragun, Ryan T. 2017. "The Declining Significance of Religion: Secularization in Ireland." Pp. 17–35 in *Values and Identities in Europe: Evidence from the European Social Survey, Routledge Advances in Sociology*, edited by M. J. Breen. Oxon, UK: Routledge.
Fazzino, Lori L., Michael Ian Borer, and Mohammed Abdel Haq. 2014. "The New Moral Entrepreneurs: Atheist Activism as Scripted and Performed Political Deviance." In *The Death and Resurrection of Deviance: Current Research and Ideas*, edited by Michael Dellwing, Joseph A. Kotarba, and Nathan W. Pino, 168–191. UK: Palgrave Macmillan.
Gamson, William. 1990. *The Strategy of Social Protest, second edition.* Belmont: Wadsworth.
Gerami, Shahin and Melodye Lehnerer. 2001. "Women's Agency and Household Diplomacy." *Gender & Society* 15(4):556–73.
Gerlach, Luther, and Virginia Hines. 1970. *People, Power, Change: Movements of Social Transformation.* Indianapolis: Bobbs-Merrill.
Grasso, Christopher. 2002. Skepticism and American Faith: Infidels, Converts, and Religious Doubt in the Early Nineteenth Century." *Journal of the Early Republic* 22(3): 465–508.
Guenther, Katja M., Kerry Mulligan, and Cameron Papp. 2013. "From the Outside In: Crossing Boundaries to Build Collective Identity in the New Atheist Movement." *Social Problems* 60(4): 457–475.

Hochschild, Arlie Russell. 1997. *The Time Bind: When Work Becomes Home and Home Becomes Work*. New York: Metropolitan Books.
Jacoby, Susan. 2004. *Freethinkers: A History of American Secularism*. New York: Metropolitan Books.
Jacoby, Susan. 2009. *The Age of American Unreason*. New York: Vintage Books.
Kemper, Theodore D. 2001. "A Structural Approach to Social Movement Emotions." In *Passionate Politics: Emotions and Social Movements*, edited by Jeff Goodwin, James M. Jasper, and Francesca Polletta, 58–73. Chicago: University of Chicago Press.
Ketchell, Aaron K. 2000. "Contesting Tradition and Combating Intolerance: A History of Freethought in Kansas." *Great Plains Quarterly* 20(4): 281–295.
Kettell, Steven. 2014. "Divided We Stand: The Politics of the Atheist Movement in the United States." *Journal of Contemporary Religion* 29(3): 377–391.
Klatch, Rebecca E. 2004. "The Underside of Social Movements: The Effects of Destructive Affective Ties." *Qualitative Sociology* 27(4): 487–509.
Kraye, Jill, ed. 1996. *The Cambridge Companion to Renaissance Humanism*. 1st edition. Cambridge; New York: Cambridge University Press.
Lamont, Michèle, and Virág Molnár. 2002. "The Study of Boundaries in the Social Sciences." *Annual Review of Sociology* 28: 167–195.
LeBeau, Bryan F. 2003. *The Atheist: Madalyn Murray O'Hair*. New York: NYU Press.
LeDrew, Stephen. 2016. *The Evolution of Atheism: The Politics of a Modern Movement*. New York: Oxford University Press.
McAdam, Doug. 1982. *Political Process and the Development of Black Insurgency, 1930–1970*. Chicago: University of Chicago Press.
McAdam, Doug. 1988. *Freedom Summer*. New York: Oxford University Press.
McAnulla, Stuart. 2012. "Radical Atheism and Religious Power: New Atheist Politics." *Approaching Religion* 2(1): 87–99.
McAnulla, Stuart. 2014. "Secular Fundamentalists? Characterising the New Atheist Approach to Secularism, Religion and Politics." *British Politics* 9(2): 124–145.
McCarthy, John D., and Mayer N. Zald. 1977. "Resource Mobilization and Social Movements: A Partial Theory." *American Journal of Sociology* 82(6): 1212–1241.
Minkoff, Debra C. 1999. "Bending with the Wind: Strategic Change and Adaptation by Women's and Racial Minority Organizations." *American Journal of Sociology* 104(6): 1666–1703.
Niose, David. 2012. *Nonbeliever Nation: The Rise of Secular Americans*. New York: Palgrave Macmillan.
Turner, James. 1985. *Without God, Without Creed: The Origins of Unbelief in America*. Baltimore: Johns Hopkins University Press.
Schulzke, Marcus. 2013. "The Politics of New Atheism." *Politics and Religion* 6(4): 778–799.
Seaman, Anne Rowe. 2006. *America's Most Hated Woman: The Life and Gruesome Death of Madalyn Murray O'Hair*. New York: Continuum Books.
Shriver, Thomas E., and Chris Messer. 2009. "Ideological Cleavages and Schism in the Czech Environmental Movement." *Human Ecology Review* 16(2): 161–171.
Smith, Jesse M. 2013. "Creating a Godless Community: The Collective Identity Work of Contemporary American Atheists." *Journal for the Scientific Study of Religion* 52(1): 80–99.

Smith, Christopher, and Richard Cimino. 2012. "Atheism Unbound: The Role of New Media in the Formation of a Secularist Identity." *Secularism and Nonreligion* 1: 17–31.

Turner, James C. 1986. *Without God, Without Creed: The Origins of Unbelief in America.* Baltimore, MD: Johns Hopkins University Press.

Williams, Rhys H. 2004. "The Cultural Contexts of Collective Action: Constraints, Opportunities, and the Symbolic Life of Social Movements." In *The Blackwell Companion to Social Movements*, edited by David A. Snow, Sarah A. Soule, and Hanspeter Kriesi, 91–115. Malden, MA: Blackwell.

Wilson, Edwin H. 1995. *The Genesis of a Humanist Manifesto.* Amherst, NY: Humanist Press.

Zald, Mayer N., and John D. McCarthy. 1980. "Social Movement Industries: Competition and Cooperation Among Movement Organizations." In *Research in Social Movements, Conflicts and Change, Volume 3*, edited by Louis Kriesberg, 1–20. Greenwich, CT: JAI Press.

Zimmerman, Kevin, Jesse Smith, Kevin Simonson, and W. Myers. 2015. "Familial Relationship Outcomes of Coming Out as an Atheist." *Secularism and Nonreligion* 4(1): 1–11.

John R. Shook
Recognizing and Categorizing the Secular: Polysecularity and Agendas of Polysecularism

1 Introduction: Seeking the Secular

What may count as a "secular" organization, or a "secular" movement? How should secular societies be studied, classified, and compared? The amount of research into group manifestations of secular energy and activism has been limited and disjointed, most likely due to a general lack of clarity and rigor.

This chapter offers a well-defined framework for classifying and contrasting the compositions and agendas of organizations for secular people. That framework must be assembled gradually and carefully, which requires initial sections of this chapter for describing how the secular and secularity can be studied scientifically. The second section shows how to liberate a free-standing conception of the secular from pre-fabricated contrasts against religious normalcies. The third section explains how to avoid the prevalent fallacies in the social sciences that distort the identities of secular people. The fourth section introduces the idea of "polysecularity" to better discriminate the many types of secular people. The fifth section introduces the idea of "polysecularism" to cover primary modes of activism chosen by some secular people in the public sphere, which need not be characterized only by negative opposition to religion. The sixth section orients research into public secular attitudes through the positive self-identities and chosen agendas of secular individuals. The highly diverse array of choices for expressing secularist views and participating in secular agendas in turn sets the stage for the seventh section, which categories a variety of prominent secular organizations in America according to their efforts to serve one or another portion of that diverse array. This chapter concludes by pointing out under-served and neglected segments of the sizable secular population in America, using the example of New Atheism to illustrate how that regrettable situation could occur in the internet age.

The terms "secular" and "secularity" lend themselves to multifaceted and multidimensional conceptions, applicable in many ways to individuals, organizations, social institutions, and whole societies (see Rechtenwald and Richter, this volume). Despite their utility for analytic frameworks in research, the work of observing secularity, tracking secularity, and explaining features of sec-

OpenAccess. © 2017 John R. Shook, published by De Gruyter. This work is licensed under the Creative Commons Attribution-NonCommercial-NoDerivatives 4.0 License.
https://doi.org/10.1515/9783110458657-006

ularity continues to be methodologically challenging. Expanding the field of Secular Studies on stably academic foundations is difficult enough; presumptions and stereotypes about the nonreligious continue to divert inquiries towards dead ends. Suppositions that the secular is the realm of crudely materialistic and utilitarian matters, secularity indicates an insensitivity or impassivity to religious or spiritual wonders, or that secularism is basically about anti-religious antagonism, continue to exert open or tacit influence across academia. Secular Studies could settle down where religious studies and theology wishes it to remain, as a subfield subordinate to their supervision. Alternatively, it can clear its own academic path with philosophical clarity and scientific rigor.

In the West, unbelief and its secularity has commonly been viewed as a deviant rebellion against theism. That perspective does simplify methodology. If the secular is only perceivable through a religious lens, then secularity seems inconceivable except in relation to religion, and secularity has no meaning apart from religious structures. Only the clarity of religious doctrine about divinity permits any shape and definition to nonreligion, this viewpoint goes on to suggest. Even atheists often assume that theism presents a doctrinally well-defined target for atheism's opposition (Clark 2015). Hence academia's approach, ever since Christian universities arose, has been to let experts in religion handle explorations into impiety and irreligion. Religious scholars have been devoted to explaining religion's reasonableness, its universality, its naturalness, and its usefulness. That devotion has conveniently set standards of normality for judging unbelief's deformities and deficiencies, and protecting society from secularity's corrosions. Historically (and presently), theology has regulated the secular.

There is an alternative. A scholarly field concerned with the secular could control its own methodologies, theoretical terminology, and interpretations of empirical findings. Inquiry into the views, values, and motivations of nonreligious people could begin with observations of them in their own lived worlds, instead of starting from theological portraits of religious people in theirs. Any presumed naturality and normality to religion (Barrett 2012; contra position in Shook 2012) can be bracketed away from sound methodology. Scholars and scientists studying nonreligious people, in non-Western as well as Western societies, can investigate the affinities and affirmations behind a person's preferred secular views and activities (Beit-Hallahmi 2007; Zuckerman 2010; Caldwell-Harris 2012; Coleman, Silver, and Holcombe 2013; Norenzayan and Gervais 2013; Guenther 2014; Burchardt et al. 2015; Bilgrami 2016). Not believing in a deity, or not behaving religiously, by itself tells us little about what a person does accept and affirm.

The field of Secular Studies and allied disciplines are ready for closer research into phenomena of individual secularity using secular methodologies and sensitivities to secularity's own histories and agendas. The reality of "polysecularity," as I term it, awaits exploration at the individual level. Polysecularity, in brief, refers to the broad diversity to secularity displayed by people throughout their mundane lives. Secular people needn't be defined in terms of deviancy any more. Some secular people are secularists offering resistance to religion, by participating in the advancement of secularism's affirmative agendas. The diversity and positivity inherent to secularist attitudes and activist agendas is here labeled as "polysecularism."

This chapter concludes by situating secular organizations in America within this polysecularity-polysecularism framework. The framework's classification of ideological niches situates where various types of secular organizations can find their corresponding sorts of supporters. The phenomena of polysecularity at the individual level is accompanied at the social level by the polysecularism of organizational diversity observed in the United States. This framework accounts for the kinds of disagreements, and even inevitable antagonisms, among secular organizations.

2 Situating Secularity

Research into secularity too often proceeds as though being secular or not being a believer is predicable upon some basic, static, and singular construct. Theology helpfully cleared the way for that procedure. With only one path up the mountain to the sacred, there is only one path down. Secularization is just de-sacralization; secular people descending to the mountain's base are secular only for having taken the path in the wrong direction. However, scholarly research into the pluralism of religions exposes difficulties for objectively defining religion or faith. Why must research into the secular wait upon any fragile consensus about which mountain is "religion" or which meaning to the "religious" is best? No religion's theology could serve as a good guide for this rough terrain.

How about history? Historians have been heard proclaiming that irreligion is but a modernist creation, emerging about the time when "religion" as a concept was invented. If "religion" is as artificially constructed as some historians of modernity think (consult Nongbri 2012), wouldn't de-centering modernist frameworks bring authentic and non-essentialized secularity back into view? Besides, atheists could not be as constructed to the same degree as "religion" by modernity, since real unbelief could not be produced by an unreal religion. Hence, historians should not classify atheism as a religion's modern spinoff or sect. Medieval scholastics read about atheism from ancient Greeks (Shook 2015), and atheists are visible during the Renaissance (Wotton 1992).

Either way, whether theology's unreliable map or history's dubious framings are followed, confused theorizing rather than methodical observation ends up dictating who is inhabiting societies. That situation is not sustainable for a scholarly field aspiring to any scientific status. Empirical research already points towards immense qualitative and quantitative variances in the beliefs, values, motivations, and psychological characteristics of individual nonbelievers. The people lacking belief in deities may be more varied than all those who do believe in a deity. Studies into personal secularity are confirming that possibility; recent research has accumulated impressive results (Hunsberger and Altemeyer 2006; Beit-Hallahmi 2007; Kosmin et al. 2009; Streib and Klein 2013; Silver et al. 2014; Keysar 2015).

Despite what religion's theologians or modernity's historians may claim, secularity is not reducible to a feature of secularism or a by-product of secularization. Trying to reduce secularity to any particular thing, much less something that exists only in relation to religion, is not proving to be empirically or explanatorily satisfactory. Secular people don't share common routes departing from religion, they don't maintain similar attitudes about religion, and many have no attitude or opinion whatsoever about religion. Secular people don't advance the same priorities for opposing religion, and they typically can't agree about effective strategies for countering religion. In fact, it appears that more secular people are not thinking about religion than those who are, and those secular people who happen to ponder religion hardly consider the matter in similar ways. It is not even the case that secularism is a uniformly definable issue, an adjunct or corollary to liberalism, or a singular ideology (Bilgrami 2014; Baker and Smith 2015; Kitcher 2015).

Despite these warnings from empirical studies, sociology and social history have been largely following a dictum accurately pronounced by Rajeev Bhargava: "It should be obvious that the 'secular' and the 'religious' are always and everywhere mutually constituted" (Bhargava 2011, 54). This dictum is false, and Secular Studies must reject it. Its role as a platitude says more about religious scholarship than anything secular. Secular and religious scholars alike should be able to register empirical facts before imposing paradigms. Most evident to objective observation are the shifting cultural forces contending for social authority over time in various countries. What constitutes religion, in the first place?

Religions are hardly the solidly permanent entities – the unmoved movers – that their followers presume or expect. They are continually reshaped and reformed by critical attention, from within and without (Berger 1967). Religions sometimes encounter such attention in the form of resistance, by those trying to modify the scope and degree of religious influence within society. When disputes over religion escalate to the point where some people are questioning its validity, legitimacy, or authority, these engagements enter the arena of secularism. While sharp criticism of religion is not the same as intentionally advocating secularity, it can nevertheless have that practical effect. No religion fails to notice. Questioning religion in public typically elicits defensive reactions, concerned for repairing any diminishment of religious conviction and public confidence in religion. That is why public criticism of religion easily arouses theological surveillance and intervention, shoring up the reputation of religion with justificatory responses. What starts out as the civil questioning of religious involvement in society can easily transition towards tendentious arguments over doctrines defended by theology and disputed by dissenters. Civic dissenters may become defensive from accusations that they dangerously deviate from the "correct" religious worldview. The mere ability of another person to consider seriously a worldview that differs from one's own is a clear epistemological threat to the religiously structured way of life (Berger and Luckmann 1966). Those courageous enough to declare their doubts about core theological creeds get cast into the role of being a religious apostate, or perhaps even being an "atheist." Critics of religious controls over society and politics are then called "secularists" but classified practically as atheists too.

So far, this account of religious-secular engagement can make Bhargava's platitude seem sensible. An account of civic dissent, as theology would shape it, revolves around unreasonable deviations from religious conviction and correctness. Nevertheless, that is not how civic dissenters necessarily describe their motivations. The religious need not be "constituting" the secular, by any means. Yes, public disputes are often dragged into theological arenas, but that hardly means that the inspiration to civic dissent is exclusively or even primarily about religion itself. Civil dissent with religion can easily erupt over civic matters of concern to all society, not merely creedal issues of theological interest. The way that theological defense mechanisms must regard civic dissent as unwelcome unorthodoxy is just a partisan perspective. It is just one way of framing the matter in a way favorable to religion, much in the same way that entrenched governing regimes can depict political dissidents as traitors motivated by unpatriotic ideology, in order to depict the government as truly loyal to the nation.

The process by which civic dissent from religion and religious influences over society are usually framed as some sort of theological schism, or even a chasm of apostasy, can make it appear that dissenters cannot be understood unless and until a measure of their theological distance from the religious hegemony is measured. The genuine motivations and goals of civic dissent can be easily overlooked by such a single-minded method, especially those aspirations having nothing to do with religiosity, but instead with secular hopes and ideals. Those wanting the least do to with religiosity, desiring to associate with similarly secular people in a more secular society, are hardly "unbelievers" – they have all sorts of secular motivations and civic goals. As far as religion can tell, however, they are just impious unbelievers and nothing more, bereft of the "correct" convictions that ought to guide everyone. That negativity, from a theological perspective, is their only reality.

Secular Studies researchers can remain beholden to that dependent negativity, in seemingly innocuous ways. A trained inability to apprehend or conceptualize the secular in any independent manner only debilitates secular research, rendering it vulnerable to religious paradigms. In two recent works, exemplary for their struggles against religion-inspired treatments of the nonreligious, we can read the following:

> Yet "secularity" is not independent of "religion" at all but is rather only meaningful in relation to it. The idea of something being secular is simply unintelligible without an understanding of something else as religious and a view as to where the (moving) boundary between the two falls. (Lee 2015, 25)

> "Nonreligion" denotes phenomena that are generally not considered religious but whose significance is more or less dependent on religion (atheists are an obvious example). (Quack 2014, 439)

With such mantras securely in place, full recognition of anything positive to religion's supposed "other" won't be possible. Allowing the meaning of the "secular" or the "nonreligious" to be controlled by religious thinking is only a (moving) measure of religion's hegemony over scholarship. Distinguishing the "nonreligious" apart from the "secular" so that one of these terms might better apply to matters more aloof from religion, all the while insisting that both terms can only ultimately be understood in relation to religion, only leaves the subject more confused and unscientific (Jong 2015). As for atheists, they are indeed of great significance to religion; appealing to them as exemplars of secularity would be expected from that same religious hegemony, not independent secular scholarship.

Instead of waiting for religious thought to explain what "secular" must mean, Secular Studies could instead study social and individual phenomena, noting those that lack religious features and whose significance is independent from anything religious. Despite the mantras now crowding religious studies, and too much of secular studies, a person can be quite secular regardless of whether that person's thoughts have ever pondered religion or that person's daily life ever contacts anything religious. To claim otherwise commits either the psychologist's fallacy or the sociologist's fallacy, explained in the next section.

3 Secular Identity

Identifying secular people is one thing; secular identity is another. A person can be quite secular regardless of whether that person ponders secularity or encounters secularism. Being secular isn't essentially about having a secular identity, any more than being secular is about having a nonreligious identity. The question must be asked, who is really controlling the assignment of identity? Mixing up social classifications with personal identities wasn't invented by theology or sociology. Society itself prefers to deal with evident stereotypes rather than subsurface identities, and politics finds it convenient to reduce self-identity to group categorization.

Social scientists can avoid reifying stereotypes. Any researcher speaking of "identity" should make clear which sort of identity is meant (Turner 2013, chap. 6). A manageable way to discriminate types of identity can include:

You are an "X" if and only if you should prefer others to regard you as an "X." [ideal identity]

You are an "X" if and only if you prefer others to regard you as an "X." [valued identity]

You are an "X" if and only if you openly agree that you are an "X." [admitted identity]

You are an "X" if and only if you sincerely think of yourself as an "X." [self identity]

You are an "X" if and only if X means Y to society and you think of yourself as Y. [social identity]

You are an "X" if and only if X means Y by definition and you happen to fit Y. [categorical identity]

For example, the classification of "atheist" is a categorical identity: so long as a person does not believe in any god, that person is an atheist, regardless of whether that person thinks much about the matter or tells anyone else. (Similarly, a person can be a theist without ever visiting a house of worship to pronounce a creed.) In a way, being an atheist is nothing personal despite being intensely personal – it isn't ultimately about who a person takes themselves to be, or about what sort of person others expect you to be. Sociology's theorists who narrow atheism down to classifications able to sort people by anti-religious signs, such as "I have lost my faith," "There's no god," or "I stand with atheism," are not learning much about atheists in general. Religion's defenders often go further, narrowing atheists to only people standing out of the crowd as anti-theists and anti-religion secularists. Sociology, by contrast, can be neutral on identity. Sociologists have every right to seek and find people fitting pre-set social identities, if that proves methodologically useful. However, pointing to admitted identities or social identities as if personal identities have been revealed, or vice-versa, is never methodologically sound.

Defending religion by taking advantage of lax psychology or sociology is nothing new, and neither is the need to point out fallacious reasoning in academia. The "psychologist's fallacy," as William James noted when psychology was emerging as a scientific field (James 1890, I, 196), occurs when the psychologist expects the analyzed matters described by theorizing to be prominent in a subject's own naive experiencing. The matters important and meaningful for refined theory are often insignificant and meaningless for coarse experience, and those matters may not even occur within any subject's experience. Correspondingly, among many fallacies from sociology, a particular "sociologist's fallacy" occurs whenever the sociologist expects that the social categories applicable to people, while confirmed by sound social theorizing, must also characterize how those people experience their immersion in the social environs around them.

The psychologist's fallacy is committed when the researcher presumes that a person intuitively and self-consciously appreciates the matters of the mental life just as described by psychological theory. This fallacy worsens when that psychologist further expects that a person's thought processes rely on those theorized matters while reaching judgments and making decisions. The fallacy is exposed when it must be denied that psychological characterizations determine the entities of one's self-consciousness. The sociologist's fallacy is committed when the researcher presumes that a person automatically and habitually appreciates matters about the social life just as described by sociological theory. That fallacy worsens when that sociologist further expects that people's judgments and actions rely on those theorized matters while conducting their social life. The fallacy is exposed when it must be denied that social categorizations determine the identity of one's self-conception. A person will not necessarily conceive of themselves in the terms imposed by psychological or sociological theorizing. They can be persuaded to do so, in some cases, but that hardly shows that they were doing so all along.

Consider this analogy. Vegetarian eating could surely be done in a world where no one eats meat, despite the fact that no one in that world would keep calling it "vegetarianism," and the fact that in our world there are self-professed vegetarians sitting next to meat-eaters. We should not fixate on a definition of "vegetarian" as "the eating of things that are not meat." Surely "vegetarian" can be categorically defined in its own right as "a vegetable diet," since vegetables can exist regardless of whether meat also exists, eating vegetation can be done without thinking about animals, and people can be vegetarian eaters without thinking about their meatless condition. The way that the popular notion of "vegetarian" immediately and primarily suggests "not eating meat" to many minds simply reveals how meat-eating is taken for normality in many cultures.

Similarly, the way that "secular" suggests "defying religion" or "disdaining religion" only tells us about what is still taken for normality in our culture. An assigned self identity or social identity within the context of a single society is not automatically a valid categorical identity for universal application. There are legitimately scientific social categories and corresponding social facts that are irreducible to social identities or self-categories, just as the reverse is true. What may characterize so-called "irreligious" people in Christendom during recent centuries is not axiomatically determinative of all secular experience and secular identity everywhere. In sum, secularity and secularization are not limited to locales where religious people are talking about them. Again, nothing religious is required to constitute secularity.

There is one type of secular person who self-consciously rejects gods and openly disdains religion: the secularist. Later sections explore the identity of secularists and their social agendas. However, the classification for "secular person" in general can be a categorical identity, and unrelated to religion, if the "secular" is correctly defined.

4 The Secular

The *Oxford English Dictionary* first lists this primary meaning for "secular":

> Of or belonging to the present or visible world as distinguished from the eternal or spiritual world; temporal, worldly.

The *OED*, like earlier dictionaries going back to the seventeenth century, assigns the meaning of "secular" through two concepts: the temporal and worldly. Both "temporal" and "worldly" are terms definable without reference to anything religious. Therefore, etymologically and logically, the "secular" is properly defined without reference to anything concerning religion. That "secular" can make sense as a terminological (not logical) contrary of the "religious" is simply due to the fact that religions usually describe their sacred and divine matters as other-worldly, eternal, and the like. In countries long dominated by Christianity, that terminological convenience within European culture has been hypostatized into an ontological constraint, as if the "secular" must depend on religion everywhere. In fact, thinking about the ontology of religious matters depends on the ontology of this ordinary world, and not the other way around (Atran 2002, chap. 4).

What is the secular? The secular is the temporal and worldly, spanning the breadth of our travels and the course of our lifetimes. Taken to its broadest imaginable extent, the secular coincides with the natural, another concept definable without any reference to religion. Religion must define itself in concepts borrowed from the secular and natural realm in order to form ideas pointing beyond temporal or worldly matters, but nothing in the secular realm must concern itself with religiosity. That includes people. People can live secular lives without thinking about anything religious or nonreligious, or doing anything religious or nonreligious. "Secular" doesn't essentially mean "non-religious" any more than "athletic" essentially means "non-sedentary." To be athletic implies being non-sedentary, but people do not consider themselves as athletic simply because they happen to not be sedentary.

To be fully secular, all one has to minimally do is to lead an entirely worldly and temporal life. One needn't ever have the thought, "My opinions and values are not religious" or "My daily experiences have nothing religious about them," or "My life's activities and associations are so worldly and temporal compared to religious living." Imputing such thoughts to secular people, in order to assuredly classify their secularity in some minimally religious terms, has no academic legitimacy. Committing the psychologist's fallacy or the sociologist's fallacy can be avoided.

Taking particular interest in secularity would be an expected feature of religion, of course. To satisfy that religious concern, inquisitors classify nonreligiosity into various types of deviances from religiosity or measured distances from religious matters. But secular people have their own concerns, not involving religion. In societies where a religion wields enough power to impact secular people's lives, secular people respond by defending their priorities. To the extent that they succeed, "secularization" may be said to be occurring there, and secular people who take action to resist religious influences and coercions may be labeled as "secularists." All the same, the lives of secular people needn't depend on secularization. Secular people can exist where no secularization is ongoing, and they can live where no secularization has happened. To imagine otherwise is to dream of a mythical time when all humanity was uniformly religious.

It is the case that identifying the "atheist" and categorizing types of unbelievers as they are understood nowadays should take into account contemporary secularity's context within the wider field of civic engagements occurring within society. Demographic research abandoned biased and essentialist views of "atheist" inherited from religion to discover much variety within that classification. Logically, not having belief in a god encompasses both the rendering of judgment against gods and the withholding of belief about gods, as well as the absence of any thought about gods. Psychologically, the condition of blank indifference feels very different from thoughtful doubt or conclusive denial. That is why a third sub-category, the "apatheist," has come to light among the Nones (noted by Marty 2003 and analyzed in Shook 2010). Apatheism serves as the "None of the above" category after religious and nonreligious identities are abandoned. The apatheist gives so little thought to religion that the label of agnostic or skeptic bestows too much credit for contemplating the matter. By declining to accept any identity label for unbelief (atheist, agnostic, etc.) as well as belief (Protestant, Catholic, etc.), and having little to no interest in opinions about religion or God, apatheists end up as the "Nones of the Nones."

Polysecularity, even if its diversity is sorted in relation to religion, stretches very broadly from atheist activists to spiritual-minded seekers. Just a sampling illustrates this point:
(i) Atheists heartily expecting that religion's disappearance would benefit humanity.
(ii) Atheists skeptically doubting that any gods really exist.
(iii) Agnostics judging that no one can know anything about god.
(iv) Agnostics simply admitting how they personally can't know what to think about god.
(v) Apatheists relieved to no longer be connected to a religion.
(vi) Apatheists who have never had the first thought about religion.
(vii) Seekers avoiding religion but wondering if some faith will arrive.
(viii) Seekers sampling religious practices and expecting some faith to grow.

Does this list illustrate how secularity requires reference to religion? Quite the opposite: all that is required are the affirmative reasons people happen to have for occupying their secular stances. They don't even have to realize how they occupy those positions. Religions can measure the distance of those stances from orthodoxy, but secular people needn't mind, or care. Remember our vegetarians – the existence of meat-eating isn't responsible for the existence of vegetarians. The existence of secular people is not necessarily the responsibility of any religions.

This point needs to be repeated. It is not religion which must establish the possibility of secular nonbelief and atheism. Affirmative grounds – such as reason, morality, and justice – supply ample reasons for adopting alternatives to religiosity. Theologians, it is true, have perpetually claimed that those grounds came from, or at least depend on, the divine. They have also proposed that unbelief is due to depraved irrationality, deception by pure evil, willful love of sin, or anarchical rebellion. Setting aside magical thinking about impiety's bases and causes, explaining secular unbelief should be grounded in research attending to secular people's own beliefs and life courses. Why do they find secular ways of thinking and living more satisfying than religious ways? Why have some never shown any interest in religious matters? Why are many leaving religious paths to travel other lifestyle paths? For those still engaging with religious matters in their thoughts, by what criteria do they pass judgment upon religion? For those choosing to engage religiosity in society, what civic goals do they try to accomplish?

5 Polysecularism

The macrocosm scale of group-level engagements involving secularity, often visible in the form of social controversies and political struggles, have been highlighted by prominent scholars for over two decades (Casanova 1994; Bhargava 1998; Asad 2003; Taylor 2009). Their robust research demonstrates how to be sensitive to the impressive variety of religious-secular stances taken by citizens in many different countries. Bhargava's (2014, 330) attention to individual scales as well as social scales has become even more pronounced. Although "secularism" is usually used in only its political sense, it nevertheless can cover multiple dimensions. He writes,

> I begin by distinguishing three senses of the term "secularism." First, it is used as a shorthand for secular humanism. The second specifies the ideals, even ultimate ideals, which give meaning and worth to life and that its followers strive to realize in their life, I call it ethical secularism. I distinguish this ethic from political secularism. Here it stands for a certain kind of polity in which organized religious power or religious institutions are separated from organized political power or political institutions for specific ends.

Secularism remains more useful for Bhargava primarily as a social and political phenomena, rather than as a feature of social processes emerging from secular individuals and their perspectives.

This top-down approach has been typical across much of secular studies, as it was inherited from sociological studies of religion. Monika Wohlrab-Sahr, as another example, has discerned correlations between personal, social, and civic-minded secularisms. Since no single pattern to such correlations could be expected across societies, one can at best speak of "multiple secularities," as she has done (2012). One kind of secularity found in one country may balance a certain distribution of religious and nonreligious people with given arrangements of civic power allotted to religions and the government. Other countries, depending on their particular development as a nation, have settled into quite different distributions and arrangements (and these patterns are dynamic over time as well). Like Bhargava, Wohlrab-Sahr ascribes secularity principally to collectives such as societies and nations, rather than to individuals. Classifying citizens and their concerns is subsequent upon categorizations for social arrangements and dynamics.

Although individuals hardly exist apart from their social roles and functions, and citizens surely have their political duties and powers, transposing socio-political classifications upon the individual level is methodologically hazardous. Such transposition can seem justifiable. Whatever is studied at the personal level should be correlatable, in some manner, with important features at group, social, and national levels. Even large-scale processes of secularization or re-sacralization concern how many people are managing their social and civic relationships and thinking about their own stances. But those people are not involved in any uniform or predictable way. Secular people do not have identical attitudes towards religion, they do not have the same priorities for opposing religion, and they will not usually agree about effective strategies against religion. A fallacy lurks in an expectation that people themselves are well-categorized for all purposes through the broad social categories for processes ongoing in their locality. The reliable exception is the secularist.

Secularism is primarily about efforts to diminish religious control over social structures and public thinking. There is no uniform or unified way that secularity manifests itself as a public agenda. There are many agendas of secularism, depending on the type of religious control to be monitored and challenged. For example, political secularism seeks adjustments to the relative control of religion and government over each other. There are multiple secular agendas, and many types of activists supporting one or another of those agendas, that do not necessarily cooperate or even cohere. That absence of unity, and ready capacity for fractiousness, calls for the recognition of "polysecularism."

The evident fact that no two countries arrange political stabilities in religion-state relations in the same manner points to multi-secularity, as we observed. The less-noticed fact that secularist agendas within a country have distinct ideals and goals, and may not care for consensus among them, points to polysecularism. Polysecularism in turn draws attention to the diversity of roles for the pro-secularism citizen, the secularist. Secularists can have allies. Participation in a particular secularism agenda, such as political secularism, is by no means limited to nonbelievers. A religious citizen who supports public education over parochial education or supports separation of church and state should not be labeled as a secularist without strict qualifications. Nonreligious citizens (atheists, in the basic sense) who advocate for some secularism agenda(s) can accurately be classed as secularists.

Core agendas of secularism, and secularist supporters of those agendas, typically align with one or more of these activities: (a) endorsing the reasonableness of personal secularity by contesting religious claims about unnatural/transcendent divinities and values; (b) grounding morality with ethical systems consistent with secular personal living and human welfare; and (c) justifying free societies having political systems promoting individual liberties and civic progress. It is no coincidence that these three secular agendas look familiar to intellectual historians recounting major kinds of popular freethought and secular thinking in western civilization (Putnam 1894; Larue 1996). Nor is it a coincidence that demographers tracking secularist attitudes in populations can also detect that familiar pattern.

The demographic study of a social phenomenon like religiosity, or secularity, can identify three primary features of an individual's outlook: one's belief, behavior, and belonging. These features are organically interfused, so an isolation of one factor is at most a useful abstraction (Day 2011), but they can suggest correlations with other social features and cultural factors. Polysecularism displays three general modes – based on belief, behavior, and belonging – concerning one's worldview, one's social ethos, and one's civic participation. As both scholars of intellectual history and social movements have noted, irreligion and antitheism are frequently motivated by objections to religiosity's reliance on faith, or to a religion's ethical lapses, or to religion's detrimental effects on societies. Three primary agendas of secularism manifest at the individual level in the secularist; three idealized types are hence available for "the secularist":
(a) The secularist is the anti-theistic and anti-metaphysical thinker denying religious dogmas.
(b) The secularist is the anti-religious moralist accusing religion and religious people of ethical failings.
(c) The secularist is the anti-clerical activist demanding that denominations renounce governing power.

Idealized manifestations of "the secularist" can also be phrased in terms of positive agendas and loyalties:
(d) The secularist is a staunch advocate of reason and science, over superstition and religious faith.
(e) The secularist is a dedicated subscriber to a secular ethics, placing humanity first instead of a god.

(f) The secularist is an equal citizen of a secular polity, keeping other group memberships subordinate.

Where religion exercises cultural dominance, the secularist can stand out as a radical freethinker, a wise sage, or a dangerous agitator. In a country already fairly secularized in many ways, such as the United States, secularists would not stand out so prominently, but they do attempt to sustain momentum inherited from past secularist efforts.

Polysecularity is one kind of phenomenon, while polysecularism is quite another. Only a minority of secular people ever become secularists and participate in one or another of secularism's agendas. That fact is often overlooked or misinterpreted, even in otherwise reliable histories of freethought and secularism. All too often, one feature of secularism is taken to characterize all of secularity, or to define the essence of atheism. Models designed to explain group behavior or make crowd action understandable seek out characteristic social identities, but they don't necessarily characterize all concerned. Social histories focusing on a single era will discern how one or another type of secularist then holds center stage, but extrapolating that starring role across other eras or cultures is unwise. The next sections describe how these three primary agendas (along with many secondary agendas) are capable of being equally potent; they are not necessarily allies, and they don't easily blend together or even cooperate in alignment with each other. Antagonisms are certainly possible, and probably inevitable, as the next section explores.

6 Polysecularity and Polysecularism Today

Too much research conducted on secularity has tended to assign nonbelievers into "atheism" for their group identity, and jointly assumed that secularist activism is characteristic of atheism, since activism is an obvious place to acquire observations of atheists. Such presumptions have allowed much research to expect many or most nonbelievers to share a common psychological profile, despite the way that common perceptions of atheism do not essentialize atheists to a high degree (Toosi and Ambady 2011). Trying to explain "the atheist," and what atheists are all doing, works better with a pre-prepared essentialization for atheism, of course. Previous sections of this chapter have raised worries about that essentialization. It is not an unreasonable concern that religious bias against atheists has been predisposing psychological research to "discover" negative personality traits in atheists in order to fit "evolution of religion" narratives composed to normalize religiosity across humanity. Disordered brains would bring disorder to society, after all. Depicting unbelievers as ready participants for disrupting civil stability with unruly secularist activism has long been a stereotype perpetuated by religion.

What do secular people actually take themselves to be thinking, and doing? Much data can be gathered from open and self-identified atheists already attending atheist, skeptic, humanist, or freethought groups, or participating in online forums sharing those interests (Cimino and Smith 2007; Pasquale 2010; Smith 2010; Baker and Robbins 2012; Williamson and Yancey 2013). Recently, Christopher Silver and Thomas Coleman (2014) led a research team investigating an even broader spectrum, looking for motivations and priorities of nonbelievers who mostly do not affiliate or participate with any group of like-minded nonbelievers. Their research findings allowed them to distinguish six main types of secular people, lending additional empirical support to the sketches of polysecularity and polysecularism in this chapter. These six types do not deviate much from prior understandings of the nonreligious gained by demographers (Kosmin et al. 2009), and they don't appear to diverge greatly from other recent hypotheses for arranging aspects and scales to secular/atheist identities (Cragun, Hammer, and Nielsen 2015; Schnell 2015; Vainio and Visala 2015). These six types are also easily recognizable to secular leaders (such as myself) who are experienced with grassroots recruiting among nonbelievers.

Earlier sections of this chapter highlight three main distinctions within polysecularity (skeptical, agnostic, and apathetic) and three main modes to polysecularism (intellectual, moral, and civic). Interestingly, Silver and Coleman's classification of six types of nonreligious people easily fit six of the boxes in a 3x3 table resulting from crossing polysecularity with polysecularism.

Table 1. Classifying the nonreligious by Silver and Coleman

	types of polysecularism		
types of polysecularity	pro-reason	pro-ethics	pro-civics
atheist	IAA		AT
agnostic	SA	RAA	AAA
apatheist		NT	

A brief overview of these six types, quoting from descriptions by Silver and Coleman (2014, 993–996), shows how to situate them.

Intellectual Atheist/Agnostic (IAA). "IAA typology includes individuals who proactively seek to educate themselves through intellectual association, and proactively acquire knowledge on various topics relating to ontology (the search for Truth) and non-belief. ... IAAs associate with fellow intellectuals regardless of their ontological position as long as the IAA associate is versed and educated on various issues of science, philosophy, rational theology, and common socio-political religious dialogue." These secular people are open about their unbelief and irreligious dissent on intellectual grounds, and they like to associate with others on those bases. The IAA type lies at the congruence of a pro-reason motivation and skeptical atheism.

Anti-Theist (AT). "[A]ntitheists view religion as ignorance ... they view the logical fallacies of religion as an outdated worldview that is not only detrimental to social cohesion and peace, but also to technological advancement and civilised evolution as a whole. They are compelled to share their view and want to educate others ... Some Anti-Theist individuals feel compelled to work against the institution of religion in its various forms including social, political, and ideological, while others may assert their view with religious persons on an individual basis." Anti-theists are primarily dissenters against religion in society, more than against god in heaven; the anti-theist type is ardently antagonistic against what religion stands for in society and what religious people do. The distinction between IAA and AT types is familiar to sociologists as something akin to the divide between High Church (intellectual) and Low Church (emotional) sides to an ideological movement or religious denomination. The AT type exemplifies combining the skeptically atheist stance with the civic and political secular agenda to limit religion's influence in society.

Activist Atheist/Agnostic (AAA). "[T]hey seek to be both vocal and proactive regarding current issues in the atheist/agnostic socio-political sphere. This socio-political sphere can include such egalitarian issues, but is not limited to concerns of humanism, feminism, lesbian, gay, bisexual, and transgender issues, social or political concerns, human rights themes, environmental concerns, animal rights, and controversies such as the separation of church and state." The AAA type often seeks alliances with other movements, prioritizing positive civic and political agenda(s) without worrying much about labeling as "atheist" or "agnostic." In the grassroots arena, this type tends to prefer non-confrontation with religion, and often seeks "inter-faith" work with religious groups on shared civic goals. The AAA type results from combining the tolerantly agnostic attitude with civic secular agendas.

Ritual Atheist/Agnostic (RAA). "The RAA holds no belief in God or the divine, or they tend to believe it is unlikely that there is an afterlife with God or the divine. ... [T]hey may find utility in the teachings of some religious traditions. They see these as more or less philosophical teachings of how to live life and achieve happiness rather than a path to transcendental liberation. Ritual Atheist/Agnostics find utility in tradition and ritual." This type perpetuates traditions of religious or "spiritual" humanism or religious naturalism, and many congregate with Unitarian Universalist churches or Ethical Culture societies, or other sorts of humanist communities. They are often intellectual, and they endorse worthy civic and political causes, but they typically put more of their energies into local communal activities rather than antagonism against religion. The RAA type connects the agnostic attitude with the secular priority of living an ethical life.

The last two categories are for people who aren't "secularists" in the strict sense of participating in the advocacy of secularization, although they do contribute to the overall secularity in a society.

Seeker-Agnostic (SA). "[R]ecognizes the philosophical difficulties and complexities in making personal affirmations regarding ideological beliefs... simply cannot be sure of the existence of God or the divine. They keep an open mind in relation to the debate between the religious, spiritual, and antitheist elements within society." These seekers often turn up in polling as "transient" Nones; they may be attending churches (irregularly) because they care about finding a reasonable fit with their flexible worldview(s). Affirming atheists can disapprove of the SA type for appreciating too many perspectives, but the SA type won't put all their faith in a single confining worldview, even science's. This type of nonreligious person represents the combination of an agnostic attitude with search for a reasonable lifestance.

The last category is the Non-Theist (NT). "For the Non-Theists, the alignment of oneself with religion, or conversely an epistemological position against religion, can appear quite unconventional from their perspective. However, a few terms may best capture the sentiments of the Non-Theist. One is apathetic, while another may be disinterested. The Non-Theist is nonactive in terms of involving themselves in social or intellectual pursuits having to do with religion or anti-religion." These individuals are prototypical apatheists, avoiding cognitive or cultural tensions about being nonreligious. They aren't anything like nonconformists or anarchists – that would require too much effort – as they participate in lifestyles they judge best.

This sort of classification for types of secular people only superficially classifies people by their evident priorities, as they explain those priorities themselves insofar as they are nonreligious. This classification cannot and does not mean to imply, for example, that IAA types aren't ethical or don't care about the civic life. An IAA or AT (etc.) may be a highly energetic promoter for a secular cause or give generously to the Red Cross or the United Way. This sort of classification is about how people connect their nonreligious attitude with their secular views and preferred activities.

There are a total of nine possible combinations. Three boxes stand empty only so far as Silver and Coleman's initial presentation of their research is concerned. There probably are nonreligious people in their data better fitting into these three boxes. The top middle box is for people too anti-religious to enjoy congregating, while preferring some sort of "lifestyle humanism" expressing their personal principles, so they affirm humanist ideals without communal validation. The lower left box is for people too apathetic to have an opinion about religion so they aren't using logic to argue against it, yet they feel strongly devoted to advancing critical thinking and rational analysis, so we can label them as "rationalists." The lower right box is for people apathetic about both religion and ethical ideas. They aren't protesting against religion using government, but they do support a civil order guaranteeing stability and liberty for everyone regardless of religiosity, so they can be called "republicans." (The lower-case "republicans" advocated constitutional democracy in the annals of politics, while "Republicans" belong to a particular political party.)

No ideal schema awaits at the "end" to this kind of research, but more detailed classifications have theoretical value in conjunction with further productive investigations. An example is provided below, taking cues from polysecularity. It provides a row for those occasionally seeking religious inspiration, and a column for those expecting science to refute and replace religion.

Table 2. Classifying the nonreligious by attitude and agenda

	Secular agenda			
Nonreligious attitude	pro-logic	pro-science	pro-ethics	pro-civics
skeptical	IAA	confrontation CON	lifestyle humanism HUM	AT
agnostic	SA	NOMA	RAA	AAA
apathetic	rationalism RAT	accommodation ACC	NT	secular republican SEC
seeking	Platonism PLA	syncretism SYN	congregational CON	deist republican DEI

With any such classification, no presumption should be made that an individual fits only a single classification, thinks of one's self as fitting a category, or understands that category's intellectual history.

Agnostics who appreciate science can be comfortable with truces sounding like NOMA: science and religion are "non-overlapping magisteria" that yield different yet valid knowledge. ("Religion knows what happens after death, something science could never refute.") By contrast, staunch skeptics relying on science demand non-negotiable confrontations with religion over the truth. Those apathetic about religion can drift into optional stances. Logic-lovers will find rationalism's neutrality quite sensible (lending appeal to stoicism), while admirers of science will expect it to admit that plenty of religious views get scientific confirmations ("It looks like evolution works best when God causes mutations.") Prioritizing civic order finds agnostics advocating, with Thomas Jefferson, a civil republic that stays strictly neutral about religion.

Looking across the bottom row, seekers have several options. Few seekers know anything about Plato, for example, but seekers expecting logic to identify god (or be god) would head towards a dualistic metaphysics like Platonism. Scientific-minded seekers will expect a synthesis of divine guidance with nature's laws, so some sort of syncretic worldview (Deism or Theosophy, for example) can appeal to them. Seekers prioritizing ethics gravitate towards eclectic religious or quasi-religious communities. Seekers prioritizing civic order may judge, as James Madison did, that a providential god favors a god-fearing republic over decadent aristocracies.

7 Organized Polysecularism

Organizations advancing the interests of secular people can be classified using these sorts of frameworks, because public support rests on those able to play the role of a secularist through their attendance at events and financial giving. Like individuals, organizations may or may not neatly fit a single box. However, few attempt to equally represent many boxes, because of the inherent discrepancies and disagreements among them, as the theory of polysecularism explains. This theory also can account for the kinds of disagreements, and even antagonisms, between secular organizations, and the fragile nature of alliances.

Research into secular movements and organizations has accelerated recently (Smith 2013; Cimino and Smith 2014; Langston, Hammer, and Cragun 2015; LeDrew 2015b). Secularists trying to find or re-shape their identities are participating in dynamic and growing organizations from neighborhood- to nation-level sizes, which are simultaneously molding their messages to attract participants. The typical type of organization at the local level is the "single-issue" secular group, so that even a small city has pro-science, atheist, and humanist meetups (see Schutz this volume). Larger organizations take a "small-cluster" approach covering a few neighboring boxes, such as American Atheists at IAA/CON/AT, or the American Association for the Advancement of Science at NOMA/ACC. Some national-level organizations are "horizontally-integrated" to represent an entire row – the Center for Inquiry, for example, from IAA to AT. Very few organizations would or could attempt a vertically-integrated approach – the American Humanist Association is the closest example by clustering at HUM/RAA/AAA (for more on these national groups, see Fazzino and Cragun, this volume).

Deep fault-lines between many of the boxes are sufficient to prevent any single secular organization from growing into a large cluster, and often obstruct alliances among secular organizations.

First, promoting a humanist ethics about equality and rights agreeable to people of all faiths can be deeply upsetting to anti-theists unwilling to set aside objections to faith just for the sake of social harmony. The anti-theism agenda can sound out of tune with the humanist ethics agenda, because humanism is unwilling to denigrate or demonize religious believers for their "foolish" faiths. Promoting a humanist ethics about equality and rights agreeable to all peoples can collide with anti-theism's typical degree of intolerance towards religious believers. Anti-theists won't see anything ethical at all about faith, despite humanism's efforts to understand religion as something quite human, and anti-theism won't award any rights to religion just for the sake of social harmony.

Second, the anti-theism agenda doesn't harmonize well with the secular polity agenda. Prioritizing open attacks against the reasonableness or even sanity of religious believers will alienate the believers who do agree on separation of church and state. Religious believers couldn't really be blamed for losing interest in a political alliance with anti-theists to reduce denominational control in government. For their part, advocates of a secular polity can tolerate non-theocratic religions as legitimate social organizations promoting the good life for their members, but anti-theism refuses to recognize churches as truly healthy for their congregants.

Third, the anti-clerical agenda can sideline the humanist ethics agenda. Prioritizing the establishment of a secular government on value-neutral principles, as liberalism proposes, demotes secular ethics to private values instead of potent political ideals. Humanist ethics are demoted from a universal framework of principled ideals down to just another lifestyle choice for people who happen to be secular. Humanism once upon a time positioned itself as the supreme arbiter of human rights and democratic values. It gave birth to liberalism, which went on to disavow its heritage while searching for non-ethical foundations to political rights and institutions. Liberalism, for its part, has staked its legitimacy on lacking any partiality towards one or another competing view of the good life or a comprehensive conception of "the good." That excludes any favoritism or reliance on humanism, so humanism is reduced to the same civic status held by every religion, and loses its distinctiveness alongside that company.

Polysecularity is the demographic backdrop to the cultural and political stage where polysecularism is enacted in multiple agendas and secularists choose their preferred roles. Polysecularity forbids any simplistic reduction of secularity to something uniform and predictable. Homogeneity and consistency will not be found anywhere. Whether secular organizations like it or not, the three main secular agendas are difficult to pursue simultaneously, and in fact they usually tend to frustrate and obstruct each other. As the second table reveals, more nuanced discriminations among secular viewpoints and secularist positions only expose additional fault-lines.

The course of "New Atheism" also illustrates both polysecularism and its challenges. Self-identified new atheists don't sound like humanists (Cragun 2015; LeDrew 2015a), but their distinctive tone conveyed substantive agendas (Kettell 2013; Kettell 2014). Few organizations seemed ready for those agendas. Secular organizations that re-arranged priorities after the rise of New Atheism in the mid-2000s, for example, promptly generated external scrutiny and internal challenges. Was the energy of New Atheism about science confronting religion's illusions (CON), or was it more about shaming religion for its social conservatism and complicity in rights violations (AT)? Perhaps both, but it caused organizational strain to divert resources to both simultaneously. (Full disclosure: this author was a staff member of two major secular organizations during the height of New Atheism.) For their part, humanists didn't see how those controversies helped deconvert religious people through values, while agnostics didn't see science disproving God or the Bible, so New Atheism left both types wondering how much they really had in common with aggressive atheists. As for New Atheism, it quickly identified traitors – NOMA, ACC, and AAA – while dismissing humanist communities as too "religious" ("They are still singing together?!"). Mobilizations in defense of AAA priorities (such as "Atheism+" and "The Orbit" initiatives) distanced themselves from New Atheism. The secular organizations focused on church-state separation clustered with AAA/SEC and tended to avoid New Atheism bombast, while larger organizations mimicking New Atheism rhetoric found fewer allies among religious organizations also defending church-state separation.

In the meantime, vast constituencies are still getting overlooked. Seekers comprise a large majority of the Nones. Types of seekers such as SYN and CON want toleration and church-state separation. They could supply vast ideological and financial support to core secular agendas, but they have been mostly ignored.

8 Conclusion

An accurate definition of the "secular" relieves it from conceptual dependency upon religiosity. The diverse secularity of individuals can therefore receive empirical study and classification independently from religious categories. Religions typically regard anything too unorthodox as atheistic, and any alternative to their social domination as anti-religious secularism. Through that biased lens, secularity would appear to owe its nature to religiosity, but academic study can reach for objectivity. The phenomena of polysecularity and polysecularism are accessible to fallacy-free psychological and sociological research. The evident diversity to positive secular agendas contradicts simplistic views offered by either religion's defenders or New Atheism.

Nevertheless, "organized polysecularism" need not be an oxymoron. That breadth to polysecularity provides many social niches for successful organizations serving their circumscribed but focused bases. Temporary alliances on specific secular agendas can be powerful in democracies that pay attention to multiple interest groups able to work together. After all, flourishing secularity and secularism in a country should exemplify more pluralism, not less.

Bibliography

Asad, Talal. 2003. *Formations of the Secular.* Stanford, Cal.: Stanford University Press.
Atran, Scott. 2002. *In Gods We Trust: The Evolutionary Landscape of Religion.* Oxford: Oxford University Press.
Baker, Joseph O., and Buster G. Smith. 2015. *American Secularism: Cultural Contours of Nonreligious Belief Systems.* New York: New York University Press.
Baker, Matthew J., and Mandy Robbins. 2012. "American On-line Atheists and Psychological Type." *Mental Health, Religion & Culture* 15(10): 1077–1084.
Barrett, Justin. 2012. *Born Believers.* New York: Free Press.
Beit-Hallahmi, Benjamin. 2007. "Atheists: A Psychological Profile." In *The Cambridge Companion to Atheism*, ed. Michael Martin, pp. 300–317. Cambridge, UK: Cambridge University Press.
Berger, Peter. 1967. *The Sacred Canopy.* Garden City, N.Y.: Doubleday.
Berger, Peter, and Thomas Luckmann. 1966. *The Social Construction of Reality.* Garden City, N.Y.: Anchor Books.
Bhargava, Rajeev. 1998. "What is Secularism For?" In *Secularism and its Critics*, ed. Rajeev Bhargava, pp. 486–520. Delhi, India: Oxford University Press.
Bhargava, Rajeev. 2014. "How Secular is European Secularism?" *European Societies* 16(3): 329–336.
Bilgrami, Akeel. 2014. "Secularism: Its Content and Context." *Journal of Social Philosophy* 45 (1): 25–48.

Bilgrami, Akeel, ed. 2016. *Beyond the Secular West*. New York: Columbia University Press.
Burchardt, Marian, Monika Wohlrab-Sahr, and Matthias Middell, eds. 2015. *Multiple Secularities beyond the West: Religion and Modernity in the Global Age*. Berlin: De Gruyter.
Caldwell-Harris, Catherine. 2012. "Understanding Atheism/Non-belief as an Expected Individual-Differences Variable." *Religion, Brain & Behavior* 2(1): 4–23.
Casanova, José. 1994. *Public Religions in the Modern World*. Chicago: University of Chicago Press.
Cimino, Richard, and Christopher Smith. 2007. "Secular Humanism and Atheism beyond Progressive Secularism." *Sociology of Religion* 68(4): 407–424.
Cimino, Richard, and Christopher Smith. 2014. *Atheist Awakening: Secular Activism & Community in America*. Oxford: Oxford University Press.
Coleman III, Thomas, Christopher Silver, and Jenny Holcombe. 2013. "Focusing on Horizontal Transcendence: Much More than a 'Non-belief'." *Essays in the Philosophy of Humanism* 21(2): 1–18.
Clark, Stephen. 2015. "Atheism Considered as a Christian Sect." *Philosophy* 90(2): 277–303.
Cragun, Ryan T. 2015. "Who Are the 'New Atheists'?" In *Atheist Identities: Spaces and Social Contexts*, ed. Lori G. Beaman and Steven Tomlins, pp. 195–211. Berlin and New York: Springer.
Cragun, Ryan T., J. H. Hammer, and M. Nielsen. 2015. "The Nonreligious-Nonspiritual Scale (NRNSS): Measuring Everyone from Atheists to Zionists." *Science, Religion and Culture* 2(3): 36–53.
Day, Abby. 2011. *Believing in Belonging: Belief and Social Identity in the Modern World*. Oxford: Oxford University Press.
Guenther, Katja. 2014. "Bounded by Disbelief: How Atheists in the United States Differentiate Themselves from Religious Believers." *Journal of Contemporary Religion* 29(1): 1–16.
Hunsberger, Bruce, and Bob Altemeyer. 2006. *Atheists: A Groundbreaking Study of America's Nonbelievers*. Amherst, N.Y.: Prometheus Books.
Hunter, Ian. 2015. "Secularization: The Birth of a Modern Combat Concept." *Modern Intellectual History* 12(1): 1–32.
James, William. 1890. *The Principles of Psychology*, 2 vols. New York: Henry Holt, 1890.
Jong, Jonathan. 2015. "On (not) Defining (Non)religion." *Science, Religion and Culture* 2(3): 15–24.
Kettell, Steven. 2013. "Faithless: The Politics of a New Atheism." *Secularism and Nonreligion* 2: 61–72.
Kettell, Steven. 2014. "Divided We Stand: The Politics of the Atheist Movement in the United States." *Journal of Contemporary Religion* 29(3): 377–391.
Keysar, Ariela. 2015. "The International Demography of Atheists." In *Yearbook of International Religious Demography*, ed. Brian J. Grim, Todd M. Johnson, Vegard Skirbekk and Gina A. Zurlo, 136–153. Leiden: Brill.
Kitcher, Philip. 2015. "Secularism as a Positive Position." In *Global Secularisms in a Post-Secular Age*, ed. Michael Rectenwald, pp. 65–70. Berlin: De Gruyter.
Kosmin, Barry, Ariela Keysar, Ryan Cragun, and Juhem Navarro-Rivera. 2009. *American Nones: The Profile of the No Religion Population*. Hartford, Conn.: Institute for the Study of Secularism in Society and Culture.

Langston, Joseph, Joseph Hammer, and Ryan T. Cragun. 2015. "Atheism Looking In: On the Goals and Strategies of Organized Nonbelief." *Science, Religion and Culture* 2(3): 70–85.

Larue, Gerald A. 1996. *Freethought Across the Centuries*. Amherst, N.Y.: Humanist Press.

LeDrew, Stephen. 2015a. "Atheism Versus Humanism: Ideological Tensions and Identity Dynamics." In *Atheist Identities: Spaces and Social Contexts*, ed. Lori G. Beaman and Steven Tomlins, pp. 53–68. Berlin and New York: Springer.

LeDrew, Stephen. 2015b. *The Evolution of Atheism: The Politics of a Modern Movement*. Oxford: Oxford University Press.

Lee, Lois. 2015. *Recognizing the Nonreligious: Reimagining the Secular*. Oxford: Oxford University Press.

Marty, Martin E. 2003. "The Triumph of 'Whatever'." *Context* 35(11): 1–2.

Meier, Brian, Adam Fetterman, Michael Robinson, and Courtney Lappas. 2015. "The Myth of the Angry Atheist." *The Journal of Psychology* 149(3): 219–238.

Nongbri, Brent. 2012. *Before Religion: A History of a Modern Concept*. New Haven, CT: Yale University Press.

Norenzayan, Ara, and Will M. Gervais. 2013. "The Origins of Religious Disbelief." *Trends in Cognitive Sciences* 17(1): 20–25.

Pasquale, Frank. 2010. "A Portrait of Secular Group Affiliates." In *Atheism and Secularity*, ed. Phil Zuckerman, vol. 1, pp. 43–87. Santa Barbara, Cal.: Praeger.

Putnam, Samuel P. 1894. *Four Hundred Years of Freethought*. New York: The Truth Seeker Company.

Quack, Johannes. 2014. "Outline of a Relational Approach to 'Nonreligion'." *Method & Theory in the Study of Religion* 26(4–5): 439–469.

Seed, John. 2014. "'Secular' and 'Religious': Historical Perspectives." *Social History* 39(1): 3–13.

Schnell, Tatjana. 2015. "Dimensions of Secularity (DoS): An Open Inventory to Measure Facets of Secular Identities." *International Journal for the Psychology of Religion* 25(4): 272–292.

Shook, John R. 2010. *The God Debates: A 21st Century Guide for Atheists and Believers (and Everyone in Between)*. Malden, Mass.: Wiley-Blackwell.

Shook, John R. 2012. "Atheists are Rejecting Today's Culturally Evolved Religions, not a 'First' Natural Religion." *Religion, Brain & Behavior* 2(1): 38–40.

Shook, John R. 2015. "Philosophy of Religion and Two Types of Atheology." *International Journal of Philosophy and Theology* 76(1): 1–19.

Silver, Christopher, Thomas Coleman III, Ralph W. Hood Jr, and Jenny Holcombe. 2014. "The Six Types of Nonbelief: A Qualitative and Quantitative Study of Type and Narrative." *Mental Health, Religion & Culture* 17(10): 990–1001.

Smith, Jesse M. 2010. "Becoming an Atheist in America: Constructing Identity and Meaning from the Rejection of Theism." *Sociology of Religion* 72(2): 215–237.

Smith, Jesse M. 2013. "Creating a Godless Community: The Collective Identity Work of Contemporary American Atheists." *Journal for the Scientific Study of Religion* 52(1): 80–99.

Streib, Heinz, and Constantin Klein. 2013. "Atheists, Agnostics, and Apostates." In *APA Handbook of Psychology, Religion and Spirituality, Volume 1*, pp. 713–728. Washington D.C.: American Psychological Association.

Taylor, Charles. 2009. "The Polysemy of the Secular." *Social Research* 76: 1143–1166.
Toosi, Negin R., and Nalini Ambady. 2011. "Ratings of Essentialism for Eight Religious Identities." *International Journal for the Psychology of Religion* 21(1): 17–29.
Turner, Jonathan H. 2013. *Theoretical Sociology*. Thousand Oaks, CA: SAGE Publications.
Vainio, Olli-Pekka, and Aku Visala. 2015. "Varieties of Unbelief: A Taxonomy of Atheistic Positions." *Neue Zeitschrift für Systematische Theologie und Religionsphilosophie* 57(4): 483–500.
Williamson, David, and George Yancey. 2013. *There Is No God – Atheists in America*. Lanham, Md.: Rowman & Littlefield, 2013.
Wohlrab-Sahra, Monika, and Marian Burchardt. 2012. "Multiple Secularities: Toward a Cultural Sociology of Secular Modernities." *Comparative Sociology* 11(6): 875–909.
Wotton, David. 1992. "New Histories of Atheism." In *Atheism from the Reformation to the Enlightenment*, ed. Michael Hunter and David Wotton, pp. 15–53. Oxford: Oxford University Press.
Zuckerman, Phil. 2011. *Faith No More: Why People Reject Religion*. Oxford: Oxford University Press.
Zuckerman, Phil, ed. 2010. *Atheism and Secularity*. 2 vols. Santa Barbara, Cal.: Praeger.

Amanda Schutz
Organizational Variation in the American Nonreligious Community

1 Introduction

Social scientists are learning more about nonreligion and those who claim no religious preference. Recent research focuses on the growth of the unaffiliated (Baker and Smith 2015; Hout and Fischer 2002), how and why individuals become nonreligious (Fazzino 2014; Hunsberger and Altemeyer 2006; Ritchey 2009; Smith 2011; Zuckerman 2012a), collective identity formation (Guenther, Mulligan, and Papp 2013; LeDrew 2013; Smith 2013), prejudice and discrimination directed toward atheists (Cragun et al. 2012; Edgell, Gerteis, and Hartmann 2006; Gervais, Shariff, and Norenzayan 2011), and the rise of New Atheism, facilitated by new media and the popularity of atheist writers (Amarasingam 2012; Cimino and Smith 2014).[1]

Some of these researchers have also addressed nonreligious organizations, or groups that offer activities and services to those who identify with nonreligious labels. Thus, these groups are specifically *not* religious, not merely religiously neutral (Eller 2010). Recent research suggests that the nonreligious community is a heterogeneous one, that nonreligious identities and the pathways that lead to them may be just as diverse as religious ones, and that "typologies" of non-belief can be developed (Cotter 2015; Mastiaux, this volume; Silver et al. 2014; Zuckerman 2012b). Given this variation in nonreligious identities, we can reasonably expect to encounter heterogeneity in organizational structures and outcomes as well. This prompts me to ask: *What are the different organizational types that exist in the American nonreligious community?* What purposes do they serve for the people who join them? What kinds of events, activities, and services do they provide? These are largely descriptive questions and answering them will provide a context in which individual and collective meaning making takes place.

Several methods of categorizing organizational activity into a typology could be employed effectively. Such groups could be organized based on the identity of individuals who join them: an organization for atheists, an organization for hu-

---

[1] Summaries of previous research on nonreligion can be found in several chapters throughout this volume.

manists, an organization for skeptics, and so on. While the names of organizations often reflect such categorization, this may not produce the most informative typology. The terminology used to describe nontheistic labels and ideologies – both by laypeople and the academics who study them – is diverse and contested (Lee 2012). These labels are undoubtedly important to nonbelievers, who often make subtle distinctions when discussing their nonreligious identities. However, if presented a laundry list of nonreligious labels, many nonbelievers would identify with multiple labels (Langston, Hammer, and Cragun, this volume).

I believe a more useful way to categorize these groups – that is, assign them *identities* – is by their functions, purposes, goals, or the chief benefits they aim to provide for their members, which can be expressed through the *types of events* that organizations offer. To determine what these functions are, I analyzed meetings and activities hosted and sponsored by several nonreligious organizations in Houston, Texas. In the remainder of this chapter, I will discuss some relevant literature on nonreligion, and how organization theory can be applied to the study of nonreligion. I will then describe methods of data collection, the organizations observed, and the sample of nonbelievers interviewed for this project. Next, I will detail a typology of the events that are hosted, sponsored, and promoted by Houston's nonreligious organizations, which I suggest can be used to determine an organization's most salient identity. Finally, I will briefly discuss the implications of gaining a better understanding of organized nonreligion.

2 Background

2.1 Nonreligion Studies

Lois Lee defines nonreligion as "anything which is *primarily* defined by a relationship of difference to religion" (2012, 131). Nonreligion is associated with a number of terms; if nonreligious individuals choose a label at all, they may use words such as atheist, agnostic, skeptic, humanist, freethinker, or secularist to describe themselves. (I refer to these individuals collectively as "nonbelievers.") In the past, researchers have been reluctant to view nonreligion as a social phenomenon rather than an individual one because, historically, it has been seen as a force that promotes individualism rather than integration, with nonbelievers being perceived as immoral, nonconforming, and alienated (Campbell [1971] 2013). However, the social significance of nonreligion is especially evident today as more people organize themselves into coherent structures that explicitly reject religious belief.

Much of the research on the nonreligious focuses on individuals' identity formation and the stigma they face, particularly if claiming an atheist identity. Nonbelievers have consistently remained a stigmatized group, despite the fact that they are slowly gaining acceptance in American society, though at a slower rate than other marginalized groups (Edgell et al. 2006; Edgell at al. 2016). Research on perceptions of atheists shows that out of a long list of minority groups, atheists consistently rank as one of the least liked and most distrusted; Americans see atheists as a cultural threat and the group least likely to share their vision of American society, compared to Muslims, immigrants, and LGBTQ individuals (Edgell et al. 2006). Other research suggests that people see atheists as a sort of "ethical wildcard" and are unsure of what they actually believe (Gervais et al. 2011, 1202).

As this stigma is discreditable and not immediately visible to others (Goffman 1963), atheists are able to "pass" as believers if they wish; in such cases, the stigmatized individual is typically responsible for signaling to others that he or she does not fit normative assumptions (Gagne, Tewksbury, and McGaughey 1997). Some nonbelievers are reticent to disclose their lack of belief, fearing they may experience disapproval or rejection from others (Smith 2011). Thus, nonreligious organizations may be a valuable resource for nonbelievers, aiding in the management and normalization of this stigmatized identity (Doane and Elliott 2014).

2.2 Organization Theory

Organizational involvement could be a significant variable in the nonreligious experience; thus, it is important to examine the *types* of organizations in which nonbelievers choose to spend their time. Within the nonreligious community, organizations will take on different roles, or, I suggest, embrace different identities that are displayed to the public via the events they offer.

Social scientists have no shortage of interpretations surrounding the term "identity." It can be understood both as an internalized aspect of one's self and as a group or collective phenomenon (Owens 2003). It can serve as a motivator of social or political action, but can also be a consequence of such action (Brubaker and Cooper 2000). It is a concept that transcends levels of analysis and can be investigated at the individual, group, or organization level (Ashforth, Rogers, and Corley 2011; Gioia 1998; Whetten 1998). Like individuals, organizations need answers to identity questions like "Who are we?" or "What do we want to be?" in order to successfully interact with and communicate their values and goals to others (Albert, Ashforth, and Dutton 2000; Albert and Whetten

1985). Organizational identity refers to what members "perceive, feel and think" about the organization they belong to (Hatch and Schultz 2007, 357). It allows an organization to distinguish itself from others that may share common goals and functions by expressing its "character," or whatever the group deems "important and essential" (Albert and Whetten 1985, 266).

Organization theorists suggest that outsiders can affect the character of an organization (Dutton and Dukerich 1991; Hsu and Hannan 2005). This is a significant point because much research has focused on the negative perceptions people have of atheists, but less has examined how nonbelievers respond to these perceptions as collectives (see Fazzino, Borer, Abdel Haq 2014; Guenther 2014; Zuckerman 2014, 11–37). Some nonbelievers may expend considerable effort toward dispelling the stereotypes attributed to them, which can be funneled through organizational channels; in other words, if nonbelievers wish to signal to outsiders that they are socially engaged, compassionate, or ethical, they may form or join an organization that prioritizes the qualities they value. Action within the context of nonreligious organizations, then, can help members manage the impressions they (as nonbelievers) give others (see Smith 2013). However, since little is known about what nonreligious organizations actually do, reactions to such groups – from both average religious Americans and the nonbelievers unfamiliar with them – can be critical. This is especially true of organizations that more closely resemble religious groups, perhaps because the idea of organized nonreligion is counterintuitive (see Smith, Frost, this volume). Research has suggested that organizations with contradictory elements can elicit aggressive responses (Galaskiewicz and Barringer 2012); since nonbelievers reject belief in a supernatural deity, others assume that they will reject other aspects of religion (e.g., a strong moral code) as well.

To this point, such organizations have been utilized primarily as a strategy of sampling for atheists, or a context where nonreligious identities are fostered (Hunsberger and Altemeyer 2006; LeDrew 2013; Ritchey 2009; Smith 2013). However, with few exceptions, researchers have not closely examined nonreligious organizations as entities in and of themselves, their variation, or how these formal and informal groups might affect (or be affected by) those who join them (see Guenther, Mulligan, and Papp 2013; Lee 2015, 106–130; Zuckerman 2014, 107–136). Research that does address nonreligious organizations usually refers to such groups abstractly and as a united collective, rather than parsing out the specific and diverse goals that each organization in a given area may have (though see Shook, this volume). Recognizing that not all organizations are created equal can allow for more nuance in our discussions of nonbelievers' identities, motivations, beliefs, and practices. Shedding light on what each of these organizations does may also broaden perceptions of nonbelievers and organized nonreligion as a whole.

3 Data and Methods

As part of a larger project, I used qualitative research methods to explore how individual and collective nonreligious experiences manifest as organizational action; this chapter describes such action. I conducted approximately 80 discrete observations among eight local nonreligious organizations in the Houston area, over a period of eight months. I conducted 125 semi-structured in-depth interviews with founders, leaders, and members of these groups, as well as people who were not actively involved. I also performed content analysis on websites, interactions on social media, and literature distributed at events. Field notes and transcripts were coded line by line and patterns emerged inductively, allowing me to discern variation in the activities and events each organization hosted. I analyzed each organization's self-description (usually published on a website or in distributed written material), what members said about the organizations, and my own observations of events and activities. In cases where these accounts differ, I defer to my observations and justify my reasoning for doing so. By triangulating observations, personal accounts, and recorded material, I was able to construct a typology of nonreligious events. The events sponsored by nonreligious organizations reflect their members' priorities, and by focusing on events (i.e., what the organizations *do*), we can determine their "essential character" (i.e., what they *are*).

3.1 The Setting

Houston seems an ideal setting to conduct research on organized nonreligion. Texas is generally socially and politically conservative, and many Texans are evangelical Protestants. Houston is also home to several of the largest megachurches in the US. It is consistently ranked by national polls as one of the most religious states, having above average levels of affiliation, belief, commitment, and religious behaviors. However, Houston also claims to host the world's largest atheist community and provides a diverse range of events for those who identify with various nonreligious labels.

The city appears to be in a "Goldilocks zone" between high and low levels of secularity that allow nonreligious organizations to thrive. Houston is the fourth-largest city in the US, set to overtake Chicago in the coming decades. It is described by its inhabitants as "cosmopolitan" and is one of the most diverse cities in the country – racially, ethnically, and culturally (Klinenberg 2016; Steptoe 2016). In order for its inhabitants to coexist, it must be tolerant of diversity to some extent. At the same time, Houston is located firmly in the Bible Belt, not far removed from the Deep South, where religion is prevalent enough that nonbelievers can expect to encounter it in everyday interactions. Nonbelievers in Houston report hearing religion in political rhetoric (both locally and nationally), seeing it make its way into public classrooms, and frequently being asked, "Where do you go to church?" upon meeting new acquaintances. Nonbelievers in places like Houston may feel a greater need to organize in response to religion than those in more secular communities like Boston, San Francisco, or Seattle, while simultaneously feeling safer openly doing so than in predominately conservative Christian or rural communities.

However, this should not suggest that cities or regions that are more or less religious than average cannot produce successful nonreligious organizations. For example, some research has described successful atheist groups in rural areas, even in the face of resistance and marginalization from religious others (Ritchey 2009). Conversely, the Sunday Assembly – a growing secular organization that emulates church services – was founded in London, despite nearly half of Britons having no religious affiliation (Bagg and Voas 2010). Further research in a range of settings is needed to confirm any concrete patterns of organizational vitality, though García and Blankholm (2016) suggest that nonreligious organizations tend to emerge in US counties with larger populations of evangelical Protestants.

3.2 The Organizations

Nearly all nonreligious organizations in Houston have a public online presence (e.g., social networking sites like Meetup.com and Facebook.com), so as to attract participants. Houston hosts several large local nonreligious organizations (totaling 5,000+ online members at the time of fieldwork) that provide a variety of gatherings for nonbelievers. I conducted participant observation among eight of these organizations, each hosting regularly scheduled, recurring events open to the public; that is, all organizations discussed here sponsor events that occur weekly, biweekly, monthly, quarterly, or annually, which anyone can attend.

The three largest nonreligious organizations – Houston Atheists (HA), the Humanists of Houston (HOH), and the Greater Houston Skeptic Society (GHSS) – host or promote a variety of gatherings (e.g., coffee socials, discussion groups, family-friendly happy hours, volunteer opportunities, meditation) that may appeal to different niches (much like the national organizations described by Fazzino and Cragun, this volume) and draw in different types of nonbelievers (like those described by Mastiaux, this volume). Another organization, the Houston Oasis (Oasis, hereafter) – dubbed a "godless congregation" due to its churchlike structure – meets every Sunday for coffee and fellowship, music, and a lecture. (At the time of fieldwork, Oasis had also launched "franchises" in Kansas City and Dallas, and were preparing to launch in Boston.) Smaller groups in the Houston area include Houston Church of Freethought (HCoF), Natural Spiritualists (NS), Houston Black Nonbelievers (HBN), and a local chapter of the national organization Americans United for the Separation of Church and State (AU). Some of these groups also coordinated action with an Austin-based organization, Atheists Helping the Homeless (AHH), though I did not directly observe this group.

3.3 Sample

My sample of interview respondents shares many demographic characteristics with those of previous research on nonreligion. Slightly over half of respondents were male, over two-thirds were white, about three-quarters had a bachelor's degree or higher, and three-quarters identified as politically left-leaning, with a median age of 43 (ranging from 20 to 84). Respondents were recruited directly from group meetings, via Meetup mailing lists or Facebook posts (depending on the recommendation of group leaders), and by word-of-mouth and snowball sampling. Most participants grew up with some degree of socialization in Protestant Christian denominations, though I also interviewed people who were raised Catholic, Mormon, Jehovah's Witness, Muslim, Hindu, and nothing in particular.

Since there is no obligation to attend meetings after joining nonreligious groups online, by sending requests for interviews using Meetup and Facebook (rather than recruiting solely from group meetings) I was able to reach people with various levels of involvement with the organizations, including founders, leaders, regular attendees, those who attend occasionally or rarely, those who used to but no longer attend, those who have not yet attended but intend to, and those who have no interest in attending face-to-face events. Speaking with nonbelievers about their organizational affiliations and preferences (or lack thereof) provided insight into how people viewed these groups and what they offer, and whether or not these impressions matched those that organizations were attempting to give.

4 A Typology of Nonreligious Events and Organizations

As the number of nonreligious organizations increases in a given area, they may develop distinctive characteristics and values in order to differentiate themselves from others. In this way, nonreligious organizations do more than provide a space where people can simply "not believe in God"; they serve specific purposes and fulfill functions (many of which echo those fulfilled by churches) that they cannot or choose not to fulfill via other means.

Table 1. Typology of Nonreligious Events and Organizational Identity

Type of event	Purpose	Examples of meetings and activities	Organization(s) displaying identity as most salient
Social	Socializing with like-minded others	Dinner, happy hour, game nights	Houston Atheists
Communal	Community building	Church-like gatherings, fundraising, potlucks	Houston Oasis
Educational	Learning and engaging in structured discussion	Lectures/presentations, debates, book clubs	Humanists of Houston, Greater Houston Skeptics Society, Houston Black Nonbelievers, Houston Church of Freethought
Political	Raising awareness of church/state issues	Protests, political discussions, rallies	Americans United for the Separation of Church and State
Charitable	Donating and volunteering	Blood drives, food bank, sorting donated items	Atheists Helping the Homeless
Spiritual	Experiencing emotions associated with religion	Meditation, philosophical discussions	Spiritual Naturalists

The typology shown in Table 1 and developed below is based on the various types of events that nonreligious organizations sponsor, which are typically organized, hosted, or promoted by leaders and/or a core group of highly active members. I classify these activities as falling into six categories: social, communal, educational, political, charitable, and spiritual. These "types of events" can serve as a proxy for organizational identity: an organization that hosts primarily social events can be considered a "social" organization, an organization that hosts primarily educational events is considered an "educational" organization, and so forth. Thus, the identities assigned to the organizations described below are ideal types. In practice, organizations may display different identities at different times by offering different types of meetings and activities that provide different purposes. This is of course true of individuals as well: we are capable of having multiple identities, but at any given moment one of our identities may be more salient than another (Stryker and Burke 2000). If an organization tends to stress a particular purpose over others, if certain events prove more popular by drawing larger crowds, or if the group sponsors a particular type of activity more frequently than others, I consider this its primary, or most salient, organizational identity.

It is also important to note that assigning identities based on events that reflect a group's primary purpose – determined by the organizations' stated missions, what members say about them (during interviews, in passing at meetings, and online), and my own impressions of the events they sponsor – is not the only way to categorize nonreligious organizations. As mentioned previously, they could be categorized based on the identities of those who join them (atheist, humanist, skeptic, etc.), though I am skeptical of the usefulness of such a typology at the organization level. Organizations could also be categorized by their leadership structures, or level of formality. They may have hierarchical leadership, with a president and board of directors who administrate all activity, or they may be structured horizontally, with responsibilities diffused among many committed members. They can be run as dictatorships or democracies. They can be formalized with 501(c)(3) status, securing the same legal and monetary benefits granted to other non-profit organizations, or pursue no such ambitions. Meetings may have strict agendas or none at all. This is an avenue certainly worth exploring further; indeed, the groups I observed did display a variety of organizational structures, though as a typology it may not capture the variation that manifests via a group's diverse membership. Ultimately, based on the data collected, I constructed a typology based on events, which I believe represents the character of the organizations and values of their members.

4.1 Social

Some nonreligious organizations are primarily *social* in nature. Houston Atheists, for example, prioritizes providing members a safe space to socialize with like-minded others, where the topic of religion will not be a point of contention. Other research has identified this as a key reason people give for joining an atheist community (Tomlins 2015). In fact, at HA events, religion often was not a popular topic of conversation. Throughout the course of fieldwork, I noticed that if someone was a first-time attendee at these types of events, they were often asked about their religious background, or how long they had been a nonbeliever. It was typically assumed that fellow attendees had "de-converted" from religion or somehow "discovered" atheism. In fact, only one interviewee of 125 explicitly indicated being raised an atheist; all other respondents were either raised in some religious tradition or as "nothing in particular" before they concluded at some point that they did not believe. As these organizations are, by name, *non*-religious, this topic often fueled initial conversations between new acquaintances. After these brief "introductory" talks, conversation usually shifted, often revolving around topics like science, entertainment, or current events.

Still, in the event that the topic of religion did come up, members could rest assured that there would be no need to "come out of the closet" like there might be in other social settings. Pat[2], a member of HA, had this to say about the group's social gatherings:

> One big thing that can make you uncomfortable if you're looking for friends and you're an atheist is, you know, if the person is religious it's inevitably going to come up, and you're going to have to deal with it. But sidestepping, skipping that whole issue is nice. So it doesn't mean you're going to like everybody or you're going to agree with everybody on political issues or anything like that, but that's one big topic that you can avoid, which is nice.

Being able to disclose a nonreligious identity without risk of judgment was a big draw for many people who chose to attend these meetings. Regardless of the sponsoring organization, these events share some characteristics: there is nearly always food, coffee, or alcohol and there is rarely an agenda. There is also no leader or designated authority figure directing action or conversation. They are usually held in public spaces like a restaurant or bar, or occasionally at a group member's home in the form of a potluck. Nearly all of the nonreligious organizations in Houston offered informal social gatherings throughout the month, though most did not prioritize these types of meetings.

---

[2] Interview respondents have been given pseudonyms. Names of organizations and their leaders (publically available information) have not been altered.

4.2 Communal

Nonreligious organizations can also be *communal*. Members strive to share knowledge, skills, and services with one another, with a focus on creating community. Over the course of my fieldwork, I began encountering events and activities that involved gathering members together in a shared safe space, but did not quite fall into the strictly "social" category described above. The idea of "community," I found, is deeper than simply meeting a basic desire to socialize.

At social events, participants meet over food or drink for conversation with other nonbelievers, which may or may not result in the same people gathering at the same place for subsequent gatherings. While a "communal" organization may host such events, its primary purpose is to function as a consistent, dependable group, where members can ask for help if they need it and take advantage of learning a new skill when offered – much like a typical church does for its congregants. The Houston Oasis is a prime example of such an organization: they do host dinners and happy hours like those described in the preceding section, but they also strive to be an enduring community that fosters a sense of belonging among nonbelievers. Someone looking for a close-knit secular community (perhaps filling a void left from leaving a church, though not necessarily) might be drawn to Oasis for this reason over a group like Houston Atheists. (However, this should not suggest that people involved exclusively in social organizations like HA cannot forge deep connections; indeed, some people I spoke to had developed close friendships or met their spouses at such events.)

These organizations can be especially appealing to young couples and families with small children, who are looking for like-minded and similarly situated people to share experiences and build relationships that will extend beyond the events hosted by the organization. These are, of course, also functions that are performed by churches and other intimate communities. During an interview, Alayna discussed the significant role church played in her life, and how difficult it was to give up when she began questioning her faith:

> Honestly, the last thing that was holding me back from fully admitting that I didn't believe in God, was the concept of community.... I need church, I need a community that has my back even if I don't know these people, right? Because I'm part of their community, they're gonna step up and help me, or they're gonna be there for me and they're gonna create a sense of home for my children. Because it did that for me as a child. Church was a really fun place for me. I loved church, I loved the friends I had at church, I loved the sports I played through church. And I was really afraid of saying I'm not gonna be part of a church anymore.... Once I realized that I could have community without God, I was gone.

While some founders, leaders, and members of organizations like Oasis do not wish to be compared to a church, others, like Alayna, recognize and appreciate the similarities. Weekly Oasis events, for example, mimic the structure of a church service. They meet every Sunday morning for coffee, cookies, music (performances, not sing-a-longs), and a lecture, sometimes given by a member of the community but often given by outside speakers. When no speaker is scheduled in advance, a presentation is given by Mike Aus: co-founder, executive director, and de facto leader of Oasis. They offer childcare during the meeting (some even call it a "service") and pass around hats to collect donations. They host family friendly events, happy hours, and discussion groups. They are a 501(c)(3) educational non-profit organization, with a salaried executive director and a board of directors.

Oasis was also working toward building a "directory of skills" that would list select group members alongside their professions or services they were able and willing to perform for other members. If, for instance, someone at Oasis needed a dentist, an electrician, or childcare, they could consult the directory and enlist the services of a fellow community member before resorting to outside recommendations. Similarly, churches – particularly those catering to immigrant and minority populations – often provide their congregations with basic resources beyond spiritual fulfillment (Cadge and Ecklund 2007; Pattillo-McCoy 1998). Having the option of relying on other group members for everyday (even trivial) needs can help foster a sense of affinity among nonbelievers that churches have successfully provided their congregations for generations.

Oasis was appealing to Alayna precisely *because* it shared these characteristics – both significant and trivial – with her conception of "church," not in spite of them. For many formerly religious nonbelievers, church is synonymous with community, and a nonreligious organization's ability to mimic these qualities can provide familiarity and comfort.

4.3 Educational

Several of Houston's nonreligious organizations could be categorized as *educational*. While some members do become involved to meet social needs, others say they are looking for "something more"; they want to learn something new or engage intellectually in structured discussions. At these types of events, members can learn about and debate the philosophical merits of atheism and shortcomings of religion, hold discussions about science, ethics, or social issues, or acquire new perspectives from outsider groups, like the LGBTQ or Black communities. The organizations may host lectures and presentations (given by community members or guest speakers) or advertise outside events of interest. These types of gatherings were the most popular among nonreligious organizations, and nearly all of the organizations I observed hosted educational events; even groups that did not host these types of events, like HA and Spiritual Naturalists, often promoted those hosted by other organizations on their Meetup and Facebook pages. Organizations specifically prioritizing these events, thus displaying an *educational* identity most prominently, include Humanists of Houston, Greater Houston Skeptic Society, Houston Black Nonbelievers, and Houston Church of Freethought (despite its tongue-in-cheek name, I categorize the HCoF as an educational organization rather than a communal one, as its events tend to focus less on community building and more on intellectual stimulation).

While the nonbelievers I observed were not always keen on restricting casual conversations to religion and nonbelief, educational events frequently dealt with these topics. For example, sociologist Penny Edgell gave a talk at Rice University, where she presented data from the new wave of the American Mosaic Project, discussing new and persistent trends among atheists and the unaffiliated. She was joined by Anthony Pinn, a Black professor of religion at Rice and author of the book *Writing God's Obituary: How A Good Methodist Became an Even Better Atheist*. This event was hosted by the university, but was promoted by several nonreligious organizations, including HA, HOH, and HBN. Pinn has also made appearances as an invited speaker at some of Houston's local nonreligious gatherings.

Topics up for discussion at these types of events varied widely. Sometimes educational events dealt with scientific topics, such as a talk hosted by GHSS about conservation programs at the Houston Zoo. Other times these events focused on social issues, like HBN's discussions about mass incarceration and homophobia in the Black community. Ethical concerns were also a popular topic of discussion, perhaps because nonbelievers are often assumed to lack a moral compass (Gervais et al. 2011; Zuckerman 2009). For example, early in my fieldwork Oasis began holding a monthly discussion group focused on ethical issues, such as the death penalty, euthanasia, and organ transplantation. As Mike Aus, former pastor and co-founder of Oasis, said preceding a Sunday morning lecture, "There's so much to talk about when you're not limited to one book."

4.4 Political

Another role these organizations can play is a *political* one: they can offer events that focus on raising awareness of church/state issues and providing members knowledge and access to political channels. Such events might aim to incite change in policies that could be interpreted as favoring religious individuals and institutions, perhaps going so far as to initiate lawsuits challenging such policies. For example, the Houston chapter of Americans United tries to host an event every quarter. One of these events featured a discussion with Ellery Schempp, plaintiff in the 1963 Supreme Court case *Abington School District v. Schempp*, which banned mandatory Bible readings in public schools. However, AU is not a nonreligious organization in the sense that other organizations discussed here are. It was founded in 1947 by Protestant Christians and caters to both the religious and nonreligious who wish to see a government free from religious influence (and religion free from government influence). Many of my respondents spoke of the separation of church and state as a cause that can be supported by believers and nonbelievers alike, an idea supported by social research (Baker and Smith 2009). Still, AU events are promoted by several of Houston's nonreligious organizations for those members who are passionate about issues tying together politics and secularism.

Such organizations can also encourage political activism, or promote events that highlight secular, political causes (see Fazzino, Borer, and Abdel Haq 2014). For example, there was a recurring protest that HOH had been hosting with Amnesty International, in which members met in front of the Saudi Arabian consulate to protest the treatment of Raif Badawi, a liberal blogger who was sentenced to 10 years in prison and 1,000 lashes for posting critical comments about Islam in Saudi Arabia. Another prominent issue plaguing secular Texans during my fieldwork involved the injection of religion into public classrooms: group members angrily spoke of a new history textbook the state was considering adopting, which cited Moses as an honorary Founding Father of the US.

Respondents often reported being frustrated with this kind of infusion of religion and public life, both at home and abroad. They spoke of seeking an outlet for such frustrations, but were also cynical about the efficacy of actions like protesting and petitioning. However, I did recognize at least 30 people from Houston who made the 165 mile drive to Austin for the second annual Texas Secular Convention, an entire weekend of talks on church/state issues specifically facing the citizens of Texas, which hosted panels and presentations with titles such as "The Importance of Secular Education," "Staying in Contact with Your Legislator," and "Effective Ways to Build Coalitions Between Progressive Religious and Secular Communities."

4.5 Charitable

Nonreligious organizations might be primarily concerned with *charitable* endeavors, such as providing opportunities to donate and volunteer as individuals or as members of a nonreligious community. Groups like HOH and Oasis hosted at least one charitable event each month (e. g., volunteering at local food banks, donation centers, and hosting blood drives), and members of these organizations often participated in monthly giveaways with Atheists Helping the Homeless, a group launched in Austin, Texas, in 2009 that had recently started a chapter in Houston. However, many nonbelievers I interviewed expressed a desire to see more activities like this, and lamented that there were too few opportunities to volunteer with nonreligious organizations. In fact, they recognized that religious groups often do charity very well, and some respondents even volunteered through churches or religious organizations simply because many charities have religious affiliations.

Some members of nonreligious organizations also recognized that disadvantaged nonbelievers might hesitate to obtain services from religious charities, especially if the recipient perceives an expectation to attend the church or somehow become involved with the religious group. Felicia, a member of Houston Black Nonbelievers, said:

> [A fellow HBN member] and I talked about the plight of the homeless. You know, a lot of these shelters around here are Christian-based, you know, it's that beat-you-over-the-head-till-you-become-a-Christian, whether you are or not, and he would like something secular. Now if you wanna go to church or whatever, that's your business, we're not gonna proselytize. And he said, "I'm pretty sure there's some atheists out there but they have to say they're Christian in order to get services." I said yeah, I'm pretty sure there are.

Not only are secular charities important in that they provide nonbelievers in need a place to go without religious strings attached, but nonreligious organizations that endorse charitable activity can also mitigate the impression that atheists are immoral or indifferent to helping other people. For instance, on our way to the Texas Secular Convention in Austin, Rose, an active member of GHSS, spoke to me about a conversation she had with a religious acquaintance. After describing volunteer work she had recently completed, the acquaintance responded, "Why do you bother volunteering if you don't believe in God?" This gave Rose the opportunity to explain that nonbelievers can be moral individuals who enjoy helping others, with no promise of an afterlife in return. By volunteering specifically as part of a nonreligious organization, nonbelievers are engaging in a sort of secular activism that aims to dispel these negative assumptions (see Fazzino, Borer, and Abdel Haq 2014; Zuckerman 2014).

4.6 Spiritual

Finally, these organizations can be *spiritual* in nature, providing a place where members can go to experience emotions traditionally associated with religion – like awe and self-reflection – where disbelief in the supernatural is not only acceptable (as it often is in Unitarian Universalist congregations), but expected. While "secular spirituality" might seem counterintuitive, there are a sizable number of people in these organizations who feel that the idea is compatible with an atheist or humanist worldview. For example, when I asked one of my respondents, Robert, if he thought there was room for spirituality in an atheistic worldview, he gave this enthusiastic response:

> When the light bulb burns out it's gone, and it's sad. Sort of. But it's also kind of awesome because I'm not gonna live forever. I get this one chance to eat ice cream and be with people I love and check out sunsets and visit Canada, and it's great. Is there room for spirituality? Yes. I meditate, that helped me get off drugs. There's room to hold someone's hand and say, you know, I'm just thankful you're in my life and I really love you and I'm really thankful you're my friend, I'm thankful you're my sister, I'm thankful for all these different things...if that's prayer, then that's prayer.... And there's also room for being crass and there's room for the banal as well. The sacred and the profane. I need both of those things. I need comedy clubs where I can go and shout obscenities, and I need moments were I can reflect on just how awesome it is that I exist.

Though Robert and several other respondents spoke of spirituality in a way that did not conflict with their non-belief, most of them did not actually attend events that specifically catered to spiritual nonbelievers. Indeed, of all the types described here, spiritual events struggled the most to maintain a critical mass of nonbelievers to justify continuing meetings. One group in Houston dedicated to secular spirituality, Spiritual Naturalists, operated on and off for several years. They resumed operations in the form of a bi-weekly meditation session and philosophy talk in March of 2015, only to disband four months later, claiming that instead of this "official organization" the group should have focused on allowing a "grassroots community to emerge organically." The group now operates via newsletters and a mailing list, announcing events of interest in the Houston area and allowing members to connect on their own terms.

This lack of participation may be due to the personal meanings that respondents attached to the idea of spirituality. In fact, research has suggested that while people interpret religiosity as incorporating the institutional aspects associated with religious belief, they interpret spirituality as being more individualistic (Zinnbauer et al. 1997); secular spirituality may be interpreted similarly. Not all nonbelievers are comfortable using the term "spirituality," and it seems to be an idiosyncratic concept in that its meaning varies from individual to individual. Some nonbelievers associated spirituality with meditation, and chose to meditate on their own terms (some with a meditation group, or even at a Buddhist temple) as opposed to specifically meditating with other nonbelievers. When my interview respondents spoke of spirituality and I asked them to explain what they meant when they used the word, they tended to define it either in terms of mindfulness and awareness, such as a realization of being a part of "something bigger than ourselves" (usually defined in a literal, scientific way, i.e., "nature" or "the universe"), or a desire to strive toward self-improvement. Zuckerman (2014) coined the term "awe-ism" to describe feelings of wonder that several of my own respondents expressed.

5 Conclusion

During her talk at Rice University, Penny Edgell suggested that public attitudes toward nonbelievers will be difficult to sway until the full range of diversity in the nonreligious community is exposed. Americans make broad, negative assumptions about nonbelievers (which have not greatly improved since the first wave of the American Mosaic Project in 2003), viewing them as immoral and un-American. These perceptions persist, despite the fact that people who claim them do not report personally knowing anyone who does not believe in God (Edgell et al. 2006); thus, the stigma attached to atheism often goes unchallenged. People may assume that nonreligious organizations exist solely for the purpose of criticizing religion – in fact, I spoke to several nonbelievers who also made these assumptions about nonreligious groups before attending themselves. Although these organizations do provide nonbelievers an outlet for venting frustrations about the prevalence of religion in everyday life, I witnessed relatively little outright hostility toward religious individuals. Many respondents reported harboring no ill feelings toward believers, some acknowledged the good that religious communities can do, and a few even empathized with those who do believe in God. Research that exposes the diversity of beliefs, behaviors, and values among the nonreligious (like that described throughout this volume) has the potential to change negative perceptions held by the general American public.

This chapter is derived from a larger project focusing on this diversity in nonreligious communities, including whether individuals with certain preferences or experiences are drawn to one type of group over another; the role organizations play in helping individuals construct and manage their personal identities; and whether organizational involvement helps to instill a set of positive beliefs, values, or characteristics that accompanies what it means to be a nonbeliever. I also suggest that individuals can shift and alter the characteristics of the organizations they join. In a span of only eight months, I saw these organizations grow and dissolve and change. Much like with individuals, organizational identity is not static. In fact, some organization theorists suggest that organizations need to be *more* flexible than individuals in how they define themselves because they must be able to adapt quickly in order to survive precarious social, political, or economic conditions (Gioia 1998; Gioia, Schultz, and Corley 2000). The Humanists of Houston provides a good example of such a shift. Since coming under new leadership in 2015, HOH has become a multi-faceted organization, offering its own social, educational, political, and charitable activities, and co-sponsoring or promoting events hosted by nearly all other nonreligious organizations in the Houston area (for more on how nonreligious organizations can support one another, see Fazzino and Cragun, this volume). While I categorize HOH as an educational organization, as its most popular events fall under this umbrella, the organization's shifting focus on building a humanist *community* – that is, a close-knit group of core active members – means HOH could be shifting its most salient identity toward becoming a *communal* organization, rather than a predominately educational one.

The organizational types described above serve an important purpose in nonreligious communities, especially to those individuals who have lost their faith and left their own religious communities (Fazzino 2014). Nonreligious organizations are very much like religious organizations in the functions they provide their members. Religious organizations have historically provided a space for their members to socialize, learn new things, engage in political discourse, volunteer, reflect and meditate, and build enduring relationships. Of course, religious organizations are not the only way to meet these needs and goals (nor are *nonreligious* organizations the only alternative), but they have arguably been the most successful. Providing a space for nonbelievers to have these fundamental human experiences is vital, especially in a society that overwhelmingly values the religious ethos. Despite religion's declining influence as a social institution over other areas of social life, scholars recognize that it remains significant in American society. Nonreligious organizations like those described in this chapter will likely continue to grow unless (or until) religion becomes such a trivial part of everyday public life that nonreligious organizations – that are nonreligious *by design* – no longer *need* to exist.

Bibliography

Albert, Stuart, Blake E. Ashforth, and Jane E. Dutton. 2000. "Organizational Identity and Identification: Charting New Waters and Building New Bridges." *The Academy of Management Review* 25 (1): 13–17.

Albert, Stuart, and David A. Whetten. 1985. "Organizational Identity." *Research in Organizational Behavior* 7: 263–295.

Amarasingam, Amarnath, ed. 2010. *Religion and the New Atheism: A Critical Appraisal.* Leiden, Netherlands: Brill.

Ashforth, Blake E., Kristie M. Rogers, and Kevin G. Corley. 2011. "Identity in Organizations: Exploring Cross-Level Dynamics." *Organization Science* 22 (5): 1144–1156.

Bagg, Samuel, and David Voas. 2010. "The Triumph of Indifference: Irreligion in British Society." In *Atheism and Secularity, Volume 2: Global Expressions*, edited by Phil Zuckerman, 91–111. Santa Barbara, CA: Praeger.

Baker, Joseph O'Brian, and Buster Smith. 2009. "None Too Simple: Examining Issues of Religious Nonbelief and Nonbelonging in the United States." Journal for the Scientific Study of Religion 48 (4): 719–733.

Baker, Joseph O., and Buster G. Smith. 2015. *American Secularism: Cultural Contours of Nonreligious Belief Systems.* New York: New York University Press.

Brubaker, Rogers, and Frederick Cooper. 2000. "Beyond 'Identity.'" *Theory and Society* 29 (1): 1–47.

Cadge, Wendy and Elaine Howard Ecklund. 2007. "Immigration and Religion." *Annual Review of Sociology* 33: 359–379.

Campbell, Colin. 2013 [1971]. *Toward a Sociology of Irreligion.* Introduction by Lois Lee, with Stephen Bullivant and Christopher R. Cotter. York, UK: Alcuin Academics.

Cimino, Richard, and Christopher Smith. 2014. *Atheist Awakening: Secular Activism and Community in America.* Oxford, UK: Oxford University Press.

Cotter, Christopher R. 2015. "Without God yet Not Without Nuance: A Qualitative Study of Atheism and Non-religion Among Scottish University Students." In *Atheist Identities – Spaces and Social Contexts*, edited by Lori G. Beaman and Steven Tomlins, 171–193. Cham, Switzerland: Springer.

Cragun, Ryan T., Barry Kosmin, Ariela Keysar, Joseph H. Hammer, and Michael Nielsen. 2012. "On the Receiving End: Discrimination toward the Non-Religious in the United States." *Journal of Contemporary Religion* 27 (1): 105–127.

Doane, Michael J. and Marta Elliott. 2015. "Perceptions of Discrimination Among Atheists: Consequences for Atheist Identification, Psychological and Physical Well-Being." *Psychology of Religion and Spirituality* 7 (2): 130–141.

Dutton, Jane E., and Janet M. Dukerich. 1991. "Keeping an Eye on the Mirror: Image and Identity in Organizational Adaptation." *The Academy of Management Journal* 34 (3): 517–554.

Edgell, Penny, Joseph Gerteis, and Douglas Hartmann. 2006. "Atheists as 'Other': Moral Boundaries and Cultural Membership in American Society." *American Sociological Review* 71 (2): 211–234.

Edgell, Penny, Joseph Gerteis, Evan Stewart, and Douglas Hartmann. 2016. "Atheists and Other Cultural Outsiders: Moral Boundaries and the Non-Religious in the United States." *Social Forces* 95 (2): 607–638.

Eller, Jack David. 2010. "What Is Atheism?" In *Atheism and Secularity, Volume 1: Issues, Concepts, and Definitions*, edited by Phil Zuckerman, 1–18. Santa Barbara, CA: Praeger.

Fazzino, Lori L. 2014. "Leaving the Church Behind: Applying a Deconversion Perspective to Evangelical Exit Narratives." *Journal of Contemporary Religion* 29 (2): 249–266.

Fazzino, Lori L., Michael Ian Borer, and Mohammed Abdel Haq. 2014. "The New Moral Entrepreneurs: Atheist Activism as Scripted and Performed Political Deviance." In *The Death and Resurrection of Deviance: Current Ideas and Research*, edited by Michael Dellwing, Joseph A. Kotarba, and Nathan W. Pino, 168–191. New York: Palgrave Macmillan.

Gagne, Patricia, Richard Tewksbury, and Deanna McGaughey. 1997. "Coming Out and Crossing Over: Identity Formation and Proclamation in a Transgender Community." *Gender and Society* 11 (4): 478–508.

Galaskiewicz, Joseph, and Sondra Barringer. 2012. "Social Enterprises and Social Categories." In *Social Enterprises: An Organizational Perspective*, edited by Benjamin Gidron and Yeheskei Hasenfeld, 47–70. New York: Palgrave Macmillan.

García, Alfredo, and Joseph Blankholm. 2016. "The Social Context of Organized Nonbelief: County-Level Predictors of Nonbeliever Organizations in the United States." *Journal for the Scientific Study of Religion*. http://onlinelibrary.wiley.com/doi/10.1111/jssr.12250/abstract (accessed June 28, 2016).

Gervais, Will M., Azim F. Shariff, and Ara Norenzayan. 2011. "Do You Believe in Atheists? Distrust Is Central to Anti-Atheist Prejudice." *Journal of Personality and Social Psychology* 101 (6): 1189–1206.

Gioia, Dennis A. 1998. "From Individual to Organizational Identity." In *Identity in Organizations: Building Theory Through Conversations*, edited by David A. Whetten and Paul C. Godfrey, 17–32. Thousand Oaks, CA: Sage Publications.

Gioia, Dennis A., Majken Schultz, and Kevin G. Corley. 2000. "Organizational Identity, Image, and Instability." *The Academy of Management Review* 25 (1): 63–81.

Goffman, Erving. 1963. *Stigma: Notes of the Management of Spoiled Identity*. New York: Simon & Schuster, Inc.

Guenther, Katja M. 2014. "Bounded by Disbelief: How Atheists in the United States Differentiate themselves from Religious Believers." *Journal of Contemporary Religion* 29 (1): 1–16.

Guenther, Katja M., Kerry Mulligan, and Cameron Papp. 2013. "From the Outside In: Crossing Boundaries to Build Collective Identity in the New Atheist Movement." *Social Problems* 60(4): 457–475.

Hatch, Mary Jo, and Majken Schultz. 1997. "Relations Between Organizational Culture, Identity, and Image." *European Journal of Marketing* 31 (5/6): 356–365.

Hout, Michael, and Claude S. Fischer. 2002. "Why More Americans Have Not Religious Preference: Politics and Generations." *American Sociological Review* 67 (2): 165–190.

Hsu, Greta, and Michael T. Hannan. 2005. "Identities, Genres, and Organizational Forms." *Organization Science* 16 (5): 474–490.

Hunsberger, Bruce E., and Bob Altemeyer. 2006. *Atheists: A Groundbreaking Study of America's Nonbelievers*. Amherst, NY: Prometheus Books.

Klineberg, Stephen L. 2016. "Thirty-five Years of the Kinder Houston Area Survey: Tracking Responses to a Changing America." *Rice University Kinder Institute for Urban Research*.

http://kinder.rice.edu/uploadedFiles/Center_for_the_Study_of_Houston/53067_Rice_Houston AreaSurvey2016_Lowres.pdf (accessed May 19, 2016).

LeDrew, Stephen. 2013. "Discovering Atheism: Heterogeneity in Trajectories to Atheist Identity and Activism." *Sociology of Religion* 74 (4): 431–453.

Lee, Lois. 2012. "Research Note: Talking About a Revolution: Terminology for the New Field of Non-religion Studies." *Journal of Contemporary Religion* 27 (1): 129–139.

Lee, Lois. 2015. *Recognizing the Non-religious: Reimagining the Secular.* Oxford, UK: Oxford University Press.

Owens, Timothy J. 2003. "Self and Identity" In *Handbook of Social Psychology,* edited by John Delamater, 205–232. New York: Kluwer Academic/Plenum Publishers.

Pattillo-McCoy, Mary. 1998. "Church Culture as a Strategy of Action in the Black Community," *American Sociological Review* 63 (6): 767–784.

Pinn, Anthony B. 2014. *Writing God's Obituary: How A Good Methodist Became an Even Better Atheist.* Amherst, NY: Prometheus Books.

Ritchey, Jeff. 2009. "'One Nation Under God': Identity and Resistance in a Rural Atheist Organization." *Journal of Religion and Popular Culture* 21 (2): 1–13.

Silver, Christopher F., Thomas J. Coleman III, Ralph W. Hood Jr., and Jenny M. Holcombe. 2014. "The Six Types of Nonbelief: A Qualitative and Quantitative Study of Type and Narrative." *Mental Health, Religion & Culture* 17 (10): 990–1001.

Smith, Jesse M. 2011. "Becoming an Atheist in America: Constructing Identity and Meaning from the Rejection of Theism." *Sociology of Religion* 72 (2): 215–237.

Smith, Jesse M. 2013. "Creating a Godless Community: The Collective Identity Work of Contemporary American Atheists." *Journal for the Scientific Study of Religion* 52 (1): 80–99.

Steptoe, Tyina L. 2016. *Houston Bound: Culture and Color in a Jim Crow City.* Oakland, CA: University of California Press.

Stryker, Sheldon, and Peter J. Burke. 2000. "The Past, Present, and Future of an Identity Theory." *Social Psychology Quarterly* 63 (4): 284–297.

Tomlins, Steven. 2015. "A Common Godlessness: A Snapshot of a Canadian University Atheist Club, Why Its Members Join, and What That Community Means to Them." In *Atheist Identities – Spaces and Social Contexts,* edited by Lori G. Beaman and Steven Tomlins, 117–136. Cham, Switzerland: Springer.

Whetten, David A. 1998. "Preface: Why Organizational Identity and Why Conversations?" In *Identity in Organizations: Building Theory Through Conversations,* edited by David A. Whetten and Paul C. Godfrey, vii–xi. Thousand Oaks, CA: Sage Publications.

Zinnbauer, Brian J., Kenneth I. Pargament, Brenda Cole, Mark S. Rye, Eric M. Butter, Timothy G. Belavich, Kathleen M. Hipp, Allie B. Scott, and Jill L. Kadar. 1997. "Religion and Spirituality: Unfuzzying the Fuzzy." *Journal for the Scientific Study of Religion* 36 (4): 549–564.

Zuckerman, Phil. 2009. "Atheism, Secularity, and Well-Being: How the Findings of Social Science Counter Negative Stereotypes and Assuptions." *Sociology Compass* 3 (6): 949–971.

Zuckerman, Phil. 2012a. *Faith No More: Why People Reject Religion.* New York: Oxford University Press.

Zuckerman, Phil. 2012b. "Contrasting Irreligious Orientations: Atheism and Secularity in the USA and Scandinavia." *Approaching Religion* 2 (1): 8–20.

Zuckerman, Phil. 2014. *Living the Secular Life: New Answers to Old Questions*. New York: Penguin Group.

Aislinn Addington
Building Bridges in the Shadows of Steeples: Atheist Community and Identity Online

1 Introduction

I met Sam and Joanna Southerland in a small conference room in the downtown branch of our city's public library. The two had known each other most of their lives but had been married only two years at the time of our interview. Both ex-Jehovah's Witnesses, Sam (48) left the religion voluntarily in his early 20s and Joanna (51) had been forced out four years before we spoke. The couple reconnected via Facebook after Sam learned Joanna was no longer with the church. When asked, they liked to joke that they "met online." As we talked about their involvement with their local atheist organizations and their experience navigating their minority worldview among a generally theistic population, the role of the Internet and social media emerged as a prominent feature of their secular lives.

For Joanna, still new to her identity outside of the insular Jehovah's Witnesses world, the community she found with the Midwest Atheist Coalition both online and in person proved to be essential to her new social life. Sam was the first to demonstrate the importance of the Internet in both their lives, explaining that the difference in their paths out of religion sometimes made it difficult for them to talk through the feelings Joanna was having, particularly early on in their relationship. The atheist communities, especially the online resources, were there for her in a way Sam could not be. He explained: "She's done a very good job of establishing these Internet friendships in a way that she has someone to talk to. I mean, I'm not going to shut her off to talk about these things. But for me it's a different path that we're on." Joanna then added her own thoughts: "And the atheist community is a whole thing online itself. They are trying to rally the troops basically because eventually people are going to wise up and see that religion is the cause of so many problems in the world." "Catharsis, I think, is the bottom line of why we participate, support, and are drawn to the YouTube, Facebook, online [atheist] community," said Sam, finishing the discussion.

Sam and Joann illustrate what others (Hunsberger and Altemeyer 2006; LeDrew 2013) have called "active atheism," i.e., individuals who actively seek out a community of other atheists. While most atheists do not physically congregate

(Bullivant 2008, Pasquale 2010), organized secular communities are becoming more common. Many such individuals participate only online; others may interact in real physical communities. Just as most atheists do not "congregate" (Bullivant 2008; Pasquale 2010), there are plenty of individuals who only participate online. The subjects of this research were unique in that they partook in atheist community *both* in person and online, indicating that the online behavior served as a piece of their larger, active atheist identity. The participation of those individuals described here reflects what research has found atheist organizations doing themselves: using an online presence to extend or supplement their physical reach (See Schutz; Smith, both in this volume). This chapter explores the specific functions of that Internet activity and finds that two patterns stand out: the Internet as a mechanism for finding and strengthening community, and social media as a tool for secular activism and outreach.

2 Literature Review

Early on in this research, it became clear that the Internet, particularly social media, was a significant site for the investigation of identity and group boundaries among my atheist respondents.

Just as technology itself has grown and changed dramatically in the last few decades, so has social science scholarship investigating the roles of these technologies and their influence on social life. Early research, as well as some contemporary work, was particularly skeptical, warning that computer mediated communication could negatively effect communication and interaction in general (Mallaby 2006; Marche 2012; Olds and Schwartz 2009; Turkle 2012), and that connections made in "virtual space" were shallow and weak compared with face-to-face interaction (Fernback 1997; Turkle 2012). Zeynep Tufekci, responding to a recent wave of popular articles that claimed social media was "eroding human connection," reminded readers that, historically, great changes in social life always produced a strong reaction. She pointed all the way back to Cicero claiming children had stopped obeying their parents – perhaps the first ever "kids these days" rant – and Plato was concerned that writing, as an invention, could "rob people of wisdom" (Tufekci 2013, p. 13–16). Clearly, as these ancient examples demonstrate, concern over changes to social life are not unique to modern innovations in technology.

Social media and technological advances have drastically changed communication and social interaction in society (Chayko 2014). Most empirical work establishes how this new era of communication helps individuals and groups to facilitate community (Baym 2000; Baym, Zhang and Lin 2004; Kendall 2010;

Parks 2011). Members of groups who interact online tend to refer to themselves as communities (Chayko 2008; Parks 2011). As online relationships become more salient in the lives of those who take part, the definitions and parameters for concepts like "community" change. As Rainie and Wellman (2012, p.12) put it: "The new media is the new neighborhood." For those seeking community, the community found online can be genuine and grant a significant sense of place (Chayko 2014; Polson 2013). In today's culture, online and face-to-face social interaction are not two separate spheres. Online activities are very much a part of lived experience for most people.

Recent research on organized atheists acknowledges the Internet as an influential resource for secular individuals and secular groups in the U.S. over the past decade (Cimino and Smith 2011 and 2012; Smith 2013). Smith and Cimino's (2012, 18) research focused on new media as an important platform for atheist concerns, particularly in the roles of "information distribution and consciousness-raising." Increased visibility among like-minded friends, as well as the public at large, has led secular individuals and groups to reframe their goals and expectations in terms of public image and activism (Smith 2013). New media changed the individual and collective identities of those involved, which in turn changed the boundaries involved (Guenther, Mulligan, and Papp 2013; Shook, this volume). As Cimino and Smith (2011, 33) stated while discussing the effects of New Atheism and new media: "We can now see how secularists feeling a greater sense of acceptance and exclusion both emerge from the same dynamics." Members of a group rely just as much on their shared commonalities with other members as they do on their differences with non-members. The Internet and social media serve as the newest field on which those boundary negotiations play out.

This chapter contributes to this growing body of work by providing empirical data on active atheists' involvement in both virtual and on-the-ground communities.

3 Methods

As a researcher based at a large, Midwestern university, I started my search for participants with the campus club for atheist and agnostic students. From there I employed purposive sampling in order to ensure my sample included representatives from as many (adult) age groups as possible. All of the interview participants preferred the label "atheist" when asked to describe their secular identity. While literature has pointed to historical tensions between secular humanism and atheism as distinct movements that may continue to clash (Cimino and

Smith 2007), the individuals I interviewed and the groups they represented did not disclose conflict over these terms and labels. In total I completed 30 interviews for this research; most of the content for this chapter came from a subset of 13 participants who discussed their use of the Internet and social media as a significant part of their involvement in the atheist community more broadly.[1]

I sought out individuals who actively participated in some sort of secular group or club. I categorized active participation as meeting with other group members, in person at least once a month. Many of my participants also interacted with other secular individuals online, but to fit my criteria they had to engage with other members of their secular community face-to-face. The findings in this piece come from a larger research project focused on identity and boundaries among active atheists in the U.S. Midwest. It is important to note that this project did not set out to make observations concerning these issues in an online context. In fact, I did not explicitly ask about online activity as a component of atheist activity. This is a subject that came up organically through the research process. As the interviews progressed, it became clear that social media and the Internet in general were a significant component of secular life for the participants of this study and, therefore, findings I could not ignore.

Interviews generally took approximately 90 minutes to complete. I conducted interviews in a variety of locations including participants' homes, my office on campus, or a quiet public place such as a library or coffee shop. Each interviewee read and signed an informed consent document, which assured them that their names, the names of their clubs and organizations and identifying characteristics would be excluded from any publication related to the project. All audio files, transcripts, and other research documents were kept in a secure location for the duration of the project. Shortly after each interview, I typed notes describing the interview to be attached as a cover sheet to the transcripts later on. After carefully transcribing each interview I began a multistage coding process. I created the first layer of the coding structure based on categories from the interview guide; the next came from themes that materialized as the research developed. As patterns emerged through the process itself I coded the data several times from multiple perspectives. A study of this nature, with this size and scope, does not bear the weight of generalizability. Even so, the findings are a step toward better understanding the issues involved.

The interview data collected reflected a specific conversation, co-created by researcher and participant. The mere presence of a researcher affects all aspects

---

[1] While all of my interviewees had access to the Internet and social media, 13 of them spoke very specifically of their interactions online as an integral part of their collective secularity.

of the research process. In my position as researcher, it was essential to be present in the project without stealing focus from the participants (Frankenberg 2004). My interviewees and I shared the interview process, but it is *their* story I aimed to tell, not my own.

4 Findings

4.1 Cyber Interactions of Active Atheists

Individuals create boundaries, drawing lines of community in many different ways – through words, actions, participation, and/or financial support (Lamont and Fournier 1992). For members of atheist groups and organizations, the Internet has become another important site for the creation and maintenance of social boundaries (Smith and Cimino 2012; Smith 2013). Almost half of my interviewees (N=13) reported some level of online engagement with secular communities as part of their atheist activity in addition to their in person participation. Once an interviewee mentioned the online world I probed for a better understanding or clarified when it was unclear what type of participation they were describing (in person vs. virtual). With these participants the discussion always began with the participant including online activity in their description of involvement in secular communities. Two themes emerged with regard to how these participants used the Internet: (1) finding community and (2) outreach/activism.

4.2.1 Finding Community

The Internet is an efficient way to find a group of like-minded individuals. Atheists and believers alike might employ an Internet search to find local groups or a church to join. This practice proved especially true for the active atheists in this research. When asking how they originally got involved with secular groups and organizations, many interviewees started with an Internet search, a search that was, for many, within social networking platforms (e. g., Facebook, Meetup.com, etc.). They typically interacted in virtual space before meeting people face-to-face. Again, researchers have noted that atheist organizations use online channels as a strategic pathway to gain attendance and participation (See Schutz; Smith, both in this volume). Meetup.com, in particular, has been a popular method for active atheists to find groups and activities (Guenther et al. 2013). For some this was the first and last foray into the online atheist community;

for others it lead to more meaningful online relationships with their like-minded associates.

One practice that spoke to how boundaries operate in an online scenario entailed people finding the initial point of contact – perhaps a Facebook page – and from there becoming linked in further and further. Martin, who discussed working toward a more secular society for the sake of his son, was a 31-year-old chef in a Midwestern metropolitan area. He explained how his atheist Internet surfing led to significant involvement with one of his city's atheist organizations:

> I first got involved with it just kind of trying to keep up with secular news. I would go onto Richard Dawkins' website from time to time and read articles. There was an article about a new website and campaign called "We Are Atheism." So I read a little about it and turns out it came from this group on a local campus essentially. I was like: *Oh wow! This is so cool and it's local!* So I kind of reached out to them on their Facebook page, like: *Look this is very important to me. It's become a big part of who I am right now. What can I do to get involved?* So the founder of "We Are Atheism" is also the director of philanthropy on the board of directors for Midwest Atheist Coalition [MAC]. So, she said I should join MAC and I had never heard of it at that point. When they said, "Check us out," I did and it just progressed from there. They recognized that I had a passion for it and, to a degree, a talent for it, so it just went from there.

Martin served on the board of the MAC at the time of our interview. Online interaction with an atheist community often overlapped into in person interaction for participants with whom I spoke. This was the pattern by which online communities often transform into face-to-face communities in general (Chayko 2014; Rainie and Wellman 2012). Consistent with Smith's (2013) research on Colorado- and Texas-based atheists, this was generally true for the atheists I interviewed. The simple act of being part of a Facebook group, listserv, or passive member of a national organization could easily open the door to myriad opportunities for participation and community building.

The Internet was not only useful in finding a secular community, but also functioned in a supportive, affirming, and sometimes therapeutic role. While scholars may be correct in that origins of online communities are shallow when compared with more traditional communities (Fernback 1997; Turkle 2012), in the case of a marginalized minority such as atheists, these shallow roots can make a significant difference in people's lives. Tom (34) made the point that the online atheist communities lend emotional support for atheists regardless of whether or how face-to-face connections exist. A self-proclaimed loner, Tom used social networking sites to stay tethered to the global secular community:

I'm around millions of different people who believe what I believe thanks to Facebook, MySpace, Google Plus, whatever. I can finally connect on at least one level with somebody in Japan or Russia. We may not be a large physical group, but we are around the world. At any given point there's somebody around the world that's going through the exact same thing that I am.

The Internet facilitated interaction with a global network of individuals who shared ideas and experiences, fellowship that might be difficult to find in geographic proximity.

Tristan, a 21-year-old college student and community theater actor, started his participation in the Plains City Atheist (PCA) group by posting questions on the organization's Facebook page. Before his deconversion from a conservative branch of the Lutheran church, he and a few friends had been novice "ghost hunters." He wondered what the atheist community thought about ghosts, and whether or not he should give up his hobby. Online communication not only helped him clarify his beliefs, but also introduced him to his new secular social network. That initial interaction led Tristan to get involved with PCA and eventually organize an atheist group at his community college. This social support from afar can be vitally important for individuals in the process of leaving religion, particularly conservative religion. Guenther et al.'s (2013) work with New Atheist Meetup.com groups emphasized the permeability of boundaries when it came to the inclusion of the ex-religious. Tristan's experience fit this pattern of permeable boundaries; the PCA community accepted his religious past and the difficulty he had leaving all things supernatural behind. As Tristan became more involved with the PCA and the satellite group he started at his community college he found he no longer had time for "ghost hunting" anyway.

4.2.2 Virtual Lines Drawn

Boundaries function not only to clarify insider status, but also outsider status (Bellah 1987; Lamont and Molnar 2002). Online interactions may build and define communities, but for my atheist participants, the Internet was also a space where individuals and groups drew lines of exclusion. Several participants discussed the social repercussions of being openly atheist online. Tristan was "un-friended" by family members on Facebook as a result of the atheist affiliations and comments he posted on his profile, a common experience for openly self-identified atheists (Guenther et al. 2013; Smith 2013). While some of Tristan's family reacted negatively, choosing to end communication with him explicitly because he was an atheist, others reacted more positively. He recalled his surprise, "A few of my younger cousins, people around my age and in high school, have 'liked' things I posted that were anti-religion. With Facebook and things it's really easy to see who is on your side or not, you know?" Tristan's status as an "out and proud" atheist in the virtual sphere consequently clarified a number of his real world relationships, particularly with extended family and acquaintances who would not otherwise have been aware of Tristan's secular worldview.

Samantha (20), the president of her University's atheist club, discussed dealing with arguments aimed at her secularly oriented online posts on a regular basis. She said, "I mean people hear atheist and are going to dislike it. I write a blog and I get a lot of flack online where people aren't seeing me face-to-face, so that's interesting. I've seen so many terrible things online. It's ridiculous!" Social networking sites made these ideological divisions transparent in a way that is different from face-to-face interaction. When a person reveals ideological affiliations via social networking profiles their worldview instantly becomes visible to whoever has access to their profile or site. This may only be friends or family *or* this may make their opinions public on a global scale, depending on the platform and the privacy settings they choose for their profiles.

Social networking sites like Facebook also produce evidence of activities, demonstrating where a person stands within their social networks. The religious/secular divide became clear to Tom (34) when he read about what his friends were doing via Facebook without him. He remarked, "I see what they post on Facebook. I see what they do. I hear about get-togethers [that] are with certain people, certain cliques. And you obviously were not invited or thought to be mentioned. So, yeah, there's negative consequences for being different." Again, the autobiographical way opinions, activities, and interactions are logged and posted via online social networking sites demonstrated social standing and clarified relationships between individuals without them ever having to directly confront one another. Tom felt he and his family were being excluded from certain events because of his/their atheism. Calling back his earlier quote though, Tom also said he was around *millions* of people going through the same thing he was thanks to the Internet. The same boundary that demonstrated what he was missing out on locally served to bolster his sense of community and solidarity with the other atheists who might have had similar experiences in their local friendship networks (Guenther et al. 2013). Tom's online interactions made visible his simultaneous acceptance and exclusion (Cimino and Smith 2011).

Conflict between individuals within online atheist forums came up in interviews as well. After 12 years as a police officer, Eric, 38-years-old when interviewed, switched gears and applied to law school. At the time of our interview he was just finishing his first year and loving the thoughtful, spirited academic environment. As a busy father and student he had a hard time attending the real life gatherings of the atheist groups in his area and preferred to interact online. Unfortunately, Eric's argumentative approach was too aggressive for the group's facilitator. He mused,

> I post a lot of stuff and make a lot of arguments. Sometimes I'm fairly funny, and sometimes I'm a bomb thrower and say just the most ridiculous thing that still fits my beliefs in the face of someone's comments [just] so I can make a point (...) they kicked me out of the online discussion. I'm too provocative for the Provocateurs group.

He continued to post comments and engage in debates from his own Facebook account, but he was asked not to participate in the "Peacemakers and Provocateurs" group's official online discussion. This particular group, which met in person and had a Facebook page, was meant to promote dialogue between believers and nonbelievers in Eric's local area. Apparently Eric's "bomb throwing" upset believers and atheists alike.

4.2.3 Secular Cyberactivism and Outreach

The other dimension of Internet-based interaction in the active atheist community that emerged from interview data was the use of online networks as a forum for debate, activism, and outreach. As narratives demonstrate, interviewees engaged in these interactions in attempts to disseminate information, to persuade others, and/or to make a public statement. Some respondents reported spending quite a bit of their online time arguing with religious believers. As Cimino and Smith point out (2012), such deliberate assertion of identity and affiliation takes place in the virtual sphere where it is uniquely public while at the same time can grant users anonymity. The ability to be anonymous in virtual interactions may allow those who are otherwise timid in face-to-face interactions the opportunity to express themselves boldly, and with little to no repercussion. This was the case for Cameron, a 31-year-old who embodied the stereotype of the shy, thoughtful individual. During our interview, he kept answers short and to the point, only adding detail and examples when requested. When asked about situations where others challenged his secular worldview, he referenced virtual interactions and declared, "I seek it out." Cameron deliberately trolled the Internet hoping to provoke a fight, but did not engage much in the real world. Face-to-face confrontations have a potential for escalation that online encounters do not.

Cameron was not alone in his antagonistic mentality of "looking for an argument online." Alex, a 29-year-old former conservative Christian turned atheist also engaged in online trolling. Alex's story was striking in that he held the same type of attitude when he was a devout Christian who, for years, lurked in chat rooms looking for non-Christians with whom to argue. The catalyst for his deconversion and eventual adoption of an atheist worldview came from one such online exchange with an elderly history professor, Dr. Russell. As a junior in college Alex encountered Dr. Russell in an online Bible discussion group. The two decided to leave the group to exchange emails directly. According to Alex, Dr. Russell was at first reluctant to engage with him too assertively, but Alex insisted on a thorough debate over the existence of God and validity of the Bible. Alex felt driven to this argument by his faith, or as he put it, "I was trying to pursue God and I ended up in this situation where I couldn't believe in him anymore!" Once comfortable in his new secular identity, Alex began the same pattern of debate and argument online, but this time from his new ideological perspective. Like Cameron, Alex preferred not to get involved in random face-to-face debates:

> I don't walk into a bar and say "Hello stranger, let's have a debate."(...) In terms of the Internet though, I have a YouTube channel. So this is a pretty big part of my life actually. I have people challenge my faith on a daily basis in terms of comments there. I can go look at a video and who wrote a comment today and debate them if I want.

With 30,000 subscribers to his YouTube channel, Alex has the opportunity to engage in debates with theists regularly. He described to me picking through comment threads from videos on his channel, often joining arguments already in progress. From Alex's perspective, his goal of advocating for the right side and sharing the truth was no different; merely the origin of that truth had changed.

Both Jennifer (34) and Eleanor (69) shared stories of striving to be more vocal and forceful in their online interactions with believers. Jennifer was a pharmacist who served on the board of directors for the PCA. For several years, living in a different town, she hid her secularity. Now that atheism was publicly part of her identity, she was trying to participate actively in online discourse concerning religion. Referencing this shift Jennifer acknowledged, "But now I'm more of an asshole atheist, or I'm trying to be. So if someone puts something stupid on their Facebook page I'm trying to be like, 'That's not true; here's where the proof is.' And there are a lot of stupid people out there! On Facebook at least." After years of self-censoring and feeling isolated because of her worldview, Jennifer has learned to embrace opportunities to stand up for what she believes. Being more vocal about her worldview has likely resulted in more conflict, which is why she classified herself as an "asshole atheist." The U.S. publics' disgust for the irreligious (Edgell, Hartmann and Gerteis 2006; Hammer et al. 2012; Zuckerman 2009) put outspoken atheists like Jennifer on the defensive, a position she used to shy away from but now welcomes. Like the others in this study, she attempted to stand up for reason and science over the perceived divine, but it had taken a while for her to find the strength to do so.

Eleanor, a 69-year-old grandmother of seven, had been involved in Midwestern atheist organizations for just under two years at the time of our interview. Eleanor claimed not to be an activist, unlike some of her fellow group members. She did not attend demonstrations to hold pro-atheism signs, nor did she distribute atheist literature in the busy city district. However, her description of interactions with others on Facebook told a different story.

Last year Eleanor posted a different creation myth on her Facebook page every week, making the point that all cultures maintain some type of origin story. She laughed and recalled, "I put things out there and get some reactions, and some of them I wonder, like, where's your head?" Eleanor posted these items knowing she would get a reaction from her religious family. When they would counter with a Biblical statement she was quick to provide links to scientific journals or other evidence-based claims that contradicted their religious arguments. Eleanor's behavior may not be considered activism in the classic sense, however, her consistent attempts to "plant seeds" of reason in the minds of those with whom she cyber-communicated is a form of cyberactivism. In their study of secularism on the Internet, Smith and Cimino (2012, 22) described similar interactions as "secularist cultural activism," which they then classified as "soft activism." Social movement scholar Bobel (2007, 149) made a distinction in her work between "being activist" and "doing activism," where a participant in social movements may *do* activism without taking the step of self-identifying as an activist. This distinction, said Bobel (2007, 157), represents a more "complicated account of identity" in the study and analysis of social movements. Eleanor's situation – stepping back from demonstrations and protests but leaning into arguments and debates online fits into the "doing activism" side of Bobel's categorization.

Many of the frequent social networking users I spoke with discussed finding a balance in how they presented themselves and their "soft activism" online. Dominic (22), in fact, had to tone down his online rhetoric in order to maintain friendships with individuals outside the atheist community. A recent college graduate in the biological sciences, he explained, "My sophomore year I got into a lot of Facebook debates where I will bring up controversial topics on my wall or somebody else's wall talking about things, and that led to a lot of issues." He, and those with whom he was arguing, had a hard time keeping the conversation amicable. Dominic discovered that, "Whenever you're talking about somebody's religion there's always a chance that they're going to be offended." Not willing to give up his virtual campaign for atheism, Dominic discovered a different tack. Rather than jeopardize friendships through Facebook flame wars, he found that conversations with strangers satisfied his desire to argue for atheism:

> I've gone onto anonymous threads and talked to people through email where it's like, for example, one person emailed our [atheist club] website once saying, "Do you know that there is no God? Because if you say you do you claim to know everything and if you claim to not know then you're really not an atheist are you." So I started emailing with them and we went back and forth.

Through trial and error Dominic found an outlet closer to that of Alex or Cameron. All three wanted to share what they knew, and what they had come to believe with other people. Internet communication has turned out to be an effective way to accomplish this. With such a wide variety of platforms available one could easily find a place to have his or her voice heard.

Both Dominic and Eric – the law student mentioned earlier who was asked to leave the online discussion forum for believers and nonbelievers who wanted dialogue with one another – found themselves in situations where their enthusiasm for the topic lead to admonishment from their online communities. Each, however, found a way to channel his zeal and continued to participate in dialogue with believers. They kept at it because it was not just about the fun of debating online; they believed they had a greater purpose. Dominic and Eric put themselves out there in an effort to raise awareness and make it easier for others to find a voice. When I asked why he engaged in online debates and Facebook flame wars Eric posited:

> I think there are a lot of atheists who are in the pew [participating in church], or who are 'in the closet,' or otherwise silenced because they don't feel like they can [speak up] and I feel like the more out there I am, and the more in your face I am, the more of them may feel more comfortable.

This talk of "closeted" atheism was a common way to describe atheists who do not publicly share their lack of belief. Scholarship on atheist identity formation has compared the process of going public with an atheist identity to the process of "coming out of the closet," with non-heterosexual sexualities and trans gender identities (Smith 2011, 2013; Siner 2011). Parallels exist between the atheist community and the LGBT community in terms of issues like stigma, societal acceptance, and identity processes. The cooptation of "coming out" language, though, is a fairly new appropriation used informally by interviewees here, and more formally by atheist organizations like Richard Dawkins' Out Campaign, as well as academically (Linneman and Clendenen 2010; Smith 2011, 2013; Siner 2011; Zimmerman, Smith, Simonson, and Myers 2015).

Alex even put his whole story on YouTube in order to share it with others. Many of my interviewees to some extent shared the goal of raising awareness, and online interaction has proven to be a good system through which to carry out that mission. According to Smith and Cimino (2012, 19), the Internet has been "both means for dissemination and mobilization" for the secular movement. The active atheists I spoke with used Internet interaction as an outreach tool. Atheism is still highly stigmatized in many segments of mainstream society (Edgell et al. 2006; Hammer et al. 2012; Zuckerman 2009). If it is not directly discouraged, non-theism is often absent from conversations about spirituality or worldviews. My participants discovered the Internet as a space where their ideas could be heard and might even be spread to others.

5 Conclusions

The active atheists I interviewed for this research engaged with social media and other Internet based platforms to find other non-believers, to discuss their minority opinion with kindred others, to argue and assert their opinions with those who did not agree, and to reach out in the name of spreading secularity. As Chayko (2014) maintained, online communities *are* real communities for those who need them. My findings indicate that some active atheists in the U.S. Midwest needed online outlets as part of their atheist identity and an augmentation to their physical secular community.

Boundary work enacted online proved particularly effective for active atheists in forming and articulating an atheist identity. The virtual world was a space where participants could explore what it meant to be an atheist individual as well as how they might fit into the atheist community. From finding a community, to building solidarity, to reaching out to those not yet in the fold, online interactions supplemented connections these individuals made face-to-face and sometimes represented situations they could not, or chose not to engage with in a physical context.

The Internet, social media, and computer mediated communication of myriad kinds permeate social life and will continue to do so. Given the extent of online interaction among atheists and the communities they have built, future research should continue to examine online atheist activities. Some elements of the atheist and secular movements have materialized and evolved predominately online; for example 2012's "Atheism Plus" component of the secular movement emerged online (Carrier 2013; McCreight 2012). Further investigation of boundary work would provide additional breadth and depth to the topics discussed here. Regardless of the theoretical backdrop, as is always the case with research concerning secular individuals and groups, there is more to know.

Bibliography

Baym, Nancy. 2000. *Tune in, Log on.* Thousand Oaks, CA: Sage Publications.
Baym, Nancy, Yan Bing Zhang and Mei-Chen Lin. 2004. "Social Interactions Across Media: Interpersonal Communication on the Internet, Telephone and Face-to-Face." *New Media & Society* 6(3): 299–318.
Bobel, Chris. 2007. "'I'm not an activist, though I've done a lot of it': Doing Activism, Being Activist and the 'Perfect Standard' in a Contemporary Movement." *Social Movement Studies* 6(2): 147–159.
Bullivant, Stephen. 2008. "Research Note: Sociology and the Study of Atheism." *Journal of Contemporary Religion* 23(3): 363–368.
Carrier, Richard. 2013. "Atheism… Plus What?" *Essays in the Philosophy of Humanism* 21 (1): 105–113.
Chayko, Mary. 2008. *Portable Communities.* Albany, NY: State University of New York Press.
Chayko, Mary. 2014. "Techno-social life: The Internet, digital technology, and social connectedness." *Sociology Compass* 8(7): 976–991.
Cimino, Richard and Christopher Smith. 2011. "The New Atheism and the Formation of the Imagined Secular Community." *Journal of Media and Religion* 10(1): 24–38.
Cimino, Richard and Christopher Smith. 2012. "Atheisms unbound: The role of the new media in the formation of a secularist identity." *Secularism and Nonreligion* 1(1): 17–31.
Cimino, Richard and Christopher Smith. 2014. *Atheist Awakening: Secular Activism and Community in America.* New York, NY: Oxford University Press.
Edgell, Penny, Douglas Hartmann, and Joseph Gerteis. 2006. "Atheists as "Other": Moral Boundaries and Cultural Membership in American Society." *American Sociological Review* 71 (2): 211–234.
Fernback, Jan. 1997. "The Individual within the Collective." In *Virtual Culture: Identity and Communication in Cybersociety,* edited by Steven Jones, pages 36–54. Thousand Oaks: Sage Publications.
Frankenberg, Ruth. 2004. *Living Spirit, Living Practices.* Duke University Press.
Guenther, Katja M., Kerry Mulligan and Cameron Papp. 2013. "From the outside in: Crossing boundaries to build collective identity in the new atheist movement." *Social Problems* 60 (4): 457–475.
Hammer, Joseph H., Ryan T. Cragun, Karen Hwang, and Jesse Smith. 2012. "Forms, Frequency, and Correlates of Perceived Anti-Atheist Discrimination." *Secularism and Nonreligion* 1:43–67.
Hunsberger, Bruce E. and Bob Altemeyer. 2006. *Atheists: A groundbreaking study of America's nonbelievers.* Amherst, NY: Prometheus Books.

Jacoby, Susan. 2004. *Freethinkers: A history of American Secularism*. New York, NY: Metropolitan Books.
LeDrew, Stephen. 2013. "Discovering atheism: Heterogeneity in trajectories to atheist identity and activism." *Sociology of Religion:* srt014.
Linneman, Thomas J. and Margaret A. Clendenen. 2010. "Sexuality and the Secular." From *Atheism and Secularity*, edited Phil Zuckerman, pages 89–112 Santa Barbara, CA: Praeger Perspectives.
Mallaby, Sebastian. 2006. "Why So Lonesome?" *Washington Post.* June www.washingtonpost.com/wpdyn/content/article/2006/06/25/AR2006062500566.html.
Marche, Stephen. 2012. "Is Facebook Making Us Lonely?" Atlantic, May. www.theatlantic.com/magazine/archive/2012/05/is-facebook-making-us-lonely/308930.
McCreight, Jen. 2012. "How I Unwittingly Infiltrated the Boy's Club and Why It's Time for a New Wave of Atheism." Freethoughtblogs.com, Blag Hag. Retrieved August 20, 2014
Olds, Jacqueline and Richard Schwartz. 2009. *The Lonely American*. Boston, MA: Beacon Press.
Pasquale, Frank L. 2 010. "A Portrait of Secular Group Affiliates." From *Atheism and Secularity edited by* Phil Zuckerman, pages 43–88 Santa Barbara, CA: Praeger Perspectives.
Parks, Malcolm. 2011. "Social Network Sites as Virtual Communities." In *A Networked Self: Identity, Community, and Culture on Social Network Sites*, edited by Zizi Paparachissi, pages 105–123. New York, NY: Routledge.
Polson, Erika. 2013. "A gateway to the global city: Mobile place-making practices by expats." *New Media and Society* 17(4): 629–645.
Rainie, Lee and Barry Wellman. 2012. *Networked: The New Operating System*. Cambridge, MA: MIT Press.
Siner, Sam. 2011. "A theory of atheist student identity development." *Journal of the Indiana University Student Personnel Association:* 14–21.
Smith, Jesse M. 2013. "Creating a Godless Community: The Collective Identity Work of Contemporary American Atheists." *Journal for the Scientific Study of Religion* 52 (1):80–99.
Smith, Jesse M. 2011. "Becoming an Atheist in America: Constructing Identity and Meaning from the Rejection of Theism." *Sociology of Religion* 72 (2): 215–237.
Stout, Daniel A. and Judith M. Buddenbaum. 1996. "Religious Beliefs and Media Adaptations." In *Religion and Mass Media: Audiences and Adaptations,* edited by Daniel A. Stout and Judith M. Buddenbaum, pages 35–38. Thousand Oaks, CA: Sage.
Tufekci, Zeynep. 2013. "The Social Internet: Frustrating, Enriching, but Not Lonely." *Public Culture* 26(1): 13–23
Turkle, Sherry. 2012. *Alone Together: Why We Expect More from Technology and Less from Each Other.* New York, NY: Basic Books.
Zimmerman, Kevin, Jesse M. Smith, Kevin Simonson, and W. Benjamin Myers. 2015. "Familial Relationship Outcomes of Coming Out as an Atheist." *Secularism and Nonreligion* 4 (1):1–13.
Zuckerman, Phil. 2009. "Atheism, Secularity, and Well-Being: How the Findings of Social Science Counter Negative Stereotypes and Assumptions." *Sociology Compass* 3(6): 949–971.

Jesse M. Smith
Communal Secularity: Congregational Work at the Sunday Assembly

1 Introduction

The Sunday Assembly is young. It is still developing as an international organization, and is in the early stages of making its mark in the broader secular community. Exactly what this mark will be remains to be seen. Despite its youth and status as essentially a 21 century secular congregational experiment, it appears to be maturing quickly and is unquestionably meeting a demand within a certain sector of the secular population in the west and other parts of the globe. Especially because of its newness, it is important to begin a discussion of the Sunday Assembly, and the idea of communal secularity more abstractly, by outlining the basics of its formation and operation in order to understand both its uniqueness within, and relevance to, organized secularism generally.

After examining the key components of its history and early development, this chapter explores the interactional details of what I call "communal secularity," (Smith 2017) with the Sunday Assembly serving as a salient case study of the concept. This involves a sociological discussion of congregational and identity dynamics, and the application of social psychological insights regarding ritual, emotion, morality, and other symbolic dimensions of this type of collective expression of the secular. I conceptualize communal secularity as the particular relationship of these elements vis-à-vis the secular, and by way of defining the process by which some secular people in contemporary culture address and express their secular identities, values, and worldviews.

2 Sunday Assembly's History and Organization

The Sunday Assembly began in the United Kingdom in 2013, a product of earlier conversations between Sanderson Jones and Pippa Evans, two young British comedians. One day while driving to a gig together, they were reportedly half-joking about the idea of a church for atheists, when they stumbled upon the conceptual seeds that would grow to become the Sunday Assembly (SA or Assembly, hereafter). On the simplest level, we can define the SA in accordance with its publicly stated intent as proffered by it co-creators. It is, as SA's website described it, a regularly scheduled gathering – an assembly – of secular-minded people for the purpose of "living better, helping often, and wondering more."[1]

The creation of an inclusive, synod-style network of secular congregations in communities around the globe became the major objective. The very first Assembly was held on January 6th 2013. About 200 congregants were in attendance at the Nave, a deconsecrated church in London. The original Assembly has since found its permanent venue at the historic Conway Hall, the home of one of the oldest ethical culture societies. The SA has seen significant growth and garnered considerable public and media attention (and some controversy) since then. As of this writing there are officially 70 established, active congregations in 8 countries across Europe, North America, and Oceania. Over half of all Assemblies are in North America. The most active Assemblies have between 50 and 250 congregants, while many smaller start-up or "warm-up" congregations (by some reports, in the hundreds) have far fewer participants and meet irregularly.

The SA is a non-profit, volunteer-based organization and has acquired legal status as a registered charity with a trading subsidiary, Sunday Assembly Limited. Each congregational chapter, regardless of its geographic location, adheres to a general set of guidelines, policies, and quality control measures as outlined by its creators, official charter, and other administrative organizers, collectively referred to as the General Assembly. Sanderson Jones holds the position of CEO. He and the SA are supported by a COO, "community creators," and a five-member board of trustees. Like the polities of some (especially liberal) religious groups, it gives a fair amount of autonomy to individual congregations regarding the specifics of their Sunday services. There is no deliberate hierarchy or central authority beyond the basic administrative body (the General Assembly), which supports the public relations, media, and marketing aspects of running an organization. There is no codified or official Assembly doctrine and no paid or trained clergy who exercise doctrinal authority over congregations. Instead, each congregation is led by a team of Assembly organizers who adhere to the Assemblies policies and general objectives. Each start-up congregation is self-produced by volunteers in the community based on local interest and demand.

Local secular activists, humanists, and nontheists interested in starting a congregation are directed to the SA's website where they are asked to review the charter, relevant policies, accept their terms and conditions, and to connect with already officially recognized congregations. This initiates the process of developing a new Assembly. Next, aspiring congregation organizers undergo a for-

---

1 Sunday Assembly's web address: www.sundayassembly.com.

mal peer-review process from SA's governing body to show evidence that a stable, regularly meeting congregation is feasible. When at least 10 committed organizers can show they are meeting regularly and gathering interest in the community (most often through various social media outlets like Facebook and Meetup) they can become a "warm-up" group, be added to the website as such, and benefit from wider promotion.

Once a regular venue has been established, musicians are brought on, and speakers have been lined up, the warm-up group can formally apply for official status, and if approved, have their first "launch" as a full-fledged Sunday Assembly. If the burgeoning congregation does well, it must then apply for accreditation from the General Assembly within two years of its launch. This accreditation process involves legal documentation to accommodate SA's U.K.-based charitable organization status, on-site visits, and video recording of live Assemblies to ensure they are meeting the objectives and are within the guidelines.[2]

Not surprisingly, most Assemblies are hosted in major cities such as London, Los Angeles, and Sydney, but there are also congregations in smaller cities and even rural areas around the globe. Specifically, there are up to 200 Assemblies (including warm-up groups) on 5 different continents. No official public records are yet available regarding membership at the SA, but it seems likely that if congregations continue to grow, greater effort will be made toward official record-keeping. Unlike most religious congregations, there is no formal documented process (e.g. baptism or member confirmation) for becoming a member of the SA, and currently organizational affiliation is entirely based on adult, voluntary self-identification.[3] Irrespective of SA's quick growth, their total numbers are a tiny fraction of those maintained by many established religious congregations. Even if each current, active Assembly had 100 regular congregants, that would bring the total global participation to around 7,000 people.

---

[2] See www.sundayassembly.com for more details regarding the technical aspects of its organization.

[3] This contrasts with many religious organizations, where much of the membership is comprised, not by adult converts, but by those raised within the religion as children who become official members through religious ordinances. With some organizations (e.g. Mormon Church), those who leave as adults must formally petition to have their names removed from member records. Otherwise they continue to be counted as members by the Church, despite inactivity or even apostasy.

3 Studying Godless Congregations

I began studying the Sunday Assembly in the summer of 2013 – just months after its formation – after receiving a small grant to travel and begin fieldwork. I participated in the San Diego, Chicago, and London Assemblies. San Diego has one of the larger Assemblies in the United States, and at the time had around 200 participants. The Chicago chapter had around 80 congregants when I attended (they had a larger turnout previously, but lost some participants because of an issue securing a regular venue). Conservatively, these numbers likely represent many of the 70 Assemblies active today.

Over 18 months I conducted semi-structured in-depth interviews with 13 congregants from the San Diego Assembly, and 8 from the Chicago Assembly. I attended, but did not interview congregants from the London Assembly due to travel and time constraints. My participation in live Assemblies in each city totaled about 10 hours, but I also analyzed the content of approximately 18 hours of live video recorded Assemblies made available on the San Diego chapter's website. Watching recorded Assemblies added to my fieldwork by expanding my familiarity with details of Assembly services. This allowed me to further develop the themes and patterns of interaction that I observed in the field. This was important for my research since U.S. Assemblies only occur once a month, which obviously limits the frequency with which I could attend.

I recruited interviewees both in person during actual Assemblies and with organizer-preapproved flyers that announced my study. The latter led to further recruits in a snowball fashion after Assembly events. Each interviewee was also asked to complete a separate survey that gathered demographic information and asked logistical questions about their involvement with the SA. Basic demographics for the 21 Assemblers are as follows: 9 identified as male, 10 as female, 1 as transgender, and 1 as gender queer. Interviewees ranged in age from 19 to 80. Eighteen respondents identified as white, 2 as Hispanic, and 1 as African American. The majority identified as middle class. All had at least some college education. Most of the interviews were conducted by phone with those I met in person or those who volunteered their time and left contact information after seeing a study flyer. The reason for phone interviews was practical; there was usually not time during my travels and after Assembly services for in-person interviews.

4 Sunday Assembly as Communal Secularity

When the SA was first taking off, the co-creators playfully suggested to an interested public and media that it was the, "best bits of church, but with no religion" (Del Barco 2014). This statement was offered a bit facetiously, but, of course, there is also truth to it. Indeed, much of the controversy surrounding the SA when it first arose had to do with whether it is, or is not "religion for atheists," and what the implications of this might be.[4] Rather than taking either media characterizations, or the SA's self-description at face value, I define the SA as, "communal secularity" to offer in more neutral terms, how it is both like, and unlike religion in relevant ways.

4.1 Promoting Secular Worldviews

Examining the Sunday Assembly's charter and the words of Assembly organizers and congregants themselves is a good starting point for understanding what attributes it shares with religious congregations, as well as its meaning, organization, and positioning within and relationship to the broader secular community. The charter offers ten short propositions that outline the manifest reasons for its existence. The first three are the most essential to the SA, and the most relevant here. "Sunday Assembly: (1) Is 100% celebration of life. We are born from nothing and go to nothing. Let's enjoy it together. (2) Has no doctrine. We have no set texts so we can make use of wisdom from all sources. [and] (3) Has no deity. We don't do supernatural but we also won't tell you you're wrong if you do."[5]

The first proposition is significant enough that the final statement of the charter simply rephrases it: "And recall point 1: The Sunday Assembly is a celebration of the one life we know we have." This is a fundamental existential claim that "doctrinally" sets the Assembly apart from religious congregations. Indeed, nearly all religious groups, whether they have a this- or other-worldly orientation, are premised on beliefs about a supernatural realm, an afterlife, however conceived, and the continued existence of the self (or soul) within it.

The implications of this perspective provide the context in which the meaning structures and congregational activities of the SA make sense and reflexively unfold. The existential premise that conscious experience ends with the death of

---

[4] One influential religious leader, for instance, called the very idea of the Sunday Assembly, "highly inappropriate," suggesting it is trivializing what makes religion a "sacred" institution.
[5] Access the full charter by clicking on the "About" link at www.sundayassembly.com.

the body informs and shapes the behaviors of the secular congregation just as beliefs in supernatural agents and eternal life inform the same with regard to religious congregations. How? Primarily through the linkage between cognitive beliefs/suppositions, a collective ethos, and the ways in which the micro interactions within congregations support, validate, and reinforce each. When Geertz (1973) wrote about the (sub)cultural construction of worldviews and the "moods and motivations" that instantiate them, he was showing how our collective behaviors, far from arbitrary, reflect and inform the things individuals value and believe. What we *do* is both cause and effect of how we *think*. An ethos is an ethos precisely because it locates the person within broader "webs of significance" that extend to collectives. Religious groups are salient illustrations of this because they explicitly respond to big questions about the cosmos and our place and purpose within it.

One might suppose this is inapplicable to organizations that overtly espouse secular claims, propose they are doctrine-free, and – as with the first proposition of SA's charter – assert a temporal-materialist cosmological view. But the purpose, organization, and activity of the SA suggest Geertz's "webs of significance" are no less applicable to secular groups that engage in meaningful, collective rituals and practices. The collective ethos the SA expresses through congregants' interactions is an important component of the broader, interrelated set of beliefs that comprise what Baker and Smith (2015, 208) call "cosmic belief systems." Based on their study of survey data and secular organizations, they outline the "cultural contours of nonreligious belief systems," arguing that organized secularism posits and advocates particular beliefs about the world in ways similar (and dissimilar) to organized religion. As such, both religion and the secular should be studied with the same conceptual tools – all focused on their broader cosmic belief systems (worldviews):

> The organization and functioning of religious, non-institutionalized supernatural, and secular beliefs can be studied in similar ways. For while some varieties of secularity are premised on *dis*believing in supernatural precepts, they nonetheless posit particular beliefs about reality and the social world, and also appeal to particular traditions and epistemic authority (Baker and Smith 2015, 208).

In other words, secular organizations, and especially secular congregations like the SA, are not so much about disbelief as they are about expressing positive beliefs about the world, even if these beliefs are framed in a way that downplays the importance of belief, as evidenced by their rhetoric of radical inclusivity and ostensible lack of interest in promoting doctrinal beliefs. Thus, whether secular or religious, what we might call *congregational culture*, by its very nature helps shape, organize, justify, and reward congregants' beliefs, and ultimately, cosmic worldviews. This is also in line with Lee's (2015) concept, based on her ethnographic study of nonreligious individuals in Briton, of "existential cultures." Such cultures, Lee suggests, involve those sets of "ideas about the origins of life and human consciousness and about how both are transformed or expire after death – what have been called 'ultimate questions' in the literature" (2015: 159–160).

4.2 Ritualizing the Secular through Congregational Practice

Religious congregations have long been the subject of academic research (Ammerman 1994), but few studies have examined the idea of the secular congregation – most obviously because they are comparatively rare. There are historical examples of secular-oriented congregations such as the Ethical Cultural Society, communal or pagan groups centered on religious naturalism (as opposed to supernaturalism), and religious congregations welcoming of nonbelievers in addition to theists, most notably seen in Unitarian Universalism. However, the Sunday Assembly represents the clearest contemporary example of an avowedly secular congregation, as it expresses a nontheistic/nonsupernaturalist identity and secular message through the deliberate adoption of a congregational model.[6] As such, we can define and study the SA as a salient form of *nontheistic expression*, which is attempting to formalize itself through the development of a new institution (Smith, forthcoming); that is, functionally they bring secular values and beliefs to life through ritualistic practice, in similar ways that religious congregations express theistic beliefs.

On the most basic level a congregation is simply a gathering of individuals for some identifiable purpose. But sociologically, congregations are complex social entities that circumscribe interrelated processes of identity, belief, and practice. Cultural (and subcultural) values come in to high definition in congregational contexts, and as significant mediums of symbolic identity expressiveness (Hetherington 1998) and ritual interaction, congregations develop the private lives and beliefs of individuals in public spaces (Tavory 2013). As Ammerman (1994) observes, religious congregations serve as important symbolic links to other cultural dynamics that can strengthen community relations, develop social networks, and encourage prosociality. As volunteer associations, they bring to-

---

[6] This form of cultural appropriation is not uncommon among religious groups themselves. "Seeker-sensitive" churches, for instance, often appropriate various aspects of secular culture.

gether community members, create solidarities, and can serve as a springboard for social action well beyond the parameters of the congregation itself.

Beyond the purely practical outcomes of congregations, they also function as powerful symbolic settings that touch upon bigger issues. They give meaning, direction, and purpose to the relationship between person, society, and cosmos. Congregations are important resources for moral identity and spiritual fulfillment (Gallagher and Newton 2009) and they bridge personal stories with collective moral narratives, and serve to dramatize the experiences of congregants' everyday lives – their aspirations, struggles, family and social values, and even political concerns. Of course, beyond these functional outcomes (but related to them), religious congregations embody particular belief systems and make religious claims about the nature of reality.

In what sense does communal secularity do the same? At the interactional level, Assembly services closely parallel the basic activities of religious congregations. A typical Sunday service includes intervals of singing and dancing to secular songs, (in some cases to a live band), "moments of reflection" and similar silent observances, talks on secular themes, testimonials from congregants, artistic performances like poetry readings and spoken word, ice breaker activities, and even the passing of a collections plate to financially support the congregation. Designed to be family friendly, Assemblies include a "kids corner" in where small children can occupy themselves with other activities while the adults focus their attention on the services.

At the San Diego, Chicago, and London Assemblies I attended, there was a palpable enthusiasm among the congregation, in part fueled by those leading the services. Each host was effective at engaging congregants, but none more than the co-creator of SA himself, Sanderson Jones at the London Assembly. He had many of the qualities of a charismatic religious leader, including the ability to elicit a range of emotions from the audience from laughter to reverence. This is why researchers Cimino and Smith (2014, 118), in their study of American secular activism in *Atheist Awakening*, compared Sanderson to a "Pentecostal preacher." Weber's (1947) description of charismatic authority centered on how the personal qualities of religious leaders can be routinized in such a way as to become an institutionalized feature of the religious organization over time. Of course, unlike Joseph Smith and other founders of new religious movements, Sanderson neither fancies himself a prophet, or makes supernaturalist claims or substantive demands of his "followers." However, the essence of his leadership style and its connection to his character bears the signature of the charismatic authority Weber identified as being central to the success of new religious movements, should such movements sufficiently integrate this authority on an institutional level.

These congregational activities effectively cultivate a setting in which a this-worldly, temporal-focused life is celebrated in communal, secular terms. It is in this sense that the idea of "secular ritual practice" gains the most purchase. Core elements of congregational ritual include: (1) emotion work (Cowen 2008), (2) symbolic and moral boundary construction (Wilkins 2008), and (3) belief systems, or ideologies (Tavory 2013). The first is apparent on multiple levels. Emotions suffuse rituals with significance by framing them in terms of some greater purpose (Corrigan 2008). When congregants employ the above elements of Assembly services, whether activating their vocal chords and bodies for singing and dancing, or listening reverentially to poetry on some humanist-naturalist motif, they are engaged in more than entertainment. These practices sacralize the secular, that is, they endow the secular with special meaning beyond what "the secular" signals in everyday ordinary living (what Durkheim called the *profane*). Put differently, Assembly services employ rituals that construct and maintain a "secular solemnity" in some sense analogous to religious congregational worship.[7] What makes this the case is not so much about songs, talks, or artistic performances themselves (after all, these happen in many contexts having nothing to do with either religious worship or secular solemnity), but their collective, emotional nature and the ways in which a shared sense of meaning and aesthetic are directed at the secular itself and given symbolic import.

Previous research on both religious congregations and atheist organizations (Guenther 2013; Smith 2013) show how emotions shape symbolic and moral boundaries. For instance, Wilkins's (2008) study of a Christian congregation found that members would use a kind of emotional exuberance – essentially a kind of "happy talk" – in their interactions within and outside the congregation as a way of demonstrating to others, and themselves, that they are happier than non-Christians. I am not suggesting Assemblers are likely to do the same, or that secular people believe they are happier than the religious, but I have observed at Assemblies and in my interviews an inclination toward, and appreciation of, the role of emotions in secular beliefs and values. More than other secular organizations, the SA attracts and cultivates an inclination for what Durkheim identified as *collective effervescence*, wherein members of a group direct emotional energy onto some object or idea, endowing it with qualities of the sacred.

As Woodhead and Riis (2010) argue, scholars (and laypersons) tend to overemphasize the cognitive, belief-based dimension of religion, which misses the

---

[7] The likeness of secular to religious congregations should not be overstated however. Belief in – and rituals directed at – the supernatural are clearly different in both their content and intention from those involving secular ideas and values.

critical role of emotion. This bias is perhaps especially salient among researchers and secular people themselves with regard to atheistic groups, where the rational, proposition-based arguments about the nature of reality are given primacy over emotion. The SA stands as an interesting counterexample of secular groups that place a premium on emotion and the experiential qualities of secularity. In Durkheimian terms, the cultivation and projection of emotion figuratively reverberates back on to the group, adding to the sense of solidarity and commitment among its members. Absent an object of worship, Assemblers nevertheless engage in emotional work that produces a similar outcome. In this way, the absence of theistic belief does not impede the more essential need for communality and belonging among this segment of the secular population (Oakes 2015).

Assemblers themselves talk about how they value ritual practice and other social aspects of congregational life usually associated with religion. This includes the "spiritual" idea of seeking the transcendent. Consider the comments of Becky, a local Assembly organizer and chapter leader. She suggested that rituals are useful for "bringing people together" and can help shape meaningful experiences that "go beyond the mundane." In talking about SA's motto, "Living Better, Helping often, and Wondering More" she went on to state:

> These [awe and wonder] are very, very important, and I would like to think I wouldn't be closed off to explorations of "spiritual things" although the way I view the nature of reality is that all of these spiritual experiences are simply human experiences. They are rare, they might be unique, they might feel transcendent or special given the nature of our everyday, mundane lives, but they are simply *human* experiences...and that's what makes them great.

It is not just those leading congregations who value ritual and seek such experiences. Stan, a rank-and-file Assembler commented:

> One thing that I do value about religion is the rituality of it. I have always been able to connect with the mystical experience portion of religion...The transcendent, or the peace and calm that comes from repeated ritualistic practice. I find that quite essential, and it ties into the meditative techniques I've come to develop...but I don't have to connect that to religious experience or to a particular set of dogmas or belief structure...If you're in a group and you're singing songs together as a congregation and everyone around you has the emotion; you look at those people and your feelings resonate and you share that experience...I feel empowered and I can find joy in that experience and to feel that sense of serenity and togetherness with fellow humans and connect to them in an emotional way is very much, for me, a transcendent experience. I find great peace in that shared emotion.

Both Becky and Stan value the emotional and ritualistic aspects of communal secularity. One may suppose they would therefore lean toward or be open to beliefs regarding the supernatural, but that is not the case. As Manning (2015) shows in her study of secular parents, there are many different internal reasons and external pressures for seeking the communal, and part of the ambiguity of seeking something beyond the mundane may have to do with how secular people define and employ terms such spirituality and the transcendent. Nevertheless, regarding the supernatural per se, when I asked specifically about this Assembler's beliefs, Stan went on to suggest:

> My worldview is based on that which can be objectively proven...a worldview based on observable reality, that is to say objective...As I developed an understanding of the world I live in I realized the only way to be certain about the reality that you and I are both experiencing is to focus on that which is objective, both sides, to measure and explain something that is not subjective. The [best] methodology of coming to a justified belief about reality is...science – a method to test and provide falsification for claims made about the world that we share. Being scientifically literate and sound are very important for both developing my worldview and for maintaining a worldview that I can feel comfortable having.

At root, Stan is a materialist and atheist. His language about "objective reality," the necessity of scientific methodology, the importance of "falsification" etc., is very much in line with studies examining the views of many atheists (Hunsberger and Altemeyer 2006; Smith 2013). Yet, his pursuit of the "peace" of the transcendent and the utility of the collective emotion and congregational rituals that provide an avenue to it, undermines the usual assumptions about nonbelievers. Of course, it is unlikely that *all* Assemblers are as open and comfortable as Becky and Stan with these "spiritual"[8] pursuits, but it does seem that Assemblers are generally those who seek what are usually thought of as religious goods, in secular, nontheistic, and most often scientific terms.

More important here, however, is the connection between congregational work and belief systems themselves. Peter Berger, in *The Sacred Canopy* (1990), famously wrote about the ways in which religious behaviors and rituals justify and reinforce specific beliefs. Through *plausibility structures* belief-systems and entire worldviews are constructed and maintained through (sub)cultural practices and institutions in ways that are intellectually *and* emotionally compelling to individuals. Becky's and Stan's ideas represent the connection of embodied ritual practice to broader belief systems. Congregational contexts in particular give substance and validation to these beliefs, whether religious or secular. In short, the SA stands as an example of how some secular people draw comfort from and validation of their beliefs, not simply through cold athe-

---

[8] It is important to note, as the literature suggests, that the term "spiritual," among the religious, can have wide-ranging meanings and uses. The interpretation of secular individuals' "spiritualty" should be qualified in a similar way.

istic reasoning in their private mental lives, but through the collective, congregational dynamics of communal secularity. This is particularly noteworthy, as contemporary studies point to the hyper-individualism that characterizes many atheists and other secular people. It is clearly useful to speak of "secular rituals" as long as the intention and meaning of *ritual* is understood in context. As Cimino and Smith (2014, 139) observed in their study of organized atheists, whereas the religious understand rituals, "as a means of transcending 'the worldly,'" and connecting to a divine realm, "secularists understand ritual as a means for celebrating oneself as human and dwelling in a contingent world." Assemblers understanding of – and search for – transcendence, thus speaks to transcendence of a different kind. It is not that which most religious theology promotes, in that it seeks to rise above the secular world through preternaturalism, the search for the divine, or that which exists beyond nature, but the active invocation of the secular world itself as a source of transcendent meaning in the here and now.

4.3 Secular Activism, Secular Mission

Earlier I suggested rituals are meaningful because they impart a sense of something bigger, or as Corrigan put it, "a greater purpose" (2008). But what is the "greater purpose" for ritual-embracing secularists who do not believe in a cosmic grand design set out by a deity? The manifest goal of the SA – to *celebrate the one life we know we have* – may seem apolitical, or to be about simply enjoying the company of like-minded people who want to live life to the fullest. But there is more to the story than this.

If we understand secularity not as a passive descriptive term referencing those who happen to be secular, but a dynamic concept that suggests it's public expression motivated by particular aims, then the question becomes more about the ways in which nontheistic congregations contribute to secular activism and secularism more generally. In other words, we do not have to understand the SA as an activist organization with global aspirations per se, to see how it contributes to the broader promotion of the secular. The socio-political and historical conditions of SA's emergence suggest this. The increased political polarization and the salience of the religious right (especially in the United States), religious and political sectarianism, and the rise of global fundamentalism(s) have each contributed to the growth of secularity (Baker and Smith 2015). Combined with social media and other communication technologies, and the availability of information generally via the Web, it should not be surprising that secular organizations – most prominently in the U.S. – have proliferated, perhaps even causing, in the words of Cimino and Smith (2014), an "atheist awakening" for the 21ˢᵗ century. The SA has been part of the wider outcome of these social and political conditions; one iteration within the broader secular community in which the timing was right for its development.

In this light, it should come in to focus how secular congregations are linked to secular activism and the promotion of the broader secular cause. In contrast to some religious organizations, the SA does not recruit new membership through active proselytization, and it is much too young to have experienced the benefits of intergenerational socialization to establish and maintain a core membership.[9] Rather, it relies on promoting itself through its website, local chapters, social media, existing secular organizational networks, and word of mouth to an already extant (and growing) population of secular-minded people interested in congregational, communal culture. Thus, aggressive marketing or the targeting of specific nonbeliever groups has not been necessary, as there is a subset of nontheists in the broader secular community already poised to participate as they have few other options for joining strictly secular congregations or for communal forms of secularity generally.[10]

In the United States in particular, demographics have played an important role in providing a viable market for secular congregations. For example, increasing religious disaffiliation, the rise of the nones, and other shifting patterns of religious (non)identity (Hout and Fischer 2002; Sherkat 2014) have opened an effective space for secular congregations and different ways of living secular lives (Zuckerman 2014). Since many American nonbelievers were raised in religious households, the SA is seen by some as a way of reconnecting with the communal aspects of religion, but without the commitment to religious claims they do not accept as true.

Despite important differences in growing their numbers and developing commitment to the organization, there are some both latent and manifest "missionizing" elements to the SA (Smith 2015). Congregational commitment is made, not through narratives of conversion or adherence to particular doctrinal claims, but through belief in the value (or necessity) of addressing the challenges of community and the anxieties of contemporary life in secular terms. This is evidenced in the online publications of the SA, where organizers write posts on con-

---

9 Given this and other shifting social patterns, it will be interesting to see if so-called millennials develop more interest in the SA than other demographic groups as might be suggested by their more liminal relationship with religion and traditional institutions generally.
10 No clear data exist on membership composition, so I cannot make objective claims about demographic patterns regarding who joins the SA. However, by most accounts, they seem to largely draw a mostly white, middle-class demographic. Average age and the proportion of men to women Assemblers is not known.

necting with others during difficult times, dealing with grief and the loss of loved ones (including through "nonbeliever funerals"), leading meaning-rich and purpose-driven lives, and always searching for experiences "beyond oneself" – all in secular terms.[11] Returning to SA's charter, the last several of its proclamations are illustrative. The SA states it will be "a force for good" via its "community mission" with congregants as "action heroes." The Sunday Assembly will "make the world a better place" and is "here to stay" (Sunday Assembly). In other words, the SA's aspirations and activities reach well beyond simply offering regular Sunday services to secular congregants. Through community outreach, volunteer activity, and working groups ("smoups") on social justice issues within local Assembly chapters, the SA essentially functions in the public sphere as the kind of community organization that Cnaan and Curtis (2013) discuss in their study of religious congregations as voluntary associations. In this view, sans theology, religious congregations are simply one prominent manifestation of the rational nonprofit sector.

Yet, we know faith and religious claims *do* in fact motivate and orient the collective actions of religious groups. They are sometimes more effective than other organizations at generating trust between participants and facilitating community engagement across and between social networks – not all of them having to do with religion (Seymour et al. 2014). What about avowedly secular, faith-*less* congregations? Is the SA no different than any other secular nonprofit charity unconnected to any particular religious institution? Given their communal rituals, goals, and symbolic positioning vis-à-vis the wider public as a deity-free congregation, the answer is no. Rather, the organizational practices of the SA suggest it is more than a celebration of life; it is a public, symbolic demonstration of the moral utility of secular values and their connection to an atheological cosmology centered on this life, rather than one to come.

Given the preceding, we can distill the following four interrelated elements regarding the activist and "mission" dimension of communal secularity. It is centered on: (1) the reaping of social and personal rewards of communal life for secular individuals, (2) normalizing and destigmatizing nontheism, (3) promoting secular beliefs, and (4) validating and legitimizing those beliefs through public congregations and organizational social action. It does this all through activities found in the more or less traditional organizational structure of religious congregational communities. It appears as though the SA has taken heed (knowingly or otherwise) of the advice offered by Baker and Smith (2015, 215) in their study of

---

[11] One blog series on the SA website, for example, is titled "M is for Meaning" and offers advice about finding meaning and happiness in both good times and the bad.

contemporary secularism that suggested, "in order to achieve long-term organizational success, secular groups would need to – dare we say it – look to religious communities."

4.4 Sunday Assembly and the Secular Community

How does the Sunday Assembly fit within the wider secular community? What role does it play, and what does this all mean for organized secularism at large? As I have suggested, the SA meets a demand among those who desire a communal secularity that, organizationally and interactionally, functions much like a religious congregation. For a subset of those in the broader secular community the SA offers meaningful ritual practices that develop a kind of emotional and expressive solidarity qualitatively different from the solidarities found in other traditional atheist and secular activist groups. There is an emerging popular interest among nonbelievers in these expressive, even nonsupernaturalist "spiritual" pursuits. Recent examples include Sam Harris's book *Waking Up: A Guide to Spirituality without Religion* (2014), and Alain de Botton's, *Religion for Atheists: A Nonbeliever's Guide to the Uses of Religion* (2013).[12] Given the interests of the SA in creating meaningful experiences in secular terms (e. g. the aforementioned secular funerals), the communal secularity it is cultivating is consistent with – and could possibly extend in the future to – the management of life cycle events usually associated with religion, such as birth ceremonies, secular marriages, and other symbolically-infused rituals.

In developing a communal secularity, the SA also promotes a secular message that contributes to organized secularism through its volunteer and service efforts in local communities. It implicitly advances secularism through practices that facilitate commitment to secular values beyond the purely rational-instrumental or intellectualized versions of nonbelief, such as those characteristic of the new atheism. This will likely contribute to any continued growth and success the SA may experience organizationally. Its cultivation of commitment from its congregants unfolds in less obvious ways when compared to groups like the American Atheists, Center for Inquiry, and other secular organizations that purse their activism through public campaigns, and sometimes legal action.

Whereas avowed secular activist groups engage the public through billboard campaigns, conventions, sponsoring debates, television programing (e. g. Amer-

---

[12] Alain de Botton even has his own secular organization, *The School of Life* that bears similarity to some of the goals of the SA.

ican Atheists "Atheist TV"), demonstrations, and political activities (e. g. church-state separation issues and other legal matters), the communal secularity of the SA has a different quality of character in its relationship to the wider public. Its Sunday services and community and volunteer actions are focused on a rhetoric of inclusivity, promoting secular ethics, and – given the continued social stigma of atheism (Edgell, Gerteis, and Hartmann 2006) and discrimination toward non-believers (Hammer et al. 2012) – normalizing nonbelief at a *cultural* level. They avoid the perceived defensive or combative posture of atheist activist organizations and in fact in some ways attempt to downplay the nonbelief component, highlighting instead the celebratory and communal aspects of their organization. In addition to what it offers participants by way of the congregational model it embraces, the SA's position in the broader secular community is in large part based on its focus and public expression of normative cultural values. In a sense, it eschews a defender-of-atheism disposition and instead adopts a do-good, lead-by-example approach to normalizing nonbelief.

None of this is to suggest all Assemblers are secular activists or are involved primarily because of their will to influence public perception of nontheists. In my interviews with Assemblers, although many were involved in secular activism of some kind, there were also those who simply wanted to enjoy the services, without intention of making a moral or public statement about the value of secularity or the importance of affiliation with secular groups (see Langston et al. this volume, in which they outline the motivational dynamics of both "secular affiliates" and secular nonaffiliates").

It is also too early to tell how the SA might evolve in the future based on the desires of it constituents,[13] but the kind of secular the SA represents – and what is different about it from other secular organizations – lies essentially in its communal character and symbolic positioning as it embraces the organizational and community-building strengths found in the religious congregational model.

5 Conclusion

Secularity, as the context of the present volume suggests, reflects a wide range of values, identities, individual viewpoints, and organizational activities. In a study of organized nonbelief and the strategic goals of secular groups, Langston, Ham-

---

[13] One notable fracture has already taken place: the Godless Revival split from the Sunday Assembly as it (SA) was seen as not having sufficient focus on an atheist message. The inclusivity and porous symbolic boundaries that currently characterize the SA could lead to further divisions in the future.

mer, and Cragun (2015) examined the affiliation patterns of nonbelievers, finding a mixed bag when it comes to why some nonbelievers, and not others, join secular groups. Those who do not affiliate cite their nonbelief as a low priority; that it is simply not an important part of who they are (although, as somewhat counter to this, the authors also found fully one-third of secular nonaffiliates say they would join a group if one were locally convenient). This suggests that for those who organize – including Assemblers – their nontheism is important to their identities and outlook on life. Most relevant here however, is the study's findings that affiliation patterns hinge on the question of how secular groups interact with the broader – and especially religious, public. Significantly more (60%) of nonbelievers had a preference for the "accommodation" of – rather than confrontation (25%) with – religion (Langston et al. 2015). It may be that nonbelievers see the SA as a novel and non-confrontational way of expressing and promoting secular beliefs.

But the *meaning* of the secular, and surrounding issues regarding identity-labels, can be complicated, and of course, not all secular-identified people see the SA as truly secular. For instance, some prominent secular humanists such as Tom Flynn, the editor of *Free Inquiry*, and Greg Epstein, the humanist Chaplain of Harvard, see the SA, not as a secular congregation, but as "congregational humanism," defined essentially as a nontheistic version of communal religiosity. This is because some secular humanists view communal activity based on a religious congregational model as being at odds with the meaning of secular. As Flynn argues, "secular humanists often disdain traditional congregational practices" (2013, 4) and therefore would not see initiatives like the SA as truly secular. To be sure, some atheists and other constituents in the nonbelieving community would take umbrage at the idea of congregational nonbelief, and thus Assemblies clearly self-select for nonbelievers open and unoffended by the notion of communal secularity. How or whether Assemblers themselves fit into any of the particular "types" that have been offered in secular-atheist typologies (see Cotter 2015; Silver and Coleman 2013) will be left to future researchers to determine after the SA has moved out of its status as a novel nonbeliever phenomenon, into an established secular organization.

What these differences – and the idea of communal secularity itself – demonstrate is further evidence of "polysecularity" (see Shook, this volume) and of the fact that increasingly, contemporary societies are characterized by multiple secularities (Wohlrab-Sahr and Burchardt 2012). That is, the contemporary secular landscape is characterized by greater diversity of secular viewpoints, interests, and complexity of meaning than is often acknowledged in prior scholarly literature. Some of the demographic patterns of atheism (see Williamson and Yancey 2013), for instance that it is a white, middle-class, male phenomenon, suggest more homogeneity in the secular community than there is. But beyond the demographics and social location(s) of nonbelievers, there is also considerable variation in the meaning of nonbelief for individuals, and this is manifested in the different strategies and goals of secular and nonbeliever organizations. From the SA to the new atheism, this challenges the notion of a united or uniform secular culture or movement (Baker and Smith 2015). But this also does not imply that accommodationists are pitted against confrontationists in the world of organized secularism. In reality, as Langston et. al. (this volume) suggest, different secular groups simply emerge from, and respond to, the diversity of motives, values, and goals of nonbelievers themselves.

Researchers have observed that congregations with strong core faith messages develop stronger congregational adherence from their members (Roberts and Yamane 2012). For instance, evangelical groups that place more demands (e. g. time commitment, confession of sin, profession of belief) generally elicit stronger commitments from congregants. Such a model usually relies on narratives of conversion, rebirth, or other kinds of personal experience that deepen religious conviction and "prove" commitment to the congregation. Absent a "core faith message" or clear doctrine, Assemblies place little by way of demands on congregants and are unlikely to draw the kind of commitments that religious congregations are known for. Notwithstanding this concern, the SA does promote a secular message, and as a public space for the celebration of secular values, it relies on individuals by way of their general convictions regarding community, science, and education, as well as their personal commitments to normalizing nonbelief and expressing a secular worldview in a public setting.

It is not yet clear what impact the SA will have on the secular-religious landscape in the decades to come. But it is clear that it is unique and offers members something they do not find in other secular organizations. Its focus on emotion and ritual are a far cry from the traditional convention meeting halls where atheists occasionally gather to polemicize in philosophical debates about God or lament the influence of religion in public life. Its focus on radical inclusivity, celebration, and solidarity sets it apart from other secular organizations. But individual nonbelievers do not simply choose one group or the other. Many are involved in multiple groups, suggesting that communal secularity is not necessarily at odds with other secular organizations, but perhaps offers a space in which nonbelievers and even "hardline" secular activists can take reprieve from the embattled politics of (non)belief and enjoy the collective effervescence that congregations by their nature offer, be they religious or secular.

Bibliography

Ammerman, Nancy T. 1994. "Telling Congregational Stories." *Review of Religious Research* 35 (4): 289–301.
Baker, Joseph O., and Buster G. Smith. 2015. *American Secularism: Cultural Contours of Nonreligious Belief Systems.* New York: New York University Press.
Berger, Peter L. 1990. *The Sacred Canopy: Elements of a Sociological Theory of Religion.* New York: Anchor Books.
Cimino, Richard, and Christopher Smith. 2014. *Atheist Awakening: Secular Activism and Community in America.* New York: Oxford University Press.
Cnaan, Ram A., and Daniel W. Curtis. 2013. "Religious Congregations and Voluntary Association: An Overview." *Nonprofit and Voluntary Sector Quarterly* 42(1): 7–33.
Corrigan, John. ed, 2008. *The Oxford Handbook of Religion and Emotion.* New York: Oxford University Press.
Cotter, Christopher R. 2015. "Without God yet Without Nuance: A Qualitative Study of Atheism and Non-religion Among Scottish Students." In *Atheist Identities-Spaces and Social Contexts*, edited by Lori Beaman and Steven Tomlins, 171–194. London: Springer International Publishing
Cowen, Douglas E. 2008. "Emotion and the Study of New Religious Movements." In *The Oxford Handbook of Religion and Emotion*, edited by John Corrigan, 125–140. New York: Oxford University Press.
Del Barco, Mandalit. 2014. "Sunday Assembly: A Church for the Godless Picks up Steam." NPR. January 7. http://www.npr.org/2014/01/07/260184473/sunday-assembly-a-church-for-the-godless-picks-up-steam.
Edgell, Penny, Joseph Gerteis, and Douglas Hartmann. 2006. Atheists as "Other": Moral Boundaries and Cultural Membership in American Society." *American Sociological Review* 71(2):211–34.
Flynn, Tom. 2013. "Religious Humanism: Is It Dead, Alive, or Bifurcating?" *Free Inquiry* Fall issue: 33(6).
Gallagher, Sally K., and Chelsea Newton. 2009. "Defining Spiritual Growth: Congregations, Community, and Connectedness." *Sociology of Religion* 70(3):232–261.
Geertz, Clifford. 1973. *The Interpretation of Cultures.* New York: Basic Books.
Guenther, Katja M., Kerry Mulligan, and Cameron Papp. 2013. "From the Outside In: Crossing Boundaries to Build Collective Identity in the New Atheist Movement." *Social Problems* 60(4):457–75.
Hammer, Joseph H., Ryan T. Cragun, Jesse M. Smith, and Karen Hwang. 2012. "Forms, Frequency, and Correlates of Perceived Anti-Atheist Discrimination." Secularism and Nonreligion 1:43–58.
Hetherington, Kevin. 1998. *Expressions of identity: Space, performance, politics.* Thousand Oaks, CA: Sage Publications.
Hout, Michael, and Claude S. Fischer. 2002. "Why More Americans Have No Religious Preference: Politics and Generations." *American Sociological Review* 67: 165–190.
Hunsberger, Bruce E., and Bob Altemeyer. 2006 *Atheists: A Groundbreaking Study of America's Nonbelievers.* Amherst: Prometheus Books.

Langston, Joseph., Joseph Hammer, and Ryan T. Cragun. 2015. "Atheism Looking In: On the Goals and Strategies of Organized Nonbelief." *Science, Religion, and Culture* 2(3): 70–85.

Lee, Lois. 2015. *Recognizing the Nonreligious: Reimagining the Secular.* New York: Oxford University Press.

Oakes, Kaya. 2015. "Belonging Without Believing." *CrossCurrents* 65: 229–238.

Roberts, Keith A., and David Yamane. 2012. *Religion in Sociological Perspective.* Thousand Oaks: Pine Forge Press.

Seymour, Jeffrey M., Michael R. Welch, Karen Monique Gregg, and Jessica Collett. 2014. "Generating Trust in Congregations: Engagement, Exchange, and Social Networks." *Journal for the Scientific Study of Religion* 53(1):130–144.

Sherkat, Darren. 2014. *Changing Faith: The Dynamics and Consequences of Americans' Shifting Religious Identities.* New York: New York University Press.

Silver, Christopher F. and Thomas Coleman. 2013. "Six Types of Atheists." Available at: www.atheismresearch.com

Smith, Jesse. M. 2013. "Creating a Godless Community: The Collective Identity Work of Contemporary American Atheists." *Journal for the Scientific Study of Religion* 52: 80–99.

Smith, Jesse. 2015. "Atheism." In *World Religions and their Missions*, edited by Aaron J. Ghiloni, 17–45. New York. Peter Lang Publishing.

Smith, Jesse. 2017. "Can the Secular be the Object of Belief and Belonging? The Sunday Assembly." *Qualitative Sociology* 40(1) 83–109.

Sunday Assembly. 2015. http://www.sundayassembly.com

Tavory, Iddo. 2013. The Private Life of Public Ritual: Interaction, Sociality and Codification in a Jewish Orthodox Congregation." *Qualitative Sociology* 36:125–139.

Weber, Max. 1947. *The Theory of Social and Economic Socialization.* New York: Free Press.

Williamson, David A., and George Yancey. 2013. *There Is No God: Atheists in America.* Lanham, MD: Rowman and Littlefield.

Wohlrab-Sahr, Monika, and Marian Burchardt. 2012. "Multiple Secularities: Toward a Cultural Sociology of Secular Modernities." *Comparative Sociology* 11:875–909.

Wilkins, Amy C. 2008. "Happier than Non-Christians: Collective Emotions and Symbolic Boundaries among Evangelical Christians." *Social Psychology Quarterly* 71(3):281–301.

Zuckerman, Phil. 2014. *Living the Secular Life: New Answers to Old Questions.* New York: Penguin Press.

Jacqui Frost
Rejecting Rejection Identities: Negotiating Positive Non-religiosity at the Sunday Assembly

1 Introduction

On a sunny Saturday morning in May of 2015, a group of over 80 non-religious Americans and Britons gathered in the basement of a Presbyterian church in the heart of Atlanta, Georgia. As individuals and groups of two and three trickled in, grabbing bagels and coffee and finding their seats, a band was setting up in the front of the room. At 9:00 a.m. sharp, the band gathered the room's attention and soon everyone in the basement was belting out the lyrics to the themesong from the 1980s comedy *Ghostbusters*. Some sang, clapped, and danced in the aisles, while others laughed sheepishly and followed along as best they could by reading the lyrics displayed on the large overhead behind the band. The band was equipped with a saxophone, a piano, a guitar, and both lead and backup vocals, and they quickly orchestrated a "call and response" dynamic with the audience during the choruses. When the band asked, "Who you gonna call?" the audience yelled back gleefully, "Ghostbusters!" Everyone was on their feet and smiling, looking around at their neighbors with knowing glances that signaled shared memories of the movie and the irony of singing about ghosts at a gathering devoted to secular worldviews.

The occasion for this secular sing-a-long was the second annual international conference of the Sunday Assembly, a growing network of "secular congregations" that selectively appropriate and replicate the Protestant church model to build community among the *non*-religious. Organizers and members had come from all over the United States and Britain to meet one another, share questions and concerns, and celebrate their successes as a growing organization. The organization, which began in London in early 2013, has quickly spread to over 70 local assemblies across the globe, though primarily within Britain and America. Local assemblies meet on Sundays, sing songs and listen to speakers, and they focus their gatherings on building community and pursuing a more meaningful life.[1] They seek out ways to volunteer and engage with their local com-

---

[1] See the organization's website for more detailed information on the organization's vision and mission at www.sundayassembly.com

∂ OpenAccess. © 2017 Jacqui Frost, published by De Gruyter. [CC BY-NC-ND] This work is licensed under the Creative Commons Attribution-NonCommercial-NoDerivatives 4.0 License.
https://doi.org/10.1515/9783110458657-010

munities and they organize small group activities among assembly members, including game nights, potlucks, and movie outings.

In this chapter, I draw on data I have collected from 21 months of ethnographic observations and interviews with a local Sunday Assembly chapter in a Midwestern American city[2], as well as observations from the larger organization's annual conference in 2015, to detail the ways in which this organization is attempting to collectively construct a *positive* non-religious community. The organization is intentionally drawing on aspects of religious ritual and practice that facilitate community building and meaning making, while at the same time selectively rejecting the aspects that are not amenable to a non-religious worldview. While I argue that the non-religious individuals who populate the assemblies are attempting to move beyond rejection identities and anti-religious activism, this does not mean that they agree on what it is that they should *affirm*.

Jesse Smith (this volume) developed the concept of "communal secularity" to describe the ways that Sunday Assembly is both like and unlike organized religion in important ways. In this chapter, I detail how this tension between being both like and unlike religion is negotiated in everyday decisions and interactions among Sunday Assemblers. Both within and among local Sunday Assembly chapters, debates and conflicts abound regarding where the organization should draw boundaries in regards to the inclusion of spirituality and ritual, as well as how much they should exclude explicit anti-religious rhetoric and activism that is prevalent in other non-religious organizations. More specifically, three major themes have emerged that highlight this boundary-making process: (1) the explicit goal to be "radically inclusive" of all individual beliefs while simultaneously maintaining a non-religious and non-theistic orientation as an organization, (2) the attempt to cultivate a "secular spirituality" and a collective transcendence that is devoid of supernatural rhetoric or beliefs, and (3) the selective appropriation of the institutional form of a Protestant church that attempts to eschew the hierarchy and dogma found in many Protestant religions while attempting to replicate their ritualized, emotionally engaged communality.

---

[2] The city has been anonymized to protect participant identifications.

2 A Shift in Non-religious Identities

Non-religious identities[3], including atheism and agnosticism, have often been seen as identities that are built on the rejection of religion and, indeed, many of the prominent organizations and figures of modern atheism in the West have fueled this image (LeDrew 2015; Kettell 2014). From the anti-religious rhetoric of the New Atheists to the image of embattled nonbelievers fighting against religious discrimination promoted by many national and local non-religious organizations, non-religion is indeed a "rejection identity" for many individuals (Cimino and Smith 2007; Smith 2011, 2013). However, as this population has expanded and evolved, there is a growing sense that an identity based on the rejection of religion and the politicization of nonbelief is insufficient for building a "positive" non-religious community. The rapid growth of "secular congregations" that focus on community, inclusiveness, and meaning making *instead* of criticism and polarization is evidence of a larger trend in which non-religious individuals are attempting to move beyond religious rejection to construct more "positive" non-religious identities and practices (Cimino and Smith 2014; Lee 2014, 2015).

While I am not the first to highlight the increasingly diverse individual and collective identities being constructed among the growing non-religious population (see Cotter 2015; LeDrew 2013; Lee 2014, 2015; Smith 2011, 2013, and Shook in this volume), there is still much work to be done in this area. As Smith (2011, 232) explains, the non-religious do not step into a "ready-made" identity with a "specific and definable set of roles or behaviors." Without the ready-made identities, rituals, and communities that the religious so often have available to them, the non-religious are forced to get creative in their search for new ways to engage with their communities and make meaning out of their beliefs and experiences. By describing the ways that one non-religious community is navigating this process, this chapter builds on previous research that "recognizes the non-religious" as a rich and diverse population full of complexity that is characterized not just

---

[3] Terminological debates abound in the nascent study of non-religious identity, so in order to be clear and consistent, I draw on Lois Lee's (2015) definition of non-religion as "any phenomenon – position, perspective, or practice – that is primarily understood in relation to religion but which is not itself considered to be religious" (32). I will use "non-religion" as an umbrella term to denote a wide variety of identities and beliefs, including atheism and agnosticism, but also less clearly defined differentiations from religious belief and practice. While many of my participants use the terms secular/ism, atheist/ism, and non-religion/ous interchangeably, I follow Lee's (2015) lead and keep these terms distinct, using "secular" to denote areligious phenomena and "non-religious" to denote phenomena built in relation to religion.

by a *lack* of beliefs and practices, but as having the potential to construct substantive, *positive* identities and practices (Lee 2015).

3 The Sunday Assembly: Changing the World with Joy and Jon Bon Jovi

The Sunday Assembly is the perfect example of the recent move to make non-religious communities more positive. The organization in many ways replicates the Protestant church model; they just simply do so with no reference to a deity or the supernatural. In fact, they avoid discussions about both religion *and* non-religion, striving to be "radically inclusive" and welcoming to people with a variety of beliefs and worldviews. The organization attempts to be non-hierarchical, and while there are a handful of paid organizers who run the international organization that manages the various local assemblies, individual chapters have no equivalent to a pastor or a leader. All the organizing at the local level is volunteer based, and speakers, who come from both inside and outside of the assemblies, rotate each month. Despite its radical inclusivity, however, the Sunday Assembly is explicitly non-religious and a majority of its organizers and active members identify as atheist, agnostic, or non-religious.

The Sunday Assembly was founded by two British comedians in 2013, Sanderson Jones and Pippa Evans. As Pippa detailed during her introductory comments at the Sunday Assembly Everywhere conference in May of 2015, the two met a few years prior on a road trip to a comedy gig in Bath. They connected on the idea of a church-like environment where non-religious individuals could sing songs and listen to inspirational talks together, offer emotional and social support for fellow non-religious individuals, and collectively construct non-religious rituals and practices that might produce a deeper sense of meaning among the non-religious. They initially set out to organize such a community in London and were met with a surprising amount of success. They began to put together a "Make Your Own Assembly Kit" online, making it widely available in order to see if they could build a network of assemblies across Britain and beyond. Since then, the number of assemblies has exploded to over 70 individual assemblies across the globe, from Hamburg, Germany, to Sydney, Australia, to Cleveland, Ohio.

The Sunday Assembly motto is "Live Better, Help Often, Wonder More," and this is reflected in what the local assemblies center their services and activities around. To "Live Better," they sing songs together, form small groups based on interests like watching Ted Talks and playing games, and they have a section in their service called "One Thing I Do Know," which is a space for members from the community to share an experience that taught them an important lesson. To "Help Often" they put on monthly volunteering activities and advocate for helping each other out by starting phone trees and cooking food for people who are sick or going through a hard time. To "Wonder More" they bring in speakers who impart knowledge about a topic, much like a Ted Talk, and a portion of their services are devoted to non-religious inspirational readings. They have a moment of silence in their services as well, asking those who came to reflect on the things they learned and how they might apply them to their lives going forward.

The organization is explicitly apolitical and avoids inserting itself into any political or social debates that might hinder the chances of collaborating with religiously-affiliated groups or individuals; while the organization and its activities are explicitly non-religious, the Sunday Assembly charter states that the organization is open to anyone who wants to join, regardless of beliefs. As such, the talks, readings, and music are, for the most part, free of any anti-religious *or* pro-atheist rhetoric. Instead, the assemblies focus on topics like science, personal empowerment, healthy lifestyle choices, and community betterment.

The organization's rapid expansion has even caught the attention of the media, and many have dubbed Sunday Assembly "the first atheist mega-church" (e.g. Walshe 2013; Winston 2013). While there are a handful of assemblies in other Western European countries like Germany, Denmark, and Hungary, a large majority of assemblies are located in the United States and the United Kingdom. The goal of the organization is to be a positive community environment for non-religious individuals and a major piece of that positivity stems from the collective singing of pop songs that the Sunday Assembly is becoming known for. As Sanderson jokingly quipped at the conference, the Sunday Assembly is attempting to "change the world with joy and Jon Bon Jovi."

4 Data and Method

I have been involved in ongoing participant observation with a local Sunday Assembly in the Midwestern United States since March of 2013 (Midwest Assembly, hereafter). I started attending their organizing meetings before they held their first assembly, so I have been able to observe the founding and evolution of this local chapter and its interactions with the founding assembly and other local chapters over time. I've gone to almost all of their monthly assemblies, I attend a majority of their organizing meetings, and I have access to their correspondence with other assemblies. In addition, I have interviewed 15 of the Midwest Assembly's organizers and active members, talking with them about their reasons for joining, their non-religious identities, and their visions for Sunday Assembly's future. I've gone to a couple potlucks and a few volunteer activities they have put on as well. Finally, as mentioned above, I attended a three day conference in May 2015 where I met numerous organizers from other chapters in the United States and the United Kingdom, spoke to and listened to the founders speak about the organization and its goals, and sat in on workshops and organizational meetings where members debated and discussed the organization's charter, motto, and the structure and content of the monthly assemblies.

Data for this chapter come primarily from my interactions and interviews with members of the Midwest Assembly, though I do draw on my observations from the conference as well. Interviews were recorded, transcribed, and coded for common themes; observations, both at the Midwest Assembly and at the conference, were transcribed into field notes and analyzed alongside the interviews. Demographic data on Sunday Assembly membership is not yet available, but the average Sunday Assembly participant I have encountered is a white, middle-class, professional in their 30s or 40s.

The main limitation of this data is that the conclusions I draw in this chapter are primarily based on my in-depth ethnography with one chapter of a much larger, international organization. Thus, my data is inevitably influenced by the specific cultural context of the Midwestern United States. However, the three days I spent observing the conference, where numerous other chapters were represented and the views and goals of the larger organization were detailed in depth over the course of the conference, offered a chance to corroborate the data collected from the Midwest Assembly with observations from the larger organization. Further, while the conclusions I draw in this chapter are representative of the Sunday Assembly as it is now, it is a new organization that is quickly growing and evolving. Its goals and vision are constantly being debated, and regional and national differences are likely to influence the trajectory of individual assemblies and the organization as a whole. With these caveats in mind, however, this chapter is meant to highlight some of the boundary making and identity construction processes at work in this new non-religious organization and the ways in which they are similar to and distinct from the ways non-religious identity in the United States has been understood in the past.

5 The Sunday Assembly in Context

While the combination of religious rituals and non-religious messages embodied in the Sunday Assembly is interesting in and of itself, it is even more so considering the prominence of the highly politicized, *anti*-religious rhetoric espoused by non-religious organizations and their leaders over the last decade. In both the U.S. and the U.K., the recent rise in visibility of atheism in the public sphere is due in large part to the popularity of New Atheism, a political movement centered around a critique of religion and the promotion of a rationalistic, scientific worldview (Bullivant 2012; Cragun 2015; Kettell 2014; LeDrew 2015). New Atheism has become a dominant ideological force driving atheist activism and non-religious organizing coming out of these two countries, and prominent atheist and secular activist groups like the Freedom From Religion Foundation and American Atheists in the United States and the Richard Dawkins Foundation in the United Kingdom promote a minority discourse and identity politics that emphasize the politicization of atheist identity and the need to battle religion's hegemony in public and political spheres (Cimino and Smith 2007; Smith 2013a; LeDrew 2015).

The often polarizing and negative message cultivated by the New Atheist movement has produced a large population of atheists who describe and enact their atheist identity as one built on religious critique (e. g. Kettell 2015; LeDrew 2015). Similarly, Smith (2011) found that atheism was a "rejection identity" for a majority of the atheists he interviewed, an identity built in direct opposition to religious beliefs and institutions. Consequently, he draws on the idea of the "not self" to describe how atheists, lacking a ready-made atheist identity to conform to, instead frame their identity as "biographical and rejection-based; a product of interaction, and an achieved identity to be sure, but one constructed out of negation and rejection, rather than filling culturally defined social roles" (Smith 2011, 232). For Smith's participants, atheism was often a way to describe what they did *not* believe in or agree with, as opposed to a marker of specific values, beliefs, or practices that they *affirmed*.

However, as the number of non-religious individuals continues to grow, researchers are finding that non-religious individuals do not always understand their identity as rejection-based. Lee (2014, 467) asserts that non-religion can also signal "substantive nonreligious and spiritual cultures more commonly than scholars and even respondents themselves appreciate" and that "we cannot therefore assume that their use indicates disaffiliation or non-identification rather than affiliation and identification." Lee (2014, 477) finds that non-religion can be used to describe "an array of concrete spiritual and nonreligious affiliations," and argues that social science research to date has been too heavily focused on atheism and non-religion as a negative, as opposed to a positive, affirmation (see also Baker and Smith 2015; Pasquale 2009). Similarly, LeDrew (2013b, 465) argues that "we should understand atheism not in terms of losing beliefs, but rather, in terms of the development of other kinds of beliefs."

Indeed, Smith (2013b, Chapter 10) agrees that not all atheism is rejection-based, and argues that the continued development and growth of organized atheism will likely lead to a wider variety of orientations to religion and identity. In line with these new empirical and theoretical developments, in their study of new non-religious communities in America, including the Sunday Assembly, Cimino and Smith (2014) describe what they call a "new new atheism" in which nonbelievers are attempting to build a positive identity around their non-religion in an attempt to move past rejection identities. Like the secular death practices (MacMurray, Chapter 13) and non-religious weddings (Hoesly, Chapter 12) described in this volume, many of Cimino and Smith's interviewees were seeking out non-theistic rituals and rites of passage, non-religious alternatives to traditional religion, and even "secular spirituality."

However, scholars like Kettell (2014), LeDrew (2015), and Baggs and Voas (2009) would warn against positing these trends as especially "new," and their historical treatments of non-religious organizing in Britain and the United States reveal that the seemingly disparate identities espoused by the New Atheists and Sunday Assembly are products of a long history of tension within the Western non-religious community. These scholars identify a major fault line within Western non-religion that was formed in many ways at its inception and continues to divide the movement today. LeDrew (2015) defines the two sides of this divide as "scientific" and "humanistic," a divide that dates back to the scientific revolution in the 19th century. At this time, LeDrew explains, two types of atheism emerged: *Scientific atheists* were affirmed and fueled by Darwin's theory of evolution and began attempting to expose religion as a biproduct of ignorance that is now superseded by science and reason. *Humanistic atheists*, however, considered religion a social phenomena; humanists were more inclined to see religion as capable of addressing social and emotional needs, and were thus less inclined to criticize religion and were instead open to compromising and working with religious individuals and institutions. And similar debates occurred between self-acclaimed "secularists" who clashed over the definitions of secularism and whether it signified an absence of religion or a substantive category in its own right (Rectenwald, this volume).

This divide is still salient today. Kettell (2014) details how disputes within the modern atheist movement are characterized by a divide between *confrontational* atheists, who utilize a combative approach to religion, and *accommodationist* atheists, who take a more conciliatory stance. Kettell explains that the internal structure of the atheist movement is diverse and absent of any central organization or ideology; some groups embody a more confrontational and political approach by engaging in legislative battles over church/state violations, while other groups are more geared toward acting as a substitution for religious institutions, providing secular celebrants for weddings and secular answers to larger questions of meaning and value. As Schutz (this volume) and Mastiaux (also this volume) describe, there are a wide variety of non-religious organizations and reasons for joining them, including social, political, communal, and intellectual. Similarly, Kettell (2014) identifies four major aims and campaigns found within this heterogeneous movement: reducing the influence of religion in the public sphere, criticizing religious belief and promoting atheism, improving civil rights and social status, and community building and group cohesion. He argues, "These disputes about identity and the use of labels also reflect more fundamental strategic frictions within the movement about the best way for atheists to present themselves and approach religious beliefs" (Kettell 2015, 383).

It is in this context that Sunday Assembly emerges, an undoubtedly distinct deviation from the anti-religious, scientific atheism of the recently prominent New Atheism, but not entirely unique from other accommodationist non-religious communities that have come before.[4] In this environment where non-religious individuals exist on a continuum of accommodation and confrontation, the Sunday Assembly has been attempting to strike a balance between the two poles – affirm a scientific, non-theistic worldview while also incorporating bits and pieces of religious ritual and spiritual practice where they are useful. In the following sections, I detail some of the ways the Sunday Assembly balances its goals of being both explicitly non-religious *and* radically inclusive, of cultivating transcendence *and* reason, and of being *like a church* while at the same time *different enough from a church* to attract the widest range of non-religious identities and beliefs possible. I will argue that these boundary-making processes illustrate how the positive non-religion that Sunday Assembly is attempting to construct is shaped by the tensions between rejection and accommodation, and while the members of Sunday Assembly are attempting to move beyond rejection identities, they are constantly negotiating what it is they should affirm.

6 Rejecting Rejection Identities

> That was something that I'd missed, I'd missed that community aspect of having a place to go to on a regular basis that was less about bashing god and religious people ... Because I'd been to [other non-religious groups] who were just so negative. And that was something

---

4 For example, the British Humanist Association that came to prominence in the 1960s embraced humanism as their rationalistic moral philosophy and focused on providing concrete alternatives to religion instead of criticizing religion and engaging in political battles to lessen its influence in society (Bagg and Voas 2009).

that I started thinking about, this whole idea of a negative identity. Of having an identity that was formed against something else. And with Sunday Assembly, now we are formed around this identity of becoming something else.

Eric, member of the Midwest Assembly

Like Eric, many of the members of the Midwest Assembly I interviewed have been or still are members of other local non-religious groups and organizations.[5] They often used their experiences with these other groups and organizations, groups Kettell (2014) would describe as more confrontational, as a foil to describe what they hoped Sunday Assembly would become. Many expressed that they found the activist and political groups useful at first, and they supported these organizations' efforts to maintain the separation of church and state and fight for non-religious citizens' rights, but they grew tired of talking about "how religion got them down" and wanted to "start seeing what else was out there."

For some, the constant rejection of religion and affirmation of nonbelief is simply not something they are interested in. Zack, a younger member who attends frequently, told me that he did not identify strongly with atheism and did not "feel the need to talk about it all the time." He joined because he liked the music and the possibility of making some new social connections. Amy, an active organizer of the Midwest Assembly, echoed Zack's sentiments, saying, "I hope we can move *post* atheism in which it's just accepted that we don't have to make our life's mission to prove there is no god. We just live secularly as if god was never presumed in the first place."

For others, however, the constant critique of religion that is prevalent in the more activist non-religious groups conflicts with the way they want to enact their non-religious identity. For Amanda, leaving Catholicism was a painful and lonely process, and to ask others to have that same experience before they were ready felt wrong. She explains:

Despite, you know, really, coming into this identity of atheism, I never felt like it was my place to dissuade others. Just because this break had been so painful for me, I did not want to inflict that on other people. If they weren't having that crisis, people were living their whole lives happily with these beliefs, who am I to take them away?

---

5 All names are pseudonyms. As this is a small community, very little identifying information is given about individual interviewees in the attempts to protect participant identifications as much as possible.

Brad, a newer member of the Midwest Assembly, also disliked what he saw as the requirement to reject all the comforts of spiritual beliefs if you become an atheist. He described himself as an agnostic, but one that still sometimes relied on the belief that "some force" was holding everything together when he was going through trying times. He said, "I want to be an atheist at some point. A lot of people I know are very comfortable being atheist, but the thing I'm holding back from is that some atheists really hate Christians. I don't want to hate anybody. I don't agree with them, but I'm not going to hate them." Brad's experience with other non-religious groups led him to believe that atheists were overwhelmingly negative toward other religions and even toward other non-religious ideologies like his. His hope for the Sunday Assembly is that it can be more open to exceptions and alternative ways of being non-religious.

Overall, the members of the Midwest Assembly express a desire to move *beyond* rejecting religion or building an identity around that rejection. Eric, like Amy above, uses the term "post-atheism" to describe this new orientation to non-religious identity. He said, "I more consider myself a post-atheist, rather than necessarily an atheist. Because my worldview really isn't defined by an absence of god. I'm really only an atheist in the presence of religious people. The rest of the time, I'm just me." For Eric, to be an *atheist* means to consciously reject religion and build your identity against that. But to be *post-atheist* means he can move beyond that rejection and live his life in a more positive pursuit of knowledge and meaning. The Sunday Assembly is a space that this new identity and community formation can take place, a space that is not built on the rejection of religion, but of "becoming something else." However, as I will describe in the next three sections, what this new positive identity should look like is much less clear, and the members of the Sunday Assembly engage in a constant process of negotiation as they attempt to balance between non-religious and non-theistic worldviews and beliefs, selective accommodation of religious ritual and practice, and a sense of the transcendent that is entirely this-worldly and devoid of the supernatural.

6.1 Negotiating Radical Inclusivity

At the beginning of every monthly organizing meeting for the Midwest Assembly, one of the five to seven organizing members in attendance reports the "Sunday Assembly Everywhere Network News." The Sunday Assembly has set up an email list-serve in which any member of any local Sunday Assembly chapter can email all the other members on the list-serve questions and concerns about their individual assembly or the organization more broadly. At each Midwest Assembly organizing meeting, we spend some time reviewing what has been discussed on the list-serve. During one such meeting, it was reported that a self-identified Christian had attended a service of the Los Angeles Sunday Assembly and sent the organizers a write-up of her experience. In her write up, this woman discussed how she did not feel like she belonged at the Sunday Assembly because she had religious beliefs, but admitted that the Sunday Assembly was not created for her and she understood why it is an important space for non-religious individuals. The result was what is now an infamously long (over 150 emails) debate between numerous members of the Sunday Assembly community regarding just *how* accommodating the Sunday Assembly should be towards religious individuals and their beliefs.

The Sunday Assembly charter, which was written by Sanderson and Pippa during the founding months of the organization, states, "The Sunday Assembly is radically inclusive – everyone is welcome, regardless of their beliefs. This is a place of love that is open and accepting."[6] This one statement has led to quite possibly *the* most debate and fallout among the different Sunday Assemblies and their members, and in many ways, shapes the other major themes discussed in this chapter as well. To start, many express confusion over what "radical inclusivity" really is and looks like, causing enough of a stir in the community to merit an entire workshop devoted to the topic at the conference in Atlanta.

During this workshop, over 30 of the conference attendees gathered in a small room to hash out what being radically inclusive meant for them as a non-religious organization. While a majority of those in attendance agreed that Sunday Assembly should welcome anyone who is interested, as long as they did not push their beliefs on anyone, some expressed that they felt it was a paradox to say you are radically inclusive while at the same time requiring that the ethos of the organization and its services remain non-theistic in spirit and in content. Others said they were in search of a *secular* community and did not want to compromise their secular commitments to be inclusive of religious beliefs. One person in attendance said, "I will feel cheated if Sunday Assembly becomes an organization that aspires to welcome the religious and the non-religious equally. The religious have plenty of opportunities to voice their concerns and their agenda. Non-believers do not." While the individuals who felt this way do not want to focus on rejecting religious ideas, they were concerned that being *too* accommodating of religious ideas would shut down real discussions about non-religious beliefs and values.

---

6 See full charter at www.sundayassembly.com/story.

These debates came up during the town hall meeting that was held on the second day of the conference as well. During this meeting, anyone at the conference who wanted could participate in discussions about making changes to the Sunday Assembly charter, motto, and mission statement. When it was founded, the Sunday Assembly charter stated that it was a "godless congregation that celebrates life," and the Sunday Assembly mission was to support a "godless congregation in every town, city and village that wants one." The media picked up on this, and began to call the Sunday Assembly an "atheist church." I noticed that many of the Midwest Assembly members took issue with this during the first few organizing meetings, both because they felt that calling it an *atheist* church was too exclusionary of non-atheists who might want to attend, and calling it a *church* risked turning off potential members who thought it would be "too churchy." Further, many felt the term "godless" was needlessly confrontational and made it difficult to connect with organizations that might be offended by the term. Despite these reservations, the Midwest Assembly continued to describe themselves as an atheist church in their press releases, and many told me that it was the term they used when they described the organization to their friends and family. However, during the town hall meeting at the conference, members of other assemblies expressed similar reservations with the terms "atheist church" and "godless congregation," and the organization ultimately voted to change their descriptor to "secular congregation" in order to be as inclusive as possible without losing their secular designation.

This conflict between accommodation and confrontation is also present within individual assembly's decision making processes. For example, the Midwest Assembly recently began volunteering once a month at a homeless shelter that is affiliated with a Catholic charity. The organizing members discussed the pros and cons of partnering with the Catholic church, agreeing that while some of the more anti-religious members might protest, the cause was worth the compromise. However, a few months later, an organizing member suggested that the Midwest Assembly partner with Habitat for Humanity for another volunteering opportunity. Although Habitat is a Christian organization, the organizer said she had a good experience volunteering with them in the past and had never been talked to about religion at any of their events. After some discussion, the board decided to hold off, deciding that they already volunteered with one religious organization and agreeing that they should seek out secular organizations to volunteer through instead.

The Midwest Assembly has also had a number of debates about whether or not to include references to god or magic in the songs they sing at their gatherings. For example, when the Midwest Assembly band wanted to cover "Rainbow Connection" from *The Muppets*, there was a debate as to whether they should keep the words "it's probably magic" in the song. The band ended up including the words, but many of the organizers expressed that the reference to magic made them uncomfortable. Sue, an organizer who disagreed with the word's inclusion, stated, "We don't stand against anything but we do stand for something. Reality."

These examples illustrate the ways that the goal to be radically inclusive requires the Sunday Assembly to constantly balance between an accommodating stance toward religious and spiritual beliefs and institutions while at the same time maintaining a boundary around the non-religious identity of the organization and its members. There are disagreements about the decisions that are made and where the lines are drawn, but this is what many say they like about the Sunday Assembly. Brad from the Midwest Assembly, for example, said that "to be radically inclusive means to make exceptions." He saw these debates about the "gray areas" as a necessary part of building something new like the Sunday Assembly. He said, "We all have so many different ideas of what this secular assembly looks like, which means that compromises will need to be made and some small transgressions like the word 'magic' in a song will have to be overlooked."

6.2 Negotiating Secular Spirituality

> The way people speak about how much they love god, I was like, that is how I feel about life. And not in a supernatural way, but in a totally materialistic way. I didn't even have the words to describe those feelings that I had...there is not language about how that can happen if you aren't religious.
>
> *Sanderson Jones, co-founder of Sunday Assembly*

The above quote comes from another workshop I attended at the Sunday Assembly conference in Atlanta, a workshop on the topic of "secular spirituality." A major goal of the Sunday Assembly is the formation of secular rituals and traditions, like those found in religious institutions, that cultivate a sense of connectedness, transcendence, and wonder. Indeed, to "wonder more" is one of the organizations main objectives, but this, too, has been met with resistance from members of the Sunday Assembly community.

At the secular spirituality workshop, around 30 of the conference attendees, including Sanderson, attempted to collectively define "secular spirituality" and if and how Sunday Assembly should try to cultivate it. Many voiced that they disliked the word "spirituality" and its association with supernatural beliefs, so one of the main objectives of the workshop was to come up with some new terminology to express feelings of secular transcendence and connectedness. After discussing some possible vocabulary options, none of which really stuck, Sanderson asked that everyone join in trying to *cultivate* a feeling of secular spirituality right there in the workshop; we tried clapping together, humming together, and some even "testified" to the group in a way similar to what you would find in a religious service. As Smith (in this volume) would say, this workshop was meant to construct new ways to "sacralize the secular" and imbue secular beliefs and practices with meaning. After these attempts, Sanderson gauged people's reactions. While some expressed that they were uncomfortable with the experience and said that it felt forced and "too much like church," others said they could see these practices really working and would be trying them in their own assemblies.

Explicit attempts to ritualize non-theistic spiritual practices and define a secular spirituality has been less of a focus at the Midwest Assembly, and some of the members I interviewed expressed a real discomfort with the idea. Angela, a more peripheral member, said that she is uncomfortable with secular rituals, saying, "I don't attend the assemblies for spiritual or personal growth. I'm enjoying it as having a party with friends, which is a very different approach than many others in the assembly." Angela is concerned that more and more members of the Midwest Assembly are coming for spiritual growth and she is hoping that they can strike a balance between their position and hers, or she might have to stop coming. However, others at the Midwest Assembly are more open to the idea of a secular spirituality. Jeff, for example, said:

> When you see atheists in the news, it's them trying to stop Christians from doing something. Their stance towards people who are not atheist is a negative stance ... It's more of an intellectual kind of a belief system, which has its purpose and maybe it's just an evolution of this community ... But a lot of people don't want to make an intellectual argument out of their reason for living. They want it to be more holistic. I don't think you ever get away from the emotional.

For Jeff, and many other Midwest members I interviewed, a purely intellectual approach to non-religious identity lacks a sense of the transcendent and the emotional connectedness that they are hoping to cultivate at the Sunday Assembly. By singing together, quietly reflecting together during moments of silence, and trying out new rituals and activities that might potentially produce a sense of wonder and collective effervescence, these Sunday Assemblers are attempting to cultivate a secular spirituality that balances their secular commitments with their desires for a more holistic approach to the pursuit of meaning and happiness as non-religious individuals.

Like the debates surrounding Sunday Assembly's stated goal to be radically inclusive, the attempts to cultivate non-theistic rituals and spirituality are met with resistance and compromise. While some members joined the Sunday Assembly in pursuit of these rituals, others have stayed in spite of them or left all together. Consequently, the organizers of the Midwest Assembly are constantly assessing whether or not their gatherings are *too* church-like or *not enough* like a church. In the next section, I will describe conversations surrounding the church-like structure of the Sunday Assembly as a final example of the ways that the Sunday Assembly operates as a space of negotiation and compromise, of both accommodation and rejection.

6.3 Negotiating Structure: Church-*Like*, But Not Too Much

The intentional replication of the Protestant church model is one of the defining features of the Sunday Assembly. The organization's primary gathering is on a Sunday, it consists of group sing-a-longs, fellowship, moments of reflection, inspirational talks, and coffee; it lasts about two hours and people often go grab lunch or drinks afterwards. As Smith (this volume) describes, the Sunday Assembly is participating in a *congregational culture* that structures the relationships and experience of its members. Not surprisingly, Sunday Assembly has received a lot of media attention for their enthusiastic appropriation of the contemporary Protestant church model, but it is in fact a common source of conflict and confusion for its members.

When I asked members of the Midwest Assembly why they liked the idea of replicating the church model to build community for non-religious people, the most common answer was: "We don't know how else to do it." At the same time, they talked about how they saw nothing wrong with the church model in and of itself; they had been disappointed by the way that the more activist non-religious communities were organized and felt like the church model had a lot going for it. For example, Eric told me, "Why not take from the best parts of religion? The things that actually work that are making us better people and just ditch the rest." Similarly, Beth, an older organizer with a long history of church attendance, said:

> I don't think the church model, in and of itself, is bad. I don't want to throw the baby out with the bathwater. It's been very successful, so to me I think there isn't anything wrong with modeling it after that. I'm not even sure what we would do if we didn't. I think the Sunday Assembly has done a good job at not having a hierarchy, like, there's no 'minister' person. So I think they've got rid of the things I don't like about the church, but I think that model is good, like I said, I don't know how else to do it.

However, others express that the Sunday Assembly is often *too* churchy for them, and there are frequent discussions about how to balance being *too* churchy and *not churchy enough* at the Midwest Assembly's organizing meetings. Luke, who has stopped participating in the Midwest Assembly since I interviewed him, told me that he liked the idea of a non-religious church but found the Sunday Assembly to be too much like a church. He said it was "too formalized" because everyone stood for the songs and bowed their heads during the moment of silence. Josie, another member who has since stopped attending, attributed the "churchiness" to the frequent music breaks and a lack of casual interactions between the assembly attendees. As a result, the organizing team has reorganized the service in attempts to cut back on the churchy aspects, while attempting to keep enough of the Sunday Assembly structure so as not to lose the concept entirely. They agreed to rename the "moment of silence" to a "moment of reflection" and began displaying a quote or question to reflect upon during these moments. They also agreed that there would be one less song during the service and more social time to increase interaction and to cut down on the transitions from siting to standing.

Like the debates about radical inclusivity and secular spirituality, the selective appropriation of the church model is rife with contradictions and exceptions that members of the Sunday Assembly continuously navigate. This sentiment is exemplified in Amanda's statement to her fellow organizers below, in which she explains to them that the discussions about how to balance being like a church and not like a church were never going to be fully resolved, and that that was okay. She said:

> We will always have the conversation that it is too much or not enough like church, but the whole purpose of this is to toe the line. And we will never get it right, and we have to be okay with that. We have to embrace the fact that this is the balancing act. I have been on both sides of the argument, and the perfect decisions are going to make up for the ones that are not so perfect.

7 Conclusion: Constructing Positive Non-religion

Like Amanda, who sees the Sunday Assembly as largely a balancing act, most Sunday Assemblers are open to compromising and negotiating the boundaries of what the Sunday Assembly is and will become. The Sunday Assembly is a space where non-religious individuals come to move beyond an identity built on rejection, but who are nonetheless unsure of what that might look like in practice. By selectively drawing on aspects of church organizational structures and spiritual rituals that they have seen work in religious settings, the members of Sunday Assembly hope to cultivate a positive non-religion that is focused on building community, pursuing deeper meaning, and celebrating life.

In this chapter, I have detailed three major themes emerging from my field work with the Sunday Assembly that illustrate how the process of constructing positive non-religion is full of compromises and exceptions; it is a constant negotiation between selectively accommodating religious and spiritual practices and simultaneously maintaining a boundary around the non-religious identity of the organization and its members. Both within the Midwest Assembly and among the members of the larger Sunday Assembly organization, debates abound about the viability of radical inclusivity, the cultivation and promotion of non-theistic rituals and secular spirituality, and the selective appropriation of the contemporary Protestant church model as its organizational structure. But despite disagreements about the shape and content Sunday Assembly, its unifying goal is to move beyond a negative non-religiosity and towards "becoming something else," something that can be positively affirmed and cultivated in practice.

However, my findings here are only one piece of a much larger non-religious landscape. The Sunday Assembly alone is made up of over 70 chapters, and future research should explore the ways that regional and cultural differences among the individual chapters influence the types of individual and collective non-religious identities and practices that take shape. Research should also explore in more depth the organizational dynamics between various non-religious groups and organizations. The organizers of the Midwest Assembly often discuss how they want to maintain a good relationship with other non-religious and atheist groups in the area, but that they are aware that they are competing with them for resources, members, and a space in the larger community. Future research should build on Kettell (2014) and Bagg and Voas (2009) to explore the ways that accommodationist and confrontational non-religious groups interact, both on the local and national level, and the extent to which there are conflicts over representation and resources. Further, do these positive and negative sides of non-religion present themselves in other times and contexts? This chapter has focused on the U.S./U.K. context, but are there other kinds of divisions among non-religious individuals in other countries and historical periods (see for example Quack 2012)? Beyond the Sunday Assembly, more research is needed that more explicitly compares accommodationist non-religious groups like the Sunday Assembly with religious organizations and groups. How do ritual practices like collective singing and moments of silence work differently in religious and non-religious settings?

In mapping the boundary work of the nascent Sunday Assembly, I set out in this chapter to contribute to the growing literature on the substantive beliefs and practices of non-religious individuals and the rich, complex identities they are constructing in relation to religion (e. g. Lee 2015). While non-religious identities have largely been understood as negative identities that indicate a *lack* of beliefs and practices, the Sunday Assembly is made up of non-religious individuals who explicitly reject rejection identities and who are working together to construct new communities and practices that allow them to express a positive non-religion. And while the shape and content of this positive non-religion is still very much under construction, the negotiations surrounding its construction exemplify the nuanced nature of non-religious identity and practice that researchers will need to attend to going forward.

Bibliography

Bagg, Samuel and David Voas. 2009. "The Triumph of Indifference: Irreligion in British Society." In *Atheism & Secularity: Volume 2: Global Experiences* edited by Phil Zuckerman, 91–111. Santa Barbara, CA: Praeger.

Baker, Joseph O. and Buster G. Smith. 2015. *American Secularism: Cultural Contours of Nonreligious Belief Systems.* New York: New York University Press.

Bullivant, Stephen. 2012. "Not So Indifferent After All? Self-conscious Atheism and the Secularisation Thesis." *Approaching Religion* 2(1): 100–106.

Cimino, Richard and Christopher Smith. 2007. "Secular Humanism and Atheism beyond Progressive Secularism." *Sociology of Religion* 68(4): 407–424.

Cimino, Richard and Christopher Smith. 2014. *Atheist Awakening: Secular Activism and Community in America.* New York/Oxford: Oxford University Press.

Cotter, Christopher. 2015. "Without God Yet Not Without Nuance: A Qualitative Study of Atheism and Non-religion Among Scottish University Students." In *Atheist Identities – Spaces and Social Contexts*, edited by Lori Beaman and Steven Tomlins, 171–196. London: Springer International Publishing.

Cragun, Ryan T. 2015. "Who Are the 'New Atheists'?" In *Atheist Identities – Spaces and Social Contexts*, edited by Lori Beaman and Steven Tomlins, 95–211. London: Springer International Publishing.

Kettell, Steven. 2014. "Divided We Stand: The Politics of the Atheist Movement in the United States." *Journal of Contemporary Religion* 29(3): 377–391.

LeDrew, Stephen. 2013a. "Discovering Atheism: Heterogeneity in Trajectories to Atheist Identity and Activism." *Sociology of Religion* 74(4): 431–45.

LeDrew, Stephen. 2013b. "Reply: Toward a Critical Sociology of Atheism: Identity, Politics, Ideology." *Sociology of Religion* 74(4).

LeDrew, Stephen. 2015. "Atheism Versus Humanism: Ideological Tensions and Identity Dynamics." In *Atheist Identities – Spaces and Social Contexts*, edited by Lori Beaman and Steven Tomlins, 53–68. London: Springer International Publishing.

Lee, Lois. 2014. "Secular or Nonreligious? Investigating and Interpreting Generic 'Not Religious' Categories and Populations." *Religion* 44(3): 466–482.

Lee, Lois. 2014. 2015. *Recognizing the Non-religious: Reimagining the Secular*. New York: Oxford University Press.

Pasquale, Frank. 2009. "A Portrait of Secular Group Affiliates." In *Atheism & Secularity: Volume 1: Issues, Concepts, and Definitions*, edited by Phil Zuckerman, 43–87. Santa Barbara, CA: Praeger Perspectives.

Quack, Johannes. 2012. "Organised Atheism in India: An Overview." *Journal of Contemporary Religion* 27(1): 67–85.

Smith, Jesse. 2011. "Becoming an Atheist in America: Constructing Identity and Meaning from the Rejection of Theism." *Sociology of Religion*. 72(2): 215–237.

Smith, Jesse. 2013a. "Creating a Godless Community: The Collective Identity Work of Contemporary American Atheists." *Journal for the Scientific Study of Religion* 52(1): 80–99.

Smith, Jesse. 2013b. "Comment: Conceptualizing Atheist Identity: Expanding Questions, Constructing Models, and Moving Forward." *Sociology of Religion* 74(4): 454–463.

Smith, Jesse. 2017. "Can the Secular Be the Object of Belief and Belonging? The Sunday Assembly." *Qualitative Sociology* 40(1), 83–109.

Walsh, Sadhbh. 2013. "Atheist 'Mega-churches' Undermine What Atheism's Supposed To Be About." *The Guardian*. http://www.theguardian.com/commentisfree/2013/nov/15/atheism-contrary-to-mega-churches. Accessed May 11, 2016.

Winston, Kimberly. 2013. "Atheist 'Mega-churches' Look for Non-believers." *USA Today*. http://www.usatoday.com/story/news/nation/2013/11/10/atheist-mega-churches/3489967/. Accessed May 14, 2016.

Joseph Langston, Joseph Hammer, Ryan Cragun & Mary Ellen Sikes
Inside The Minds and Movement of America's Nonbelievers: Organizational Functions, (Non)Participation, and Attitudes Toward Religion

1 Introduction

Both Campbell's *Toward a Sociology of Irreligion* (1971) and Budd's *Varieties of Unbelief* (1977) described how some members of the secular/freethought movements in late 19th century Britain took a militant approach to religious doctrines, theology, the Bible, and the authority of the church. To these individuals, religion was, at best, nonsense, and, at worst, harmful. Other members preferred a more conciliatory approach characterized by politeness and civility. The latter's goal was obtaining respectability and social acceptance for secularists and atheists. It was their view that the former hostile approach barred those who possessed "advanced religious opinions" from the desired circle of increased social status and thus out of positions of political influence. Indeed, Budd described this division in terms of "militant" and "respectable" wings (Budd 1977, 46, 49, 69), referring to them also as "negative" and "positive" secularism, respectively (also see Rectenwald, this volume).

There are similar divisions between conciliatory and militant views and approaches to secular, humanist, atheist, and freethought (SHAF) movement activism in America today (see Fazzino and Cragun, this volume; Kettell 2013). The noted similarity between this issue today and as described by Campbell and Budd served as the impetus for the study that follows. Has this tension persisted across time, space, and culture? If so, why? Obviously the context covered by Campbell and Budd was quite different from contemporary America, and yet, the term "accommodationist" has come to characterize the conciliatory position for modern American nonbelievers. This term is often applied pejoratively to nonbelievers who *are* accommodationists by nonbelievers who *are not*,[1] whereas

---

[1] The term "accommodationist" was previously and still is used to refer to those who think that science and religion can be accommodated with one another. We point this out to avoid confusion with the term's other, more contemporary usage in referring to accommodation of nonbelievers with the existence of religion.

OpenAccess. © 2017 Joseph Langston, Joseph Hammer, Ryan Cragun & Mary Ellen Sikes, published by De Gruyter. [CC BY-NC-ND] This work is licensed under the Creative Commons Attribution-NonCommercial-NoDerivatives 4.0 License. https://doi.org/10.1515/9783110458657-011

those who wish for the elimination of religion have come to be known as "New Atheists"—whether or not such individuals self-consciously subscribe to this label. Campbell (1971, 37–38, 43, 54) referenced these attitudes with the terms "eliminationists" (or "abolitionists"[2]) and "substitutionists" (or the "replacement" view), although it should be clear that Campbell's substitutionists need not be today's accommodationists, and vice versa. Modern discourse in American SHAF communities does not identify substitutionism and accommodationism as necessarily commensurate, although some contemporary examples of substitutionists in America would include Ethical Culture, some Unitarian Universalist congregations or individuals, and the Sunday Assembly (see chapters by Smith and Frost in this volume). We offer that modern New Atheism in America can still be understood in the same manner described by Campbell in expounding on eliminationism/abolitionism; that is, for our purposes, these terms describe the same attitudinal approach to religion.

Regarding the similarity across place and time, we wondered: what is the "big picture" when it comes to conflicts, schisms, or divisions that might characterize movement participation and SHAF groups in modern America? Nonbelievers in America have been described as a particularly contentious group, prone to fragmentation, and an inability to be organized (although see Smith 2013, 84, who suggests that such problems are becoming a thing of the past; also see Cimino and Smith 2011, 36). Yet, it is not clear how or why this makes them any more disintegrated than other social forms of organization, ecclesiastical or otherwise; in fact, we would observe that instability, inter- and intra-organization contentions, and in-fighting are characteristic of most social movements. Pointedly, Cimino and Smith (2011, 36) stated that "publics open to internal antagonism are publics that are active, not fractured." But, in the specific case of nonbelievers and their movement, certain unanswered questions remained. What do nonbelievers who are *or are not* members of these groups think about the actual or hypothetical goals of these groups? What were these groups doing that might attract or repel greater support? What were groups, leaders, or activists doing that turned people away or polarized either participation in or opinion about the movement? Why didn't nonbelievers who were not members, and never had been, join these groups? When we noticed that the dynamic of eliminationism and accommodationism was present then, in Britain, and now, in the United States, these were the kinds of additional questions that sprang to mind. While

---

2 "Eliminationism is the belief that religion has proved to be erroneous and harmful and thus needs to be abolished" (345). "Substitutionists...are more concerned with building a movement which can effectively displace religion in all its major functions and thus they favour a less centralised structure capable of meeting the needs of its members" (345).

some non-empirical literature spoke to these issues, empirical investigations of these questions were nowhere to be found in previous studies of atheism and nonbelief, so we set out in a pioneering effort to address these questions.

1.1 Previous Research

A few contemporary studies address the eliminationist-accommodationist dynamic. Kettell (2013, 2014), LeDrew (2012, 2014, 2015), and Cimino and Smith (2007, 2010, 2011) all described contention among individual nonbelievers and their groups since the inception of New Atheism in the first decade of the 21st century. Their work points to differences between New Atheists and those nonbelievers who seek, at the most, cooperation and solidarity with religious groups and individuals on social and political issues of mutual concern, or at the least, polite coexistence. While these two positions are not necessarily mutually exclusive, they can be identified as separate strategies or approaches endorsed by different individuals (Kettell 2013).

Kettell (2014, 381), regarding "the atheist movement" in America as a whole, suggested that it had four aims: reducing the influence of religion in the public sphere; criticizing religious belief and promoting atheism; improving civil rights and the social status of atheists; and community building and group cohesion. Echoing Kettell, but referring to New Atheism specifically, Schulzke (2013) described it as "a loosely defined movement that [...] is not a clearly stated ideology and [...] lacks clear leadership as a social movement. Nevertheless, it is possible to identify points of agreement that many or most New Atheists share, as well as their disagreements with other variants of atheism" (780). New Atheists aggressively and unapologetically challenge both the metaphysical claims made by different religions and religious influence on social life, science, and politics. This approach sets them apart from previous forms of nonbelief, in terms of their high-publicity critiques of both Christianity and Islam, and an unwillingness to compromise or coexist with monotheistic religion (Csaszar 2010; Kettell 2013; McAnulla 2014). Notably, for Schulzke, the New Atheists are differentiated from both pre 20th century atheists and modern atheists inclined toward accommodationism by a greater emphasis on political instead of theological opposition to religion (i.e., the New Atheists advance "a form of political liberalism that coheres to core liberal doctrines" [2013, 779]) and by their confidence in science, particularly the natural sciences (Cragun 2014). By contrast, then, New Atheism seeks to supersede traditional atheism by attacking religion's incursion into the public sphere; by preventing religion from being an "alternate discourse" alongside science; and by elevating atheism as a political cause rather than merely a personal, and thus private, perspective (Schulzke 2013).

Kettell (2013, 66–67) described a more moderate approach to religion within the broader nonbeliever movement. Individuals endorsing this position tend to criticize the New Atheist approach for being an "anti-position" that subordinates "the affirmation of ethical values, humanistic virtues, and democratic principles" (Cimino and Smith 2011, 35). Some members of the SHAF/nonbeliever movement who are not New Atheists could be said to desire a neutral public arena that is equally shared by all (or at least one devoid of any undue bias toward one specific religious tradition). Their approach is characterized more by tolerance, coexistence, and a greater focus on the positive as opposed to negative constitutive attributes of nontheism. Both New Atheists and the more moderate nonbelievers appear to equally share a desire for the separation of church and state, but there is conflict over the style or character of approach that should be used in dealing with religious others, as well as conflict over whether it is more important to improve the image and reputation of nonbelievers (Cimino and Smith 2011; Kettell 2013) versus achieving progress toward a religion-free public sphere. In general, then, New Atheists, as eliminationists, are more likely to think overt hostility is both necessary and justified in the struggle against both the *influence and existence* of religion, whereas other nonbelievers, as accommodationists, think that a more respectful or less hostile approach is likelier to achieve the desired end of reducing undue religious influence, while leaving religion extant.

Because no research to date has collected data on nonbeliever attitudes regarding movement goals and how best to approach religion, we set out to examine issues that might serve as the arenas of conflict—the "fractures" that exist among American nonbelievers—as opposed to their agreements. Our study was referred to as *Atheism Looking In* (Langston, Hammer, and Cragun 2014); we were interested in what secularists, humanists, atheists, freethinkers, and nonbelievers in general thought about the broader nonbeliever movement and its aims, and their relation to it. In particular, we were interested in examining attitudes indicative of hostility, or lack thereof, toward religious influence and religious beliefs. As such, we loosely saw our study as a kind of *organizational* study, but our approach was to examine the movement and its groups through the perceptions of the members who made them up, whether affiliated or not, rather than groups themselves as units of analysis.

2 Method: Survey and Sample

We sent a recruitment email to over 100 American SHAF organizations that were located on the Internet and in various directories on, or maintained by, these groups. The email requested participation in our study and contained a hyperlink to our Qualtrics survey. The first page of the survey contained an informed consent, which specified who was eligible to participate (i.e. those who had resided in the U.S. at least five years or who were U.S. citizens; 18 years of age or older). The survey was operational from January 11th, 2014, to February 9th, 2014. A total of 2,527 respondents started the survey, with 2,006 completing it. After coding and cleaning the data, a total nonrandom sample of 1,939 cases remained, all of which had complete responses to all questions. All data reported in results here are based on these cases, except where noted. Respondents from every U.S. state were represented, from a low of three in Hawaii to a high of 149 from Texas. Thirty-two respondents said they did not live in the United States, but data for these were kept under the assumption that these were U.S. citizens living abroad.

In order to analytically address organizational involvement and identity, we divided our final sample into four categories: members of many SHAF groups ("MGs" for "Many Groups"; $n = 581$, 29.9%); members of just one group ("OGs" for "One Group"; $n = 356$, 18.3%); respondents who were once members of at least one group but were not members of any groups at the time of the survey ("FMs" for "Former Members"; $n = 222$, 11.4%); and respondents who had never been members of such groups ("SNAs" for "Secular Nonaffiliates"; $n = 780$, 40.2%). This distinction served as a primary means to analyze differences on other questions asked in the study.

First, we asked nonbelievers about their preferred identity labels, and about their preferences for the goals, activities, and functions of nonbeliever groups (some of which reference within-group activities, with others referencing external activities oriented toward religion or the public). Second, we asked MGs, OGs, and FMs why they thought SNAs did not join nonbeliever groups, and we compared their answers side-by-side with the actual reasons given by SNAs. Third, we examined a series of attitudinal questions about approaches to religion, religious believers, and religious beliefs. Fourth, we asked about respondent willingness to include in their communities what may be unpopular social or political opinions, and we also asked how many secular nonaffiliates the respondent personally knew. Fifth, we ran post hoc analyses to examine a variety of gender and identity label differences in opinions and attitudes. Finally, we obtained external data from the American Secular Census, which further illuminated our focus and offered corroboration for some of our findings.

3 Results

3.1 What were the age, gender, and racial demographics of our sample?

Table 1. Age, Gender, and Race by Group Membership

Demographics	Secular Nonaffiliates ($n = 780$)	Former Members ($n = 222$)	One Group ($n = 356$)	Many Groups ($n = 581$)	All (N = 1939)
Age					
Mean	36.02	35.82	38.98	43.62	38.82
Median	33	31	36	43	36
Mode	24	26	21	27	21
Range	18–82	18–86	18–85	18–88	18–88
Gender					
Male	62.4%	61.5%	58.3%	61.4%	61.9%
Female	37.6%	38.5%	41.7%	37.9%	38.1%
Race					
Nonwhite	8.8%	6.8%	5.3%	5.5%	7.0%
White	91.2%	93.2%	94.7%	94.5%	93.0%

Note: Nine respondents reported "Other" for gender and are excluded from gender reporting in this table.

A one-way ANOVA determined that there was a significant age difference between groups ($F [3, 1939] = 31.4$, $p < .001$). However, because Levene's test for homogeneity of variances revealed that group variances were not equal ($F [3, 1939] = 14.6$, $p < .001$), we employed a Welch Test, which does not assume equal variances ($F [3, 1939] = 30.5$, $p < .001$). Because this result indicated statistically significant differences between group means on age, post hoc comparisons using the Games-Howell procedure were conducted to determine which pairs of the group membership means differed significantly. MGs ($M = 43.62$, $SD = 16.16$)

were statistically significantly older than the other three groups ($p < .001$); OGs ($M = 38.98$, $SD = 16.6$) were statistically significantly older ($p = .01$) than SNAs ($M = 36.02$, $SD = 13.64$). A Chi-Square test further revealed that there was a statistically significant relationship between age and group membership (χ^2 [3, 1939] = 59.06, p < .001, V = .17). More MGs ($n = 355$; 61.1%) were part of the older group than the younger group (when splitting age by the median for the total sample). More SNAs (57.4%) and more FMs (62.6%) were part of the younger group than the older group.

3.2 What did these nonbelievers call themselves?

Table 2. Identity Labels by Group Membership

Label	Secular Nonaffiliates ($n = 780$)	Former Members ($n = 222$)	One Group ($n = 356$)	Many Groups ($n = 581$)	All (N = 1939)
Atheist	78.5%	83.3%	84.0%	90%	83.5%
Humanist	51.4%	67.1%	56.7%	72.8%	60.6%
Secular	51.5%	63.1%	54.5%	68.2%	58.4%
Skeptic	45.6%	60.4%	45.5%	60.2%	51.7%
Nonbeliever	45.4%	51.8%	48.3%	56.1%	49.9%
Freethinker	37.8%	40.1%	46.1%	61.6%	46.7%
Rationalist	31.2%	29.7%	30.1%	40.1%	33.5%
Agnostic	30.3%	26.1%	23.9%	26.7%	27.5%
Non-Theist	19.2%	22.5%	22.2%	34.4%	24.7%
Anti-Theist	18.7%	18.9%	21.9%	32.5%	23.5%
Spiritual But Not Religious	10.1%	9.9%	4.8%	4.6%	7.5%
Other	4.2%	9.5%	5.6%	7.9%	6.2%

Table 2 reports identity labels by group membership level. Selections of labels were mutually inclusive. Even though we used the term "nonbeliever" as an umbrella term, many identity labels can be found in use within SHAF communities. Because these labels, which we assembled from various online sources, were not meant to be exhaustive, we provided an "Other" category in case our respondents did not see their preferred identity labels among the list. It is encouraging that only 6.2% of respondents selected "Other"; even fewer selected none of the 11 labels but only "Other" (eight out of 1,939 respondents, to be exact). Thus, the labels we offered seemed largely adequate to our respondents in order to describe themselves.

3.3 Which goals, activities, or functions of local, regional, or national groups would these nonbelievers support?

Table 3. SHAF Group Goals, Activities, and Functions (GAFs) by Group Membership

GAF	Secular Nonaffiliates ($n=780$)	Former Members ($n=222$)	One Group ($n=356$)	Many Groups ($n=581$)	All ($N=1939$)	Chi Square/ Cramer's V
Charity	73.1%[a]	77%[a]	75.3%[a]	86.1%[b]	77.8%	$\chi^2=34.4$, $V=.13$
SJ Activism	69.4%[a]	68%[a]	66.6%[a]	79.3%[b]	71.7%	$\chi^2=24.9$, $V=.11$
Socialize	57.8%[a]	73%[b]	77.5%[b]	84.2%[c]	71.1%	$\chi^2=122.6$, $V=.25$
Politick	64.9%[ab]	71.6%[b]	61%[a]	84%[c]	70.7%	$\chi^2=78$, $V=.20$
Discussion	52.4%[a]	68%[b]	71.3%[b]	83.8%[c]	67.1%	$\chi^2=152.5$, $V=.28$
Litigate	58.1%[ab]	64.9%[b]	54.2%[a]	79%[c]	64.4%	$\chi^2=83.7$, $V=.20$
Officiate	41.5%[a]	44.1%[a]	46.3%[a]	56.8%[b]	47.3%	$\chi^2=32.4$, $V=.12$
Moral Education	43.7%[a]	41.4%[a*]	39.3%[a]	50.4%[b*]	44.7%	$\chi^2=13.1$, $V=.08$
Proselytize	16.9%[a]	17.6%[a]	19.9%[a]	32.2%[b]	22.1%	$\chi^2=50$, $V=.16$
Other	7.4%	9.5%	9.3%	12.9%	9.7%	N/A

Note: Percentages reflect respondents who support each item as a goal, activity, or function of groups at any organizational level. Response options were mutually inclusive. Percentages within rows that do not share superscripts are significantly different at $p < .01$ or lower, with the exception of "Moral Education" (p = .02) between MGs and FMs, denoted by (*). Because each GAF was collected as its own variable (i.e. selected or not selected), Bonferroni adjustments in pairwise comparisons were not employed in subsequent pairwise comparisons for 2 (selected or not selected) by 2 (group membership x or y) analyses. All omnibus Chi Square and Cramer's V reports for each row are statistically significant, $p < .001$. For all, $df = 3$, $N = 1939$. According to Gravetter and Wallnau (2008), with 3 degrees of freedom, a Cramer's V of .06 or above represents a small effect size; .17 or above represents a medium effect size; and .29 or above represents a large effect size, meaning that Cramer's V for Discussion (.28) and Socialize (.25), as the largest effect sizes for GAFs, approached the threshold of large effect sizes. Discussion = "I think such groups should hold regular meetings for discussing topics related to critical thinking, rationalism, religion, science, philosophy, and other intellectual topics"; Moral Education = "I think such groups should develop and teach programs of moral education and positive values and ethics, or I think such groups should serve as a platform to improve people morally"; Politick = "I think such groups should lobby Congress and lawmakers for secular causes, and, in general, be involved in promoting political views, with the goal of advancing secular views and causes via political processes; such groups should be involved in politics"; Litigate = "I think such groups should litigate and be legal advocates on behalf of secular individuals and causes; such groups should be involved in legal cases"; Socialize = "I think such groups should offer regular social events, recreational outings, and opportunities to socialize and build a sense of community among their members"; Officiate = "I think such groups should provide officials who can conduct life cycle ceremonies such as weddings, funerals, and births"; Proselytize = "I think such groups should use their influence to deliberately convince others to adopt secular or nontheistic views"; Social Justice Activism = "I think such groups should be explicitly involved in social justice efforts to combat racism, sexism, economic inequality, hate crimes, and to support civil rights, equal opportunity, and social equality"; Charity = "I think such groups should be involved in humanitarian activities and charitable contributions".

Compared to the other three groups, MGs over-selected on every goal selection. SNAs only differed from FMs and OGs in SNAs' lower preference for Discussion and Socialize, whereas FMs and OGs only differed on FMs' higher preference for Politick and Litigate. Notably, OGs under-selected compared to SNAs on Social Justice Activism, Politick, Litigate, and Moral Education.

3.4 Why didn't secular nonaffiliates join groups? What did affiliated and formerly affiliated nonbelievers think were the reasons that SNAs did not join?

Table 4. SNA Reasons for Not Joining Groups, Compared to Perceptions of MGs, OGs, and FMs

Reasons Given	Secular Affiliates/ Former Members ($n=1159$)	Secular Nonaffiliates ($n=780$)
Low Priority	55.7%	43.6%
Not Local	54.4%	32.6%
Nonbelief Not Big Part Of Self-Identity	77.5%	30.8%
Too Much Like Atheist Church	49.6%	25%
Too Focused On Attacking Religion	55.2%	24.7%
Intellectual Independence	23.6%	17.8%
Other	13.7%	14.7%
Silly, Pointless, Contradictory	43.1%	12.2%
Too Ideological, Dogmatic, Close-Minded	29.5%	11.8%
Stigma	65%	10.5%
Misguided Or Wrong Goals	22.4%	5.9%
No Interest In Discussion Types	34.6%	5.1%

Note: Multiple selections were allowed. Similar questions were asked of both groups; response options listed here were the same for both groups, with the exception of the proper pronoun replacement (e.g. "I" for Secular Nonaffiliates instead of "they" for Secular Affiliates and Former Members). Nonbelief Not Big Part Of Self Identity = "They don't see nonbelief as a primary part of their self-identity; being a nonbeliever is just not a big deal to them". Silly, Pointless, Contradictory = "They think organized forms of nonbelief are silly, pointless, or self-contradicting". Misguided Or Wrong Goals = "They think such groups have misguided or wrong goals". Too Focused On Attacking Religion = "They think nonbelieving groups are too focused on religion, i.e. attacking and criticizing it". Intellectual Independence = "They value their intellectual independence so much that they are not willing to be told by others what to believe or not believe". Too Ideological, Dogmatic, Close-Minded = "They think such groups are too ideological, dogmatic, or closed-minded about their views". Too Much Like Atheist Church = "They think organized nonbelief mimics organized religion too much, i.e. 'atheist church'". Stigma = "They don't want to risk the social stigma that might come with being a public nonbeliever". Low Priority = "They would join but they simply have better or more important things to do with their time, i.e. it is low priority". Not Local = "They would join but such groups are not locally or immediately available to them". No Interest in Discussion Types = "They have no interest in having philosophical, metaphysical, or intellectual conversations about science, religion, etc."

The guesses of Secular Affiliates and FMs placed the most emphasis on stigma, and on nonbelief not being an important part of SNA self-identity. However, SNAs reported that they mostly did not join because they have more important things to do with their time. Roughly a third of SNAs indicated that they would join if groups were local to them, whereas nearly a third of SNAs said that being a nonbeliever simply wasn't that important to them. Among the "Other" responses, which triggered open-ended short responses in the survey apparatus, 21 respondents indicated "Not enough time"; 14 said that they were "introverted, shy, not social"; another 13 said that they were unaware of available groups nearby, and another 11 indicated that they were "non-joiners". Lastly, 10 respondents indicated that atheists and/or their groups "promoted negative views".

3.5 How willing were nonbelievers to endorse nonbeliever groups openly attacking or not attacking religion?

Table 5. Willingness to Attack or Not Attack Religion by Group Membership

Response	Secular Nonaffiliates (n = 780)	Former Members (n = 222)	One Group (n = 356)	Many Groups (n = 581)	All (N = 1939)
Attack	4.9%	4.5%	4.5%	6.5%	5.2%
Depends	61.7%[b]	67.6%[b]	65.7%[b]	74.7%[a]	66.9%
Refrain	7.3%	6.8%	4.8%	4.3%	5.8%
Focus Within	19.2%[b]	15.3%[b]	18%[b]	9.6%[a]	15.6%
None Of Above	6.9%	5.9%	7%	4.8%	6.1%

Note: Omnibus χ^2 (12, 1939) = 41.3, $p < .001$, V =.08. Subsequent z-score comparisons for each row, employing Bonferroni corrections (p = .001), revealed that MGs were statistically significantly different from the other three groups on selections for "Depends" and "Focus Within". Attack = "Nonbelieving groups should always or usually openly criticize and attack religion". Refrain = "Nonbelieving groups should always or usually refrain from openly attacking religion". Depends = "What nonbelieving groups should do depends on context and various other factors; sometimes they should openly attack religion, and sometimes they should refrain from openly attacking religion; it depends on various considerations". Focus Within = "Nonbelieving groups should not even worry about openly attacking religion, but should instead focus their attentions and efforts within their own groups".

A majority of nonbelievers said that groups should neither refrain from nor always choose to attack or criticize religion and religious beliefs. While small minorities said that groups should always engage in one of these options (5.2% Attack vs. 5.8% Refrain), three times as many said that groups should not worry about attacking religion, but should instead focus their groups' efforts within the group itself.

3.6 How willing were nonbelievers to seek the eradication of religion, if possible, or to seek common ground with believers and not try to eradicate religion?

Table 6. Willingness to Eradicate or Accommodate to Religion by Group Membership

Response	Secular Nonaffiliates ($n = 780$)	Former Members ($n = 222$)	One Group ($n = 356$)	Many Groups ($n = 581$)	All (N = 1939)
Eradicate	22.6%[a]	19.8%[a]	24.4%[a]	29.1%[b]	24.5%
Accommodate	63.3%[a]	64.9%[a]	57.6%[a]	56.1%[b]	60.3%
Ignore	3.6%	4.5%	6.2%	4.1%	4.3%
Unsure	10.5%	10.8%	11.8%	10.7%	10.8%

Note: While omnibus Chi Square testing was marginally statistically significant different (χ^2 [9, 1939] = 16.5, p = .057, V = .05), subsequent z-score comparisons for each row, employing Bonferroni corrections (p = .002) revealed that MGs were statistically significantly different from the other three groups on selections for "Eradicate" and "Accommodate", indicated by superscripts across rows. Eradicate = "If possible, religion should be eradicated entirely". Accommodate = "Secularists, nontheists, and atheists should seek accommodation with religious people to achieve common goals; beyond that, they should leave religious people alone and not seek to eradicate religion". Ignore = "Secularists, nontheists, and atheists should neither work with religious people on common causes nor should they seek to eradicate religion in its various forms".

A majority of nonbelievers said that nonbelievers should not only work with religious people to accomplish common goals, such as the separation of church and state, but that no attempt should be made to eradicate religion. A quarter of respondents opted for the elimination option, whereas very few said that nonbelievers should pursue neither course of action. While we cannot say anything definitive about the relatively high number of "Unsure" responses on this question, this could be indicative of ambivalence about how to approach religious people and religious beliefs. It could also be indicative of an attitude which suggests that nonbelievers should work with believers to achieve common goals while simultaneously seeking to eradicate religion, an opinion offered by at least one respondent in post-study feedback.

3.7 How willing were nonbelievers to mock or ridicule religious beliefs, or to refrain from doing so?

Table 7. Willingness to Use or Not Use Mockery/Ridicule of Religion by Group Membership

Response	Secular Nonaffiliates ($n = 780$)	Former Members ($n = 222$)	One Group ($n = 356$)	Many Groups ($n = 581$)	All ($N = 1939$)
Avoid	37.2%[a]	31.5%[a]	34.6%[a]	22%[b]	31.5%
Depends	54.9%[a]	58.6%[a]	57.9%[a]	69%[b]	60.1%
Don't Avoid	6%	6.3%	5.9%	7.7%	6.5%
Unsure	1.9%	3.6%	1.7%	1.2%	1.9%

Note: Omnibus $\chi^2 (9, 1939) = 44.1$, $p < .001$, $V = .08$. Subsequent z-score comparisons for each row, employing Bonferroni corrections ($p = .002$) revealed that MGs were statistically significantly different from the other three groups on "Avoid" and "Depends", indicated by superscripts across rows. Avoid = "Mockery and ridicule of religious people and religious beliefs should be avoided; they are counterproductive or make nonbelievers look bad". Don't Avoid = "Mockery and ridicule of religious people and religious beliefs should be encouraged or used; it is the treatment that religious beliefs deserve, and to avoid using them is to give religious people and religious beliefs a free pass that they don't deserve". Depends = "Some degree of mockery and ridicule are acceptable and/or recommendable, but it just depends on various different things".

A majority said that whether mockery and ridicule should be applied to religious people and religious beliefs simply depends on various considerations. A relatively large minority of respondents said that mockery and ridicule should be avoided because they are counter-productive or make nonbelievers look bad, although fewer MGs than any of the other groups selected this option.

3.8 How willing or unwilling were nonbelievers to include or exclude unpopular social or political opinions from their communities or the movement in general?

Table 8. Willingness to Accept or Not Accept Unpopular Social and Political Opinions in Secular/Atheist Communities by Group Membership

Response	Secular Nonaffiliates (n = 780)	Former Members (n = 222)	One Group (n = 356)	Many Groups (n = 581)	All (N = 1939)
Incompatible	17.8%[a]	14.0%[a]	20.8%[a]	24.3%[b]	19.9%
Compatible	71.7%	74.3%	65.7%	66.3%	69.3%
Not Sure	10.5%	11.7%	13.5%	9.5%	10.9%

Note: Omnibus χ^2 (6, 1939) = 17.7, p = .007, V = .06. Incompatible and Compatible options refer to whether the respondent thought that unpopular social or political opinions were incompatible or compatible with a secular view of the world, and thus acceptable or unacceptable views to be held in SHAF communities. Subsequent z-score comparisons for each row, employing Bonferroni corrections (p = .002) revealed that MGs are statistically significantly different (p < .05) from the other three groups on "Incompatible", indicated by superscripts across rows.

The nonbeliever movement has sustained problems with diversity issues (Hassall and Bushfield 2014; Kettell 2013, 67; Miller 2013; Schnabel et al. 2016), including racism, sexism, and social justice issues. On this question, we were not able to specify *which sorts* of social or political opinions we intended, without leading respondents. If we had been very specific, these answers may very well have changed, but, the question as we asked it was meant to be taken by the respondent as meaning whatever they imagined regarding "social" and "political" opinions. This may account for the relatively high amount of "Not Sure" responses. At any rate, the majority attitude of nonbelievers here was characterized by inclusion rather than exclusion.

3.9 What did nonbelievers think about the compatibility, or lack thereof, between science and religion?

Table 9. Compatibility of Science and Religion by Group Membership

Response	Secular Nonaffiliates ($n = 780$)	Former Members ($n = 222$)	One Group ($n = 356$)	Many Groups ($n = 581$)	All ($N = 1939$)
Incompatible	48.7%[a]	49.1%[a]	56.7%[a,b]	60.1%[b]	53.6%
Pretend Compatible	25.5%	25.2%	26.1%	25.5%	25.6%
Compatible	25.8%[a]	25.7%[a,b]	17.1%[b,c]	14.5%[c]	20.8%

Note: Omnibus χ^2 (6, 1939) = 34.8, $p < .001$, V = .09. Subsequent z-score comparisons for each row, employing Bonferroni corrections ($p = .002$), revealed that MGs differed from FMs and SNAs but not OGs on "Incompatible". MGs differed from FMs and SNAs but not OGs on "Compatible", whereas OGs differed only from SNAs on this option. Incompatible = "Science and religion are obviously incompatible; faith is irrational, and endorsing the unity of science and religion only enables delusion". Pretend Compatible = "Science and religion are not truly compatible but we should pretend that this is the case so as not to lose public support for science; it is valuable for nonbelievers to work alongside religious believers to pursue shared goals, and an individual's religious belief is irrelevant unless it leads them to distort or misrepresent science". Compatible = "Science and religion may answer different questions but they are compatible in certain ways; failing to see this is either unimaginative or intolerant".

Extending the accommodationist versus eliminationist argument to discussions of science and religion, we tried to formulate questions that would reflect these varying approaches. Attitudes about science and religion among members of the SHAF movement have ranged from compatible (Gould 1999) to incompatible (Stenger 2009). The Pretend Compatible response was our attempt to provide an option for those who, while not seeing science and religion as compatible, would not choose to make an issue out of this disjunction as long as it did not threaten the integrity of the scientific process. Given these selections alongside Incompatible responses, which came from a majority of each group membership category, most nonbelievers do not think science and religion are compatible, though the gap between MGs and SNAs on Compatible is particularly salient.

4 Additional Analyses: Gender

The statistically significant demographic differences that emerged across our questions primarily centered upon gender rather than age or race, thus we present the gender differences of interest only.

4.1 What were the gender differences, if any, for GAF selections?

Table 10. Gender Differences on Goals, Activities, and Functions (GAF) Selections

GAF	Male ($n = 1185$)	Female ($n = 745$)	Chi Square/ Cramer's V
Proselytize	29.1%	10.7%	$X^2 = 90$, $V = .21$
Litigate	69.7%	56%	$X^2 = 37.6$, $V = .14$
Politick	73.3%	66.4%	$X^2 = 10.4$, $V = .07$
Officiate	44.9%	51.3%	$X^2 = 7.4$, $V = .06$

Note: For all, $df = 1$, $p < .001$, except Officiate, $p = .006$. GAFs were only included here if they reached statistical significance with gender.

Females had a lower preference for Proselytize, whereas more minor gender differences emerged in the lower female selections of Litigate, Politick, and Officiate.

4.2 What were the gender differences, if any, on opinion and attitudinal questions?

Table 11. Gender Differences on Questions 3.5, 3.6, 3.8, and 3.10

Attack or Not Attack	Male (n = 1185)	Female (n = 745)	Chi Square/ Cramer's V
Attack[a]	7.3%	1.7%	
Depends[a]	71.2%	60.4%	χ^2 (4, 1930) = 81.5, $p < .001$
Refrain[a]	4.2%	8.6%	V = .20
Focus Within[a]	12%	21.5%	
None of the Above[a]	5.2%	7.8%	

Eradicate or Accommodate	Male (n = 1185)	Female (n = 745)	Chi Square/ Cramer's V
Eradicate[a]	30.5%	15%	
Accommodate[a]	54%	70.3%	χ^2 (3, 1930) = 64.9, $p < .001$
Ignore	4.4%	4.2%	V = .18
Unsure/Undecided	11.1%	10.5%	

Use of Mockery and Ridicule	Male (n = 1185)	Female (n = 745)	Chi Square/ Cramer's V
Avoid[a]	24.6%	42.7%	
Depends[a]	65.1%	52.2%	χ^2 (3, 1930) = 89.1, $p < .001$
Don't Avoid[a]	8.9%	2.7%	V = .21
Unsure	1.5%	2.4%	

Science and Religion	Male (n = 1185)	Female (n = 745)	Chi Square/ Cramer's V
Incompatible[a]	59.3%	44.4%	
Pretend Compatible	25%	26.6%	χ^2 (2, 1930) = 58.2, $p < .001$
Compatible[a]	15.7%	29%	V = .17

Note: [a] Indicates statistically significant differences between column percentages, at least $p < .05$.

Although majorities chose to circumstantially criticize or ridicule/mock religion, wherever respondents had the opportunity to decide between eliminationist and accommodationist attitudes, females exhibited the latter more so than males. The fact that the nonbeliever movement is majority male may especially contribute to public perceptions (or the actuality) that it is a hostile or militant movement (cf. also Silver et al., 2014, on descriptions of anti-theism and views of "types" of nonbelievers of one another).

5 Identity Labels: Evidence That They Matter

We endeavored to provide additional analysis for "atheist", "secular", and "humanist" identity labels because some literature suggests potential "approach" differences between secular humanists and atheists (e.g. Kettell, 2013, 2014; Cimino and Smith, 2007, 2011; Smith and Cimino, 2012). Only 75 respondents (3%) selected, at least, both "secular" and "humanist" but not "atheist". On the other hand, 387 respondents (19.9%) selected, at least, "atheist" but neither "secular" nor "humanist". A majority of 822 respondents (42.3%) selected all three of these labels, whereas 142 respondents (9.9%) selected, at the least, none of these three labels. This left 513 ALI respondents (26.4%) who did not fall into any of these four reconstituted categories. What were the differences, if any, between these four categories?

5.1 How did these identity labels compare on GAF selections?

Table 12. Identity Label Differences on Goals, Activities, and Functions (GAF) Selections

GAF	SH Not Atheists ($n = 75$)	Atheists Not SH ($n = 387$)	All Three ($n = 822$)	None of the Three ($n = 142$)	All ($N = 1426$)	Chi Square/ Cramer's V
Politick	64%[a]	65%[a]	80%[b]	48.6%[c]	72.5%	$X^2 = 80$, $V = .23$
Discussion	74.7%[a]	56.6%[b]	77.1%[a]	50%[b]	68.7%	$X^2 = 77.9$, $V = .23$
Litigate	58.7%[a]	59.2%[a]	74.8%[b]	41.5%[c]	66.4%	$X^2 = 76.4$, $V = .23$
Charity	82.7%[a]	68.5%[b]	86.6%[a]	64.1%[b]	79.2%	$X^2 = 74.8$, $V = .23$
SJ Activism	86.7%[a]	64.3%[b]	79.8%[a]	52.8%[b]	73.3%	$X^2 = 70.9$, $V = .22$
Socialize	66.7%[a]	61.2%[a]	79.2%[b]	55.6%[a]	71.3%	$X^2 = 62$, $V = .21$
Officiate	54.7%[a]	34.4%[b]	56.3%[a]	36.6%[b]	48.3%	$X^2 = 60.2$, $V = .20$
Moral Education	46.7%[ac]	33.9%[b]	51.5%[a]	41.5%[bc]	45.4%	$X^2 = 33.9$, $V = .15$
Proselytize	10.7%[a]	19.4%[a]	27.6%[b]	12.7%[a]	23%	$X^2 = 27.7$, $V = .14$

Note: For all, $df = 3$, $p < .001$. Percentages in rows that do not share the same superscript are statistically significantly different, at least $p < .05$. "Secular Humanists" was constructed by combining those who chose, at least, both "Secular" and "Humanist" from identity labels, despite the fact that not everyone who selected one selected the other; see Table 2. From ALI, at least 1,132 respondents chose, at least, "Secular" and 1,175 chose, at least, "Humanist".

Those who selected "All Three" identity labels were different on every goal selection from both "Atheists Not Secular Humanists" and "None of the Three". "Secular Humanists Not Atheists", when compared to "Atheists Not Secular Humanists", showed higher selections on each goal for which they were statistically significantly different. In this regard, "Atheists Not Secular Humanists" were more similar to "None of the Three" than were "Secular Humanists Not Atheists", whereas this latter group was more similar to "All Three". Those selecting "All Three" labels out-selected the other three groups on all goals, except for Social Justice Activism, which was most selected by "Secular Humanists Not Atheists". Thus, secular humanists who did not also call themselves atheists were more similar to those who identified with all three labels, whereas those who only called themselves atheists, and not secular humanists, were more similar to those who chose none of these labels, though the differences between all four groups are also apparent (cf. Cotter, 2015).

6 Additional Data: The American Secular Census

In the course of carrying out our study, we became aware of another data source which shed additional light on our topic: the American Secular Census (ASC). Launched on November 7, 2011, the ASC describes itself as an independent national registry of demographic and viewpoint data recorded on secular Americans. Census registrants are U.S. citizens or permanent residents over 18 years of age who are skeptical of supernatural claims, including those generally associated with religion. Each registrant maintains an ASC website account used to complete 13 Census forms which collect personal and household information, a secular profile, a religious profile, political activism and voting patterns, philanthropy habits, parenting information, military service, experiences with discrimination, public policy and social views, and opinions about secular advocacy.

For the purpose of making comparisons to our own data, we acquired data from Personal and Secular Profiles in the ASC online database on November 14th, 2015. At that time, the sample size for registrants who had completed both forms was 1,340 respondents. Table 13 shows a comparison of age, gender, and race between ALI and ASC samples. Notably, the ASC respondents were older than ALI respondents. Outside of this, although we cannot make statistical comparisons, both sets of data seem surprisingly similar, though both are composed of nonrandom, self-selected samples.

6.1 What were the demographic similarities or differences between ALI and ASC?

Table 13. Age, Gender, and Race Comparison between ALI and ASC

Atheism Looking In (N = 1939)		American Secular Census (N = 1340)	
Age			
Mean	38.8	Mean	42.3
Median	36	Median	40
Mode	21	Mode	31
Range	18–88	Range	19–86
Gender			
Male	1185 (61.1%)	Male	778 (58.1%)
Female	745 (38.4%)	Female	539 (40.2%)
Other	9 (0.05%)	Other	23 (1.7%)
Race			
Nonwhite	135 (7%)	Nonwhite	123 (9.1%)
White	1804 (93%)	White	1217 (90.8%)

6.2 How active in the nonbeliever movement were ASC respondents?

Table 14. ASC Respondent Level of Involvement in the Nonbeliever Movement

Level of Involvement	Frequency (N = 1340)
I'm aware of organizations and events but have not participated	40.7%
I'm slightly active in the movement	27.9%
I'm pretty active in the movement	8.8%
None; I'm vaguely aware it exists but haven't explored further	6.1%
I'm an insider (e.g. leader, employee, major donor)	5.5%
None; this is the first I've heard of it	5.2%
I'm a former participant who is currently inactive	5%
Something not listed here	0.8%

SNAs comprised 40.2% of the ALI sample. In the ASC sample, those who are comparable make up 52%, if adding the first, fourth, and sixth categories from Table 14. If respondents indicated that they were not active in the atheist/secular movement (in this case, however, using only Options 1 and 7 from Table 14), this triggered a conditional question in the ASC questionnaire which asked about their reasons for not being involved.

6.3 What reasons did inactive ASC respondents give for lack of participation?

Table 15. ASC Inactive Respondent Reasons for Lack of Nonbeliever Movement Participation

Reason	Frequency ($n = 613$)
Insufficient time	57.9%
Events inconvenient	37.4%
Insufficient money	36.4%
Not a joiner	31%
Some other reason	16.5%
Events uninteresting to me	10.8%
Not really sure	10.4%
General disinterest	9.6%
Fear of damaging my relationships	8.8%
Lack of childcare	8%
Bad experience with group, person, or event	7.8%
Don't see relevance to my life	6%
Not open about my secularism	5.2%
Health issues	4.7%
Publications uninteresting to me	2.3%

Even though ALI provided an "Other" category so that respondents could list reasons that were not part of the formal listing, 36% of inactive ASC respondents said that "Insufficient Money" was a reason for lack of participation; this did not emerge at all in our study. Because selections for "Events Inconvenient" and "Insufficient Money" were very close, we further determined that 112 respondents (18.2%) selected both options, meaning that for a majority, these were distinct selections. The top reason for inactivity, "Insufficient Time", would support our own finding that respondents did not prioritize participation. This raises the question of whether these respondents would join or participate more often if they did have the time. Also, though lack of time is comparable to participation being a low priority, neither of these compares to nonbelief not being a salient component of self-identity (see Stryker 2000). Nonbelief could be a primary part of self-identity even in the event of insufficient time or if one has higher-priority life obligations (e. g. family, work, practical projects, hobbies, friends, etc.). Roughly a third of respondents from ALI said that they would join groups if they were local; this compares to 37% of non-active nonbelievers from ASC saying that events are "inconvenient", though inconvenience could also refer to schedule conflict, not physical proximity or lack of local groups. This point also dovetails with lack of time as a top reason. Lastly, 31% of ASC non-affiliates said they were not joiners, which comports with the qualitative responses we received from 14 ALI respondents (see Table 4), indicating that they were introverted, shy, not social, or not interested in socializing.

6.4 What did ASC respondents find beneficial about their involvement in nonbeliever groups?

Table 16. Benefits of Participation Experienced by ASC Respondents

Benefits	Frequency ($n = 641$)
Friendships and community	74.9%
Personal development	47.3%
Social or cultural acceptance	43.2%
Educational resources	32.8%
Service opportunities	25.4%
Moral guidance	15.3%
Political influence	15.3%
Support with family issues	11.2%
No benefits at all	8.1%
Support with other problems	6.6%
Something not listed here	6.2%
Career opportunities	4.8%
Youth programs	3.3%
Support with substance abuse	0.5%

An alternate strategy to our own would have been to ask secular affiliates about the advantages of participation in the movement and membership in its groups.

As Table 16 shows, the most frequently derived benefits were friendships and community; personal development (e.g. leadership, confidence); and social or cultural acceptance, a factor that we would suggest probably relates to stigma against nonbelievers in America (see Table 4).

6.5 What did ASC respondents find disadvantageous about their involvement in nonbeliever groups?

Table 17. Disadvantages of Participation Experienced by ASC Respondents

Disadvantages	Frequency ($n = 641$)
No disadvantages at all	51.3%
Problems with family members	24.6%
Problems with friends	15%
Problems within the organization itself	12.8%
Problems in the workplace	9.2%
Problems in my community	7.3%
Conflict with mission or values	7%
Something not listed here	6.2%

Yet another approach alternate to ours would have been to ask about disadvantages that came with movement and group participation. In Table 17, a majority reported no disadvantages due to their participation, whereas, consistent with Cragun et al. (2012), the most likely disadvantages occurred for social relationships with family members or friends. With regard to internal conflict, 12% said they had problems within their own groups, while another 7% said they had conflict with the nonbeliever movement mission or values.

7 Conclusion

Some nonbelievers don't have time to join groups but would if they in fact did have time, and if these groups and related events were readily available and convenient. For these nonbelievers, nonbelief is a part of their identity; for others, nonbelief is not a part of their identity, and they would not join such groups even if they had the time or if such groups were available. Though using a small sample, Cimino and Smith (2011) found that an appreciable number of their respondents engaged in activism and participation exclusively online. A separate but relevant issue concerns historical anti-authoritarianism and the tendency toward a decentralized organization of humanist, atheist, and freethought groups (Budd 1977). The Internet provides the opportunity, for those for whom nonbelief is important, to engage in movement participation and activism; this may comport well with a preference for individual, or non-institutional activism carried out on the individual's own terms. On this basis, many SNAs likely eschew formal organizational participation in favor of private, individual participation. This is similar to Cimino and Smith's (2011, 32) "cultural secularists", who "[try] to discredit religious belief and advocate for change on more personal and individual terms, outside the channels created for this purpose by the dominant secular organizations."

Our gender differences in particular proved interesting. The lesser hostility of women betokens consequences for a movement that is male-dominated in both its membership and its leadership; it stands to reason that a female-led movement might result in noticeable differences in strategies, and thus also outcomes. It is possible that such a movement might more readily achieve social acceptance in the American public at large, or at least diminished stigma—although this in turn depends on what one thinks about the efficacy of an accommodationist strategy over an eliminationist strategy (see Cragun and Fazzino, this volume, concerning the organizational leadership of Madalyn Murray O'Hair). Certainly, females in our data demonstrate a willingness to engage in mockery/ridicule and criticism of religion and religious beliefs, regardless of whether they selected "elimination" or "accommodation". To the extent that female leadership increases, this may result in a more gender-balanced membership. Although this seems obvious, such change in leadership may also have the effect of increasing the number of women in the movement by virtue of the fact that "hostile" attitudes turn them away. Noticeably, 33% of our SNA female respondents said that one reason they didn't join groups was because of how focused such groups were on attacking or criticizing religion (compared to 19% of male respondents).

We cannot suggest that gender differences in attitudes toward hostility, mockery, and criticism of religion are a *strong* ground of contention that exists in and between groups that make up the nonbeliever or secular movement (pointedly, most of our males also fall into the more accommodating half of this attitudinal divide). Some data indicate that the gender ratio among nonbelievers has shifted in favor of a growing number of women (cf. Hassall and Bushfield 2014; cf. also Barna Group, 2015). Nevertheless, it is possible that part of this increasing diversity in membership is a result of strategy differences where women have come to gain greater and more positions of leadership. If not actual, the effect is at least feasible.

The questions we asked and the data we analyzed were part of our effort to ultimately understand *differences* between nonbeliever ideas, preferences, and attitudes across a variety of affiliative statuses. Despite a nonrandom sample, the greatest value provided by our study comes from descriptive insights that can be examined *when and if* a viable random sample becomes available. For example, perhaps nonbelieving men and women in the larger population do not truly differ regarding eliminationist and otherwise hostile attitudes toward religion, but, as we found the opposite here, future research can investigate a random sample to see if this relationship would hold. The same notion applies to any descriptive insights generated from this study. Future studies should take note of the fact that some nonbelievers could be described as the opposite of "MG/All Three" individuals. In other words, we can identify this category of nonbeliever as someone for whom nonbelief is highly inconsequential, a facet of their lives that likely does not shape or influence behaviors and activities (these would be "apatheists" per Shook's chapter in this volume). It seems likely that this group could only be reached through a nationally representative random survey (e.g. GSS, ARIS, etc.), although at present such nationally representative datasets do not contain data concerning secular and atheist organizations. It would be interesting to see if and/or how this category differed from our four groups. Future studies might further benefit from determining why it is that former members of groups are, in fact, *former* members, that is, the circumstances or reasons for their disaffiliation. We speculate that such reasons would largely resonate with the more pragmatic, as opposed to ideological, concerns that were expressed here.

One assumption we employed was that dividing respondents into the four group categories would produce meaningful analyses. While this is obvious, there are finer group membership conceptualizations that might have been used to greater analytical effect, such as those found in the ASC (see Table 14). In the sociology of religion, categories such as belief, belonging, identification, behavior, and salience are employed in the quantitative analysis of religion; we would suggest that similar categories, if considered dynamically (and dimensionally?) rather than statically, might prove useful in analyzing nonbelievers and distinctions among them (see Cotter 2015; Silver et al. 2014). Because we sought to gauge "approach" attitudes toward religion, a better method for measurement in the future might be to develop a survey instrument with standardized responses, measured at least ordinally so that other, more sophisticated assessments could be made. Lastly, Mastiaux's chapter in this volume is a fine example of how organization members and their "participation motives" may be characterized; as a qualitative study, it is a welcome complement to our own quantitative approach.

It is worth bearing in mind that the nonbeliever movement did, in fact, exist prior to the year 2000, yet it has more vitality and visibility today than before. What ultimately becomes of it will depend, in part, on the vitality and condition of American religion. Despite the fact that Christianity in America has been forecasted to decline (Hackett et al. 2015; Stinespring and Cragun 2015), it seems unlikely that a minority of American nonbelievers would wish to back off from a chance to either effectively rid their country of religion, or at least secure a victory for neutrality in the public and political spheres. If American Christianity does decline as predicted (as other organizational participation has; Putnam, 2001), then this might attenuate types and magnitudes of divisions between various nonbelievers, especially to the extent that such decline might bring about reduced religious influence in the political sphere, or greater social acceptability of nonbelievers. It could also have the effect of shifting SHAF strategies and approaches to eliminationist or accommodationist sides, such that one approach becomes more dominant than the other. Until then, as Kettell (2013, 2014) and Cimino and Smith (2011) have noted, both eliminationist and accommodationist approaches fulfill niches that match the desires of respective movement members. Kettell (2014, 388) offers that this may be to the advantage of such a movement:

> The absence of a consistent or uniform approach furnishes the movement with a high degree of flexibility and dynamism, enabling the formation of loose and adaptive alliances in response to specific issues of concern that may arise, providing multiple sites of access and points of entry to atheist groups and ideas and numerous ways of getting its messages across to a variety of audiences.

Our results not only echo this sentiment, but suggest a blending of these two views on the part of many individual nonbelievers, despite the fact that most responses concerning hostility in our study ranged from moderate to minor. Even majorities of those in our study who took an accommodationist stance did not opt out of circumstantially attacking, mocking, or ridiculing religion and religious beliefs. In the end, a more apt metaphor to accurately capture the situation may be one that does not describe "camps" but rather a sliding scale tempered by circumstance.

Bibliography

Barna Group. Mar 2015. State of Atheism in America. Accessible at https://www.barna.org/barna-update/culture/713-2015-state-of-atheism-in-america#.Vw7wVzArKhc
Budd, Susan. 1977. *Varieties of Unbelief: Atheists and Agnostics in English Society, 1850–1960*. London: Heinemann.
Campbell, Colin. 1971. *Toward a Sociology of Irreligion*. London: Macmillan.
Cimino, Richard, and Christopher Smith. 2007. "Secular Humanism and Atheism Beyond Progressive Secularism." *Sociology of Religion* 68: 407–424.
Cimino, Richard, and Christopher Smith. 2010. "The New Atheism and the Empowerment of American Freethinkers." In *Religion and the New Atheism: A Critical Appraisal*, edited by Amarnath Amarasingam, 139–156. Leiden: Brill.
Cimino, Richard, and Christopher Smith. 2011. "The New Atheism and the Formation of the Imagined Secularist Community." *Journal of Media and Religion* 10: 24–38.
Cotter, Christopher R. 2015. "Without God yet Without Nuance: A Qualitative Study of Atheism and Non-religion Among Scottish Students." In *Atheist Identities-Spaces and Social Contexts*, edited by Lori Beaman and Steven Tomlins, 171–194. London: Springer International Publishing.
Cragun, Ryan. 2014. "Who are the New Atheists?" In *Atheist Identities: Spaces and Social Contexts*, edited by Lori Beaman and Steven Tomlins, 195–211. Springer International Publishing.
Cragun, Ryan T., Barry Kosmin, Ariela Keysar, Joseph H. Hammer, and Michael Nielsen. 2012. "On the Receiving End: Discrimination Toward the Non-Religious in the United States." *Journal of Contemporary Religion* 27: 105–127.
Cragun, Ryan, and Lori L. Fazzino. 2014. "Splitters: Lessons from Monty Python for Nontheist/Freethought Organizations in the US." Presentation at the Annual Meeting of the Society for the Scientific Study of Religion in Indianapolis, IN.
Csaszar, David. 2010. "Standing on the Shoulders of Giants: The Voice of the 'New' Atheists." *Over Dinner: The Laurier M.A. Journal of Religion and Culture*, 1.
Gravetter, Frederick, and Larry Wallnau. 2008. *Essentials of Statistics for the Behavioral Sciences* (6th ed.). Belmont: Thomas Wadsworth.
Gould, Stephen Jay. 1999. *Rocks of Ages: Science and Religion in the Fullness of Life*. New York: Harmony Books.
Hackett, Conrad, Marcin Stonawski, Michaela Potančoková, Brian J. Grim, and Vegard Skirbekk. 2015. "The Future Size of Religiously Affiliated and Unaffiliated Populations." *Demographic Research* 32: 829–842.
Hassall, Christopher, and Ian Bushfield. 2014. "Increasing Diversity in Emerging Non-Religious Communities." *Secularism and Nonreligion* 3: 1–9.
Kettell, Steven. 2013. "Faithless: The Politics of New Atheism." *Secularism and Nonreligion* 2: 61–72.
Kettell, Steven. 2014. "Divided We Stand: The Politics of the Atheist Movement in the United States." *Journal of Contemporary Religion* 29: 377–391.
Langston, Joseph, Joseph Hammer, and Ryan T. Cragun. 2015. "Atheism Looking In: On the Goals and Strategies of Organized Nonbelief." *Science, Religion and Culture* 2: 70–85.
LeDrew, Stephen. 2012. "The Evolution of Atheism: Scientific and Humanistic Approaches." *History of the Human Sciences* 25: 70–87.

LeDrew, Stephen. 2014. "Atheists are Believers," NSRN Blog, March 21, 2014, http://blog.nsrn.net/2014/03/21/atheists-are-believers/. Accessed on 31 May 2014.

LeDrew, Stephen. 2015. "Atheism Versus Humanism: Ideological Tensions and Identity Dynamics." In *Atheist Identities-Spaces and Social Contexts*, edited by Lori Beaman and Steven Tomlins, 53–68. London: Springer International Publishing.

McAnulla, Stuart. 2014. "Secular Fundamentalists: Characterising the New Atheist Approach to Secularism, Religion and Politics." *British Politics* 9: 124–145.

Miller, Ashley F. 2013. "The Non-Religious Patriarchy: Why Losing Religion HAS NOT Meant Losing White Male Dominance." *Cross Currents* 63: 211–226.

Putnam, R. D. (2001). *Bowling Alone: The Collapse and Revival of American Community.* Simon and Schuster.

Schnabel, Landon, Matthew Facciani, Ariel Sincoff-Yedid, and Lori L. Fazzino. Forthcoming. "Gender and Atheism: Paradoxes, Contradictions, and an Agenda for Future Research." *Annual Review of the Sociology of Religion.*

Schulzke, Marcus. 2013. "The Politics of New Atheism." *Politics and Religion* 6: 778–799.

Silver, Christopher F., Thomas J. Coleman III, Ralph W. Hood Jr, and Jenny M. Holcombe. 2014. "The Six Types of Nonbelief: A Qualitative and Quantitative Study of Type and Narrative." *Mental Health, Religion & Culture* 17: 990–1001.

Smith, Christopher, and Richard Cimino. 2012. "Atheisms Unbound: The Role of the New Media in the Formation of a Secularist Identity." *Secularism and Nonreligion* 1: 17–31.

Smith, Jesse M. 2013. "Creating a Godless Community: The Collective Identity Work of Contemporary American Atheists." *Journal for the Scientific Study of Religion* 52: 80–99.

Stenger, Victor J. 2009. *The New Atheism: Taking a Stand for Science and Reason.* New York: Prometheus Books.

Stinespring, John, and Ryan Cragun. 2015. "Simple Markov Model for Estimating the Growth of Nonreligion in the United States.". *Science, Religion and Culture* 2: 96–103.

Stryker, Sheldon. 2000. "Identity Competition: Key to Differential Social Movement Participation?" In *Self, Identity, and Social Movements*, edited Sheldon Stryker, Timothy Joseph Owen, Robert W. White, 21–40. Minneapolis: University of Minnesota Press.

Björn Mastiaux
A Typology of Organized Atheists and Secularists in Germany and the United States

1 Introduction

The typology proposed in this chapter is the result of a transnational study that was carried out in the years from 2006 to 2013. It had been motivated by media reports on atheist activism in Germany, in particular the staging of so-called "religion-free zones" during the *Catholic World Youth Day* festival in Cologne in 2005. It was reported that this activism was carried out by secularist organizations, some of which had been in existence for many years. Initial research made it clear that little was known about these organizations, their networks, activities, and supporters, despite the fact that they might qualify as a social movement. Furthermore, the early stages of the conception of this project coincided with the popularization of the term "new atheism" by Gary Wolf (2006) and the ensuing reports and debate on the authors and books labeled as such. This, too, pointed to the existence of a secularist movement, an international one at that, which seemed to be experiencing a wave of mobilization at the time.

The aim of this research project, as it was conceptualized back then, was twofold. On the one hand, it was conceived to map and delineate the field of secularist, humanist, atheist, and freethought (what the previous chapter called SHAF) organizations in parts of the Western world, and to argue for its classification as a social movement. Germany and the United States, with their marked differences regarding private religiosity and church-state separation, were chosen as representative cases from both sides of the secular/religious divide within the West. On the other hand, the aim was to investigate the motives and biographies of the members of a certain type of those organizations in both countries. Who are those people who, despite having grown up and living under very different socio-religious conditions, feature the commonality of not only being nonreligious, but of being a member of organized atheism?

Over the years during which this particular study was carried out, the research landscape on nonreligion, secularity, and organized atheism has changed dramatically. While at the study's inception such an academic field was almost nonexistent, the phenomenon of "new atheism" prompted an explosion of research activity in this area within a number of different scientific disciplines (for an early report on this development see Bullivant and Lee 2012). Besides studies on the "new atheist" writings and campaigns themselves (e.g. Amarasingham 2010; Zenk 2010; Taira and Illman 2012), research so far has dealt with the terminology for nonreligion and secularity (e.g. Cragun and Hammer 2011, Lee 2012), the nonreligious' biographies, demographics, and opinions on social issues (e.g. Hunsberger and Altemeyer 2006), their deconversion stories (e.g. Zuckerman 2012), their identity construction as atheists (e.g. Foust 2009; Smith 2011; Beaman and Tomlins 2015), as well as their participation in various forms of organized secularity (e.g. Pasquale 2010; Cimino and Smith 2011). Meanwhile, the field of atheist, secularist, freethought, and humanist organizations and its adherents is more routinely conceived of as a social movement (see e.g. Cimino and Smith 2007, 2014; LeDrew 2016), as evidenced also by this volume. At least, it has been treated as such within the fields of religious studies and the sociology of religion, while curiously the sociology of social movements is only beginning to take note (see e.g. Guenther, Radojcic and Mulligan 2015). Also, the movement's ideological roots as well as conflicting ideological currents that run within it have been detailed (see e.g. LeDrew 2012, 2016). Accordingly, these aspects of the study at hand will not be focused on in this chapter.

While several of these and other studies have begun to explore who organized atheists are, the research presented here has followed some new paths and is able to offer additional insight in this respect. *One* important contribution of this study is that it extends its perspective to continental Europe. The study of nonreligion and secularity has, up to this point, largely concentrated on the English speaking world. This is also true of the existent member studies of atheist organizations, most of which were conducted in the United States of America and Canada – a few in Great Britain and Australia (e.g. Black 1983; Mumford 2015). The secularist movement(s) in continental Europe has (have) hardly been explored so far. For the case of Germany, the study at hand is a first foray to remedy this situation.

Yet, as mentioned before, the typology aims to be inclusive and is based on organized atheists from Germany *as well as* the United States. In addition to a first insight into the German secularist movement, the transnational comparison this approach allows for is the *second* innovation of this research.

Thirdly, much of the prior research on the motives of nonbelievers to join atheistic or freethought-secularist organizations has concentrated on informal meet-up groups or freethought organizations which, through socializing and lectures, mainly serve the identity construction and the treatment of a "nonnormative identity" (Fitzgerald 2003) of atheists who are viewed as "other" in a highly religious society (e.g. McTaggart 1997; Heiner 2008; Foust 2009; LeDrew 2013). Even though there are studies on the political activism of the secularist movement (see e.g. Cimino and Smith 2007, 2014; Kettell 2013), the protagonists of this kind of activism, their biographies and motives, have been explored much less. The research presented here is based on the exploration of organizations which offer their members both community and education *as well as* political activism and protest.

Finally, the material from which the typology was constructed represents a new approach in the exploration of organized atheism and allows for a novel or additional way to perceive and structure the movement's membership. The typology is based on the identification of narrative patterns (Kruse 2011, 2014), meaning the leading motives or topics that emerged in the open-style interviews that were conducted with members. These, in combination with the reported styles of participation, served to identify eight ideal types of members, which have been named: the "political fighter", the "indignant", the "collectivist", the "alienated", the "intellectual enlightener", the "silent intellectual", the "dissociate", and the "euphoric". These types of members are going to be portrayed in some detail further down in this chapter. Before that, the following section will introduce the sampling and methodology of the study.

2 Sample and Methodology

As at the time of the study's initiation the field of nonreligion and secularity had hardly been explored, a qualitative approach was chosen. Also, semi-structured in-depth interviews were considered the optimal method for the exploration of organized atheists' personal views on their activism, their ways into the organizations, as well as their worldviews and religious / nonreligious biographies – questions which stood at the heart of the study.

Sampling

A first step toward that goal consisted in the sampling of potentially relevant cases on two levels: the level of organizations, and the level of members. In order to capture the variety of cases "out there", regarding members, the aspiration was to find maximally different cases. Yet, in order to allow for comparability, on the level of organizations it was necessary to limit variation to a certain type of groups. Accordingly, organizations that would qualify for the sample had to meet the following criteria:

With respect to the intended variety of members' socio-religious backgrounds, they had to be located in substantially different regions, particularly as relates to the role of religion – though my interest was exclusively on Western countries. Besides practical reasons of accessibility, this was the major reason for choosing Germany and the United States as countries for consideration. Both offer considerable internal plurality regarding socio-religious landscapes, with the predominantly Catholic Bavaria, the Lutheran North, and the largely secular East in Germany, as well as the religiously mixed and relatively liberal West Coast, the mainline Protestant Midwest, and the evangelical Baptist South or "Bible Belt" in the United States. In addition to this intended variation in location, on the other criteria the chosen organizations were supposed to be similar to one another.

One important demand was that the targeted organizations shared similar goals. As outlined above, one aim of the study was to find organizations which offered their adherents not only a place for socializing and identity formation via community and education, but also the chance for political activism, e.g. via participation in protest, work on press releases, or in other public relations or outreach projects.

Another demand was for the organizations to take a medium or center position regarding their topical scope and targeted population. Some groups follow only a defined narrow goal within the realm of atheism and secularism or are open only to a subset of nonbelievers, such as *Camp Quest* (that organizes secular summer retreats), or the *Secular Student Alliance*. Organizations at the other end of the spectrum, while being critical of religion and church at times, address much wider issues and, accordingly, attract a more general audience. Examples for this include civil rights organizations like the *American Civil Liberties Union* (*ACLU*) and the *Humanistische Union* (*HU*), or rationalist and skeptics groups. In contrast to both of these "extremes", the organizations that were to be sampled needed to be open to all the nonreligious and to be concerned with issues relating to atheism and secularism exclusively.

In the United States these criteria were easily met by a large number of locally active atheist groups that were either affiliated with or chapters of the *Atheist Alliance International* (today: *Atheist Alliance of America*) or *American Atheists* (compare Fazzino & Cragun in this volume). These groups typically hold a monthly meeting, where they will often have a guest speaker – such as a scientist, political activist, or author – as well as other regular meetings, for example book clubs, discussion groups, or charitable activities. But they also act out, either in the form of protests against (usually locally relevant) infringements on the separation of church and state, in the form of writing letters to the editor, or in the form of regular radio or TV programs that they produce for free access cable channels. U.S. organizations which found their way into the sample were *San Francisco Atheists* and *Atheists and Other Freethinkers* of Sacramento from

California, *Minnesota Atheists* from Minneapolis / Saint Paul, and the *Atlanta Freethought Society* from Georgia.

In Germany, it turned out to be a bit more difficult to find matching organizations. My criteria were met best by the Munich chapter of the *Bund für Geistesfreiheit Bayern* (*BfG, Freethought Association of Bavaria*). Even though the *BfG* is officially recognized by the Bavarian state as a "worldview congregation" with roots in the 19th century free-religious movement, the Munich based group in particular had become known for its political activism in opposition to the pronounced influence of religion – particularly Catholicism – on the operations of the state at the time of my research. The other group from Germany that was included has a decidedly political orientation. As its name suggests, *IBKA* (*Internationaler Bund der Konfessionslosen und Atheisten, International League of the Non-Affiliated and Atheists*) commits itself to fighting for the political rights of citizens without religious affiliation or religious belief – contrary to its name, though, its activism is not international, but focused mainly in Germany. As for socializing, some of its regional chapters, at the time of this study, offered meet-ups, movie nights, or sporadic guest lectures as well. Therefore, *IBKA* members from different parts of Germany were selected for the sample, too.

Individual members of these organizations were sampled with the idea of maximum variation in mind. While the short research time of only two months in the United States did not allow for the interplay between sampling, interviewing, analyzing, and only then further sampling and interviewing that is characteristic of the strategy of "theoretical sampling" (see e. g. Ritchie and Lewis 2003, 80 – 81), the large number of interviews conducted with very diverse members nonetheless afforded the opportunity to contrast very different cases *ex post facto*, which is in line with this research strategy as well. Members were contacted via various paths. In the case of most of the American organizations, my visit to the area and my call for interviewees was announced well in advance in the organizations' newsletters. Also, this research journey involved a visit to the respective organizations' monthly meetings, which allowed for the introduction of the research project as well as on-the-spot recruitment of interviewing subjects.

In the case of the German organizations, the Munich based *BfG* group and nationally active *IBKA*, their annual main assemblies served the same purpose. Another occasion for recruiting interviewees was a monthly meet-up of the Cologne-based *IBKA* group. In order to find members more spread out over the country, who did not regularly participate in group activities, a call for interviewees was placed in *IBKA*'s online forum. This as well as the announcements in the U.S. organizations' newsletters ensured the participation not only of highly active, but also of more or less passive members. In order to counter a potential bias due to self-recruitment or recruitment only via "gatekeepers" (such as the organizations' presidents), who sometimes helped to find interviewees, several members were approached by myself and asked for participation in interviews. This also helped to increase the socio-demographic variety of participants.

All in all, 63 interviews were conducted, 58 of which were used for the analysis. Of these 58 interviews, 36 were with members of American organizations, and 22 with members of German organizations. The ratio of men to women was 39 to 19. Regarding age, seven interviewees fell into the range of 21–30 years, 11 each into those of 31–40 and 41–50 years, nine members were between 51 and 60 years old, 16 between 61 and 70, and finally four were 71 years old or older. Even though the sample was not drawn for statistical, but rather theoretical representativeness, the gender and age ratios are somewhat typical of secularist organizations, which are known for a predominantly male and older membership (Hunsberger and Altemeyer 2006, 106; Pasquale 2007, 47). Also, the educational level in these groups is usually above average, and Pasquale reports a predominance of educational occupations for the members of a secular-humanist group in the American Pacific Northwest (Pasquale 2010, 50). Both of these patterns were observed in this study's sample as well. Aside from teachers and university educators, there was some diversity regarding the interviewees' (former) occupations: they ranged from scientists, lawyers, and physicians, to architects and IT specialists, to paramedics, secretaries, and booksellers. While some of the younger participants were still attending college, most of the older respondents had already retired from their jobs. A few of the interviewees were unemployed, with one living in an alternative commune. A peculiarity of the American sample was that two of the members used to be priests in their earlier careers. Ethnically, most participants were Northern European or of Northern European descent, with the exceptions of an Italian, a Greek, a Brazilian, and one Iranian. Only one interviewee was African-American and another one of Asian descent.

Data collection and analysis

The interviewing technique used was semi-structured interviews in the tradition of the "problem-centered interview" (Witzel 2000). In contrast to totally open, narrative interviews, the purpose of this interviewing tradition is the exploration and collaborative reconstruction of a fixed "social problem" or "issue" that the researcher has already acquired some familiarity or "theoretical sensitivity" with. This familiarity paired with the desire to learn about different dimensions of the problem at hand structures the interviewing guideline by providing a number of topical fields that are to be addressed. The interviews for this study started out with a warming-up phase, in which respondents were asked to introduce themselves and to talk about their general biographies. After this, the main topical fields that were explored were (1) the interviewees' ways into their organizations, (2) their worldview or religious / nonreligious biographies, and (3) their experiences, activities, and opinions as members of their organizations.

These three fields of interest also structured the first step of the analysis: the use of the "qualitative case contrasting method", as detailed by Kelle and Kluge (2010). Building upon the practice of open coding in grounded theory (e.g. Strauss and Corbin 1998), in this approach categories and subcategories are devised deductively from the pre-structure of the interviews as well as inductively from the text and contrasted, refined, and restructured systematically by comparison of a range of cases, until the variation within the field is sufficiently delineated.

The aim of the second step of the analysis was to reduce the overwhelming variety found – regarding organized atheists' ways into the movement, their worldview formation, as well as their views on and experiences of activism – with the construction of a typology of very basic, exemplary, or ideal types of members. This typology was constructed using an analytical method delineated by Jan Kruse (2011, 2014). It builds on the identification of certain "narrative patterns" that are deemed to be characteristic of the individual respondents, which are made up of central motives and discursive habits that occur consistently throughout the interview – especially in so-called "rich" or "dense" passages as well as in the opening monologues (Kruse 2011, 176). The identification of four such narrative patterns in combination with the reported activism, behavior, and ambitions of the interviewees led to the construction of eight ideal types of organized atheists.

3 The Diversity of Organized Atheists

Investigating the members of atheist organizations, the study presented here has focused on the fact of their membership. It has studied organized atheists *as members*. What do they do as members of their organizations? What do they think about the activities of their groups and about other members? How did they get to be a member in the first place? And what has been the history of their worldview formation leading up to becoming a member? As it turns out, the diversity of answers to these questions is overwhelming. This section will explore some of this diversity and will put into focus those results which either contradict or amplify our knowledge of organized atheists from prior studies.

Worldview and Worldview Formation

There is some debate, both among scholars and within organized atheism, over whether agnostics should count as part of the atheist movement (see Cimino and Smith 2007, 416; McGrath 2004, 174; Hunsberger and Altemeyer 2006, 25). But considering that agnosticism, rather than an independent worldview position which is softer or less radical than atheism, actually constitutes a method of reasoning by which one may arrive at either an atheist or theist position (Eller 2010, 8–9), it is not surprising that agnostics have always been involved in atheist organizations – and several members identify that way primarily. In general, many – even though by no means all – of the members of atheist or secularist organizations give a lot of thought to how to position themselves regarding their worldview and what to call themselves. This was evidenced by the inscription on Paul G.'s (Atheists and Other Freethinkers, AOF, 76) – the creator of the "Brights" – business card. It read:

> I am a bright (my naturalistic worldview is free of supernatural / mystical elements). I am agnostic in regards to unverifiable claims (including gods), humanistic in morals, pragmatic in actions, freethinking in regards to authority, existentialistic in philosophy, sartrienne in regards to purpose, scientific in regards to what constitutes knowledge, contrarian in demeanor, and skeptical with respect to all the aforementioned.

Whether they call themselves "atheist", "agnostic", "secular humanist", "naturalist", "bright", "Jewish atheist", "mystic", or some other term I found in my sample, such as "liberal" or "realist", organized atheists presumably share at least the commonality of being nonreligious in some form and also critical of (at least certain aspects and variants of) religion.

Yet they have arrived at this common place via very different routes of worldview formation. Some of these routes have been outlined by Stephen LeDrew (2013), who, in his research on atheist activists in Canada and the U.S., has differentiated five "different trajectories to atheist identity and activism". Of the five paths he describes, two have secular socialization as their starting point, while three start out from religious socialization. All five eventually lead to atheism and only from there to atheist activism. While this typology of different routes of worldview formation matches the experiences described by most of the interviewees from my study, there are at least a few cases in which this model is not sufficient. In several cases there was ambiguity regarding the classification of a participant's socialization as having been either "religious" or "secular". Some of the respondents grew up in a home that was only nominally religious. Others experienced cognitive dissonance early on, either because their parents were not both equally religious, belonged to different churches, or changed religious affiliation continuously over a short period of time. Others grew up in a strongly religious household within a secular environment or in a secular household within a religious environment.

Additionally, a few cases had not even acquired an atheist identity or a position critical of religious belief at the point at which they entered their atheist organization. Dietmar H. (BfG, 50), for example, was recruited as a member for *BfG Munich* only after being interviewed on the group's radio program. The group had invited him to their show as a victim of purported church-state entanglements. At the time, Dietmar had made local headlines after a gay pride float mocking Pope Benedict for his anti-gay rights policies, which he and his colleagues had created, had been confiscated by the Bavarian police under dubious charges of "insulting a foreign head of state". Up until meeting the *BfG* group and learning more about their positions, Dietmar had never considered himself an atheist, but was only critical of different religious traditions for their views on gay rights. He had even studied theology in college and had been employed as a public school teacher for Protestant religious education for many years, a job he only quit for a more promising career option, not for a lack of religiosity. Even though he said that he did not believe in a personal god, he still regarded Jesus as an ethical role model and expressed spiritual ideas.

A similar case was that of Brigitte S. (BfG, 42). Even though she had disaffiliated from the Catholic Church long ago, as she was at odds with its conservative positions on many social issues, she had never thought about cultivating a more pronounced secular identity. This only changed when she made friends with two active members of the *BfG* group and decided to join in order to do "something meaningful". One explanation for these cases may be the widespread perception of a strong privilege and influence of the Catholic Church in Bavaria. As *BfG Munich* does not only act as a secular "worldview congregation" ("Weltanschauungsgemeinschaft"), but as an activist group fighting for the separation of church and state, it is conceivable that the group and its goals are deemed attractive also for citizens who do not identify as atheists primarily.

Ways into Organized Atheism

While Dietmar and Brigitte found their way into *BfG* through personal contacts, atheist organizations also employ more conscious and systematic attempts at "frame bridging": making people who share similar views aware of the organizations' existence (Snow et al. 1986, 467–469). They may advertise in progressive media, practice outreach via their own media channels, or employ the strategy of "bloc recruitment" (Oberschall 1973) by cooperating with other movements or, at least in the case of the American organizations, Unitarian Universalist churches, which provide some membership flow. Even though the literature on social movements stresses such active efforts at mobilization by movement actors, in the case of atheist organizations "self-recruitment" – i.e. the active search for a group one can join – seems to be even more important. Goodwin and Jasper (2009) describe self-recruitment as a common reaction to so-called moral shock. This kind of shock may set in when "events or information raise such a sense of outrage in people that they become inclined toward political action, with or without a network of contacts" (Goodwin und Jasper 2009, 57–58). Outrage may be generated by so-called "suddenly imposed grievances" (Walsh 1981, 2), which can be events or new developments, perceived as scandalous, that are reported on in the media. To Steven F. (Atlanta Freethought Society, AFS, 50), for example, the publically staged prayer for rain after a drought period by the governor of Georgia on the steps of the state capitol constituted such an event. Friedrich G. (BfG, 71) of Munich got agitated when he read that posters of demonstrators against the local visit by the Pope were confiscated by the police: "It was in the newspaper. And so... (,) I wasn't there myself, but still this infuriated me. And so I wrote to the paper. And in the course of this I became aware of BfG and became a member". Personal experiences that contradict a person's values and expectations may also be experienced as a suddenly imposed grievance. Rainer P. (IBKA, 41), for example, had always believed that religion was nothing to worry about in modern-day, highly secularized Germany, until he asked for the removal of a large crucifix in the classroom of the public elementary school that his young son attended, who seemed to be afraid of the object:

> How a mayor conspires, more or less, with the school district of Cologne in order to keep the crucifixes on the walls of a ridiculously small school of a hundred and fifty kids, how a priest from the pulpit calls for protest marches in front of this school until the crosses get reapplied, and similar things, ...how the local paper deems it worthy of a full page report and their front page that these crosses got removed, well, that... surprised me quite a bit. I didn't expect that. I really didn't expect that. That the opinion of the granny at home regarding the crucifixes in the children's classroom may count more than a supreme court ruling, I didn't expect that either. ...And when I realized all of this, I thought that, indeed, it might make sense to get active.

In other cases, the active spread of information by movement activists in combination with their interpretation of the situation may cause moral shock: "Moral shocks do not arise only from suddenly imposed grievances; organizers try hard to generate them through their rhetorical appeals" (Jasper and Poulsen 1995, 498). Lukas G. (IBKA, 30) and Martin H. (IBKA, 23), for example, consumed the organization's magazine and newsletter for a while before they decided that it was time to get more involved. But, of course, this framing can only be successful if potential recruits "already have certain visions of the world, moral values, political ideologies, and affective attachments" (Jasper and Poulsen 1995, 496) that match those of the movement. In cases such as these, moral shock does not set in in reaction to a singular event or experience, but in reaction to the perception of a slow and creeping development, a change in cultural values perhaps, which, apart from outrage, causes the feeling of alienation. Typical for the American experience is the observation of the rise of the Religious Right in the years prior to and during the presidency of George W. Bush (see also Fazzino, Borer, and Haq 2014, 176–181). Alice C. expresses well how, prior to her joining of *AOF*, she felt increasingly uncomfortable:

> Early on it was not... something I... gave much... thought to. I would say, in the last fifteen years, though, I've become very aware of it... and... /eh/ almost annually increasingly shocked. And... /eh/ the whole country feels like... East Texas, oughh, pushing this (,) this incessant... need to convert everybody. There's only one religion, and it's theirs and... (,) you know, the sooner you acknowledge that, the better off you'll be. It's uncanny. It's everywhere now. ...Just as it... used to be forty years ago.

Similar to moral shock, and often in combination with it, alienation is a feeling that may lead to self-recruitment. It is an experience which may motivate people to look for others to help them relieve the tension. In addition to the feeling of being at odds with the surrounding culture at large, alienation may also result from more limited experiences of new, confusing, or frustrating situations, from the loss of an old or the adaptation of a new worldview and identity, or simply from moving to a foreign, possibly more religious place.

Whatever their motives for joining, most of the respondents from this study reported that once they had learned of the existence of these organizations they immediately became a member. But in those rare cases, in which doubts were reported, it was often the influence of other persons which convinced them to join eventually. Lee S. (Minnesota Atheists, MNA, 69), a former Evangelical preacher, for example, was originally biased against atheists, and it took him some time and courage to finally attend a few meetings of the organization whose TV programs he had already watched and enjoyed. What finally convinced him to join as a member was the presence of a person he knew, respected, and considered similar to himself:

> And so... my first reaction was: well, I wouldn't want to have anything to do with those... people, but... the more I listened, the more I thought: you know [laughs slightly], I think I have more in common with them than I have with any Christians. So I attended a few meetings. ...And as a matter of fact [...] I walked in the door [...] and I... see a person there and I

suddenly [...] recognize him. ...He was somebody that I went to high school with. [...] And he was a very popular guy in high school. And... so we got to talking. And it turns out, he, too, had been in the ministry [laughs]. And he, too, was ordained. And now he was a member of Minnesota Atheists.

Other doubts about joining had to do with fears that the group might be too similar to religion, that it might be ineffective, or that members might be either too eccentric or intolerant. In some examples, these doubts could be dispelled by the influence and convincing presence of a charismatic leader. Steven F. (AFS, 50) and his wife, for example, had known for a long time of the existence of secularist organizations in the Atlanta area, but had never bothered to join, since they thought that people there might be strange. This changed when they saw an interview with *AFS*' Ed Buckner on TV:

> And... Ed was very articulate. An intelligent man. And, so, what he said was (,) was great. I mean, he wasn't shouting, he wasn't pounding his chest, and he wasn't screaming or yelling or any of that kind of thing. He was just very (,) it was a very reasoned and rational... statement that he made. And that immediately appealed to us. And... we just kind of went: hmm, Atlanta Freethought Society? So we wrote that down. And we went and did a google search and found their website.

Finally, Stan C. (San Francisco Atheists, SFA, 45) was impressed by Madalyn Murray O'Hair, the notorious founder of *American Atheists*, who spurred in him the enthusiasm to become an activist:

> You know, a lot of these separation organizations don't have much of a sense of humor. You know, somebody like me walks in the room, they go: oh, you know, you should get a haircut! With American Atheists it was just very (,) yeah: you're one of us! Welcome on board! And part of that was the Madalyn O'Hair attitude. So, if Madalyn O'Hair had not been around with her free-wheeling, you know, fuck-you attitude, I probably would not be doing this... myself. But she made it seem cool. She made it seem fun. She made it seem exciting. And she made it seem important. You know? So that's a large part of why I'm doing what I'm doing today.

Activism within the Organization

Due to conscious sampling decisions, interviews were conducted with members with varying degrees of activity in the groups: passive members, whom McCarthy and Zald (1977, 1228) in their member typology call "isolated constituents", as well as weakly, medium, and highly active members. In some cases, the degree of activism may depend on people's experiences with other members. Mariva A.

(SFA, 38), for example, who only sporadically attended meetings of her organization, explained that she could not relate to some of the other members and criticized them for their public demeanor, sharing her experience at a public debate as an example:

> I kind of, ...like, was a little bit embarrassed by the behavior of some of my fellow atheists, for... they were just kind of laughing really loud... and just kind of making comments during the debate. And... all the, like, the Christians were, you know, fairly well behaved. And I was just (,) I was thinking, like: okay, ...you know, if... (,) if we're gonna show that we're as good as these people, like, let's behave that way!

In general, the diversity of characters found in these groups is often cited as a drawback and reason for restraint in commitment. But even those who are the most committed may evaluate this diversity differently. Assunta T. (BfG, 46), for example, criticized the majority of casual members for lacking enthusiasm and sincerity in their atheism:

> Our biggest problem is the nonreligious themselves. [...] They'll actually have the nerve and tolerate that their wives, friends, children... have a different conviction. They treat it as their spare time... (,) their hobby. And hobby only in the sense that if they find the time they may go and attend a meeting. But never make a fuss! They'll only speak up where they feel safe and know that everybody is of the same opinion. That's our trouble!

Stan C. (SFA, 45), on the other hand, felt rewarded by the less active members for his efforts in providing them a place to feel at home at:

> Well, the monthly meetings basically just give people a chance to meet other atheists, give them a chance to relax. Those of us who have been working on it for an entire month get a chance to talk to people who actually care what we're doing [laughs slightly]. You know? So (,) so, it's nice.

These statements show that within the movement there are different expectations regarding organized atheists' openness and candor about their lack of religion. While Assunta expected of her fellow atheists a self-confident demonstration of their rejection of religion, Stan was more tolerant of some of the atheists' fear of ostracism.

Just as these expectations vary, so do the actual practices of concealment or disclosure. Some respondents kept their atheism completely to themselves, while others decided to reveal it only selectively, such as Sharon W. (AFS, 57), who was careful not to appear as a member of *AFS* as long as she was working as a school teacher in the U.S. South. Others, who did not have to fear work-related sanctions, liked to admit to their atheism and seemed to enjoy some of the reactions they would get. Adrienne M. (SFA, 34), for example, sometimes liked to be seen as a *femme fatale* when going out to bars in her home state of Texas and meeting men:

> and of course they'd be Republican, they would be *so intrigued*... by that fact that I was a (,) a Democrat, and that I was a liberal and that /hughhh/ [gasps] I didn't believe in *god!* That was like I was like this (,) like they were flirting with danger just by hanging out with me or something.

Similarly, Michael C. was amused about a common reaction to his answer for people's question about his church affiliation:

> And you can (,) and you can watch it. Right in their eyes. You can see them like going through... (,) /eh/ it's almost like a computer (,) going through all their files, looking for an appropriate (,) like: what do I do with that? You know? He's an atheist? What? And they're trying to be... polite. Because that's the big thing in the South. You have to always appear to be (,) you can be the biggest bastard in the world, but you have to appear to be polite. And /eh/... (,) you know, they're like: o-o-h...(.) They always make that sound. They're like: o-o-o-h, ...okay. You know? And (,) and I can tell, ...they're like: ...I wonder if he's about to kill me [laughs].

Other than simply answering people's questions about their religion, some respondents talked about regularly confronting people with the fact of their atheism more or less directly. Chuck C. (SFA, 60):

> I travelled a lot when I was working. I would *intentionally*... on an airplane have a book. You know: 'Atheism Understood'. Or something about atheism. That would be my book to carry on the plane. And it wasn't that I really wanted to read that book, but I wanted to invite conversation.

Finally, Assunta (BfG, 46), the leader of *BfG* who advocated for some atheist pride – similar to that of the gay movement – and liked to wear atheist t-shirts and caps in everyday life, even reported that she regularly put invitations to events and political pamphlets by her organization into the business mail of her family's medium-sized company in the car-manufacturing industry.

The organized atheists from this study did not only use different strategies regarding the disclosure of their atheism in everyday life, but they also preferred different strategies for their organizations. Cimino and Smith (2011) argue that the American secularist movement was torn in this respect: "The tension between, on the one hand, spreading secularism and attempting to expose the fallacies of belief and, on the other, seeking acceptance in a largely religious society runs through the recent history of secular humanism" (28). LeDrew (2013,

18–19) argues that favoring either a "confrontational" approach, in which criticism of religion and satire are used in order to produce attention and to push certain political goals, or an "accomodationist" approach, which is deemed to further respect and acceptance of atheists, would mirror different ideas about a collective self (see also Fazzino & Cragun in this volume). To my observation, these divergent strategies do not only separate secular humanists from atheists, but they are also associated with different umbrella organizations within the atheist sector. This regularly causes debates within local atheist groups, as described by Don K. (AOF, 53) for the case of *AOF:*

> You know, do we... (,) do we join American Atheists, who for so many years have been (,) who have lived by... ridiculing... religion? ...Or do we take a more... understanding approach, I guess you could call it? The way... the Atheist Alliance International... approaches it, saying: we need to develop... a better connection... with society, so that they will accept us as equals. ...And, you know, so, yeah, it's a (,) it's a constant... conflict that we have in our board meetings. You know, which direction do we go?

At the time this study was conducted, a similar debate took place in the Munich based *BfG* group. Some of the members criticized the group's president, Assunta T., for her provocative style and activism, such as the implementation of a blasphemy contest. Friedrich G. (BfG, 71):

> In any case, she is not a conventional character. Let's put it that way. And she does exhibit that quite a bit. [...] You know, I don't have a problem with that at all. But the fact is, we want to change things. And for that we need the regular citizens. And therefore my opinion is that the current politics are not very favorable, the politics of provocation. ...Because that way we scare away the regular citizens.

Yet, Assunta countered with the opinion that citizens in a democratic society should be able to stand criticism and satire. Accordingly, she advocated a provocative, attention-grabbing strategy, arguing that noble values alone "are not sexy" for the media:

> Those so-called humanistic, secular values, ...they should have actually been societal consensus for a long time. It shouldn't take anything for that. [...] You know? So it's sad enough that we still have to work our asses off for that. And we can only be successful [...] with provocation, of course! ...What else? With provocation. How else do you want to reach anything? That's how the world works. As long as there are things going wrong, we must provoke and trust that in a democratic society democratic-humanistic people will be able to bear that.

But just as atheist blogger Greta Christina (2010) argued that one should "let firebrands be firebrands" and "diplomats be diplomats", voices that saw advantages in both strategies and even the need for a movement to be pluralistic could also be found.

4 A Typology of Organized Atheists

It has become apparent that goals, strategies, identity labels, as well as worldview biographies vary drastically among organized atheists. The saying commonly used in the movement that "organizing atheists is like trying to herd cats" finds some validation in these results. Still I want to argue that this bulk of highly diverse cases can be reduced to a fair number of characteristic exemplars or ideal types of members.

The typology proposed was achieved by the identification of narrative patterns or "central motives", which consist of typical figures in verbalizations as well as in topical choices and which heavily inform and shape the character of an interview while putting it in line with select others. In order to be seen as central motives these patterns must appear recurrently throughout an interview and especially be present in its "richest" passages (Kruse 2011, 176–179). I have identified four such narrative patterns, which in combination with one of two behavioral patterns or modes of action – one more other-, the other more self-oriented – constitute eight ideal types of organized atheists.

Diagram 1: The eight ideal types of organized atheists

Narrative Pattern / Central Motive	Ideal Type	
	Other-Oriented	*Self-Oriented*
Political Conflict	Political Fighter	Indignant
Belonging	Collectivist	Alienated
Philosophical, Scientific, and Religious Knowledge	Intellectual Enlightener	Silent Intellectual
Identification with Organization	Dissociate	Euphoric

The Narrative Pattern of "Political Conflict"

The common motive in narrations of members who I will call the "political fighter" and the "indignant" is the narrator's conviction that in the current situation democratic or constitutional principles are violated, as religious ideas or actors are being granted undue influence on the operations of the state or as atheists and the nonreligious are being discriminated against. This concern is at the heart of these persons' activism, while epistemological questions of religious belief or unbelief are seen as less important or dismissed completely. This overriding principle is represented fairly well in a statement by Adrienne M. (SFA, 34):

> I refuse to debate people on the existence of god. I don't care. Believe whatever you want to believe! Whatever makes you happy, I want you to do it! But you need to keep it out of my government... and off of my body and away from me! ...That's the only reason I do what I do. [...] I've never even read the bible! Okay? I don't care. I can't get past page two. It's boring. ...So I refuse to debate the existence. ...What I do is civil liberties.

Apart from this *political orientation*, the two types of members who are united by this motive show further distinct characteristics which distinguish them from one another.

The Political Fighter: Representatives of this type are characterized by their *disputability*, their conviction of a high degree of *self-effectiveness*, as well as their preference for a *confrontational strategy*. Their activism is strongly outward- or other-oriented. Ed B. (AFS, 62), for example, said that what he loved most about his activism was "to do public speaking and debates". When, during the interview, he reproduced the disputes that he regularly has with people who want the Ten Commandments to be posted in public buildings, he self-ironically remarked: "You can get me on some soap boxes now. I'll preach for a while, if you want me to [laughs]". Similarly, Assunta T. (BfG, 46) described herself as "streitlustig" (cantankerous – literally "argument jolly"), "with an emphasis on 'lustig'" ("jolly"). She shrugged off fears of retributions for an outspoken secularism, as voiced by other members of her organization, with a "pfff" sound, characteristic of her and used many times throughout the interview. As long as nothing worse happened than having ones car's tires punctured, one needed to speak out against religiously motivated violations of individual rights. Assunta, as well as other representatives of the political fighter, stressed that this should be done by oneself rather than waiting for others, such as political parties, to do the job. She said that it was not her style to bemoan a bad situation, but, rather, to do something about it. Besides believing in the effectiveness of political action, political fighters typically also exhibit a strong will and a tendency to make decisions unilaterally. Accordingly, they often take up leading roles in their organizations. As they strongly believe in the legitimacy of their project, they advocate the use of a confrontational strategy in order to get attention.

The Indignant. Representatives of this type are characterized by their indignance. Just as the political fighters, they are *appalled about new developments* regarding the relationship between state and religion or regarding religious intrusions on individual liberties. Yet, different from the political fighters, their ambition is less to look strategically for ways to change the political situation in the long run, but rather to look for an outlet to their disgust, for a way to *vent* their *frustration*, which they find in their organizations. Accordingly their activism is of an expressive nature and often rather low-key and sporadic, such as writing letters to the editor, as Jay B. (AFS, 77) does:

> We also have in our local newspaper on a daily basis... a column called vent. And the vent means really, literally, for people to let off steam. ...And it's a... series of what might be called one-liners, in which people would make some comment. And... I have, again, been very (,) pretty successful in having a number of vents printed.

Some other indignants do not get active themselves, but rather want to support financially and give *voice* to political activists, even though they may not believe in the realization of their instrumental goals, as for example Lisa K. (IBKA, 32):

> I don't believe that they can actually achieve a lot. But knowing that there is a voice that says: hello, here, we have an opinion on this, too, does help. That's why I find the work that they do tremendously important.

Representatives of the indignants are often new members as their indignation is usually fresh and connected to a specific current issue. Yet, in other cases, outrage and frustration may be kept up and alive for years, not least by the religion-watch and news services of the organizations themselves.

The Narrative Pattern of "Belonging"

Another central motive that surfaced regularly in some of the interviews is that of belonging. Interviewees who represent the types of the "collectivist" and the "alienated" articulated experiences of estrangement and a – sometimes profound – desire to (re-)connect with others. Mariva A. (SFA, 38), a "Jewish atheist" who, after a religious quest, became a member of *San Francisco Atheists*, but who still enjoyed attending services at a progressive church on Christmas and Easter, got at the heart of this pattern when she remarked:

> And I came home from one of these services, and I told my husband: you know, I think, one (,) maybe *the* reason I've gone to all these different religious... outlets and... services and traditions and rituals is, ...you know, between like the Native American sweat lodge and the Buddhist retreats and, you know, the Quaker meeting house and the gay Jewish synagogue and Glide Memorial Church (,) you know, maybe what I...(.) I thought I was looking for god, but, I think, what I was really looking for and what I *found*... was a connection to

humanity. [...] And that was sort of a profound realization for me that... you could look at almost any religion and it's sort of a different expression of humanity. You know, the Buddhist tradition is an expression of becoming quiet and becoming grounded and becoming very meditative. And the Native American expression of religion is... about becoming very connected to the earth and to nature. ...You know, and the Jewish expression is (,) is very intellectual. It makes us think. It makes us, you know, buzz with ideas. And, you know, the San Francisco Atheists dinner [...] sort of brings out the misfit in me and makes me feel like, you know, finally we're part of a community where we're not being ostracized.

The term "community" is used frequently in the narratives of both the collectivist as well as the alienated. Both may use the term in two senses – meaning either society at large or the smaller group of the secular community. Yet, for the collectivist the wish to belong is directed more at the former, while for the alienated it is directed more at the latter.

The Collectivist. As atheists, representatives of the collectivist type feel alienated from and misunderstood by the general population. They are driven by the desire to bridge that gap and by the wish to find *community with the greater collective.* As a co-founder of *Atheists and Other Freethinkers*, Mynga F. (AOF, 63) defines this as the group's original goal: "The purpose of AOF... is to... promote civic understanding of atheism... and acceptance of it in our community". Collectivists are looking for common ground with the religious population of their society. One starting point for this is their refusal to criticize religion at large, which, as Paul G. pointed out, did not mean not to protest at all:

It's not that we won't ever criticize. ...It's simply that we do not lump religion... in one giant lump and therefore say: religion's bad! We can't say that [chuckles], 'cause there are religions that are good. And so... that (,) that's the basic idea.

This differentiating and *benevolent treatment of religion* is not necessarily motivated by strategy. Instead, it may result from personal positive experiences with religion, such as in Paul's case. He did continue his passion for singing in church choirs long after his loss of faith and still enjoys singing church songs together with his wife. Yet, the collectivists ask for the same kind of acceptance by the religious in return. They try to earn this respect, for example, with the help of *charitable activities* that they pursue or that they want their organization to engage in, such as highway cleanups or food drives. In addition, they promote *openness about their worldview* in personal relations. This, according to Don K. (AOF, 53), should help to dispel stereotypes about atheists as anti-social beings, which "church-going people" may have: "They will also learn then to accept atheists as... equal participants in... society, and that we can share... our common humanity... without... embracing a deity".

The Alienated. Others who share the experience of alienation from their surrounding society with the collectivists are less concerned with trying to bridge that gap. Rather than hoping to prove that atheists are respectable members of society, too, their narratives tell of a desire to find a new "home" – be that in social or intellectual terms – a small *community of like-minded people*. This motive is common for (but not exclusive to) members who grew up and used to live in an area where religion mattered little or not at all and who, after moving, suddenly were confronted with a higher degree of religiosity or with religion at all. Heiko T. (MNA, 40), for example, had grown up as the son of a nonreligious father and a moderately religious Lutheran mother in the secularized German Democratic Republic (GDR) / Eastern Germany. After he got divorced from his American wife, whom he had followed to Minnesota after their wedding, he felt lost and foreign there. He reported that during the first two years of his stay in the United States he had mainly been working on his doctoral dissertation and got to know American society mostly via television. What he was presented there on several religious channels was decidedly different from what he knew of religion from back home:

> I actually saw hate there. This was not the kind of Christianity... which teaches love and understanding, you know. It was decidedly directed against atheists... and nonbelievers. You know? Well, to me this was shocking. Also, there were certain aspects of Christianity that I had never heard about, like the Second Coming of Christ and... the rapture, ...things like that. [...] And also, of course, the cultural war of the intelligent design movement. And then there's me with my scientific background. So that hits (,) that hits close to home.

Also, trying to find a new partner after the divorce turned out to be difficult for Heiko, as women were regularly put off by the fact of his nonreligion. Both experiences prompted him to go online and search for other "atheists" in "Minnesota". Martina R. (BfG, 35), who also grew up in the GDR and lived in East Germany for the better part of her life, did not have any experience with religion until she took a job in Bavaria. There she was not only confronted with Catholic street processions, but also with new colleagues who claimed to be religious. This at first unsettled her and she wondered whether, as an atheist, she was missing an important source of support in her life. Yet, she started to develop some atheistic self-esteem after she learned that religion had not saved a particularly faithful colleague of hers from committing suicide. Finally, after seeing a representative from *BfG* in a discussion on television, she soon joined this organization, in order to learn more about a well-reasoned secular position. As in these two cases, the feeling of alienation can be a short-term experience, resulting from a new situation. But it may also become a permanent condition, as for atheists who are surrounded by strongly religious people in their jobs and private lives. To them, their organization feels like a safe haven, where they can be "themselves", as Stu T. (MNA, 46) explained:

> In our society religion is (,) you know, like in the workplace and in social settings (,) so it's just largely: hands-off! People don't say anything rather than risk offending somebody. And so it was... (,) I think it was... energizing to just be able to be myself, ...be more of myself and be able to say what I think and to be able to talk about those kinds of subjects and hear, you know, different perspectives and views without... people getting upset.

The Narrative Pattern of "Philosophical, Scientific, and Religious Knowledge"

The two types who, as their main narrative pattern, share an interest in philosophical, scientific, and religious knowledge have a lot in common otherwise, too. Their narrations show a *high degree of self-reflection* and structure. They appear as critical thinkers and they exhibit intellectual curiosity. Both, the "intellectual enlightener" as well as the "silent intellectual", also share the experience of a *religious deconversion*, which they usually interpret as a consequence of their inquisitiveness. David F. (SFA, 43) portrayed this as a necessary connection:

> And... it's just ironic that, if you take... your Christianity seriously enough... to investigate that and to really hold that up, you know, to look for the truth, it will [claps hands] fall apart, if you look at it too close, in my humble opinion.

Joseph H. (MNA, 46), for example, traced his deconversion back to his high school education, for which he attended a Catholic school:

> Now, whereas most high school students didn't particularly care and they just did enough to get by, ...like other subjects, I was really interested. I asked questions. ...Sincerely concerned... teachers and priests gave me books to read. And in doing so, I learned the history of my religion, ...in particular, and all religions in general, and discovered that they all had... very... reasonable, rational histories. Like the history of any... philosophy or political movement or city state or... economic system or whatever. They had a beginning. They had a cause and effect. ...And it wasn't something that was dumped out of the sky. It wasn't something handed down by a deity. And more and more the idea gelled in my mind that... (,) that it had to be that the exact same causative forces that created... the ancient Egyptian gods... and the Roman gods and the Greek gods and the Chinese gods... had to have been the exact same causative forces that had created the Christian god. ...It made sense. ...Ironically, if I had never gone to a Catholic school, I might never have questioned anything.

Others started to investigate religion more closely only later in life, such as Rüdiger C. (BfG, 69), who in private developed a growing interest in the bible, or former evangelical preacher Lee S. (MNA, 69), who, over the years, discovered more and more contradictions in the scripture. What they all have in common, though, is that after their deconversions they continued their "search for the truth" and kept up an interest in questions of philosophy, science, and religion.

The Intellectual Enlightener. In addition to this pattern of an interest in philosophy, science, and religion, some of these intellectuals exhibited in their narrations a drive and *desire to actively educate*. Trained biologist and educator Mynga F. (AOF, 63), for example, who also represents the type of the "collectivist", viewed the public's education about evolutionary theory as a service to all of society. For this reason she took the Darwin Day event, which her *AOF* helps to set up each year, to be of premier importance. Others are more concerned with the provision of knowledge about religion, such as Steve Y. (AFS, 54), president of the *Atlanta Freethought Society* at the time, who saw this as the organization's most important purpose:

> We want people to learn (,) especially people like myself back in 1998, when I was still trying to figure things out… about religion… and nonreligion… and matters like this. […] Our organization might be able to help them to understand better. And so that's a good thing. I *love* (,) I love it when people… come to… that realization and they learn more every day about how there are some real problems with religion.

This motive of the "intellectual enlightener" is typical for members who have had a religious past of their own or who went through an *intense religious quest*. One example is Grant S. (MNA, 63), a former school teacher, who after 30 years as a Jehova's Witness converted to Catholicism and wrote a doctoral dissertation about cults at a Jesuit university. After having lost religious faith altogether he joined *Minnesota Atheists*, despite his aversion against joining organizations, only in order to be able to educate others about religious cults. In particular, he had hoped to be able to provide active Jehova's Witnesses with a dropout's point of view on their religion via *Minnesota Atheists'* media outlets, such as their cable TV show. Also, he entertained the idea of conducting a tutorial:

> Sort of a class 101, atheism 101, that would give you books and then it would give study questions and sort of set it out that you could follow it through and study it. …Fine books that would… aim at where you're at. Because… in my own approach it was sort of: catch by catch, whatever happened to be the most accessible. […] But I think that most people are not here. They're here. …They're not as… educated. And so they need to have a program or a way of approaching it. […] I'm always the teacher, I'm always the educator. And… that's what I want to do… (,) is trying to educate people and to help them.

One reason for the fact that "intellectual enlighteners" seem to be predominantly those members of atheist organizations who used to be strongly religious in their past may be found in Laurence R. Iannaccone's concept of "religious human capital". It builds on the idea that the time, money, and effort spent on religion for religious believers amount to an *investment* in techniques and knowledge, which makes it less likely for them to leave their faith behind:

> The skills and experience specific to one's religion include religious knowledge, familiarity with church ritual and doctrine, and friendships with fellow worshippers. It is easy to see that these skills and experiences, which I will call *religious human capital*, are an important determinant of one's ability to produce and appreciate religious commodities. (Iannaccone 1990, 299, italics in original)

Iannaccone's argument is that these investments over time would make it more and more irrational – and therefore unlikely – for an individual to change his or her religious affiliation, to marry someone of a different faith, or even to deconvert from religion altogether. Obviously this did not hold true for those atheists who used to be very religious in the past. But while, despite all costs, reason and conscience compelled them to leave behind their faith in which they had invested so much, they still discovered a chance to apply at least parts of their religious human capital in sharing their religious knowledge with others. David F. (SFA, 43), a former evangelical Christian who at the time of the interview participated in religious-secular dialogue projects and authored a book on the historicity of Jesus, even voiced his wish to convert this element of his religious capital into economic capital:

> What I hope to do (,) you know, if the magic career fairy came down and granted me my wish, I would be on, like, the lecture circuit... or some sort of teaching position, you know. ... I think I'd be... really good as a teacher and...(,) I mean, people really seem to enjoy my public speaking. ...And that's what I'd like to get paid for.

The Silent Intellectual. The adjective "silent" characterizes the representatives of this type only regarding their treatment of philosophical, scientific, and religious knowledge. Compared with the intellectual enlighteners, interviewees who exhibited this narrative pattern were far less eager to share their knowledge, but rather to be educated further themselves. They showed a high and generalized *ambition to learn*. One case in point is Joseph H., who answered the general biographical question about the most important stages in his life so far by talking extensively about experiences that shaped his way of thinking. Other biographical events, like meeting and marrying his wife or having a daughter, instead, appeared only as an afterthought:

> For some reason they don't... jump out exactly as turning points in my life, because in certain ways they didn't really... affect my world outlook, perhaps. They weren't... (,) they were very important and emotional... parts of my life, but they really didn't... teach me anything. I really haven't learned anything. I really wasn't *transformed*... by the experience of becoming a father or being married.

The silent intellectuals like their organizations for the chance to meet others that may be of a similar intellectual orientation as well as for being able to attend presentations on various scientific and philosophical topics. Some, like Rüdiger C. (BfG, 69), particularly enjoy their group's library, which enables them to study criticism of religion and its history systematically. Accordingly, Kenneth N. (AOF, 56) believed that he would leave *AOF* only in the case that he would not be able to learn anything new there any longer:

> I like AOF because I'm always learning things. And that's when I'm happiest, when I'm learning something. ...Yes, it's an educational... pursuit. It's a way of expanding my mind. And I think, if I ever left AOF, it would be because... I felt that my mind is no longer growing.

The Narrative Pattern of "Identification with the Organization"

While the narrative patterns introduced so far were characterized primarily by members' motivations for affiliating with their organizations (political protest, community, education), the narrations of the two remaining types of members were shaped more strongly by how they positioned themselves toward their groups. All of these interviewees felt compelled to negotiate the relationship with their organization as a means of performing a segment of their personality that they identified with very strongly. Substantially, these interviews were diametrically opposed to each other, though, as they were characterized either by vehement rejection of or full-blown compliance with the atheist organization.

The Dissociate. All of the organizations explored have a fair share of nominal or passive members. With their membership, they only wish to support the goals of the movement symbolically or financially or they merely wish to be informed by their group's newsletter or magazine. This does not make them "dissociates" in the sense discussed here. Rather, the members classified as such actively *reject identification* with their atheist group, some of its practices, and members. This rejection results from a *value central to the person's identity* which he or she does not see fulfilled or represented by the other atheists and their organizations. Interviewees who exhibit this pattern also exhibit a certain amount of generalized distrust and accuse the atheists of some of the same mistakes that they accuse the religious of. Marco P. (AFS, 65), for example, identified predominantly as a mystic. By this he meant a person who did not believe without questioning, but who was open still to new experiences and insights. Persons, who would jump to conclusions or unconditionally cling to their convictions, he called "stupid" – a term that occurred frequently throughout his interview. One of his fields of interest was that of near-death experiences. He had offered the board of directors at *AFS* to give a talk on the topic, but at the time of the interview he was certain that this would be rejected, as many atheists deemed the field to be unscientific. This "closed-mindedness", Marco said, made him just as angry as bans on the teaching of evolution, which he experienced in his career as a lecturer in anthropology:

> I don't react well to people who try to limit my freedom. And, essentially, what you've been hearing me say about the Atlanta Freethought Society... is that... it seems to me that there are some... in there that have their own very, very narrow view of what free is. ...If they really were free*thought*... they would be *really* open to all thought. But... I don't have the opinion that they are.

While Marco P. felt threatened by "stupid people" who wanted to limit his freedom, the central issue in Mona T.'s (IBKA, 69) narration is her rejection not only of Christians, but also of conservatives and sexist men – who, in her experience, tended to appear in personal union and who she deemed responsible for most bad things that ever happened to her. Even though in *IBKA* there were no Christians, she reported that she still grew critical of the group:

> Because I think the *only* ones who can *really* do anything against those dreadful religions are the leftists... and women. They have the most reason. And both are heavily discriminated against in this organization. ...Being leftist is treated as bad. And women are in the minority. [...] I pity that. But I am still going to stick with IBKA, because otherwise it would only be one less – one leftist and one woman.

Finally, Wolfram B. (IBKA, 55), who was mainly active in the anarchist and pacifist movements, was discouraged from further attending *IBKA* meetings not only by procedures there, such as podium discussions, that he deemed too hierarchical for his taste, but also by the fact that he was not able to recruit new members for the pacifist movement:

> Well, of course, who votes for Social Democrats is not interested in peace and who votes for the Greens goes to war as well. Let me put it that way [laughs slightly]. So, my topic is a minority issue, I know. ...That was obvious. No one showed any interest in it.

Therefore, Wolfram himself developed no interest in engaging with atheism more actively and remained distant. Polletta and Jasper (2001) see a reason for the phenomenon that people sometimes associate themselves with movements whose members they criticize in the fact that "(c)ollective identity is not the same as common ideological commitment. One can join a movement because one shares its goals without identifying much with fellow members (one can even, in some cases, despise them)" (298). To that effect, Marco P. (AFS, 65) stressed that before joining *AFS* he did not think "{{with feigned voice, soft} ooohhh, I'm going to meet people like me. And I'm gonna feel so at home and so comfortable.} Bullshit!" Instead, he said, he only wanted to make a statement:

> I have no... interest in stupidity. ...So, I don't run around looking for stupid groups. I joined... this particular... Atlanta Freethought Society not because I thought these people were... smart and had any answers, but because I (,) ...mainly I thought it was a way of me doing... what I think is morally proper. Me saying: hey, here's another number you can put on your membership list to show that not everybody in this god-damn country is a simple-minded evangelical.

The Euphoric. In contrast, representatives of the euphoric feel completely at home in their atheist activism. Their *identity as atheist* is at the center of their personality. With the freethought-secularist movement they have found a platform with the help of which to act out on this aspect of their identity. This ideal type is characterized by three motives: the *public self-presentation as atheist* in activist as well as everyday situations, the *conviction of being part of a victorious movement*, and the characterization of *religion as psychosis* and mental imprisonment. David M. (SFA, 77) represented the prototypical euphoric:

> I got an atheist cap. It says American Atheists up here. I got that at one of the conventions. And... a reporter from the Chronicle interviewed me... and took my picture and... (,) and this actually was at an atheist meeting, I believe, in Berkeley. They were discussing something... about atheism or something the government is doing. And this reporter was there and... took my picture. And I've been in parades. I've been in a lot of parades... holding... a banner or something. And I give out these pins [pins with the word "GOD" crossed out].

It is obvious that David enjoyed presenting himself as an atheist in public. In contrast to many other American atheists, he happily had his picture taken for a newspaper. Also, he liked to be present and honk his horn at demonstrations, the actual cause of which seems to be less important to him. He fashioned himself an "atheist preacher", who, for example, sings atheist blues songs and plays his harmonica at a night club or who advertises his book, "Atheist Acrimonious", in everyday situations, such as while inquiring about car insurance on the phone. This ambition results from his idea that atheism constitutes a superior and, in the long run, victorious worldview. David typically argued for this view with a mixture of serious and tongue-in-cheek arguments:

> Atheists have more fun. You have more enjoyment being an atheist. You're happier being an atheist. ...And [laughs] (,) and, of course, if you're talking to another guy, says: you can drink more without guilt. I mean, you can have another beer! ...And drink more whiskey! Shit, you got 'em right there [laughs]! ...Or you talk to the women and says: ...did you know that the atheist men are the handsomest men in the world? They're a lot more handsomer than these Catholics. You know? ...Tell 'em any god-damn thing! It don't matter. As long as you get their attention.

Of these arguments, David was at least convinced of the greater happiness that atheists would enjoy. His happiness about his own atheism and his enthusiasm to advertise for it result from his past, when, he claimed, he suffered from "god phobia". Having finally concluded that the god he used to be afraid of did not exist, to him, accordingly, felt like an enormous liberation: "And I've been elated and happy about it... ever since that... I just can't get over it. I am so happy [laughs]."

5 Conclusion

The phenomenon of "new atheism" at the beginning of the 21 century has led to a growing academic and public visibility of a freethought-secularist movement, whose protagonists have sometimes been called "militant" or "zealous atheists" (Gray 2008; Platzek 2011). Apart from the general problem that "militancy" is a mischaracterization of stringent criticism, my exploration of German and American atheist organizations has revealed that the membership of these groups is much more pluralistic – regarding degrees of and motivations for members' activism, their views on strategies and openness, as well as their worldviews and worldview formation. A certain degree of zeal may only be ascribed to members that I characterized as the "political fighter", the "euphoric", and, to some degree, the "intellectual enlightener". In general, organized atheists' activism may be either other- or self-oriented, it may follow political, communal, or educational goals, and it may seek confrontation or accommodation. Also, some of the members may be very critical not only of religion, but also of their fellow atheists and atheist organizations.

This plurality was present in both the American as well as the German organizations. One exception, at least in my sample, was the ideal type of the "euphoric", whose prototypical representative I only found in one of the American groups. While this may be mere coincidence, I would like to argue that a systematic difference between organizations from the two countries can be found with respect to the narrative pattern of "belonging". Even though the study's design does not allow for quantitative comparisons, it is noteworthy that this narrative pattern was much more common in the American interviews. There may be a structural reason for this tendency, and it may have to do with the "ubiquity of theism" (Smith 2011) in U.S. society and the more charismatic and expressive character of American religiosity. It has been reported that these factors make the American atheist identity a rejection identity faced with stigma and ostracism. Accordingly, the main reason for joining atheist organizations so far (looking at American cases only) has been seen in the management of a non-normative identity through association with like-minded people – either with the aim of fighting the stigma, or with the aim of banding together. While important in the American context, this is less of a motive in the case of Germany, where non-religion and atheism are not uncommon and faced with less of a stigma. Accordingly, this exploration has shown that there exist further motivations for secularist activism – namely political outrage and intellectual curiosity – which can be found in both countries alike.

Finally, the difference in religious vitality between the two countries overall may be responsible for the most striking difference between the German and the American atheist organizations. The latter proved to be a lot more vivid. Even though in both countries I consciously sampled organizations that offered their members chances for getting active politically as well as for socializing, the German groups studied offered social events and meetings much less regularly and less frequently than the American ones. Efforts at organizing informal meet-ups within the German groups were generally short-lived and charitable activism not considered necessary. Therefore, except for the preparation of the newsletter, the more active members tended to only meet irregularly, such as for occasional political protest, for outreach at progressive festivals (such as Labor Day or gay pride events), for an occasional lecture or book discussion, and for their groups' annual conferences. In contrast, the American groups featured not only their monthly meetings, but also dinner clubs, book clubs, charitable as well as a plethora of other activities. Even though national differences in civic cultures may also play a role here, it seems more likely that the degree of religiosity present in a culture determines heavily the degree of activism in atheist organizations, which on all other counts are so similar to one another.

Bibliography

Amarasingam, Amarnath, ed. 2010. *Religion and the New Atheism. A Critical Appraisal.* Boston: Brill.

Beaman, Lori G., and Steven Tomlins, eds. 2015. *Atheist Identities – Spaces and Social Contexts.* New York: Springer.

Black, Alan W. 1983. "Organized Irreligion: The New South Wales Humanist Society." *Practice and Belief: Studies in the Sociology of Australian Religion*, edited by Alan W. Black and Peter E. Glasner, 154–166, Sydney: George Allen & Unwin.

Bullivant, Stephen, and Lois Lee. 2012. "Interdisciplinary Studies of Non-religion and Secularity: The State of the Union." *Journal of Contemporary Religion* 27 (1):19–27.

Christina, Greta. 2010. "What Can the Atheist Movement Learn from the Gay Movement?" *Greta Christina's Blog.* February 15, 2010: http://gretachristina.typepad.com/greta_christinas_weblog/2010/02/what-can-the-atheist-movement-learn-from-the-gay-movement.html.

Cimino, Richard, and Christopher Smith. 2007. "Secular Humanism and Atheism beyond Progressive Secularism." *Sociology of Religion* 68 (4):407–424.

Cimino, Richard, and Christopher Smith. 2011. "The New Atheism and the Formation of the Imagined Secularist Community." *Journal of Media and Religion* 10:24–38.

Cimino, Richard, and Christopher Smith. 2014. *Atheist Awakening. Secular Activism & Community in America.* New York: Oxford University Press.

Cragun, Ryan T., and Joseph H. Hammer. 2011. "'One Person's Apostate is Another Person's Convert.' What Terminology Tells Us About Pro-Religious Hegemony in the Sociology of Religion." *Humanity & Society* 35:149–175.

Eller, Jack David. 2010. "What Is Atheism?" *Atheism and Secularity. Volume 1: Issues, Concepts, and Definitions*, edited by Phil Zuckerman, 1–18, Santa Barbara: Praeger.

Fazzino, Lori L., Michael Ian Borer, and Mohammed Abdel Haq. 2014. "The New Moral Entrepreneurs. Atheist Activism as Scripted and Performed Political Deviance." *The Death and Resurrection of Deviance. Current Ideas and Research*, edited by Michael Dellwing, Joseph A. Kotarba, and Nathan W. Pino, 168–191, New York: Palgrave Macmillan.

Fitzgerald, Bridget Ann. 2003. *Atheists in the United States. The Construction and Negotiation of a Nonnormative Identity.* Dissertation. Albany, NY: University of Albany.

Foust, Christine H. 2009. *"An Alien in a Christian World": Intolerance, Coping, and Negotiating Identity among Atheists in the United States.* Master Thesis. Winston-Salem, NC: Wake Forest University.

Goodwin, Jeff, and James M. Jasper, eds. 2009. *The Social Movements Reader: Cases and Concepts.* 2nd edition. Oxford: Wiley-Blackwell.

Gray, John. 2008. "Religionskritik. Was führen die Atheisten im Schilde?" *Frankfurter Allgemeine Zeitung*, April 1st 2008 (online edition): http://www.faz.net/aktuell/feuilleton/debatten/religionskritik-was-fuehren-die-atheisten-im-schilde-1512472.html.

Guenther Katja M., Natasha Radjocic, and Kerry Mulligan. 2015. "Humor, Collective Identity, and Framing in the New Atheist Movement." *Research in Social Movements, Conflict and Change* 38: 203–227.

Heiner, Robert. 2008. "Nones on the Run. Evangelical Heathens in the Deep South." *Deviance Across Cultures*, edited by Robert Heiner, 201–216, New York: Oxford University Press.

Hunsberger, Bruce, and Bob Altemeyer. 2006. *Atheists. A Groundbreaking Study of America's Nonbelievers.* Amherst: Prometheus Books.

Iannaccone, Laurence R..1990. "Religious Practice: A Human Capital Approach." *Journal for the Scientific Study of Religion* 29 (3): 297–314.

Jasper, James M., and Jane D. Poulsen. 1995. "Recruiting Strangers and Friends: Moral Shocks and Social Networks in Animal Rights and Anti-Nuclear Protests." *Social Problems* 42(4): 493–512.

Kelle, Udo, and Susann Kluge. 2010. *Vom Einzelfall zum Typus. Fallvergleich und Fallkontrastierung in der qualitativen Sozialforschung.* 2nd edition. Wiesbaden: VS Verlag für Sozialwissenschaften.

Kettell, Steven. 2013. "Faithless: The Politics of New Atheism." *Secularism and Nonreligion* 2:61–72.

Kruse, Jan. 2011. *Reader – Einführung in die qualitative Interviewforschung. Version Oktober 2011.* Freiburg: Universität Freiburg, Institut für Soziologie.

Kruse, Jan. 2014. *Qualitative Interviewforschung. Ein integrativer Ansatz.* Weinheim, Basel: Beltz-Juventa.

LeDrew, Stephen. 2012. "The Evolution of Atheism: Scientific and Humanistic Approaches." *History of Human Sciences* 25 (3):70–87.

LeDrew, Stephen. 2013. "Discovering Atheism: Heterogeneity in Trajectories to Atheist Identity and Atheism." *Sociology of Religion* 74(4):431–453.

LeDrew, Stephen. 2016. *The Evolution of Atheism. The Politics of a Modern Movement.* New York: Oxford University Press.

Lee, Lois. 2012. "Research Note: Talking about a Revolution: Terminology for the New Field of Non-religion Studies." *Journal of Contemporary Religion* 27(1): 129–139.

McCarthy, John D., and Mayer N. Zald. 1977. "Resource Mobilization and Social Movements: A Partial Theory." *American Journal of Sociology* 82(6): 1212–1241.

McGrath, Allister. 2004. *The Twilight of Atheism. The Rise and Fall of Disbelief in the Modern World.* London: Rider.

McTaggart, John Mitchell. 1997. "Organized Humanism in Canada: An Expression of Secular Reaffiliation." *Religion and the Social Order. Volume 7: Leaving Religion and Religious Life*, edited by Mordechai Bar-Lev and William Shaffir, 61–75, Greenwich: JAI Press.

Mumford, Lorna. 2015. "Living Non-religious Identity in London." *Atheist Identities – Spaces and Social Contexts*, edited by Lori G. Beaman and Steven Tomlins, 153–170, Heidelberg: Springer.

Oberschall, Anthony. 1973. *Social Conflict and Social Movements.* NJ: Prentice-Hall.

Pasquale, Frank L. 2007. "The 'Nonreligious' in the American Northwest." *Secularism & Secularity: Contemporary International Perspectives*, edited by Barry A. Kosmin and Ariela Keysar, 41–58, Hartfort: Institute for the Study of Secularity in Society and Culture, ISSSC.

Pasquale, Frank L. 2010. "A Portrait of Secular Group Affiliates." *Atheism and Secularity. Volume 1: Issues, Concepts, and Definitions*, edited by Phil Zuckerman, 43–87, Santa Barbara: Praeger.

Platzek, Arik. 2011. "Die Legende vom militanten Atheismus." *Humanistischer Pressedienst*, January 12th 2011: http://hpd.de/node/10955.

Polletta, Francesca, and James M. Jasper. 2001. "Collective Identity and Social Movements." *Annual Review of Sociology* 27: 283–305.

Ritchie, Jane, and Jane Lewis. 2003. *Qualitative Research Practice. A Guide for Social Science Students and Researchers*. Los Angeles: Sage.

Smith, Jesse M. 2011. "Becoming an Atheist in America. Constructing Identity and Meaning from the Rejection of Theism." *Sociology of Religion* 72(2): 215–237.

Snow, David A., E. Burke Rochford, Jr., Steven K. Worden, and Robert D. Benford. 1986. "Frame Alignment Processes, Micromobilization, and Movement Participation." *American Sociological Review* 51(4): 464–481.

Strauss, Anselm L., and Juliet Corbin. 1998. *Basics of Qualitative Research: Grounded Theory Procedures and Techniques*. 2nd edition. Thousand Oaks: Sage.

Taira, Teemu, and Ruth Illman 2012. "The New Visibility of Atheism in Europe." *Approaching Religion* 2(1): 1–2.

Walsh, Edward J. 1981. "Resource Mobilization and Citizen Protest in Communities Around Three Mile Island." *Social Problems* 29(1): 1–21.

Witzel, Andreas. 2000. "The Problem-Centered Interview." *Forum Qualitative Sozialforschung / Forum Qualitative Social Research* 1 (1), article 22: http://www.qualitative-research.net/index.php/fqs/article/view/1132/2521.

Wolf, Gary. 2006. "The Church of the Non-Believers." *Wired* 14 (11):182–193: http://www.wired.com/2006/11/atheism/.

Zenk, Thomas. 2010. "Die Erfindung des 'Neuen Atheismus'. Relgionswissenschaftliche Anmerkungen zu einem Phänomen der religiösen Gegenwartskultur." *Aufklärung und Kritik* 17(3): 127–135.

Zuckerman, Phil. 2012. *Faith No More. Why People Reject Religion*. New York: Oxford University Press.

Dusty Hoesly
Your Wedding, Your Way: Personalized, Nonreligious Weddings through the Universal Life Church

1 Introduction: The Growth of Personalized, Nonreligious Weddings

Wedding ceremonies in the United States are increasingly personalized and nonreligious, a trend facilitated in part by the Universal Life Church (ULC), which will ordain anyone nearly instantly. While it does not identify as a secular or nonbeliever organization, the ULC provides a popular pathway for self-described nonreligious couples to achieve a unique wedding that honors their beliefs and relationships. As a church, its ministers are capable of solemnizing marriages legally; and as a religion that allows anyone to become a minister, it permits secular people to perform legally valid weddings. Although civil ceremonies are secular, they are not often customized for specific couples. Secular celebrants who are certified by nonbeliever organizations are few and far between, and in most states their weddings are not recognized legally. Given that nonbeliever organizations have not prioritized secular alternatives to religious rites of passage, nonreligious couples find alternatives that facilitate such rituals, even paradoxically yet pragmatically by utilizing a religious resource such as the ULC. The ULC thus complicates notions of "organized secularism" because it shows how many avowedly secular people take up a strategic religious identity in order to achieve a desired nonreligious ritual in an individualized manner.

The rise of nonreligious weddings in the 21st century tracks with several developments in American society and technology, particularly the rise of the "nones" and widespread use of the internet. Since 1990, more Americans have declared that they have no religious affiliation, rising from 8% in 1990 to 21% in 2014, according to the General Social Survey (Hout and Smith 2015, 1). A 2014 Pew survey claims that 23% of Americans are religiously unaffiliated (2015, 3). Younger cohorts are more likely to be unaffiliated, with 33% of those aged 18–24 claiming no religious affiliation (Hout and Smith 2015, 3). During this same time, the rates of Americans who earn bachelor's and graduate degrees, engage in premarital sex, cohabit before marriage, delay marriage and childbirth, and forego marriage entirely have increased. In 2010, the median age for first marriage was 29 for men and 27 for women, up from 26 and 24 in

1990 (Cohn et al. 2011). As newer generations get married, they want their weddings to reflect their increasing secularity. Those with no religion tend to marry partners also with no religion (Baker and Smith 2015, 163–164; Merino 2012, 8). Alongside these trends, the growth of the internet as a site for exchanging and marketing wedding concepts and vendors has changed how Americans marry. The development of wedding websites and blogs, such as The Knot, A Practical Wedding, and Offbeat Bride, has steered middle class tastes regarding wedding fashions and DIY alternatives. The internet has also made it easy for people to become ministers in religions that allow near-instant ordination online.[1] The primary institution offering such ordinations is the ULC, which has ordained nearly 23 million people since 1962 by mail and online.

Rates of weddings performed by conventional clergy have declined as couples opt instead for friends or relatives who get ordained online or else hire professional wedding officiants, an emerging industry in the 21st century (Gootman 2012).[2] According to The Knot's 2009 survey of its members, 29% of member couples were married by a friend or relative; by 2015, that number jumped to 40% (Sun 2016). The Wedding Report similarly shows that the ratio of weddings performed by friends or relatives (from 10% in 2008 to 17% in 2012), or by professional officiants who advertise as wedding vendors (from 13% in 2008 to 17% in 2012), is growing (McMurray 2012, 2–3). Simultaneously, the ratio of weddings performed by priests (27% in 2008 but 18% in 2012) and by pastors, ministers, and rabbis (43% in 2008 but 39% in 2012) is declining, while the proportion of civil ceremonies has remained steady (about 6%) (2–3).[3] Despite the statistical variations between The Knot and The Wedding Report, both show a clear and fast-growing trend toward friends and relatives officiating weddings rather than traditional clergy. Nonreligious people increasingly want a personalized ceremony that reflects their values, led by someone they know. Most of the indi-

---

[1] Internet-based religions offering near-instant online ordination, usually for free, include American Marriage Ministries, Open Ministry, Universal One Church, Church of Spiritual Humanism, Rose Ministries, American Fellowship Church, First Nation Church & Ministry, Church of the Latter-Day Dude, United Church of Bacon, Church of the Flying Spaghetti Monster, and more, in addition to the Universal Life Church.

[2] The New York City Clerk's office "processed 1,105 marriage licenses last year for ceremonies officiated by Universal Life ministers, a small fraction of the total, but more than twice as many as in 2009" (Gootman 2012).

[3] There are almost no government or academic surveys of how people marry or of the numbers or ratios of civil to religious wedding ceremonies. Counties and states rarely input data regarding whether marriages were civil or religious into state records databases, although that information is marked by officiants on individual marriage licenses in most jurisdictions. Rates of civil ceremonies likely climbed after the nation-wide legalization of same-sex marriage in 2015.

viduals ordained online for this purpose receive their ministerial license through the ULC.

American weddings have become more individually-centered, alternatively spiritual, and overtly secular since the 1960s, as couples have sought alternatives to traditional religious rituals. This personalization and detraditionalization of American weddings is linked to the ULC, which began as a mail-order ministry. News media (Curtis 1970; Gootman 2012; Lehmann-Haupt 2003; Price 1993), wedding guidebooks (Ayers and Brown 1994, 117–118; Bare 2007, 180–181; Francesca 2014, 22–24; Roney 1998, 78, 98; Roney 2013, 24; Stallings 2010, 116; Toussaint and Leo 2004, 39), and scholars (Dunak 2013, 80; Mead 2007, 138, 161) have explicitly cited the ULC as part of the growth of personalized weddings. Same-sex couples, now legally permitted to marry across the U.S., typically want nonreligious weddings, with many led by ULC ministers (Freedman 2015). These sources report that couples seeking nontraditional and nonreligious weddings often ask a friend or relative to officiate for them, using the ULC as a way to ensure their marriages' legality while reflecting their choices for how they want to celebrate their special day.

This chapter explores how nonreligious couples celebrate their weddings using the ULC as a case study, and how ULC weddings complicate simplistic secular-religious binaries. Since nonbeliever organizations, as well as most religious organizations and civil officiants, are unable to meet the demand for personalized, nonreligious weddings, nonreligious couples seek alternatives such as the ULC. The ULC is a religious institution that will ordain nonreligious people, who can then officiate personalized, nonreligious, and legally-valid weddings. In order to be recognized by the state, a secular or "spiritual but not religious" friend who officiates a ceremony is counted as a religious minister, and the nonreligious ceremony is counted as a religious one, even though all of the parties to the wedding understand it and themselves to be thoroughly nonreligious. According to my original survey and interview data, most ULC ministers and the couples who engage them self-describe as nonreligious, typically as "spiritual but not religious" but also as humanist, secular, agnostic, and atheist. Similarly, they describe their weddings as nonreligious, consciously excluding traditional religious language and locations. Examining ULC weddings thus reveals not only the diversity of nontheistic self-identification and lifecycle ritualization, but also the interpenetration and co-constitution of religious and secular categories. The ULC, its ministers, and its weddings blur the presumed boundary between religious and secular, showing their constant entanglement.

In next four sections, I discuss my research methods, the history of American wedding personalization and secularization, secular options for nuptial celebration, and the ULC's history particularly as it relates to weddings. I then analyze a sample ULC wedding (section 6) before placing it in the context of general ULC wedding trends (section 7). Finally, I conclude by examining further how ULC weddings, in instantiating a sort of "secular sacred," demonstrate the mutual entanglement of the religious and the secular.

2 Methodology

In order to investigate how nonreligious couples marry through the ULC, I conducted mixed-methods research including participant observation, interviews, a survey, and archival research.[4] I was ordained by the ULC in 2000 while I was a college undergraduate; I had heard about it from classmates and thought it would be fun to become a titular minister. I did nothing with my ordination until 2009 when two friends asked me to officiate their wedding. Over the next six years I officiated twelve more weddings for friends and relatives: two in 2011, three in 2012, two in 2013, two in 2014, and three in 2015.[5] Weddings took place in California, Oregon, Washington, Louisiana, Connecticut, and England. For each wedding, I took notes about what kind of ceremony the couple wanted, where it took place, what kind of language and rituals they wanted included and excluded, how they met and fell in love, why they wanted to get married, and what compromises (if any) the couple made amongst each other and with their parents or other family members who expressed preferences for the ceremony. All but one of the couples agreed to interview with me about their wedding for my research, and all names and identifying characteristics are anonymized.

From November 2013 to May 2014, I distributed an online survey of ULC members and couples married by them through personal chain referral email and Facebook contacts, ULC Seminary and ULC Monastery monthly email newsletters and Facebook pages, and eighteen other Facebook pages which used the

---

[4] Parts of this methodology section repeat descriptions from an earlier publication (Hoesly 2015).

[5] For full disclosure, I also began a wedding officiant business in Santa Barbara, California in 2012 and have since officiated over 80 additional weddings in that capacity. No data from those weddings is included in my research, however, because I opted not to solicit those couples' consent to participate in my study and because I was paid for officiating their weddings. My research question primarily focuses on couples who consciously select someone they know to officiate their ceremony as a ULC minister, rather than couples who select an officiant-for-hire who is otherwise a stranger and who just happens to be ordained by the ULC. While this is an interesting population and a phenomenon worthy of further study, it is not the focus of this chapter.

name "Universal Life Church." Questions covered each respondent's past and current religious, spiritual, or secular beliefs, practices, and self-identifications; reflections on their affiliation with the ULC; knowledge about and characterization of the ULC; descriptions and labeling of ULC weddings in which they have participated; and demographic information. Some questions allowed for an open-ended response. All responses were anonymous. 1,599 people completed the survey. Answers were coded and analyzed for patterns related to respondents' (non-)religious self-identifications, motivations for affiliating with the ULC and characterizations about the church, and (non-)religious characteristics and labeling of ULC wedding ceremonies. At the end of the survey, respondents could opt-in to participate in a follow-up interview by providing their contact information. No compensation was provided to any survey or interview participant.

I conducted in-depth, semi-structured interviews with 62 ULC ministers and 31 couples married by ULC ministers from October 2012 to May 2015. Participants were gathered through chain referral sampling and through the opt-in question at the end of the online survey. As it is not possible to determine what a representative sample of ULC ministers and couples wed by them would be, given the respective ULC churches' lack of demographic data collection, I sought interviewees via purposeful sampling, looking for "typical cases" as well as significant variants (Patton 2002, 230–242).[6] Most chain referral participants lived in California, Oregon, and Washington, so most of my interviews occurred in those states. Interviews took place in person, by phone, and online via Skype or Google Hangouts. All participants have been given pseudonyms. Questions covered the same topics as the survey. Interviews were transcribed, coded, and analyzed for patterns related to the same themes as the survey.

I also interviewed the president of the Universal Life Church (Andre Hensley), as well as leaders of several ULC-affiliated and spin-off organizations, such as the Universal Life Church Monastery (George Freeman), the Universal Life Church Seminary (Amy Long), and the Universal Life Church Online (Kevin Andrews), among others. These interviews covered the history, activities,

---

[6] Typical case sampling is one kind of purposive/purposeful (nonprobability) sampling. In typical case sampling, the researcher looks for themes that recur frequently or that are not extreme or unusual. These cannot be used to make generalized statements about the experiences of all participants, but rather are illustrative. Other kinds of purposeful sampling include extreme/deviant case sampling, maximum variation (heterogeneity) sampling, homogenous sampling, convenience sampling, chain referral, etc. I looked for recurring themes and narratives until I reached data saturation. By significant variants, I mean seeking extreme or deviant cases as well as covering a spectrum of perspectives (maximum variation).

and organization of each group, and the leaders' involvement in and thoughts about each church, in addition to the same topics discussed in the other interviews. These interviews were designed to augment the information I gathered from ULC archival sources, newspaper and magazine databases, and court decisions. The original ULC in Modesto, California allowed me to study their church records, newsletters, and publications. Online, I visited ULC websites, subscribed to various ULC email newsletters, followed official and unofficial ULC Facebook pages, and read official and unofficial web-based discussion forums.

3 Your Wedding, Your Way

Personal choice reigns supreme in how couples construct contemporary weddings.[7] Just as modern couples choose their marital partners, they also want to craft a wedding that manifests their particular desires, tastes, and beliefs. Although couples often negotiate some aspects of their weddings with parents or other concerned parties, the couples' expressive choices are paramount. Underlying contemporary American wedding culture, Rebecca Mead argues, is the idea that "a wedding ceremony, like a wedding reception, ought to be an expression of the character of the couple who are getting married, rather than an expression of the character of the institution marrying them" (2007, 139). Specifically linking this trend with ULC-ordained ministers, Mead attests that growing numbers of "unchurched" people desire "freelance, part-time" ministers who can offer "an aura of spirituality without the regulations of an organized religion" (138). Such weddings are an "expression of their taste when it came to religious ritual—their selection among an array of elements" they could include (136–137). As Howard Kirschenbaum and Rockwell Stensrud noted over forty years ago, "The personal wedding has revolutionized our society's way of thinking about rites of passage" (1974, 15). The ideology of personal choice continues to ground and shape American weddings today, including for nonreligious couples.

Starting in the 1960s, scholars documented a cultural turn away from more established religions (Wilson 1966), observing new forms of religious experimentation, spiritual seeking, and secularization (Roof 1993; Roof 2001; Wuthnow 1998; Wuthnow 2010). Progressive, anti-establishment attitudes challenged traditional religious institutions and orientations. Feminists and civil rights movements insisted on full equality, inclusion, and social justice. Increased social

---

[7] Christel Manning has shown that personal choice also guides how nonreligious parents raise their children (2015).

mobility and higher education further threatened local affiliations and social mores. For many, the individual self became the locus of authority. This new era of "expressive individualism" affected all facets of American life, including marriage (Bellah et al. 1985, 33). Karen Dunak describes this trend toward "individual expression, personal authority, and cultural reinterpretation" as central to modern weddings, which eschew patriarchal forms of wedding ritualization and marriage, passé religious or parental expectations, and rigid conformity to social conventions (Dunak 2013, 6).[8]

Since the 1970s, books titled *Your Wedding, Your Way* (Ingram 2000; Naylor 2010; Newman 1975; Stoner 1993; Vincenzi 2003) have celebrated growing individualization in American weddings while noting declining religious elements. In 1975, Carol Newman offered tips for "planning and executing a personalized ceremony," capturing a moment in the history of American weddings that increasingly emphasized prioritizing a couple's choices for their ceremony above traditional wedding etiquette, parental concerns, and religious traditions (13).[9] Her book included suggestions about outdoor wedding venues, modern spiritual readings, and "where to find a flexible officiant" who would be "open to the concept of the new wedding" (128). Clergy allowed couples to include less patriarchal or sexist language in ceremonies, for example, or to write their own vows. "Even within the traditional wedding," Newman wrote, "personalization has become common practice" (134). The growth of personalized weddings went hand-in-hand with a turn toward spiritual and secular self-identifications, leading couples to evacuate religion from their ceremonies.[10] As Marcia Seligson

---

8 Karen Dunak states, "Spirituality trumped organized religious belief. Personal selection and contribution were paramount" (2013, 85). Couples incorporated nonsexist language in their ceremonies, Kahlil Gibran's *The Prophet* or the "Apache Wedding Prayer" instead of biblical quotes, alternative clothing, outdoors locations, and other elements reflecting the new era. This "individualized approach to their weddings" reflected couples' desires for "honesty and authenticity" as much as leftist politics or alternative lifestyles (92).

9 Leah Ingram similarly advised couples: "Forget what convention tells you to do. This is your day and you should have a wedding that truly reflects who you two are as a couple" (2000, xi).

10 Sharon Naylor encouraged couples to "break from tradition and create a one-of-a-kind celebration," emphasizing that the wedding ceremony is "where you join your lives together in the manner of *your* choosing, with the words and the music *you* want, the rituals that mean the most to *you* [emphasis in original]" (2010, 31). This is in contrast to the "strong-handed direction to follow religious protocol, to include the types of rituals that mean the most to *them* [emphasis in original]" (15). Her oppositional view of religion shaped her recommendations for wedding location ("Look at nature as the ultimate religious location") and officiant (suggesting the Celebrant Foundation & Institute, a civil servant, or "having a friend or relative ordained to perform your ceremony"), as well as many other wedding elements (34–35). In her list of values that shape couples' desires for non-traditional weddings, "Religion is not a big part of your life"

noted of the "new wedding" of the 1960s, "Whatever the script created, most kids of the new world prefer that God be mentioned as little as possible" (1973, 278).[11] Similarly, today's nonreligious couples—whether "spiritual but not religious" or secular—prefer to leave religion out of their weddings, even if they draw upon some religious ritual forms or otherwise bend traditions to their personal likings.

4 Secular Wedding Options

Nonreligious couples in America who do not want to be married by a traditional religious authority have limited options apart from a civil ceremony if they want their wedding to be legally valid. In the United States, each state regulates marriage differently, although all require a marriage license issued by civil officials. The vast majority of couples who wish to marry have only two options: a religious wedding performed by clergy (often labeled a "minister of the gospel" in state marital statutes) from a recognized religious organization or a secular wedding performed by a designated civil official (such as a judge). Religious ceremonies are often performed in churches or other religious buildings, but can also take place at other sites, depending on the flexibility of the clergy person performing the ceremony and the requirements of the religious tradition. The specific content of these ceremonies depends upon the dictates of the religion and the choices of the individual minister. Civil ceremonies usually take place in city halls or courthouses, although some civil officials may choose to perform ceremonies at other locations and times, depending on where and when a couple wishes to marry. Due to the constitutional prohibition on government establishment of religion, and since civil officiants are agents of the state, these ceremonies are supposed to be secular. Some states allow additional alternatives for couples, such as getting married by a notary public,[12] by someone who becomes

---

came first, followed by ecological living, a preference for unique or personalized elements, and other values (6).

11 Robert Bocock argued that there is a general trend away from religious ritual and toward secular forms in industrial societies, including in weddings and funerals (1974). Bryan Wilson also documented declines in religious weddings (1966). Nicholas MacMurray and Lori L. Fazzino discuss secular funerals in this volume.

12 Four states authorize notary publics to solemnize marriages: Florida, Maine, Nevada, and South Carolina. Kelle Clarke, a member of the National Notary Association, reports on the *Notary Bulletin* website that notaries in other states can get ordained online in order to officiate weddings (2014).

deputized for a day,[13] or by self-solemnization,[14] but these are not options in most states.

Secular wedding options usually do not provide the personalization that modern couples desire, or else are not legally valid. While tens of thousands of couples marry in civil ceremonies each year, courthouse weddings are typically standardized ceremonies led by a stranger with little tailoring for the individual couple. Aside from civil ceremonies, there are several secular organizations that authorize trained celebrants to perform weddings, including the Center for Inquiry (CFI), the Humanist Institute,[15] the Humanist Society,[16] and the Celebrant Foundation & Institute. The Unitarian Universalist Association (UUA) will also perform atheist weddings. Although many couples get married by using such celebrants each year, several issues limit their reach and appeal: the process of becoming certified is lengthy and costly, few states recognize marriages solemnized by secular celebrants, and couples who want a personalized wedding prefer someone they know to officiate it.

In order to become a celebrant with one of these secular organizations or the UUA, one has to undertake a period of training, pay fees, and submit to the rules of the certifying body. For example, to become a CFI secular celebrant, an individual must become a member of the CFI, attend a training, obtain letters of recommendation, write an essay describing one's worldview, interview with CFI directors, obtain approval, and pay initial and yearly fees.[17] Similarly, the Humanist Institute requires applicants to complete online training; the Humanist Society requires an application, a fee, and membership in the American Humanist Association; and the Celebrant Foundation and Institute requires lengthy training and higher fees in order to become a "Certified Life-Cycle Celebrant™." These rules make it hard for nonreligious couples to have someone they know

---

13 Alaska, California, Massachusetts, Vermont, and Washington, D.C., for example, allow people to become a "deputy marriage commissioner for a day" or "temporary officiant" (or similar title) so that they can perform a particular civil ceremony. There are several requirements in order to become deputized, such as paying a fee and obtaining paperwork from the county clerk's office, with specific requirements dependent on local statutes.
14 Colorado, Pennsylvania, Wisconsin, and Washington, D.C., allow couples to self-solemnize (perform their own marriage), for example.
15 The Humanist Institute is an affiliate of the American Humanist Association.
16 The Humanist Society is an adjunct of the American Humanist Association.
17 The CFI further notes that it "does not allow anyone acting as a CFI Secular Celebrant to solemnize a marriage under any religious designation or pretense, or using the certification of any religious organization," including the Humanist Society and "so called 'mail order' ordinations such as the Universal Life Church." "CFI Celebrant Certification," Center for Inquiry, accessed March 1, 2016, http://www.centerforinquiry.net/education/celebrant_certification/.

become certified to perform their ceremony. Furthermore, most states do not permit celebrants trained by secular organizations to solemnize legal marriages, and there are very few secular celebrants in states where this is permitted.[18] The UUA, by contrast, is recognized by every state as a religious organization whose marriage solemnizations are valid.

More importantly, none of the couples I interviewed considered a secular celebrant because such celebrants pose the same problem as clergy and civil officiants: lack of a personal relationship with the couple. The driving motivation for nonreligious couples to ask their friends or family to become ULC ministers is so that they can have someone they know well perform an intimate, heartfelt wedding tailored to that specific couple, while reflecting their nonreligious worldviews. A celebrant trained by one of the aforementioned secular organizations or a UUA minister could offer a customized ceremony, but she likely would not be someone with whom the couple had a prior relationship; instead, she would be a stranger who the couple contracted for a service. A friend ordained online by the ULC, for free, without any creedal commitment or organizational oversight, allows nonreligious couples to marry however they wish assured that their ceremony will be recognized as legally valid. It can be a romantic, perhaps humorous, and personally-meaningful celebration led by a close friend or relative of their choosing.

5 The Universal Life Church

The story of the ULC is a prism for contemporary American religion, reflecting trends in emerging forms of spirituality, secularization, individualization, and state regulation of new religions. Kirby J. Hensley (1911–1999) incorporated the ULC in 1962 in Modesto, California, offering free ordinations to anyone

---

[18] In 2013, Washington, D.C., began allowing "civil celebrants" trained by a secular or nonreligious organization to perform marriage ceremonies, and New Jersey became the first state to authorize "civil celebrants" to solemnize marriages in 2014. Oregon followed suit in 2017. The CFI won a federal lawsuit, *Center for Inquiry v. Marion Circuit Court Clerk*, in 2014 forcing Indiana, Illinois, and Wisconsin to recognize CFI secular celebrants as lawful marriage officiants. In 2014, Nevada changed its marriage statutes to permit notary publics to perform weddings after humanists and atheists filed a lawsuit. As of 2015, due to a lawsuit, Washington County, Minnesota became the fourth county in that state to allow atheists accredited by a nonbeliever organization to perform weddings; bills that would allow atheists to officiate weddings have also been introduced in the state legislature. Movements in the United Kingdom similarly advocate that governments recognize humanist weddings (Engelke 2014; Law Commission 2015). New York has long permitted Ethical Culture Society leaders to solemnize marriages.

who wanted one. He had preached earlier in Baptist and Pentecostal congregations, but they dismissed him due to his unorthodox beliefs and provocative preaching style. In founding his own church, Hensley wanted to "make it possible for *anybody* to be ordained... No matter *what* he believes [emphasis in original]" (Ashmore 1977, 21). The ULC had no doctrine except to do *"that which is right... and every person has the right to decide what is right for himself* [emphasis in original]" (24). Hensley's church is a religious institution flexible enough to accept all manner of beliefs and practices, including Christianity, Judaism, Asian religions, UFOs, New Thought, metaphysical spiritualities, and atheism.[19] In addition to shielding ministers from any doctrinal orthodoxy that might be imposed by church hierarchies, the ULC defends individual religious freedom from state regulation. As he told one college audience, "We don't stand between *you* and your *God*, but between *you* and the *State*. The purpose of the Church is to bring *absolute Freedom of Religion* to *all* people [emphasis in original]" (52). Hensley called the ULC a "buffer zone" for religious liberty, protecting ministers from the encroachments of both church and state while ensuring that no outside authority would dictate or delimit a person's beliefs or practices (1986).

The unconventional form and content of the ULC helped it grow rapidly, ordaining over one million ministers by 1971, but it also brought challenges from government regulators and skeptical media. Draft boards complained that the church encouraged Vietnam War draftees to resist conscription by claiming the draft's ministerial exemption. California's tax agency argued that the church served as a for-profit diploma mill, since it offered honorary doctorate degrees for a fee without state accreditation. The IRS refused to grant the church tax-exempt status. However, the ULC sued and a federal judge ordered the IRS to recognize it as a tax-exempt religion in *Universal Life Church v. U.S.* (1974). The court also declared that states cannot require accreditation for honorary theological degrees. Hensley and the ULC touted this ruling in publications, subsequent legal arguments, and in the media, including during their long-running dispute with the IRS after it revoked the ULC's tax exemption in 1984 for advocating tax avoidance schemes. By that year, the ULC had ordained over 12 million ministers. In the 1970s-1980s, a number of legal cases challenged the legitimacy of ULC weddings in state courts, but over time judges have generally ruled in favor of their validity (Rains 2010).[20] Unlike childbirth or puberty rituals or funerals, wed-

---

19 For example, Hensley ordained Madalyn Murray O'Hair, the founder of American Atheists, awarded her honorary degrees, and issued a charter for her Poor Richard's Universal Life Church in Austin, Texas (Ashmore 1977, 39; LeBeau 2003, 148–150).
20 The first of these, *Ravenal v. Ravenal* (1972), centered on a New York couple's divorce wherein the man argued that he owed no alimony due to the fact that they were never legally married.

dings must conform to state marital statutes in order to count as legal marriages; they are governed by laws in ways that other lifecycle rituals are not (Cott 2000). Despite the few states where ULC weddings were litigated, the vast majority of states have always accepted ULC weddings as legally valid.[21] The ULC encourages ministers to check with each county in which marriages will be performed to ensure their legal validity.[22]

The judge agreed, declaring the marriage void since the ULC minister and the ULC itself did not meet the state's definitions of a church or of a minister eligible to solemnize marriages. Many laws governing marriage require ecclesiastical bodies to have some structure managing their clergy and for ministers to maintain a regular house of worship, meeting times, and membership. The ULC's loose ecclesiology did not fit these state definitions of religion and ministry, judges ruled. This early decision would be affirmed in later cases, *Rubino v. City of New York* (1984) and *Ranieri v. Ranieri* (1989), although a different New York court, in *Oswald v. Oswald* (2013), ruled recently that the ULC counts as a religion and its ministers are eligible to solemnize marriages. The judge in the latter case argued that the ULC, while unconventional, is a religion if it says it is and that courts should not second guess church decisions about their own ordination processes. The logic of these two positions, for and against the ULC, played out in several other cases. In *Cramer v. Commonwealth* (1974) and *State v. Lynch* (1980), Virginia and North Carolina's supreme courts ruled that the ULC is not a church and that its ministers are not clergy according to their state statutes defining these terms, while Mississippi's supreme court ruled in favor of the ULC in *Last Will and Testament of Blackwell v. Magee* (1988). Judges in Washington, D.C., ruled against the ULC in 1981 (*In re: Dixon*) but for it in 1998 (*In re: Stack*). Judges in different Pennsylvania counties ruled against the ULC in 2007 (*Heyer v. Hollerbush*) and for it in 2008 (*In re: O'Neill*). A 2001 Utah bill prohibiting recognition of marriages performed by ministers who are ordained by mail or online was ruled unconstitutional by a federal judge in *Universal Life Church v. Utah* (2002). In 2006, the New York City Clerk's office issued a rule allowing ULC ministers to officiate weddings in the five boroughs. Additionally, a New York Assemblywoman has tried to pass a bill from 2005 to at least 2012 that would grant online officiants legal power to solemnize marriages throughout the state. The overall trend is that the more recent decisions recognize the ULC as a religion and its weddings as legally valid.

21 Indeed, the few jurisdictions where ULC weddings are not honored due to judicial rulings are Virginia, North Carolina, and parts of Pennsylvania and New York. In personal phone calls with clerks and recorders in each jurisdiction in which ULC marriages are supposedly invalid, I was told that marriage licenses are recorded without inspection as to the ecclesiastical body ordaining the minister. In effect, ULC weddings in these jurisdictions are processed successfully nearly all the time.

22 New Haven County in Connecticut refused to accept my ULC ordination as valid for performing a marriage there when I called in the summer of 2015. This seems to run counter to an official opinion of the Connecticut General Assembly's Office of Legislative Research, which declares that "Nothing in statute or case law appears to prohibit mail order ministers from performing marriages in Connecticut" (OLR 2003-R-0490). I have officiated legally valid weddings in four states. New Haven and Frodsham, England are the only two jurisdictions that did not accept my ULC ordination; nevertheless, I performed ceremonial weddings for each of these two couples, even though they were married legally in civil ceremonies earlier in the day.

The expansion of the internet in the 1990s broadened the ULC's reach and further connected it to wedding personalization. In 1995, the ULC created a website offering online ordinations and retailing ministerial products under a subsidiary called the Universal Life Church Monastery (ULC Monastery). Newspapers ran stories about journalists getting ordained online, celebrity ordinations, and nontraditional weddings led by ULC ministers, further promoting the ULC as a way for nontraditional or nonreligious couples to personalize their weddings. After Kirby Hensley died, the ULC settled with the IRS. Internally, it lost control of the ULC Monastery, which was reincorporated as an independent entity in Seattle, Washington by George Freeman, a ULC minister who thought that the church was not harnessing the power of the internet as much as it should. Today, the ULC Monastery owns hundreds of online ordination websites, directing web searches to the ULC Monastery; most people ordained online today are ULC Monastery ministers.[23] In the early 2000s, two ULC ministers created the Universal Life Church Seminary and the Universal Life Church Online, both affiliated with the original ULC. These sites offer ordinations and sell their own ministerial products; they united into one organization, also called the Universal Life Church Seminary, in early 2016. In this chapter, I will use the name Universal Life Church or ULC to refer to all of these churches, unless I am referring to a particular church, in which case I will identify that specific church by name.

6 A ULC Wedding

In this section, I present an example of a nonreligious couple who got married by a friend who was ordained online by the ULC so that she could perform their wedding. Given the diversity of the types of couples and weddings I encountered in my study of ULC weddings, no single story can capture this variety. Still, Scott and Sadie's worldviews and wedding include many of the characteristics that appeared frequently in accounts of personalized, nonreligious ULC weddings.

Scott and Sadie got married in 2010 in Portland, Oregon. They had both moved to Portland to attend college and then remained in the city after graduation. Even though they were just acquaintances during school, their friendship eventually grew into something more, as camping trips and regular hikes became stepping stones to developing their romantic relationship. They dated for

---

[23] The ULC Monastery ordains around 1,000 people per day, according to my 2014 interview with its president, George Freeman. In 2009, Andre Hensley said that the ULC ordained 8,500 – 10,000 ministers per month (Nowicki 2009).

six years before getting married, which they agreed "brought us together more as partners." Even though they had lived together before marrying and had already committed themselves to each other, they felt that having a legal marriage and ceremony "substantiated the relationship." They are now in their mid-30s and raising a son.

Sadie grew up near Boston in an Italian-Irish Catholic family, attending church regularly, but she left the church in high school after a class inspired her critical evaluation of religion in general, leading her to refuse confirmation rites. "I started learning about religion and religious history and decided—I was never really that into going to church anyways—and I didn't really want to be a part of the church and so I separated myself from that," she said. "I have not embodied any religion since then. I'm not really interested in it," she added. Instead, in Portland, she has developed a strong circle of interpersonal support and a deeper connection with nature.

> I know a lot of people love their churches for things like community, but I feel like, living here in Portland, we have so many awesome friends and neighbors and colleagues that we just have such a strong community in all *that* that I don't feel like I need a church in addition to that. And so, I'm not a religious person at all, but I love nature and science, and I feel like I get all my spiritual needs fulfilled by all that.

For Sadie, being outside in nature is peaceful and rejuvenating, a "place of meditation": "I feel like that's what church is. It's a break from reality where you can get a little peace and reset, and I feel like I find that in other ways." Describing herself as a "very rational, practical person," Sadie asserts that she does not believe in religion and that it is not something she thinks about much. "It's not a part of my life," she said, adding that she would not involve their son in religion either. Sadie described her view as both "anti-religion" and indifferent to religion in her everyday life.

Scott was raised in a liberal Methodist church near San Francisco but he quit religion soon after his confirmation ceremony. Like Sadie, a high school course where he learned "all the awful things the institution has done" catalyzed his change. Additionally, "the concept of feeling spiritual and feeling connected to something else just... drifted away. Without a thought." Over time, he drifted further away from religion or spirituality and towards indifference.

> For a long time, I thought, "Oh, I'm agnostic." I'm almost more atheist now? Like, I would defend the argument that there is no god. It's not like, all of a sudden, there's going to be evidence at some point that there is some god so I should be agnostic. I just say, whatever comes, comes. But at the same time, I don't think about it a lot, so maybe that is more agnostic, right? It's kind of like whatever. To be atheist is to, like, really, think about it, process it. I don't think I really do that much.

Neither Scott nor Sadie are sure about what terms like agnostic mean, but they also do not care about such labels, asserting that these identifications are not salient for them. Family and friends are most important in their lives, alongside other commitments and pleasures such as sustainability, good food, and the natural world. Scott added, "Sometimes I feel like we don't have a formalized process for reflection, which kind of is too bad, but going out hiking allows for that, I think, just as much as sitting in church. You know? I dunno. I listen to *Fresh Air.* Terry Gross is my pastor [*Laughs*]. *This American Life* is our church service." Sadie echoed: "Terry Gross is our pastor." Both Scott and Sadie articulate a language of meditation and reflection that is connected to nature, and which they consider a secular analogue to church, but irony and ambiguity also suffuse their use of culturally-typical terminology for religious polity and practice. Ultimately, quibbles about terms such as agnostic or atheist are unimportant to them, as is the topic of religion. They share a secular orientation but it is one that operates on an implicit level, which becomes operationalized during the context of my interview with them.

Given their nonreligious worldviews and desire for a personalized, outdoors wedding, Scott and Sadie immediately gravitated towards asking a friend to obtain ordination online from the ULC. Scott first learned about the ULC through a high school friend who had gotten ordained in high school or college. As far as he was aware, the only purpose of the church was to facilitate weddings. He said, "I remember it being kind of like a gag-y thing where you're like, 'Oh. I could become an ordained minister and marry people? Huh!'" His wife Sadie had a similar understanding of the church and its utility: "neither of us are religious or practice any religion, so we were just looking for something that was... not affiliated with a religious practice, and so... that's why we went with the Universal Life Church." For Scott and Sadie, the ULC is a nonreligious religious organization, one which they do not consider to be religious in terms of dogmas or community, but which they think is considered a religion legally in order for the weddings conducted by its ministers to be counted as legally valid. Sadie added an additional reason for choosing the ULC: "We also wanted our friend to marry us. And that provided a way for her to be able to do that." They quickly settled on their college friend, Niki, asking her to get ordained by the ULC in order to perform their wedding ceremony.

Despite their appreciation for the ULC as a vehicle for personalized weddings, Scott and Sadie are critical of the institutional structures leading them to ask their friend to get ordained in the first place. As Scott said, "I think anybody should just be able to marry you and then submit the paperwork, and be on record as having married a person." Couples should not have to choose between a secular civil official or a religious minister, they claim, even if that minister is a friend who is avowedly nonreligious and only technically a minister by virtue of having been ordained online in a religion they know almost nothing about. The ULC, Scott said, is "more of a contemporary fix to an out-of-date kind of procedure, y'know? Maybe not out-of-date, but... it's like a patch, y'know?" Similarly, Sadie did not like the fact that the ULC connection tinged their wedding with the veneer of religiosity. "I don't see why they have to be ordained. It sort of puts a religious... edge on it that... I'm not really that interested in," she said. It would be better, they argued, for the marriage solemnization process to be simplified such that any adult can perform marriage ceremonies and sign the legal paperwork, not just certain civil or religious officials. But given the current marital relations statutes, for them the idea of asking a friend to get ordained has become an unfortunately necessary step in legitimizing their marriage in the eyes of the state.

When I asked Scott and Sadie about what other options they considered for legally solemnizing their marriage, they said the only option they had considered was having a friend do it. When pressed about why they did not select a civil ceremony, Sadie said, "I wanted to get married with friends and family. I don't even know how many people you could have in a courthouse." Scott added, "I think probably the biggest thing is it being somebody... you know. The idea of somebody marrying you who doesn't even know you... or performing a civil ceremony and it's someone you don't know..." The idea of a ceremony presided over by a stranger, a civil functionary, seemed weird to them and out of steps with the spirit of an intimate, communal event such as their wedding. Similarly, a more traditional religious wedding was never on the table. "We would not have ended up at a church, that's for sure," Scott said, before stating that churches have "doctrines and dogmas" to which he does not subscribe. In Oregon, where they live and got married, the only options for legally valid weddings are those conducted by civil or religious figures. Given that they are not religious and desired greater personalization than a civil ceremony would allow, they opted for the ULC as a convenient work-around since its status as a recognized religion guaranteed their marriage's legal validity while also ensuring their ability to obtain a secular wedding ceremony that celebrated their values and community. Their friend network espouses similar values. In their time as a couple, they have attended only one traditionally religious wedding and no civil ceremonies. All of their other friends were married by the nonreligious friends of nonreligious couples, under the auspices of the ULC.

The process of creating their wedding ceremony, with their friend Niki presiding, was significant for Scott and Sadie. Niki "was just a perfect fit," Sadie said. "She's really creative and funny, and... she just pretty much had all the qualities we wanted." Well-spoken in public, funny, thoughtful, creative, and a close friend—these are the traits Scott and Sadie cherished in Niki, and which led them to ask her to officiate their wedding. "Niki asked us all the things that we wanted to include in the ceremony. It was really our own creation that we made with her, and it was.... special that way," Sadie said. Moreover, she added, "It was nice to see that people really supported us and were happy to be there, happy to be a part of making that happen." Cherished bonds of friendship and intimacy proved the foundation for their wedding and for their choice of officiant. It would have been incongruous and impersonal had they chosen a civil official or a more traditionally religious minister. The process of crafting their ceremony with Niki "created a bond" between them that they said made them "feel closer" to Niki.

Their wedding took place outdoors on an island in the Columbia River just north of Portland. The outdoor setting was important to them because they love being in nature and outdoors activities were central to their early relationship. "Ultimately, we wanted a place that was meaningful to us... and we had previously, when we were dating, we had a whole day adventure out there, and had had a picnic at this park before," Sadie said. Desiring a casual, intimate wedding, they invited a small group of friends and family, who sat on picnic blankets. One friend, who came dressed in lederhosen, served as an impromptu ring bearer. Two others offered readings tailored for the couple. Sadie loved how much joy infused their ceremony. Niki's wedding outfit was a "librarian-esque style getup, with her big glasses, and she came up with a huge book as her notebook—it was really funny," Sadie said. The text of the ceremony was nonreligious, reflecting their secular orientations. "I think that what we both read were just expressions of whatever experiences and memories and things that... make us right for each other. Speaking from the heart, y'know? As spiritual as *that* is, right? But nothing formally spiritual," Scott said. He added, "Niki did a really good job. She took it seriously, y'know? And I think that could be a concern. I think that's why we made sure we thought about who we wanted, and why she really stuck, was because she's somebody who is fun and casual but knows how to take things seriously and speak from the heart." It was important to them to balance humor and creativity with thoughtfulness and sincerity in their wedding ceremony, as well as to celebrate with close friends and family. The ULC offered them a way to have the wedding of their dreams while also ensuring its legal validity.

7 General Trends in ULC Weddings

The primary reason people join the ULC is to officiate weddings for friends or family. In my survey and interviews, couples repeatedly expressed a desire for someone they knew to officiate their ceremony. Seventy-eight percent of survey respondents who are ULC ministers (N=1,584) reported that they liked that they could officiate weddings after being ordained, and 79% of couples married by a ULC minister (N=207) said that they were friends (61%) or relatives (18%) of their officiant. Seventy-seven percent of couples married by a ULC minister did not consider getting married by traditional clergy, and 67% did not consider getting married by a civil official. Ministers described how meaningful it was for them to help their friends or relatives celebrate their weddings. Adelaide said, "I think having somebody that knows you a little better makes it more meaningful" than a random clergyperson or civil official. An officiant who had gotten ordained as a joke but later officiated his friend's wedding remarked, "I didn't realize how deeply, deeply meaningful it actually is when you actually do this." Gabe, who has officiated three weddings for friends, said that it is "very empowering to feel that I as an ordinary person can perform recognized religious ritual functions, recognized by the state or my larger community, and that's something that doesn't require me to be a spiritual person." A groom who was married by a friend later joined the ULC himself in hopes of performing a friend's wedding: "It would be a great honor," he said. The gravity and intimacy of presiding over the wedding of a loved one deepens bonds of affection not only between the couple but also amongst the couple and their officiant, and into their wider social networks.

Most of the couples married by ULC ministers who participated in my research reported that they are not religious, although over two-thirds said that they are spiritual. Of those married by a ULC minister (N=207), 69% reported that they do not consider themselves a member of any religious organization. Given the chance to select multiple identifications, 72% described themselves as spiritual, 64% as humanist, 47% as secular, 37% as agnostic, 32% as apathetic or indifferent, and 27% as atheistic. Gordon, who has officiated for nearly thirty couples in thirty years, almost all through personal connections, said, "The people that I've married, they're all secular. None of the people are practicing any religion—that I know of. So they're doing this because they don't want it to be a religious ceremony." Only a minority of my interviewees articulated unambiguous atheist, agnostic, or spiritual identities, with most shifting between different categorizations, ultimately claiming that they are "not religious" and that religion is not central to their lives. For example, one bride described herself this way:

> I'm definitely not religious. But I would say I'm spiritual. I associate more with, like, the Eastern religions, you know, like Buddhism and... I don't know. I like their tenets more. But yeah, but I don't like, I'm not very spiritual. I go to yoga... I meditate, and I try to like commune with nature and stuff. So I don't, I guess I just don't think about it much.

Scott and Sadie similarly played with various identifications—atheist, spiritual, agnostic, disinterested—without settling on any single label, except perhaps for consistently articulating themselves as generically nonreligious. This may reflect an ambiguity in the terms themselves, an indifference toward choosing precise terms or ignorance of various meanings of such terms on the part of participants, or a fuzziness, hurriedness, or weariness brought about by the out-of-the-ordinary interview/survey context that called for such identifications on the spot.

ULC weddings were described as nonreligious and usually as not spiritual either. Seventy-one percent of peopled married by a ULC minister said that their ceremony included no language or readings from religious or spiritual texts. In my interviews, very few respondents reported getting married in a church or another religious building; instead, the vast majority were married outdoors or at a rented wedding venue. While most of the weddings used the traditional form of a generic Protestant wedding, including walking down an aisle and exchanging vows and rings, they also innovated by evacuating the ceremony of supernatural referents and incorporating words and/or rituals unique to their own relationships and sensibilities.[24] Only a couple of the weddings I performed for friends or family included readings from religious or spiritual texts, with couples opting instead for no readings or for secular poetry, such as by e. e. cummings or Pablo Neruda. Most of the weddings I officiated took place outdoors, on farms, by rivers or lakes, under tall trees or in a clearing on a sunny day; the others took place at venues such as concert or reception halls. Other couples, like Scott and Sadie, loved the humorous yet serious ceremony their friend Niki wrote with and presented for them at a picnic wedding. One couple I inter-

---

[24] Ronald Grimes is skeptical about alternative weddings, arguing that they are "culturally constrained" with recognizable themes and predictable sentiments (2000, 208). However, he also notes that, "At marriage, more intensely than at any other Western passage, primary participants become ritually active in designing, deciding, and choosing elements for the rite... they conduct research, scour their traditions, consult friend and relatives, negotiate values, and invent ceremonies" (213).

viewed, avid bicycle commuters both, invited guests to ride with them in a procession through the city to their venue, an industrial warehouse turned into an events center. All of the ceremonies I experienced or heard about expressed each couples' nonreligious worldviews and personal visions for their wedding days, and each couple told me how special their ceremony was and how meaningful it was for their friend or relative to help them through the process of becoming married.

8 ULC Weddings as Religious-Secular Entanglements

Consideration of the ULC and weddings solemnized by its ministers presents problems for certain classificatory schema in religious studies and in the social scientific study of religion, especially the religious/secular binary. There already exists a healthy literature criticizing this dichotomy (e.g., Asad 2003), yet in closing I want to explore four areas where I see religious and secular labels blurring and interpenetrating in connection with the ULC. These areas include: the ULC's double mission, ministers' self-identifications, couples' valuations of their weddings, and valuations of spirituality and intimate relationships. These entanglements occur because of a complex web of state and federal laws, ULC ministerial structures and processes, and social and cultural transformations such as the growth of "spirituality" and other "third term" designations denoting something between or against religion and secularism, but always in relation to them (Bender 2012; Bender and Taves 2012).

The ULC's twin mission for religious freedom implicates it as both secular and religious simultaneously. Hensley's vision for the ULC as a bulwark for liberty of conscience and religious practice over against any *church* regulation of religion coexists alongside the ULC as a protector of religious liberty over against any *state* regulation of religious belief and practice. Its litigation history in federal and state courts demonstrates the difficulty governments and judges have had in deciding whether the ULC counts as a *bona fide* religion or not. Was its church polity too amorphous, its ordination process too easy, and its doctrine too short to be taken seriously as a religion worthy of all the rights and benefits accorded to religious organizations in American law and society? Judges and regulators at both state and federal levels arrived at different conclusions, with some ruling that the ULC was not a religion and its clergy were not ministers while others decided in favor of the ULC by analogizing it to mass revivals or Martin Luther's priesthood of all believers. In insisting on being treated equally with other religions, the ULC reveals the limits of religious freedom while also expanding them for itself and others. ULC legal cases demonstrate the church's commitment to defending its own religious prerogatives as well as those of its ministers against state action, all while making no theological or other demands upon its members. The ULC was founded to protect First Amendment freedoms as much as to resist the imposition of dogmatic orthodoxies.

A majority of ULC ministers self-identify as nonreligious, usually as "spiritual but not religious," yet they are technically religious officials of the ULC—and it is in this very capacity that the weddings they perform are considered to be legal marriages. Their self-identifications bleed from one category to another, including multiple yet seemingly contradictory simultaneous labels, such as when Scott said that he is nonreligious, agnostic, atheist, and spiritual all within the span of a few minutes.[25] Such ambiguous articulations already imply problems with rigid religious/secular dichotomizations, but adding the fact that these ministers perceive themselves as nonreligious calls into question not only what it means to be a religious leader in the ULC but also what it means to be a minister capable of solemnizing marriages legally. For many ULC ministers, they are nonreligious except for the moment they check the box marked "religious" on a marriage license, write down their denomination and title, and complete the form. In that moment, they agree that they are indeed religious ministers, if only nominally and fleetingly. Most couples married by ULC ministers are self-described nonreligious people who want a personalized, nonreligious ceremony performed by someone they know well, yet they acknowledge that for the purpose of making their wedding legally valid it must be considered religious in the eyes of the state. In terms of emptying their weddings of explicitly religious content, these weddings are nonreligious and on par with a secular civil ceremony. However, their ritualization choices largely mirror traditional Christian wedding practices, including a leader standing at the front of the assembly, the couple processing down an aisle, introductory remarks welcoming guests and discussing love and marriage, readings from texts, perhaps a ritual (such as lighting a unity candle), exchanges of vows and rings, and the pronouncement and presentation followed by a recessional.[26] The content may be secularized but the form largely

---

[25] Religious, spiritual, secular, and nonreligious identities are not stable, unitary formations (Chaves 2010; Hackett 2014; Lee 2014). Terms like religion, spirituality, secularism, and nonreligion are discursive constructions contingently articulated in particular locations at specific times for particular purposes, that is, in a contextualized "religion-related field" (Quack 2014; von Stuckrad 2013).
[26] This description closely matches that of the wedding script suggested for CFI weddings (Cimino and Smith 2014, 130–131) and the *Humanist Wedding Service* written by renowned human-

copies religious ceremonies. ULC weddings are both religious and secular: nonreligious in intention yet religious in structure and by state classification.

ULC weddings are also sites of sacralization, valued by participants as experiences of high honor, as deeply personally meaningful, as sacred.[27] One groom, who described himself as "spiritual but not religious" and who had also officiated a wedding for a friend, told me, "[T]he institution of marriage is not something I find sacred but I do find sacred love and being committed to the one I love." Love holds a special place for people involved in weddings—for the couple marrying, for the gathered friends and family who support their union, and for the friend-officiant who conducts the ceremony. Another groom, an atheist who had also officiated one wedding, told me that he was attracted to the ULC because, "This is how we make things sacred." Terms like "sacred," "honor," "deeply meaningful," and "spirituality" mark a set of terms that elide the arbitrary bifurcation between religious and secular (Bender and Taves 2012; Huss 2014).[28] Kim Knott has labeled marriage, and values such as the right to marry, as "the secular sacred" (2013).[29] By studying self-conscious "processes

---

ist Corliss Lamont (1972). New York Society for Ethical Culture leader Khoren Arisian similarly formats weddings this way (1973). The British humanists Matthew Engelke has studied "do not want belief, but they do want belonging" in their wedding ceremonies (2014, 300).

27 Sacralization refers here to the process of deeming or valuating something as "sacred," special, or set apart from ordinary life. I use it to categorize first-order ascriptions of "specialness," not an inherent or *sui generis* quality of things (Taves 2009, 17). In *Living the Secular Life* (2014), sociologist Phil Zuckerman observed, "People—even the most ardently secular—still want, need, and enjoy structured moments of reflection, recognition, and consecration... But they don't want these to be religious in nature... But they still yearn for a meaningful, authentic ceremony that allows them to come together and be a part of a ritualized gathering that marks the occasion as special, set apart, sincere, heartfelt" (186).

28 Boaz Huss argues, "I think there is a considerable decline in the cultural power of the disjunction between the religious and the secular, and a growing tendency to blur the distinctions between these two (postulated) oppositional realms. The decline of religion and the secular as key cultural concepts comes to the fore in the growing number of people who refuse to define themselves as either religious or secular, in the growing popularity of the folk concept of 'spirituality' that transgresses this binary opposition, and in the formation of new social institutions and practices (mostly belonging to New Age culture) that indeed challenge and defy the distinction between the religious and the secular" (2014, 100–101).

29 According to Knott, "...those forging social identities in secular contexts—who draw on non-religious commitments and beliefs, including atheism, humanism, and secularism—mark as 'sacred' those occasions (such as marriage), persons (a lover), things (a ring), places (a registry office) and principles (equality and justice) that they value above all others, and that they see as set apart and inviolable: those things that may be deemed to be *both* secular *and* sacred [emphasis in original]" (2013, 160). Similarly, ritual studies scholar Ronald Grimes claims that the "eclecticism and bleeding of boundaries that characterize the alternative wedding scene testify

of valuation and meaning making" in particular contexts, we can see how messy and entangled events are on the ground (Bender and Taves 2012, 2). We can also then see how nonreligious material practices and ritualizations complicate simplistic understandings of what secularity and nonreligion mean, such as if they are taken to mean merely atheism and agnosticism instead of a wider assortment of frames, seemingly contradictory self-identifications, and religo-secular interpenetrations (Lee 2012).

The ULC is a "religion of convenience," as one interviewee called it, a "cultural resource" (Beckford 1992, 171; Swidler 1986, 281) which allows nonreligious individuals and couples to create personalized, nonreligious weddings that are legally valid. Getting ordained online is a "pragmatic religious practice" (Smilde 2013, 44) for these nonreligious ministers, one that leads them toward a "sacred" goal of uniting two people who love each other in marriage.[30] Even if nonbeliever organizations and secular celebrants are allowed to solemnize marriages legally, they will encounter the same limitation as civil ceremonies: lack of a meaningful relationship with the couple. Modern nonreligious couples seeking personalized celebrations are willing to strategically adopt a religious label in order to achieve their wedding, their way.

Bibliography

Arisian, Khoren. 1973. *The New Wedding: Creating Your Own Marriage Ceremony.* New York: Knopf.
Asad, Talal. 2003. *Formations of the Secular: Christianity, Islam, Modernity.* Palo Alto: Stanford University Press.
Ashmore, Lewis. 1977. *The Modesto Messiah: The Sensational Story of Kirby J. Hensley, the Famous Mail-Order Minister.* Bakersfield: Universal Press.
Ayers, Tess, and Paul Brown. 1994. *The Essential Guide to Lesbian and Gay Weddings.* San Francisco: HarperSanFrancisco.
Baker, Joseph O., and Buster G. Smith. 2015. *American Secularism: Cultural Contours of Nonreligious Belief Systems.* New York: New York University Press.
Bare, Kelly. 2007. *The DIY Wedding: Celebrate Your Day Your Way.* San Francisco: Chronicle Books.
Beckford, James A. 1992. *Religion and Advanced Industrial Society.* New York: Routledge.

---

to the permeability of what were once regarded as impenetrable social and religious barriers" (2000, 208).

30 David Smilde holds that pragmatic religious practices are "oriented toward addressing concrete dilemmas in the here and now, and they are evaluated by their success in doing so" (2013, 44).

Bellah, Robert N., Richard Madsen, William M. Sullivan, Ann Swidler, and Steven M. Tipton. 1985. *Habits of the Heart: Individualism and Commitment in American Life.* Berkeley: University of California Press.

Bender, Courtney. 2012. "Things in Their Entanglements." In *The Post-Secular in Question: Religion in Contemporary Society*, edited by Philip S. Gorski, David Kyuman Kim, John Torpey, and Jonathan vanAntwerpen, 43–76. New York: New York University Press.

Bender, Courtney, and Ann Taves, eds. 2012. *What Matters? Ethnographies of Value in a Not So Secular Age.* New York: Columbia University Press.

Bocock, Robert. 1974. *Ritual in Industrial Society: A Sociological Analysis of Ritualism in Modern England.* Edinburgh: George Allen & Unwin.

Center for Inquiry. "CFI Celebrant Certification." Accessed March 1, 2016. http://www.centerforinquiry.net/education/celebrant_certification/.

Chaves, Mark. 2010. "Rain Dances in the Dry Season: Overcoming the Religious Congruence Fallacy." *Journal for the Scientific Study of Religion* 49(1): 1–14.

Cimino, Richard, and Christopher Smith. 2014. *Atheist Awakening: Secular Activism and Community in America.* New York: Oxford University Press.

Clarke, Kelle. 2014. "How Notaries Can Add 'Wedding Officiant' to Their List of Services." *Notary Bulletin*, May 14. Accessed March 1, 2016. https://www.nationalnotary.org/notary-bulletin/blog/2014/05/how-notaries-add-wedding-services.

Cohn, D'Vera, Jeffrey S. Passel, Wendy Wang, and Gretchen Livingston. 2011. "Barely Half of U.S. Adults are Married – A Record Low." Pew Research Center. Accessed March 1, 2016. http://www.pewsocialtrends.org/2011/12/14/barely-half-of-u-s-adults-are-married-a-record-low/.

Cott, Nancy F. 2000. *Public Vows: A History of Marriage and a Nation.* Cambridge: Harvard University Press.

Curtis, Charlotte. 1970. "'Dearly Beloved,' the Clergyman Used to Intone, but Today?" *New York Times*, 8 November.

Dunak, Karen M. 2013. *As Long as We Both Shall Love: The White Wedding in Postwar America.* New York: New York University Press.

Engelke, Matthew. 2014. "Christianity and the Anthropology of Secular Humanism." *Current Anthropology* 55(S10): S292–301.

Francesca, Lisa. 2014. *The Wedding Officiant's Guide: How to Write & Conduct a Perfect Ceremony.* San Francisco: Chronicle Books.

Freedman, Samuel G. 2015. "Couples Enlist Online-Ordained Officiants, Redefining Nuptials." *New York Times*, June 27.

Gootman, Elissa. 2012. "The Officiant Among Us." *New York Times*, March 11.

Grimes, Ronald. 2000. *Deeply into the Bone: Re-Inventing Rites of Passage.* Berkeley: University of California Press.

Hackett, Conrad. 2014. "Seven Things to Consider When Measuring Religious Identity." *Religion* 44(3): 396–413.

Hensley, Kirby J. 1986. *The Buffer Zone.* Modesto: Universal Life Church.

Hoesly, Dusty. 2015. "'Need a Minister? How about Your Brother?': The Universal Life Church between Religion and Non-Religion." *Secularism and Nonreligion* 4(12): 1–13.

Hout, Michael, and Tom W. Smith. 2015. "Fewer Americans Affiliate with Organized Religions, Belief and Practice Unchanged: Key Findings from the 2014 General Social Survey."

National Opinion Research Center, March 10. Accessed March 1, 2016. http://www.norc.org/PDFs/GSS%20Reports/GSS_Religion_2014.pdf.
Huss, Boaz. 2014. "The Sacred Is the Profane, Spirituality Is Not Religion: The Decline of the Religion/Secular Divide and the Emergence of the Critical Discourse on Religion." *Method and Theory in the Study of Religion* 27(2): 97–103.
Ingram, Leah. 2000. *Your Wedding Your Way*. Lincolnwood: Contemporary Books.
Kirschenbaum, Howard, and Rockwell Stensrud. 1974. *The Wedding Book: Alternative Ways to Celebrate Marriage*. New York: Seabury Press.
Knott, Kim. 2013. "The Sacred Secular: In between or both/and?" In *Social Identities between the Sacred and the Secular*, edited by Abby Day, Giselle Vincett, and Christopher R. Cotter, 145–160. Burlington: Ashgate.
Lamont, Corliss. 1972. *A Humanist Wedding Service (Third Edition Revised)*. Buffalo: Prometheus Books.
Law Commission. 2015. "Getting Married: A Scoping Paper." UK Law Commission, December 17. Accessed March 1, 2016. http://www.lawcom.gov.uk/wp-content/uploads/2015/12/Getting_Married_scoping_paper.pdf.
LeBeau, Bryan. 2003. *The Atheist: Madalyn Murray O'Hair*. New York: New York University Press.
Lee, Lois. 2012. "Locating Nonreligion, in Mind, Body, and Space: New Research Methods for a New Field." In *Annual Review of the Sociology of Religion: New Methods in the Sociology of Religion*, edited by Luigi Berzano and Ole Preben Riis, 135–157. Boston: Brill.
Lee, Lois. 2014. "Secular or Nonreligious? Investigating and Interpreting Generic 'Not Religious' Categories and Populations." *Religion* 44(3): 466–482.
Lehmann-Haupt, Rachel. 2003. "Need a Minister? How about Your Brother?" *New York Times*, 12 January.
Manning, Christel. 2015. *Losing Our Religion: How Unaffiliated Parents Are Raising Their Children*. New York: New York University Press.
McMurray, Shane. 2012. "A Detailed Look at Who Performs the Ceremony." In "Trend Talk: Week of 9/9/2012." The Wedding Report, Inc.
Mead, Rebecca. 2007. *One Perfect Day: The Selling of the American Wedding*. New York: Penguin.
Merino, Stephen M. 2012. "Irreligious Socialization? The Adult Religious Preferences of Individuals Raised with No Religion." *Secularism and Nonreligion* 1: 1–16.
Naylor, Sharon. 2010. *Your Wedding Your Way: Break with Tradition and Create a One-of-a-Kind Celebration You'll Never Forget!* Avon: Adams Media.
Newman, Carol. 1975. *Your Wedding, Your Way: A Guide to Contemporary Wedding Options*. Garden City: Doubleday.
Nowicki, Sue. 2009. "Universal Life Goes On." *Modesto Bee*, March 7.
OLR Research Report. 2003. "Regulating 'Mail Order' Ministries." Connecticut General Assembly, Office of Legislative Research, 2003-R-0490. Accessed March 1, 2016. https://www.cga.ct.gov/2003/rpt/2003-R-0490.htm.
Patton, Michael Quinn. 2002. *Qualitative Research and Evaluation Methods (Third Edition)*. Thousand Oaks: Sage.
Pew Research Center. 2015. "U.S. Public Becoming Less Religious." Accessed March 1, 2016. http://www.pewforum.org/files/2015/11/201.11.03_RLS_II_full_report.pdf.

Price, Richard. 1993. "Couples Leaving Church out in Search for 'Fun' Weddings." *USA Today*, 30 August.

Quack, Johannes. 2014. "Outline of a Relational Approach to 'Nonreligion.'" *Method and Theory in the Study of Religion* 26(4–5): 439–469.

Rains, Robert E. 2010. "Marriage in the Time of Internet Ministers: I Now Pronounce You Married, But Who Am I to Do So?" *University of Miami Law Review* 64(3): 809–877.

Roof, Wade Clark. 1993. *A Generation of Seekers: The Spiritual Journeys of the Baby Boom Generation*. San Francisco: HarperCollins.

Roof, Wade Clark. 2001. *Spiritual Marketplace: Baby Boomers and the Remaking of American Religion*. Princeton: Princeton University Press.

Roney, Carley. 1998. *The Knot's Complete Guide to Weddings in the Real World: The Ultimate Source of Ideas, Advice, and Relief for the Bride and Groom and Those Who Love Them*. New York: Broadway Books.

Roney, Carley. 2013 [2000]. *The Knot Guide to Wedding Vows and Traditions: Readings, Rituals, Music, Dances, and Toasts (Revised Edition)*. New York: Clarkson Potter.

Seligson, Marcia. 1973. *The Eternal Bliss Machine: America's Way of Wedding*. New York: Edward Morrow.

Smilde, David. 2013. "Beyond the Strong Program in the Sociology of Religion." In *Religion on the Edge: De-Centering and Re-Centering the Sociology of Religion*, edited by Courtney Bender, Wendy Cadge, Peggy Levitt, and David Smilde, 43–66. New York: Oxford University Press.

Stallings, Ariel Meadow. 2010. *Offbeat Bride: Creative Alternatives for Independent Brides*. Berkeley: Seal Press.

Stoner, Carroll. 1993. *Weddings for Grownups: Everything You Need to Know to Plan Your Wedding Your Way*. San Francisco: Chronicle Books.

Sun, Winnie. "18,000 People Surveyed by The Knot: Where to Splurge and Where to Save on Your Big Day." *Forbes*, April 6. Accessed May 1, 2016. http://www.forbes.com/sites/winniesun/2016/04/06/wedding-18000-people/#107f1dad6364.

Swidler, Ann. 1986. "Culture in Action: Symbols and Strategies." *American Sociological Review* 15(2): 273–286.

Taves, Ann. 2009. *Religious Experience Reconsidered: A Building-Block Approach to the Study of Religion and Other Special Things*. Princeton: Princeton University Press.

Toussaint, David, and Heather Leo. 2004. *Gay and Lesbian Weddings: Planning the Perfect Same-Sex Ceremony*. New York: Ballantine Books.

Vincenzi, Sophie. 2003. *Your Wedding, Your Way*. London: Ebury Press.

von Stuckrad, Kocku. 2013. "Discursive Study of Religion: Approaches, Definitions, Implications." *Method and Theory in the Study of Religion* 25(1): 5–25.

Wilson, Bryan. 1966. *Religion in Secular Society: A Sociological Comment*. Baltimore: Pelican.

Wuthnow, Robert. 1998. *After Heaven: Spirituality in America since the 1950s*. Berkeley: University of California Press.

Wuthnow, Robert. 2010. *After the Baby-Boomers: How Twenty- and Thirty-Somethings Are Shaping the Future of American Religion*. Princeton: Princeton University Press.

Zuckerman, Phil. 2014. *Living the Secular Life: New Answers to Old Questions*. New York: Penguin Press.

Nicholas J. MacMurray & Lori L. Fazzino
Doing Death Without Deity: Constructing Nonreligious Tools at the End of Life

1 Introduction

A growing body of literature is considering secularity and nonreligion from a variety of scholarly perspectives. In this volume, we see both the diversity of efforts towards secular organizing as well as of the diversity of strategies for researching these topics. To this discussion, we would like to contribute research on nonreligious organizing at the end of life. Nonreligious organizing at the end of life is not new, historically, but the ways in which these actions play out in the contemporary American context are novel and have much to teach us about broader discussions of secularization and the standing of nonreligion in U.S. society more generally.

In this chapter, we use the terms "nonreligious" and "nonreligion" to refer to both the identities and worldviews of our research participants, though we recognize that other authors in the collection are using varying and potentially more specific language. For this project, we collected data from a broad array of individuals in a variety of settings. As such, it was not possible to learn of exact belief structures, identities, or more specific personal information that would allow us to typify our research participants in more nuanced ways. We use the term "nonreligious" as an umbrella term to cover those individuals who identify with various Atheist, Secularist, Humanist, Free-Thinker and Agnostic classifications in this project. A further note on language in this chapter is we are using terms such as "nonreligion", "religion", and "science" as generalities within this project in order to frame our discussion, but are sensitive to the notion that the empirical realities of these subjects are far more complex than our labels imply, as noted by Harrison (2006).

Several centuries have passed since the Enlightenment, when religion began to be superseded by science and reason as the primary method for understanding and addressing problems in the natural and social world. Decline in the reliance on mysticism, magic, and God, and the rise of rationalization and intellectualization was referred to as the "disenchantment of the world" (Weber 1905). As explanatory religious frameworks continued to be challenged by science, religion was said to be pushed further out of public and into private life. As modernity progressed, the inclusion of religious meaning and symbolism in the public sphere continue to decline through processes of secularization (Berger 1967).

OpenAccess. © 2017 Nicholas J. MacMurray & Lori L. Fazzino, published by De Gruyter.
This work is licensed under the Creative Commons Attribution-NonCommercial-NoDerivatives 4.0 License. https://doi.org/10.1515/9783110458657-014

More recent research has problematized the notion of a steady, linear process of secularization across Western society, noting that the process occurred in segmented, uneven and diverse ways (Martin 2007). Though not occurring in the uniform pattern once theorized, scholars agree that the rationalizing and secularizing of society transformed the whole of social life in the West. That transformation encompasses the social managing of death. Historically, handling the dead was both a personal and public affair with the family in charge of the social and corporeal aspects (i.e., one's body), while the church was in charge of the spiritual aspect (i.e., one's soul). Modernity has seen, in a Weberian sense, the rationalization of the management of dying and death, a trend often equated with secularization (Mellor and Shilling 1993). Death in society today occurs largely outside of public view (Lofland 1978), sequestered from daily life and daily concern, handled by a cadre of death-specialists (Mellor and Shilling 1993). Similarly, the location of the deathbed has shifted in modern times from one's home to institutional settings, primarily the hospital (Kellehear 2007). If death has been professionalized, routinized, and institutionalized, we must ask, "Do these rationalized aspects equate to the secularization of death?" Our research indicates that in American culture, the dynamic is not so simple.

In this research, we examine death and bereavement among nonreligious Americans. Our study emerged from Fazzino's (second author) dissertation work, which examined lived nonreligion in Las Vegas. While in the field, a member of the local atheist group, Betty, died shortly before a scheduled interview. Fazzino was unable to attend Betty's funeral, but learned that when her sister, who is Mormon, closed the service she said, "You know, I don't care what my sister believed. I know she's in Heaven, and when I get up there, I'm going to tell her 'I told you so!'" As a Mormon-turned-atheist, Betty forbade in writing the inclusion of any religious sentiment in her memorial. Nonbelievers in attendance described this as a slap in the face. They were offended by the disregard for Betty's final wishes in her sister's expression of religious sentiments. They also expressed how this event both amplified and delayed their grief. They felt compelled to decide whether and how to respond to the sister, and how they would live with the consequences of that choice.

While talking about this situation, we realized that the intersection of our research areas, religious/secularity studies and death and dying, was fertile ground for research. The events that transpired at Betty's funeral left us with questions about how nonbelievers manage dying and death in a highly privatized religious culture, what resources are available specifically for a nonreligious worldview, and if end-of-life is an area where marginalization occurs. We decided this topic deserved attention, so we chose to investigate further.

In this chapter, we present a qualitative analysis of nonreligious understandings, coping strategies, and organizational efforts towards managing death and dying. We draw from sociology, cultural studies and social justice theories to form a perspective uniquely suited for exploring death and bereavement among the nonreligious in the contemporary American context. Our analysis reveals several key findings. First, we find that our respondents frequently encountered religion at the end of life. While a resource for many Americans, religious language, narratives, symbols and ideas were not helpful to our respondents in coping with their grief, as these cultural forms do not hold the same meaning for nonbelievers as for believers. Beyond this, several respondents noted conflict with theology at the end of life, such as Betty's funeral, in which religious sentiment was imposed on that service against their will.

We also found that death is an area where the nonreligious are disadvantaged by a lack of an institutionalized nonreligious death culture. We find that the nonreligious lack the ready-made "cultural tools," such as ceremonies, rituals, rites, language, and grief resources widely available to those of a religious worldview. Our final finding addresses how the nonreligious have and are producing and disseminating death cultural resources geared specifically to those with a nonreligious orientation. We conclude that, taken together, these challenges both problematize and politicize death and dying for nonreligious Americans. We close by discussing the implications of our findings.

2 Brief Review of Literature

In the following sections, we review literature pertinent to our research as well as describe the theoretical concepts and frameworks we use to craft our lens for this research. In the opening section, we discuss how death intersects with religion and nonreligion, and describe how the end of life causes the nonreligious to intersect with religion as well. Following that, we discuss a number of theories for understanding nonreligious organizing from a cultural perspective.

2.1 Death, Religion, and Nonreligion

The end of life presents challenges for persons of all worldviews. It is often assumed that dealing with death would be more difficult without religion. However, Seale (1998, 76) situates contemporary death culture by arguing that "modern rationality... [provides]... guidance for a meaningful death that are at least as powerful as those of earlier traditions." For example, from the perspective of western medicine, death is the failure of the biological systems necessary for one's survival. Medical rites give death a corporeal meaning as a bodily process, which generates a sense of death as something scientifically accurate or knowable. Some research has noted that it is the strength of one's worldview, not the content that matters. Among older adults, strong adherence to atheism operates much like religion does for believers, providing meaning, explanation, consolation, and support when coping with ageing (Wilkerson and Coleman 2010). Perhaps medicalizing death explains differences in psychological distress. Secular caregivers exhibit significantly higher levels of communication about mortality with patients and reported significantly lower levels of fear of death compared to their religious counterparts (Bachner, O'Rourke, and Carmel 2011).

The nonreligious and religious alike must construct meaning to deal with the inevitability of death. Despite being governed by a secular democracy, "the will to religion" (Beaman 2013, 151) permeates American culture, creating a "new normal," or what Lori Beaman refers to as the assumption that all persons are religious and have spiritual needs (Beaman 2013, 151). Nowhere is this more apparent that in the reliance on religion for relating to death. One might say that death is inescapable on several levels. Manning's (2015) research on unaffiliated parents reminds us that meaning-making around the topic of death is not relegated to illness, aging, or some distant time. Death is unavoidable for parents who must answer when asked by their children, "What happens when we die?" As the end of life raises issues of personal philosophy on mortality, interacting with others around the topic of death may bring one into contact with the worldview of another. While the nonreligious do not take stock in religious narratives of post-mortem existence, advancements in technology and medicine raise questions of extending one's life and the possibility of someday conquering death. These scientific narratives offer hope of immortality to the nonreligious, as the potential for these occurrences fit within the nonreligious worldview as potentially possible (Fontana and Keene 2009).

Do scientific advances reduce fear and anxiety concerning death among the nonreligious? Sociologist Ryan Cragun argues that the nonreligious are, in some ways, better at dying than the religious. His national and international analysis of death and dying among religious fundamentalists, moderates, liberals, and the nonreligious found that across all religious categories, the nonreligious were less afraid of death, less likely to have anxiety about dying, and less likely to use aggressive means to extend life (Cragun 2013, 166). Moreover, nonreligious persons also report higher levels of support for death with dignity measures (Smith-Stoner 2007). It appears, then, that perhaps nonreligious interpretations of death lead to differing relationships with end-of-life matters than do religious interpretations.

The impact of religion on the nonreligious varies. For instance, people who do not believe in God with some degree of certainty tend to experience religious environments more negatively than those who do (Speed and Fowler 2016). Many of the narratives compiled in Melanie Brewster's (2014) *Atheists in America* highlight religion as unhelpful when it comes to providing consolation for death. In Bakker and Paris' (2013) study of baby loss, religion was inadequate for helping nonreligious women who suffered the pain of baby loss. Imposed religion, or what Lin (2014) refers to as a bereavement challenge, can often impede healthy grief trajectories. The likelihood that any person will encounter theist sentiments or practices is largely contingent on one's social environment; in this case of the United States. Though not prepared to generalize our findings to national or international contexts, our data indicates encounters with religion at the end of life are common, at least in the contexts we investigated.

2.2 Cultural-Justice Approach to Studying Death

In crafting our theoretical lens, we draw on Swidler's (1986) cultural tool-kits, Griswold's (2003) cultural production theory, Young's (1990) oppression theory, and Buechler's (2000) cultural politics. Swidler (1986) conceptualizes culture as a toolkit of strategies and repertoires which comprise a system of meaning through symbols, a set of beliefs, values, and practices, and shared communication. This "toolkit" concept may be applied at the societal level or to smaller groups, such as a bowling team, and may also be applied generally or in a particular context, such as managing end-of-life matters. Griswold's collective production theory synthesizes the micro interactional production of culture through symbolic interaction with the macro-organizational nature of culture, specifically in terms of cultural producers and consumers. From this perspective, culture is not sui generis; it is a production. Taken together, these concepts of producing a cultural toolkit allow us to look deeper at how modern nonreligious Americans, much like the secularists in Victorian era Europe who found themselves outside the normative death and dying culture (Nash 1995), are finding ways to construct meaning regarding mortality without the cultural toolkit (Swidler 1986) offered by faith-based traditions.

We must also account for why non-religious individuals so often find themselves excluded from normative death culture, especially when the ways in which Americans relate to death and dying have shifted and vary across time and place (Kellehear 2007). To this end, we employ the concept of cultural imperialism, which refers to "the experience of living in a society whose dominant meanings render the perspectives and point of view of one's group invisible, while also stereotyping one's group and marking them as 'other.' [It] is the universalization of one group's experience and culture and its establishment as the norm" (Young 1990, 58–59). Participants in our study voiced feeling marginalized and belittled for their worldview.

Cultural imperialism provides a framework within which Christian-centric hegemony and anti-atheist discrimination are situated. Recent research on prejudice toward (non)religious minorities suggests that there has been growing tolerance and/or acceptance for most religious minorities in the US. However, as Edgell, Gerteis, and Hartmann's 2006 study suggests, the same may not be true for atheists. We argue that there may be other – as yet undescribed – factor(s) that explain the continued prejudice against atheists. Recent social psychological research may have uncovered one such issue. Perceptions of threat have been identified, albeit under-theorized, as a contributing factor in anti-atheist sentiments. Findings delineate three specific types of threat – value threat, threat to cultural worldview, and existential threat that people may experience with regard to atheists (Cook, Cohen, and Soloman 2015; Cook, Cottrell, and Webster 2015). Distrust, disparagement, and social distance have been shown to substantially increase when existential threat was activated by increasing people's concern for death. Likewise, existential concern was increased when people simply thought about atheism (Cook, Cohen, and Soloman 2015). In short, anti-atheist prejudice may be exacerbated in end-of-life situations. This suggests to us that even though death itself may less anxiety-provoking for nonreligious people in comparison to their religious counterparts, feeling marginalized may increase anxiety at times surrounding the end of life.

Finally, the concept of "cultural politics" (Buechler 2000) is used to describe political efforts directed towards the cultural realm, as opposed to efforts directed at the state. In drawing this distinction, Buechler notes that no action is inherently state- or cultural-politics, as elements of both forms are always intertwined. An example would be the green funeral advocates who work to bring ecological reform to the American way of death. Similarly, we believe the ongoing negotiation of cultural meaning at the end of life represents this form of politics, as nonreligious individuals resist defaulting to Christian-centric norms through the creation of explicitly nonreligious end of life cultural tools. The norms which preside over the end of life are inherently political, as they reify some worldviews while marginalizing others. Similarly, efforts to create nonreligious end-of-life cultural tools and repertoire are political, as those projects represent efforts to reform the American way of dying to include spaces and tools which nonreligious individuals will find meaningful. While not inherently critiquing religion, these projects do critique a status-quo in the United States in which nonreligious end-of-life resources have traditionally been scarce.

3 Data and Methods

Data for this chapter comes from observations at several monthly events hosted by various non-religious groups, including the Humanists and Atheists of Las Vegas (HALV), the Las Vegas Atheists Meetup (LVA), the United Church of Bacon (UCB), and Sunday Assembly Las Vegas (SALV). Interview data come from informal and focus group interviews. We collected textual data by conducting a series of online searches through search engines such as Lexis/Nexis and Google. We were intentionally narrow, searching only for the terms "death," "dying," "grief," and "bereavement" for all the various nonreligious identity labels (e. g., Atheist; Humanist). We read books by prominent atheist authors, collected blogs, popular print media, video media, and we joined the Grief Beyond Belief (GBB) private group on Facebook. We intentionally did not collect data from that site because of privacy restrictions, but used it instead as a validity measure against which we compared our codes. Our analytic strategy was inductive, following the precepts of grounded theory (Charmez 2014).

For the sake of transparency, it should be noted that both authors bring to this material some insider experience. Fazzino has been involved with organized nonreligion in Las Vegas, as both an insider and researcher, for six years (2010 – 2016). Our collaboration on this project began in March 2014. At that time, Mac-Murray (first author) began participating in a regular Tuesday night Meetup event, where Fazzino introduced him to the people at the meeting. In this way, Fazzino's insider status facilitated MacMurray's entre to the groups, making introductions and both organizing and participating in interviews (as interviewer, not interviewee). Two very active group members had recently died within three months of one another, just prior to MacMurray's entrance into the field. These events provided a foundation for discussing death and dying with participants. In an attempt to be reflexive about our own standpoint, we would like to mention that we have been actively involved in the creation and dissemination of nonreligious end-of-life cultural tools ourselves, which is part of our focus in this research (the specifics of this project are described in detail in our findings section). Our politics on the matter support the notion of equitable death, in which individuals of any worldview have equal access to the resources which might help them navigate the often-troubling times at the end of life. We view both the subjects of this research and this research itself as contributing to the secular organizing at the end of life.

4 Findings

The nonreligious respondents we spoke with typically described death as the end of individual existence. Interpreting death in this way is quite different from traditional religious interpretations. Death is, as one participant told us, "...just different for us." This difference in worldview may go largely uncontested through much of daily life, but during times of death, varying or even opposing interpretations of what death "is" may come into conflict. As many of the cultural norms for social interaction at the end of life contain theist symbolism, the American way of death often fails to assist the nonreligious. Beyond being of little use as a resource, religious symbolism at times became a hurdle to our participants, as they felt that their worldview was ignored, downplayed or otherwise marginalized.

It appears that the lack of nonreligious end-of-life culture is motivating a variety of individuals to create and spread resources which are meaningful from within the nonreligious worldview. Both in the Las Vegas field and in our broader content analysis, nonreligious organizing at the end of life is an active project. We argue that these challenges and responses problematize and politicize the end-of-life for the nonreligious. In the following pages, we attempt to support and defend this position, providing a glimpse into the lived reality of doing death without deities.

4.1 The Inadequacy of a Theistic Death Discourse

Worldviews among the nonreligious are incredibly diverse (Lee 2014). Despite ideological differences, two themes emerged in our data. The first is the inadequacy of religion as a means to manage death for the nonreligious. This finding is supported by prior research (Bakker and Paris 2013; Vail III et al. 2012). Religious answers may bring comfort to religious people, but many nonreligious individuals draw little from these explanations. In some cases, death can lead individuals who had previously identified as religious to question their faith. This happened to one of our respondents, Gina, who prayed for the healing of two ill family members. She recalls:

> I grew up in a home that left the option of religion up to me. However, I was sent to a private Catholic school and was exposed to that belief system. For a while it was nice to believe that everything could be fixed by kneeling in your pew and praying your heart out. Then, within the course of one year, an uncle passed away...a few months later my grandfather very suddenly passed as well. While my uncle was wasting away, I was told to pray,

and he would be well again. Obviously, it [prayer] didn't have any effect. Then when my grandfather was in a coma, I was told the same thing. I put all my heart into praying so he would wake up. Again, [prayer] not helpful. After that, I knew. I just KNEW that religion was nonsense, and I would never tell someone to just "pray for it."

Another respondent, Amber, traces her deconversion from Christianity to when she was 11-years old. Her father was sick and her entire family would gather night after night to pray. For Amber, her father's death meant either God refused to answer their prayers or he simply did not exist. She concluded the latter and abandoned her faith. She now sees religion as nothing more than a way for people to deal with their feelings rather than face the truth. This link between experiencing death and rejection of religion is also illustrated in the documentary *Hug an Atheist*. As one woman narrates: "When my husband was hit by the elderly driver, he spent three days in the hospital dying, and I spent a lot of time in the chapel on my knees praying to God that he'd be okay. And, of course, in the end he wasn't, and part of me felt like that was all time I wasted. I should've been by his side. I shouldn't have bothered with the chapel." In all these examples it seems that religion justified time spent looking for divine intervention, which for some pulled them away from loved ones with little time left. In the moment, seeking god's intercession seemed like the right thing to do, but when it failed to work, deep regret ensued.

Although some nonreligious individuals wished they could accept religious narrative to help them cope with death, this does not lead them back to religion. In the same documentary a man speculates about how much easier dealing with his father's death would have been with religion, "It's been ten months since my dad died. In times, I think it would have been a whole lot easier if I would have been a person of faith because it's just so much easier to strike it up to God's will: 'It was his time,' 'He's in the arms of Jesus now,'...Those kind of clichés... that to me felt like a cop-out." The perception that religion, as a means to cope with death and loss, is "a cop-out" is a second pattern in our data. It supports a prominent theme in previous research on non-religion, namely the importance of living authentically (Fazzino 2014; Zuckerman 2015). For the nonreligious, truth (or more accurately their perception of big "T" truth) is more important than mitigating the negative emotions from existential threat. While understanding that neither religious or nonreligious identities are entirely rational choices, we find that death is often a time when one's worldview is put to the test. The unavoidability of mortality forces humans to manage its inevitability in some way. To this end, the nonreligious are constructing their philosophy of death independent of the theism.

4.2 Accepting Death as Final End

The nonreligious philosophy of death that emerges from our data is best expressed by our respondent, Joe:

> Put as simply as possible, death makes life worth living. By understanding and accepting death, we can understand that our time here is finite, and that this is our only chance of being alive and making the most of it. This isn't just a life you can ruin and then get a second chance after you die. This is it. If you don't want your last moments of existence to be spent considering your regrets, death should be the inspiration to get out there and live your life.

Joe's quote expresses three main ideas that transcend ideological differences among the nonreligious: (1) the cessation of life is death; (2) this life is the only life there is; there is no afterlife or rebirth; and (3) the finality of death makes life more meaningful, not less. Here, we see a connection between how death is interpreted and how that interpretation informs one's personal philosophy of how life ought to be lived. As death is thought of as the final end, the social life of here and now become more important, as one's time is limited by death.

Part of understanding one's identity as nonreligious means accepting the inevitability of death. When we asked, either individually or in focus groups, "What is death?", we heard the same three or four responses repeatedly, most of which were expressed in the same matter-of-fact manner. Death was described as the end of consciousness, simple non-existence, and as a natural process. In one focus group, this question generated a dialogue about fear that we did not expect, but were nevertheless pleased with this direction because of the nuance that emerged – namely the difference between fearing death and fearing dying. Joe again articulates this clearly:

> ...any fear I have had in the past was of dying, rather than being dead. Some people don't seem to understand the difference. Dying could very well be a terrifying experience as you contemplate the fact that you are coming to the end of your existence. Dying is a process that the living go [sic] through. I can see why many people would be scared of dying, and having to say goodbye to loved ones. But death itself? That's the easy part.

Another respondent, Gino, acknowledges: "As a secular/non-religious person, I would be lying to state that death doesn't bother me. As much as I accept the inevitability of death, it's not something I look forward to and hope to put off for as long as possible." While death, as non-existence, means one no longer feels anything, it is the process of dying or watching others die that is painful. As another respondent, Sheila, explains: "It's like you fear other people's death more than your own, 'cuz [sic] it's like, 'I'm dead. Whatever. I don't care!'" Sheila's point, too, highlights the difference between death and dying.

Dale McGowan, a secular activist and author of *Parenting Beyond Belief*, writes: "One of the things it is important to recognize is that death isn't easy for anyone. There is a myth that religion quells the fear of death; that if we can only accept the idea of heaven, then we won't be afraid anymore." Another secular author and activist, Jerry DeWitte, writes: "When you can truly put yourself in that position and realize that the only thing to fear may be the moments leading up to it, there's absolutely nothing to fear afterwards. It's truly accepting death that gives you a new lease on life. It really does." It appears that both professional writers and ordinary seculars like Joe, Gino, and Sheila, are able to articulate a coherent non-religious philosophy of death.

4.3 Nonreligious Conceptions of Life After Death

A common perception is that the nonreligious reject any notion of an afterlife, but this is incorrect. In his 2013 TEDx talk, "The Four Stories We Tell Ourselves about Death," Steve Cave identified four stories that people employ that allow us to escape death, cognitively at least. The majority of nonreligious people reject the idea of a supernatural afterlife, rendering spiritual and resurrection immortality stories invalid, but this is not the end of the story. Two stories deemed legitimate by the nonreligious are those proposing scientific or symbolic immortality. The former espouses the idea that death can be cured through science. Among those we spoke with, the degree to which this idea was accepted depended on views about whether or not conquering death was a good thing. Consider the following exchange from one focus group:

> **Nick:** Will we ever overcome death?
> **Mary:** Be able to live forever?
> **Nick:** Yes.
> **Jimmy:** And would you want that?
> **Mary:** Paul Kurtz thinks maybe...
> **Jimmy:** Yeah! The singularity...
> **Phil:** I think that technology could get us there, you know? We've heard about all sorts of advances in anti-aging, however, there's also a very big problem, and that is, who gets to take advantage of it? And, there's quality of life to consider, of course, but at the same time, if everybody's doing it, what's that going to do to our resources?
> **Mary:** Are people going to stop mating? Stop having kids?
> **Phil:** And that's why I personally think if you're gonna [sic] do it, you should sign a waiver that says you're not going to procreate and add to the extra shortening of resources.

Given the opportunity, though, would these participants extend life? Responses were mixed. Jimmy opposed the idea for himself for individualistic reasons, namely the loss of doing things he enjoyed and becoming bored. Phil took the opposite stance, stating he would want to live on given the opportunity just "to see how knowledge develops." Being skeptical of science resolving the problem of mortality and logical about their positions may lend support to our claims that the nonreligious fear dying, not death.

Symbolic immortality, the idea of living on through the legacy one has created in life, was much more common across our data. The following quote from Humanist Manifesto II summarizes this popular view, "There is no credible evidence that life survives the death of the body. We continue to exist in our progeny and in the way that our lives have influenced others in our culture." Among many who identify as nonreligious, the viable means for achieving immortality is through the legacy established in life. The evidence of one's existence is found in the contributions that person makes, big and small, in the lives of all those who go on living. Any notion of an eternal life lives only in the memories of loved ones and in how they hold the deceased in their memory, or in other words, is a social legacy.

It is important to note that the legacy story is not exclusive to the nonreligious. The problem death and legacy poses for social media has been the subject of much commentary in recent years. Options for users to name a "legacy contact" who will be granted access to one's Facebook account in the event of death, along with headlines like, "What Will Your Social Media Legacy Be?" from the Huffington Post, have driven the push to secure one's virtual immortality. While these options are available to the religious and nonreligious alike, we find the nonreligious have fewer cultural resources to manage and cope with death in general.

4.4 Finding Meaning in Death

The general sentiment among our respondents is that death is an experience that can provide them with meaning, purpose, and peace. Contrary to any conception that nonreligious people have "nothing to live for", our data indicates that nonreligious individuals make meaning within the parameters of their worldview, through the company of loved ones, satisfying their love for learning, experiencing new things, and taking in the wonders of the world. Mortality is an inescapable part of the human condition, and research has shown that reminders of death activate cognitive defenses and uphold cultural worldviews (Greenberg, Solomon, and Pyszczynski 1997). Applying this idea to our respondents, we find it easy to understand how death becomes a motivator for making the most of this life, as for them, there is no other.

Our respondents expressed this desire to live life fully. Thus, the way one's spends their time greatly informs their interactions and behavior. Tito explains, "It was the finality of death that motivated me to find peace in my life. Death motivated me to make amends with estranged family members, like my father. I felt like it was such a waste of energy to hold on to all of the anger and hate that was pent up inside of me. I accept that we're all here for only a short time. Ultimately, death is what motivates me to live, love, and enjoy every second of my life." It would seem that quality of life is an important consideration among the nonreligious for determining what it is to have a "good life" (see Toscani et al. 2003).

Tito's quote suggests that one's quality of life is not determined by others' adoration, approval, or by the absence of conflict and pain. Whereas many turn to religion to reconcile the problem of suffering that exists in the human condition, the nonreligious try to accept the reality of life's ebbs and flows. Rather than asking why bad things happen, they focus on how to live in spite of bad things happening. Secular activist and author Ayaan Hirsi Ali highlights this idea, "The only position that leaves me with no cognitive dissonance is atheism. It is not a creed. Death is certain, replacing both the siren-song of Paradise and the dread of Hell. Life on this earth, with all its mystery and beauty and pain, is then to be lived far more intensely: we stumble and get up, we are sad, confident, insecure, feel loneliness and joy and love. There is nothing more; but I want nothing more." To live a good life is to have a high quality of life, which for the nonreligious, is measured by their ability to live effectively, authentically, and autonomously. With this in mind, we now turn to the unique problems death poses for the nonreligious.

4.5 Negative Encounters with Theist End-of-Life Culture

The formal and routine processes around managing the dying and the dead have largely been professionalized, rationalized, and thus secularized in the United States. But religion is far from absent. Our respondents reported many encounters with theism throughout their end-of-life-experiences. Both personal interactions and institutional support structures illustrate how nonbelievers experience religion as cultural default at the end of life.

4.5.1 "Your Religion Only Makes My Grief Harder!"

Talking openly about death has long been considered taboo in U.S. culture (Walter 1991). While that is beginning to change, we found a pattern of deferring to cultural scripts when interacting with the bereaved. A common experience among our nonreligious participants was receiving religious condolences. Well-meaning religious phrases, such as "She's in a better place," or "His spirit is all around you," were not interpreted as words of comfort by our respondents, often instead serving as a reminder of their minority status in society. A participant in Hug an Atheist recalled a particular exchange after her husband passed away, "I got a lot of – 'He's in a better place,' and I was like, 'He was a healthy 32-year-old man in the prime of his life. He was in a pretty good place!' We had just gotten married, and he had just had a nephew. Things were really good and he was killed."

In the same vein, our respondents expressed not knowing how to interact in a way that was comforting to religious friends and family coping with loss that was authentic to their worldview. Stephanie explains, "An atheist can't lie and utter the immortal words: 'She/he will be in my prayers.' It would be untrue. It would come across as disingenuous sympathy." Both the (un)intentional denial of their nonreligious worldviews and lacking a way to communicate support that is both effective and authentic to all involved made social interactions unwelcome and/or upsetting. Here, we see what seems to be an interactional divide across worldviews. As these groups fundamentally interpret death in differing, or even opposing ways, interacting around this topic becomes difficult.

4.5.2 "Here's to the Hereafter: Last Respects at...Happy Hour?"

As religious toolkits for death are insufficient for the nonreligious, new meanings, understandings, and practices are created, often in times of distress. Those who were previously religious acknowledged this can be a difficult process, sometimes made more so when additional hurdles are present. Fazzino experienced this first hand in the field, despite being disassociated with formal religion for 10 years. When Erich, a 30 something-year old "baconist"[1] passed

---

[1] The United Church of Bacon is a legal "church" that utilizes the cultural "bacon craze" phenomena to challenge all abuses of religious privilege and put an end to atheophobia and secularphobia. The organization was started in 2010 by celebrity magician Penn Jillette and a group of his friends, which included John Whiteside. UCB claims no tax exempt status and pay their taxes. By "baconist," we mean those who are members of the United Church of Bacon.

away, she was challenged by not knowing the norms of an atheist funeral. Consider the follow excerpt from her field notes:

> The memorial took place on a cloudy afternoon on the first Saturday in March. I bought a new dress from Ann Taylor because what does one wear to a memorial service being held at the VFW (a veterans' organization and bar)? For all intents and purposes, this was a funeral...a funeral at a bar. I had two choices – casual or classy. I chose the latter. It was the wrong choice. Many in attendance wore their Church of Bacon t-shirt to pay their respects to Erich. Many said he would have wanted it that way. When I saw David Silverman, President of American Atheists, in a suit, I let out a sigh of relief. What the heck was the protocol for an atheist funeral anyway? I didn't know what to expect before I got here and I don't know what to expect now. I'll just follow everyone else's example and go get a drink at the bar.

Erich's funeral was held in a bar, which was unusual to Fazzino initially. While it seemed this space would meet our needs, that would not be the case. Consider, for example, the following conversation between Prophet John Whiteside (veteran, Atheism advocate, and founder of The Church of Bacon -an Athiest organization based in Las Vegas) and Fazzino about the memorial service lead by Whiteside, which Fazzino attended for professional *and* personal reasons, as a member of the group:

> When we [United Church of Bacon] had the memorial service for Erich, the bartender told David Silverman and I that they triple booked the room. When she said we triple-booked the room I said, "Oh, I don't believe this. Look, let me tell you something. This is an atheist...you got to close the bar. You got to get these people out of here. This is an atheist funeral and I'm going to talk bad about the military. I'm going to talk bad about Erich's experiences in the military. This is a horrible idea." People from the birthday party using the room before us refused to vacate so we could have Erich's memorial. We waited around for about an hour, and finally Erich's mom comes over and says, "Let's just do it." And so we started. I was very upset...extremely upset the whole time. David did a good job, and Erich's mom did a wonderful job, but I was upset. I was mad! I started blocking the door to the meeting room with my foot, so they're going around the long way to get more beers and they're knocking over flowers. They're doing all kinds of things. Somebody at the front door, and I don't know who it was said, "Would you mind waiting until the memorial service is over?" And the guy said no. That pissed him off. Here we were being civil even though they refused to leave. This is Church of Bacon's first memorial, and they are being disrespectful. Well, that guy from our group made a comment about this guy's girlfriend, then he cold-cocked (i.e. punched) him. The other guy cold-cocked our guy. He made a comment and the reaction of this drunk guy was to cold-cock him. His girlfriend said, "Are you going to let him say that to me?" And then he cold-cocked him. It was my first memorial and there's a fight outside the bar. After the funeral was over, the guy who ran the place, who by the way was just reeking of alcohol...in fact, he's one of the guys who was stumbling around and knocked over flowers. He comes up to us and says, "Yeah, I'm VFW," I

think he says, "I'm the president. I'm really sorry about this, but I couldn't get my friends out of the room."

Whether or not those attending the party refused to vacate out of a sense of antagonism towards atheists is unknown. It may be that a bar is simply a difficult place to hold a funeral ceremony. This in itself indicates a lack of institutionalized end-of-life culture, as location and dress were tenuous. Instead, we argue this experience was an outcome of not having a formal space for the atheists to express their grief. As the nonreligious formalize and institutionalize components of the American funeral, such as spaces, presiders, norms for dress, the potential for confusion, disorganization, and conflict with other groups seems likely to decrease.

4.6 Organizing Secular Death and Bereavement

If necessity is the mother of invention, then theist dominance on the American way of death seems to be motivating the creation of new cultural forms. Consider this Tweet from atheist comic Keith Lowell Jensen, "When I die, cremate me, put the ashes in walnut shells, close them, and give them to my friends so they can say "Well that's Keith in a nutshell." Whether or not this statement is meant literally, we can see the potential for flexibility, creativity, and even humor towards nonreligious death. Without the prescriptive aspects of religious ritual, individuals are able to not only choose once-deviant options such as cremation, but to add personal touches to their death, for the satisfaction of themselves and their bereaved loved ones. The loosening of religion's dominance of death opens a space for a personal agency at the end of life.

4.6.1 Nonreligious Crutches

In "Grief Beyond Belief", a website intended to provide the nonreligious a space to support one another online, Rebecca Hensler writes:

> When you're engaged in mutual grief support you discover that the emotions you're having that make you feel crazy are very common and so it really was helpful to find out that I wasn't the only person who was going around the long way in the market 'cause I didn't want to walk down the baby aisle and things like that. Or who couldn't cope with seeing baby clothes. We do have to accept that someone we love is gone forever. They're not coming back. We can carry them forward in memory. We can let our own actions be motivated

by our emotions about that person or by what that person taught us. There are a lot of things that we can do that are comforting ...

Nonreligious people are beginning to build their own cultural toolkit to find that comfort. As the retelling of the memorial at the bar indicates, the nonreligious require spaces in which their death practice may proceed uninterrupted. We found the most evidence for the creation of spaces online, in the form of message boards. These forums were created out of a frustration with the ongoing use of religious crutches in other grief and bereavement support boards. Spaces like Grief beyond Belief indicate the value of religion-free discourse for the nonreligious. They offer the following statement of purpose: "The aim of Grief Beyond Belief is to facilitate peer-to-peer grief support for atheists, Humanists, and other Freethinkers by providing spaces free of religion, spiritualism, mysticism, and evangelism in which to share sorrow and offer the comfort of rational compassion."[2] These virtual places provide a space in which the nonreligious worldview is normative, which counters the Christian-centrism they risk facing in mainstream end of life culture.

As previously mentioned, social norms at the end of life contain aspects of religious symbolism and cultural meaning which are of minimal condolence to the nonreligious in even the best of situations. To move around these impediments, the nonreligious require "crutches," or what we have referred to as tools through which to express and represent their worldview. We find that a common method for constructing these crutches is through the secularizing of religious crutches. In the following examples, the form of the crutch is borrowed from conventional forms while the content is replaced with nonreligious meaning[3]. This is consistent with prior research on the topic (Engelke 2015; Garces-Foley 2003).

The traditional religious funeral in the West routinely contains elements of eulogizing the deceased. For the nonreligious, this eulogy will be meaningful if the content of the eulogy aligns with their worldview. Discussion of a religious afterlife or being "in a better place" will hold little comfort. Instead, nonreligious individuals craft eulogies from the cultural symbolism that they find meaningful, often drawing on scientific knowledge. The "Eulogy from a Physicist" by Aaron Freeman draws on the knowledge of the physical universe to explain how our energy is not destroyed upon death, but goes on existing in some other form. Here, a sort of after-death-longevity is defined from within the accepted scientific

---

2 http://www.griefbeyondbelief.org/about-us/mission-statement/.
3 http://openlysecular.org/toolkits-and-resources/.

worldview, intending to bring comfort and peace to those for whom religion is unable to sooth. While science has not conquered death, as is hoped for by some, it is providing resources for making-meaning, as the principle of energy conversion serves as the basis for this particular eulogy. Moreover, much of the meaning-making that brings the nonreligious consolation comes in actually celebrating the life of the loved one, not mourning their death.

Another outlet for these creating and disseminating crutches is the Openly Secular Coalition (OS). OS is a national campaign headed by Todd Stiefel from the Stiefel Freethought Foundation, which aims to eliminate anti-secular stigma by normalizing nonbelief. The coalition has several tool kits on a variety of topics for different demographics, and have added two additional resources, created by the authors, on managing and coping with death. These toolkits contain general information for the specific audience they are intended for, such as lists of resources, readings, complicated grief warning signs, and a host of other content, intended to provide support at the end of life. These resources contain things as simple as the types of phrases the nonreligious will find comforting and the types of phrases they will not, on the basis of their worldview.

Finally, the book *Funerals Without God* by Jane Wynne Wilson provides insight into presiding over nonreligious ceremonies. The main purpose of this booklet is help with end-of-life service planning for bereaved loved ones, as well as to help humanists thinking of going through training to become secular celebrants. Another group who may find parts of it useful are funeral directors, primarily when the family of the deceased has no wish to play an active role. By creating and disseminating this resource (Griswold 2003), Wilson has added another symbolic crutch to the nonreligious end-of-life toolkit (Swidler 1986).

These crutches are important for those who preside over death ceremonies, as they accomplish the necessary aspects of the ritual while presenting content that is meaningful to the nonreligious. Based on Fazzino's field notes (as described above concerning attire), normative expectations at atheist funerals are somewhat tenuous. While this provides a certain freedom of expression, this can also increase the potential for uncertainty at an inopportune time there are already high levels of stress and anxiety due to the loss of a loved one. Cultural crutches provide the often taken-for-granted schema of social interaction. With crutches in-hand, those who preside over nonreligious ceremonies have greater tools and resources with which to fulfill their social requirements.

5 Conclusion

Our research indicates that, in America, religious cultural tools are of little use to the nonreligious when it comes to managing the end of life. Furthermore, we have seen how differing interpretations of death problematizes and politicizes this already difficult aspect of life. This highlights the importance of creating secular death management infrastructure that is explicitly nonreligious. Such infrastructure will allow nonreligious individuals greater agency, with more resources readily available, and more cultural crutches waiting to be implemented, augmented and/or adapted for personal use. Our findings indicate that the nonreligious are in the process of expanding their cultural toolkits for dealing with death, making them better equipped to confront and cope with death.

While death at the macro level of society has been secularized in a number of ways, through processes of rationalization, medicalization, and the professionalization of the end-of-life, the interaction at and around the death remains potentially contentious, as members of varying (and at times, opposing) worldviews attempt to ritualize death in accordance with their worldview. Secular organizing has already provided a far greater cache of resources than existed even a decade or two ago. The problem of mortality can be thought of as yet another "terrain of resistance" (Routledge 1996, 517), in which an interwoven web of contested meanings, symbols, and ideologies between the religious and nonreligious have politicized the end of life, situating the nonreligious and their struggle for meaning, recognition, and resources within the domain of "cultural politics" (Buechler 2000). On one hand, the lack of an institutionalized death culture affords the nonreligious some freedom to manage death however they see fit, which is often appealing to the nonreligious with their strongly-held secular values of authenticity and individualism. On the other hand, recent efforts to establish a nonreligious death culture by the broader secular movement may unmask a historical legacy of cultural imperialism, as their end-of-life needs have previously been rendered invisible.

As nonreligious end-of-life-tools enter the wider cultural realm, they bring with them the potential to practice death and dying in new ways. If we imagine those instances in which our respondents encountered religion negatively at the end of life, these nonreligious tools bring the potential to overcome negative encounters with theism and to practice death in ways the nonreligious find meaningful. While palliative medicine searches for definitions of a "good death", we advocate that an equally important concept is the notion of "equitable death", or equal representation and access to resources at the end of life for all people. Our data indicates that the nonreligious often face an additional burden at death on the basis of their nonreligion. If our goal is equitable death and dying, then the nonreligious require access to the same cultural crutches which are currently available to religious individuals. We see nonreligious organizing at the end of life as an attempt to carve out a space in American culture for themselves and others who share their worldview, so that when others come to find themselves in similar situations, they have more resources at their disposal. As the nonreligious end-of-life-toolkit is expanded, we hope that nonreligious individuals will increasingly be able to find the resources they need during those difficult times.

Bibliographpy

Bachner, Yaacov G., Norm O'Rourke, and Sara Carmel. 2011. "Fear of Death, Mortality Communication, and Psychological Distress among Secular and Religiously Observant Family Caregivers of Terminal Cancer Patients." *Death Studies* 35(2): 163–187.
Bakker, Janel Kragt, and Jenell Paris. 2013. "Bereavement and Religion Online: Stillbirth, Neonatal Loss, and Parental Religiosity." *Journal for the Scientific Study of Religion* 52 (4): 657–674.
Beaman, Lori G. 2013. "The Will to Religion: Obligatory Religious Citizenship." *Critical Research on Religion* 1: 141–157.
Berger, Peter L. 1969. *The Sacred Canopy: Elements of a Sociological Theory of Religion*. Garden City, NY: Anchor Books.
Brewster, Melanie E., ed. 2014. *Atheists in America*. New York: Columbia University Press.
Buechler, Steven M. 2000. *Social Movements in Advanced Capitalism: The Political Economy and Cultural Construction of Social Activism*. Oxford: Oxford University Press.
Charmez, Kathy. 2014. *Constructing Grounded Theory*. Sage Publishing.
Cook, Corey L., Florette Cohen, and Sheldon Solomon. 2015. "What If They're Right About the Afterlife? Evidence of the Role of Existential Threat on Anti-Atheist Prejudice." *Social Psychological and Personality Science* 6(7): 840–846.
Cook, Corey L., Catherine A. Cottrell, and Gregory D. Webster. 2015. "No Good without God: Anti-Atheist Prejudice as a Function of Threats to Morals and Values." *Psychology of Religion and Spirituality* 7(3): 217–226.
Cragun, Ryan T. 2013. *What You Don't Know about Religion (but should)."* Durham: Pitchstone Publishing.
Edgell, Penny, Joseph Gerteis, and Douglas Hartmann. 2006. "Atheists as "Other": Moral Boundaries and Cultural Membership in American Society." *American Sociological Review* 71: 211–234.
Engelke, Matthew. "The Coffin Question: Death and Materiality in Humanist Funerals." *Material Religion* 11, no. 1 (2015), 26–49
Fazzino, Lori L. 2014. "Leaving the Church Behind: Applying a Deconversion Perspective to Evangelical Exit Narratives." *Journal of Contemporary Religion* 29(2): 249–266.
Fontana, Andrea, and Jennifer Reid Keene. 2009. *Death and Dying in America*. Cambridge, UK: Polity Press.
Garces-Foley, Kathleen. 2003. "Funerals of the Unaffiliated." *Omega* 46(4): 287–302.

Greenberg, Jeff, Sheldon Solomon, and Tom Pyszczynski. 1997. "Terror Management Theory of Self-esteem and Cultural Worldviews: Empirical Assessments and Conceptual Refinements." *Advances in Experimental Social Psychology* 29: 61–139.
Griswold, Wendy. 2003. *Cultures and Societies in a Changing World.* Thousand Oaks: Pine Forge.
Harrison, Peter. 2006. ""Science" and "Religion": Constructing the Boundaries". *The Journal of Religion.* 86(1): 81–106.
Kellehear, Allan. 2007. *A Social History of Dying.* New York: Cambridge University Press.
Lee, Lois. 2014. "Secular or Nonreligious? Investigating and Interpreting Generic 'Not Religious' Categories and Populations." *Religion* 44(3): 466–482.
Lin, Tiffany. 2014. "The Invisible 'Religious' Minority: Working with the Nonreligious Bereaved." MSW Thesis, California State University, Long Beach.
Lofland, Lyn. 1978. *The Craft of Dying: The Modern Face of Death.* Beverly Hills: Sage.
Manning, Christel J. 2015. *Losing Our Religion: How Unaffiliated Parents Are Raising Their Children.* New York: New York University Press.
Martin, David. 2007. "What I Really Said about Secularisation." *Dialog.* 46(2): 139–152.
Mellor, Philip A., and Chris Shilling. 1993. "Modernity, Self-Identity and the Sequestration of Death." *Sociology* 27(3): 411–431.
Nash, David S. 1995. "'Look in Her Face and Lose Thy Dread of Dying': The Ideological Importance of Death to the Secularist Community in Nineteenth-Century Britain." *The Journal of Religious History* 19(2): 158–180.
Norenzayan, Ara, Ilan Dar-Nimrod, Ian G. Hansen, and Travis Proulx. 2009. "Mortality Salience and Religion: Divergent Effects on the Defense of Cultural Worldviews for the Religious and the Non-religious." *European Journal of Social Psychology* 39(1): 101–113.
Routledge, Paul. 1996. "Critical Geopolitics and Terrains of Resistance." *Political Geography* 15: 509–531.
Seale, Clive. 1998. *Constructing Death: The Sociology of Dying and Bereavement.* Cambridge: University Press.
Smith-Stoner, Marilyn. 2007. "End-of-life Preferences for Atheists." *Journal of Palliative Medicine* 10: 923–928.
Speed, David, and Ken Fowler. 2016. "What's God Got to Do with It? How Religiosity Predicts Atheists' Health." *Journal of Religion and Health* 55(1): 296–308.
Swidler, Ann. 1986. "Culture in Action: Symbols and Strategies." *American Sociological Review* 51(2): 273–286
Toscani, Franco, Claudia Borreani, Paolo Boeri, and Guido Miccinesi. 2003. "Life at the End of Life: Beliefs about Individual Life After Death and "Good Death" Models: A Qualitative Study." *Health and Quality of Life Outcomes* 1:65–75.
Vail III, Kenneth E., Jaime Arndt, and Abdolhossein Abdollahi. 2012. "Exploring the Existential Functions of Religion and Supernatural Agent Beliefs among Christians, Muslims, Atheists, and Agnostics." *Personality and Social Psychology Bulletin* 38(10): 1288–1300.
Walter, Tony. 1991. "Modern Death: Taboo or Not Taboo?" *Sociology.* 25(2): 293–310.
Weber, Max. 1905. *The Protestant Ethic and the Spirit of Capitalism.* New York: Charles Scribner's Sons.
Wilkinson, Peter. J., and Peter G. Coleman. 2010. "Strong Beliefs and Coping in Old Age: A Case-based Comparison of Atheism and Religious Faith." *Ageing and Society.* 30(02): 337–361.

Young, Iris Marion. 1990 *Justice and the Politics of Difference*. Princeton: Princeton University Press.

Barry Kosmin
Old Questions and New Issues for Organized Secularism in the United States

1 Introduction

American secularism is a feature of American exceptionalism.[1] It is unique in its origins as well as its composition. I have suggested that American history since 1776 has produced alternations between eras of Christian religious 'awakenings' and periods of 'secular' or non-religious dominance and so, in effect, a continuous 'culture war' over the nature and purpose of the American nation (Kosmin 2014a). Recently national social trends seem to suggest the country is entering a new secular phase (Kosmin 2013). The ARIS 2008 findings showed that half of U.S households did *not* currently belong to a religious congregation and on the average Sunday 73% of Americans did *not* go to Church. While 27% of Americans did *not* anticipate a religious funeral, 30% of Americans did *not* believe in a personal biblical style God (Kosmin et al 2009). And more recent surveys have confirmed these data and trends so we may be at an important tipping point in U.S. history. The evidence demonstrates that the Zeitgeist, if not the Force, is with the secular and secularizing Nones and this development makes the analysis and study of secularism *per se* of major relevance for American social science.

Religious conservatism, faith-based initiatives, religion-related terrorism, the New Atheist texts, and increasing use of digital and 'social' media have energized and emboldened secularist advocates, networks, and organizations at both local and national levels. Accelerated growth in membership has been reported in recent years by nationwide organizations with clear secularist agendas including the Freedom From Religion Foundation (FFRF), Center for Inquiry (CFI), American Atheists (AA), American Humanist Association (AHA), Secular Student Alliance (SSA) and the Military Association of Atheists and Freethinkers (MAFF). On the intentional side, public advertising campaigns and events have been mounted in major cities. This new secularist surge of activism has been framed, in part, as an identity politics issue and movement in the United States. Some present themselves as members of a marginalized and maligned minority

---

[1] The terms secular, secularist/secularism, secularize, and secularization here are used in the sense discussed in the Introduction to this volume; referring respectively to non-religious, ideology that endorses non-religion, activities or process of reducing the influence of religion, and the outcome of that process.

(not unlike gays and lesbians) whose rights have been curtailed or denied (Cragun et al. 2012). Such efforts may be having an effect. References to atheists (or nonbelievers), even in the American 'public square', have become noticeably more frequent and prominent – such as, for example, President Barack Obama's inclusion of nonbelievers in his first inaugural address (Grossman 2009) and references to 'agnostic and atheist brothers and sisters' by speakers at anti-capitalist rallies (Landsberg 2011).

Nevertheless, until quite recently sociological work on secularization virtually ignored active or organized forms of atheism and the myriad of other secularist constructs or those that share criticism or rejection of religious ideas, behavior, or institutions, such as freethought, secular humanism, skepticism, positivism, and philosophical materialism or naturalism (Pasquale 2007; 2010). Colin Campbell noted '[t]he fact that irreligious movements act as agents of secularization has strangely enough been overlooked by sociologists in their contribution to the continuing secularization debate [...] one has to search hard to find examples of sociologists referring to material about irreligion in this context' (1971: 7). As Beckford summarized the matter:

> [T]hey have tended to overlook, omit or deliberately ignore the significance of both organized and diffuse attacks on religion. It is as if the progress of secularization could be adequately accounted for in terms of the effect of abstract cultural forces, such as class struggle or functional differentiation, without consideration of the agents and agencies that actively campaigned for secularism and secular societies. Given that a wide range of campaigns, movements and voluntary associations promoted secularism, rationalism, atheism and humanism in Britain and elsewhere, it is important to consider their direct and indirect contributions to secularization *and* to interpretations of secularization. (2003: 36)

It could be argued that in the U.S. the paucity of scholarly attention to organized secularism until recently was justified because it reflected the societal reality of the lack of institutionalization and divisions that has bedeviled free thinkers and secularists in the U.S. for more than a century. Only a small percentage of the millions who could be identified as Seculars belong to explicitly secularist groups. In fact, secularism could be described as a classic leaderless movement in America (Cragun & Fazzino, this volume). Despite accelerating growth in recent years, numbers of atheist and secularist group affiliates have always been, and remain, extremely small—not only with respect to the populations of the societies in which they emerge, but with respect to those people who reasonably may be characterized as substantially or thoroughly nonreligious (Budd 1977; Campbell 1971). Historically even during periods of substantially declining religiosity such as the 1930s and 1960s, secularist organizations failed to capitalize on their opportunity with even remotely proportionate growth rates (Demerath and Thiessen 1966; Warren 1943). As Steve Bruce (2002) and John Shook (this volume) have suggested, the natural resting state of secularity tends to be passive indifference to religion, apatheism, rather than active atheism or irreligion.

Secularist organizations (like the American Humanist Association, Council for Secular Humanism, Freedom From Religion Foundation and American Atheists) have been advocating secularization in the United States for decades, particularly as watchdogs regarding infringement of constitutional church-state separation. While their activities has triggered skirmishes with religious advocates along the way, incremental increases in the population of Nones seem more attributable to cultural, political, or demographic factors than to organized intentional activity. A surge of religious abandonment in the 1960s and 70s, for example, was largely attributable to developmental adolescent apostasy in the Baby Boom generation (Putnam and Campbell 2010). Some Baby Boomers returned to organized religion but many did not, giving way to increasing proportions of 'Nones' in succeeding cohorts as future generations were not raised in a religion. Hout and Fischer concluded that 'change in the religious preferences of believers in the 1990s contributed more to the increase in no religious preference than disbelief did' (2002: 178).

Much like organized religion, secularism is a diverse and pluralist tradition producing competing visions and organizations. Or, alternatively and negatively, it can be pictured as a weak worldview movement rent by lack of consensus on definitions and goals from its inception (Rectenwald, Mastiaux, this volume). Secularism has had a sectarian quality since its beginnings because of the manner in which diversity of philosophical approach to "human consciousness" as demonstrated in the Shook's elaborate taxonomy (this volume) were translated into calls for social and political action with regard to religion. This uncertainty has produced a variety of binaries that can be described as "soft" and "hard" secularism (Kosmin 2007). On one side is the "substitutionist" or "accommadationist" tradition of Holyoake, Huxley and Dewey, and before them the "soft" thinkers of the Enlightenment, such as John Locke, Adam Smith, and Thomas Jefferson, whose view of humanity led them to doubt that secularization would be sweeping, thorough and total. The Sunday Assembly (see chapters by Smith and Frost in this volume) may be seen as a contemporary illustration of this tradition. On the "hard" side stands the "eliminationist" and "confrontationist" tradition of "out Atheists" like Bradlaugh, Marxist-Leninists and nowadays the New Atheists (Campbell 1971, 54). The Atheist Alliance and the American Atheists (see chapters by Mastiaux, and Fazzino & Cragun in this volume) are contemporary examples of this second type.

Disagreements over strategy and style reflect these longstanding and deep ideological divisions among secularists (Richter and Langston this volume). In the contemporary U.S. the degree to which active atheism, particularly as advocated by the New Atheism, may have contrary effects – prompting religious backlash, promotion, and reactionary adherence – cannot be discounted (Bullivant 2010; Kosmin 2014b). This hostility to atheism as a result of its radical image, of course, is longstanding and consistent with the teachings of John Locke in *A Letter Concerning Toleration* (1689). As in the past, this negative reaction prompts debate and disagreement among secularists of varying stripes (e.g., Baggini 2007; Kurtz 2010; Uhl 2011). 'Moderates' often advocating a positive free standing secularism complain that acerbic or absolutist 'shock and awe tactics...polarize identities' and push otherwise moderate religious allies 'into the arms of the extremists' (Baggini 2007: 42, 44).

In the U.S. only a tiny percentage of freethinkers have ever been affiliated with secular organizations whereas around 60% of the religious population currently belongs to a congregation (Kosmin and Keysar 2009). The low rates of affiliation, mobilization and participation is even more problematic in the current circumstances of a rapid increase in the potential constituency for organized secularism. This deficiency is a familiar theme in secularist gatherings where the "faithful faithless" lament the failure of non-theist organizations to realize their full political and cultural potential– their inability to penetrate and mobilize their natural market. Secularist organizations today as in the past do indeed face a social marketing problem as the preceding chapters directly and indirectly evidence. Organized secularism in the U.S. has failed to affiliate even a fraction of the more than 10 million strong core constituency of self-identifying non-believers – the "hard secularists" (Kosmin 2007), those willing to self-identify as atheists and agnostics. Using wider theological or (un)belief criteria as by set out in Shook's "polysecularism" this target group could be even a larger and more sizeable demographic amounting to one in four Americans according to the findings of recent national surveys. Secularist organizations have no real need to proselytize since they already have a 50 million strong potential constituency of Nones. Organic economic and societal forces have created this social momentum towards mass secularity. Thus the present challenge for secularist organizations is not to produce growth but building the self-awareness and the mobilization of this population. The result of this lack of mobilization and structural weakness is most evident in the political arena where identifying Nones are almost non-existent and so the most under-represented population in the country in terms of political office holders.

2 Recruitment and Organizational Challenges

The religiosity of the United States, compared with other developed societies, can be attributed to a 'supply-side' proliferation of religious products in a comparatively free market. Secularism seems to have a similar trajectory (Kosmin and Keysar 2006). We can explain the sectarian syndrome of proliferating small secular groups, by applying an economic market model to secular choices that parallels the religious marketplace. When free of monopolistic or governmental control, religious products naturally proliferate to satisfy multiple needs and varying tastes. The demographic profile of secularist activists is heavy with educators and intellectuals. This means secular organizations spend lot of time and energy on mission statements and discussion of principles often without reaching consensus. But many more non-activist secularists remain unaffiliated.

There is an obvious need to explain the paradox of rapidly growing numbers of Nones alongside only a slight uptick in secular organization affiliates and so the weakness of organized secularism. The most significant cause is that most Nones are Apatheists as indifferent and uninterested in secularism as they are in religion (see Langston, Shook this volume). Individually they have undergone a secularization of consciousness in that they have lost any sense of sin, concern for day of judgement, afterlife, heaven and hell and many traditional social taboos. Yet paradoxically the rise of "individuation and personalization" (Hoesly this volume) has inhibited affiliation with overtly secularist organizations. Presumably, one constraint for most Nones is that many of their immediate family and friends are believers. In fact, in U.S. society most discrimination and hostility against non-believers arises from family and friends rather than strangers in institutional settings (Cragun et al. 2011).

The lack of consensus over nomenclature and boundaries highlighted in this volume reflects the tensions among secular people over secular identities. A typology based on "state of individual consciousness" produces a binary model of hard and soft secularisms (Kosmin 2007). This bifurcation of secular perspectives on philosophy and religion comprises only one dimension of this typology. The second dimension is based on the distinction between individuals and institutions. Here the individual aspect primarily pertains to states of consciousness while the institutional aspect relates to social structures and their cultural systems. In reality, these are not closed cells but ranges stretched between the polarities of the dimensions. A range of intermediate positions can and does exist between soft-soft and hard-hard secularism. In addition, the boundary between the individual and the institutions is not firm in real life. There is interplay that involves social expectations and constraints originating from institutions on the one hand and extreme subjective mental states that are individually based on the other. Given the intellectualism of secularists the outcome of all this is a predilection for sectarianism (Fazzino & Cragun, this volume).

The pioneering research on affiliation and membership patterns among secularists by Frank Pasquale (2007) highlighted this trend towards sectarianism. Nones tend to be individualists and skeptical of the value of organizations. They were never the types who joined the Elks, Rotarians and Masons, the traditional fraternal membership organizations, which are on the decline in the contemporary world of bowling alone. The character of the secular impulse itself tends to militate against institutional participation specifically on the basis of metaphysical world views. Pasquale goes as far as to suggest that many non-believers are "conflicted" about their own individual preferences and motives (Pasquale 2010: 2). Another factor that militates against affiliating most Nones is their individual psychological profile. They tend to be rather analytic and critical. They have difficulty endorsing standard statements of opinion. They would rather dissect and discuss than offer straight positions. Most dislike labels and labeling. Whereas atheists tend to be confident in their identity and hold strident opinions, by way of contrast the more numerous agnostics, humanists, and 'softer secularists", hold to more moderate and qualified opinions. Their openness to alternatives and unwillingness to commit to a single viewpoint makes them particularly hard to organize. Thus secularism unsurprisingly has no official hierarchy or leadership. The obvious contrast to this semi-anarchic situation among free thinkers is the authoritarian personality types found in fundamentalist religious groups (Ellison and Sherkat 1993), composed of individuals who are anxious to submit to an authority and to follow a charismatic and often disciplinarian leader.

The notion that secularization is linked to a preference for autonomy finds support elsewhere as well. Langston's research (this volume) tends to discredit ideological barriers and point out the psychological disposition and structural weaknesses and fractures that characterize secular organizations. Similarly, Bruce (2002) views the process of secularization as an individual process. While it can be characterized as affecting large collectivities, the decision to be secular is not a decision that is made at the group level. For Bruce, this decision is reached on an individual level. Each single individual makes up his or her own mind, however affected they may be by others, and therefore they all experience secularization as affirming their individual autonomy. The relationship of leaders to led is difficult because Nones tend to be suspicious of charisma and authority. Heightened individualism creates a mentality (if not the politics) whereby a majority is more libertarian than communitarian in organizational outlook. For example, Mastiaux (this volume) showed there is a large pool of secular sympathizers but there is a lack of secular missionaries.

Obviously, the small size of secularist organizations means a lack of resources and professionals (clergy). This in turn weakens recruitment efforts so there is little outreach activity. Another indicator of institutional weakness is a paucity of donors, particularly large givers, to subsidize outreach. This deficiency means secular organizations have to rely on self-recruitment largely (Mastiaux, Schultz, Smith, Frost, this volume) and on social media. As a result there is little face to face engagement. De Tocqueville saw voluntary organization as a strength and uniqueness of American society. Yet most types of membership organizations e.g. trades unions, fraternal organizations such as Elks, Masons etc. are in decline and suffer from the bowling alone syndrome that weakens many voluntary organizations today (Putnam,2000). Still, this is a particular problem for a contemporary movement that lacks inherited infrastructure and plant.

Added to those problems is the fact that most voluntary organizations are hit by burn out and turnover. This is a feature even of the student organizations SSA and CFI on college campuses. They operate in friendly markets with a constituency unburdened by family and job responsibilities but they face a difficult migratory structure namely a fast turnover of volunteer leadership (McGraw 2016). Today organized secularism faces a challenge in how to decide how to use to best advantage the groundswell of popular sentiment and opinion and the organic, secular trends in society and economy. We have to realize that membership organizations are hard to maintain and resource in today's society if you are not offering tangibles, power or salvation to your followers; if the goal is to fight for their hearts and minds but not their souls. Rational choice theorists (Stark 1999; Stark and Bainbridge 1985) argue that human beings pervasively depend upon the supernatural 'compensators' offered by salvational religion for unfulfilled worldly expectations and rewards. If true, that reality requires secularists to learn new ways and techniques to acquire people's loyalty.

The role of the Internet in creating networks of seculars into new organizational forms is a paramount concern for secular organizations. But how does that translate into changing people's sense of belonging or identification, which is necessary to grow a movement? The emergence of digital technologies (internet, social media) – another structural (or infrastructural) factor – is likely playing a role, particularly among the young (Addington, this volume). A young demographic is not hidebound by tradition so they are early adopters of technology. Atheists are a rare population, a geographically dispersed minority in many locations. Younger cohorts, in particular, who were weaned on the Web are considered ideal for creating 'imagined communities' and virtual movements through blogs, Internet-organized 'meet-ups', 'tweets' and 'open posts' (Cimino and

Smith 2011; Smith and Cimino 2012). These new media are enabling atheistic messages to reach larger audiences, no matter how remote or culturally insulated. How far this trend can overcome the face-to-face deficiencies only time will tell.

Another methodology which has been adopted by organized secularism recently is public signaling –stickers, flags, tee-shirts, advertising posters on buses and on the highways and Reason Rallies. In 2014 several secularist organizations joined together to create a new "Openly Secular" initiative (Openlysecular.org). The outrage and grievance peddling described by Mastiaux (this volume) as "moral Shock" is best seen in the FFRF strategy of seeking legal fights in middle America, suing local governments, school boards and police departments over prayers and religious symbols infringing the separation of church and state.

As we have noted, Nones tend to be individualists, not joiners. Most Nones also tend towards being political independents but that is not entirely true of secular activists. The profile of the leaders and members of secular organizations is an important factor in the image and appeal. Activist secularists and the leadership are overwhelmingly male, white, well educated, older, and affluent (Keysar, 2007). The social majority of secular activists in terms of race, education, age and income, regardless of where they live, has all the characteristics consistent with political conservatism and country club membership, or so one would think. The reality is otherwise. For example, 64% of the readers of the Council for Secular Humanism's of *Free Inquiry* self-identified in 2015 as Liberals or Progressives (Tom Flynn 2016). AA and AHA members tend to be even more likely to be social and political progressives (Fazzino & Cragun, this volume). This overlap between political liberalism and public secularity can be expected to deepen under the Trump administration.

Nevertheless, gender differences and minority representation are important differentiators that help explain the profile of identification groups and organizations. Men tend to be more militant than women and that factor is said to inhibit female recruitment. This has led to calls for more diversity by gender and race. So CFI has sponsored three Women in Secularism Conferences and AHA and CFI have established sub-groups for African-Americans. There is some recognition among secular activists of generational issues and an emphasis on recruiting Millenials. Indeed the student generation is very sympathetic to secularism but few seem to have the time or inclination to be activists, the interest to purchase secularist publications, or the resources to be donors (Kosmin 2014c).

As regards Hispanics and Asians, secular organizations are myopic. Research such as the Institute for the Study of Secularism in Society and Culture's (ISSSC) report on Latinos, has been ignored by secular organizations (Navarro et al). This failure epitomizes the short-sightedness problem of secularist organizations and their obliviousness to important facts and opportunities. The findings show that despite the stereotype of Latinos being a naturally religious community there is a new and expanding constituency of Nones among college educated and English-speaking Latinos. These people are totally invisible to the media, scholars and unfortunately to most secular organizations. The explanation is that they fail to fit the common stereotype of the religious Latino. That prejudice is explicable for the media that loves stereotypes and values exoticism and photogenic Catholic processions but secular organizations lose when they ignore social reality. The same deficiency reappears in their failure to outreach to Asian-Americans who ISSSC research has repeatedly identified as the most secularized population group in the country. In short, the leadership profile and membership ranks of organized secularism appear unlikely to be transformed in the near future.

3 Congregation and Community Models

The membership of religious congregations in the U.S. has a demographic profile very different from that of the secular organizations – older white males – as described above. The churches tend to disproportionally attract rural dwellers, African-Americans, older women and young families (Kosmin and Keysar 2006; Manning 2015). The secular Sunday Assemblies' constituency described by Smith and Frost (this volume) appears different again, having a distinct social background and psychological profile mainly composed of urban young singles, the proverbial Yuppies. Yet these "seekers" of groupness and community are very much a minority of the secular Nones (Schutz, Smith, this volume). This population's need for the support of others is often derided by the majority of the activist seculars, with their more individualistic and autonomous personalities particularly by "out Atheists" with grievances against religion or escaping what they see as personal trauma caused by religion. As we have noted expressive individualism is more common than collectivism among Nones. Nevertheless the Sunday Assembly movement has attracted attention from the media. It is regarded as a strategy that might overcome the problems and constraints of organized secularism with recruitment described above. Apparently the new technology and media work well for Sunday Assemblies as they do for Evangelicals. These movements are not as burdened by complicated and clergy-focused rituals as are Catholic and Orthodox Christianity, Judaism and Hinduism (Addington, this volume).

Historically the American population has been socialized to see the Protestant congregational model as normative. The cultural hegemony of organized religion and Christianity means that Non-Christian traditions, Jews, Buddhist, Muslims and Hindus have adopted this congregational structure in America. The Sunday Assembly's particular organizational structure is the lay led Protestant denomination with a liberal model of standardized services and notions of voluntary work towards the "common good". The medium is the message. The Sunday Assembly has adopted a familiar Protestant Christian format and style geared to its constituency of young Recovering Protestants meeting in a deconsecrated church on a Sunday morning.

Of course an organizational model of secularized congregations parallel to organized religion has been tried before by Ethical Culture, Humanistic Judaism and the Unitarians but it did not taken off as a mass movement. One reason is that Secular Humanism and atheism have found it difficult to easily reproduce the family and generational nexus of ties that religion offers. If the Sunday Assembly is to succeed it will need to provide the social provision typical of religious congregations such as welfare and charity work and early childhood education (Manning 2015). Secular ceremonies and life cycle rituals are obvious next steps. The Assemblies' predicament is whether to follow the Humanistic Judaism and Ethical Culture model and label themselves as a religion with clergy, thus gaining the attendant tax and legal advantages, or to utilize the Universal Life Church fiction (Hoesly this volume). Yet many secularists value radical purity and the sectarian and fissiparous tendencies that plague secularism have already affected the Assembly movement with the rise of the "splitters" of Godless Revival (Smith; Fazzino and Cragun, this volume)

It is worth placing the Sunday Assembly in the comparative context of the earlier efforts at secular congregationalism because it provides insights into the particular dilemmas organized secularism faces. Ethical Culture (American Ethical Union) was founded by Felix Adler in New York City in 1877. Adler was a deconverted rabbi and son of a Reform Rabbi. Very much a "progressive" he organized Sunday meetings in an attempt to offer a more universalistic, ethnicity free inclusive organization. Ethical Culture offered life cycle rituals. Its motto was "deed not creed" and it was geared to urban social action sponsoring a kindergarten, school and housing and philanthropic projects (Radest 1969). Humanistic Judaism, the "Saturday Assembly" – a Judaism without God- was founded in Michigan in 1963 by Rabbi Sherwin Wine (Rowens 2004). It has 30 congregations and 10,000 members in the U.S. Compared to Ethical Culture and the Sunday Assembly its services offers more ritualistic ceremonies that reflect the heritage of the audience, including censored traditional Hebrew texts. It is socially progressive, welcomes "intermarried" couples and operates gender equality (Chalom 2010).

The secular congregations may be viewed as close to Comte's vision of religions of humanity. And their placement on the soft side of secularism makes them open to joining ecumenical religious coalitions and civic alliances with liberal religious traditions and so fitting into the civic life of mainstream America. The public's demand for life cycle rituals and particularly state recognized marriage ceremonies encouraged Humanistic Judaism and Ethical Culture to claim official status as religions and recruit clergy as state recognized marriage officers. That strategy provides tax privileges (e.g. clergy parsonage tax relief) and legal autonomy for the congregation (the same fiction described by Hoesly for the ULF). The exploitation of unique U.S. constitutional provisions particularly freedom from financial supervision (e.g. exemption from the the need to submit IRS Form 990 that applies to other non-profit organizations) favors organized religion and disadvantages organized secularism unless it compromises. One response is to establish secular celebrant training program and several secularist organizations have begun campaigns for state recognition (e.g. Indiana 2016). Alongside that, they can fight for a level playing field and true equality e.g. the FFRF claim for parsonage tax relief (*Freethought Today*, Vol 33 No 5 June/ July 2016).

Burial and death rituals are less subject to state intervention than marriage licensing but consumerism and market forces are more at play. The ARIS 2008 finding, which discovered that 27% of Americans do not expect to have a religious funeral, was a surprise. But it was noted by funeral directors and that industry has responded to market forces such as the rising demand for cremation (*The Pittsburgh Post-Gazette*, 8.21.2015) Structural forces such as the existence of an established industry makes it difficult for secular organizations to exploit the rising preference for non-religious interment. A secular community can offer support and consolation in bereavement but this remains a family arena and most families still have a religious majority that sees secular "toolkits" as having an emotional deficit (MacMurray, this volume) compared with traditional religious burial and mourning rituals.

4 Appropriation of the Civic Square

One of the weaknesses of organized secularism is its lack of imagination and opportunism in claiming territory and furthering its cause using the existing agencies that advance the common good in society. Organized secularism's myopia is probably due to its fractured nature and poor leadership. In fact, a wider notion of secularism with more extravagant claims is possible and this could make it more recognized and mainstream in society. For example, secularists have not focused recently on the role of the public school as a mass secularizing and secular organization. The philosopher John Dewey saw this opportunity to use the American public school to promote a democratic secular education based on freedom, equality, social cohesion and commitment to Human Rights as against the separatism and religious segregation of faith schools (Dewey 1916).

Campbell concluded that '[t]he irreligious movements of the nineteenth and twentieth centuries assisted in the secularization of society in the sense that they promoted and accelerated the disengagement of various social institutions and activities from the legitimation and control of religion' (1971: 121–122). Most sociologists who studied these phenomena characterized them as loose-knit or ideologically 'diffuse' (Budd 1967), organizationally 'precarious' (Demerath and Thiessen 1966), frequently short-lived, and of negligible significance overall. Campbell attributed these judgments to a tendency to approach these phenomena with religious (read: Christian) organizations in mind. This, he argued, is inappropriate. It obscures the distinctive social forms and activities through which such constructs have played secularizing roles. These tend to be task-specific, educational, political, or associational (rather than communal). As such they have more in common with labor unions, political movements, or advocacy groups than with church congregations or communities. Campaigns against religious blasphemy laws, challenges to science, or moral legislation and for church-state separation or rights to privacy and alternative lifestyles have undoubtedly had some secularizing (and liberalizing or individualizing) effects.

An obvious arena for enhancing secularization has been sports and recreation. In 1934 religion, i.e. the churches, lost the struggle against Sunday professional baseball (Bevis 2003). The growing influence of major sports corporations in the transformation of Sunday is best expressed in the history of the National Football League's Super Bowl. It has been played on Sunday since 1967 and it is now widely recognized as a national secular holiday (MacCambridge 2004). The Olympic Movement, with its ethos and hymn, can also be envisaged as part of the international secular realm. Sports compete with religious activities in time use and under Title IX it emancipates women to the detriment of conservative religions.

Whether the emphasis is on science, politics or any other area of life, it seems that secularists support efforts, public or private, that justify their belief systems and advance society in the direction they believe it should go, which is almost without exception in the way of progress. In this view, old and outdated ways of thinking, often entrenched in religion, are just anchors that hold society back from that progress. Secularists' relationship to the arts and culture is a key area of potential strength—and one that challenges the German sociologist Max Weber's dictum that the process of secularization in the West was part of the disenchantment of the world, a process whereby magic and mystery were banished from the mainstream of our culture (Weber 1905). Such criticism of modernity and the associated triumph of science and rationalism, maintains that a secular society and culture has no place for the spiritual, the sublime or the romantic. Yet a visit to any of the nation's museums and art galleries dispels this conclusion. These public institutions are secular shrines and places of deep meaning in contemporary culture. Americans view museums, art galleries and public libraries as places of awe and reverence characterized by silence and decorum. The secularizing influence of science and natural history museums is obvious, otherwise there would be no need for a rival Bible-oriented Creation Museum in Kentucky.

Most public museums' mission statements reflect the heritage of Renaissance-style humanism and the Enlightenment, the essential harbingers of secularism. Museums do an excellent job of conveying secular values by stating their hopes to inspire people of all backgrounds by imbuing them with a greater appreciation for human achievement and diversity. The nation's cultural institutions espouse pluralistic values and court broad audiences implicitly offering visitors, from every background a chance to connect with one another through dialogue and shared experiences with the arts. The impulse to universalize goes hand in hand with the tendency to secularize. One can see museums as temples of a sort: temples of culture and memory. Older museums are notable for their classical i.e. pre-Christian architecture. The contemporary museum is often heavy on glass, suggesting the absence of boundaries, again a very secular concept.

Similarly early public expressions of the secular with a clear aim and purpose, both personal and civic, were the higher educational institutions, inspired by the Enlightenment. Again visually, they tended to looked back to classical pre-Christian Greek models symbolized in architecture e.g. Doric columns. The prime example is Jefferson's University of Virginia 1818, an "academical village" and "temple of knowledge" inspired by his passion for Palladian architecture and Greek philosophers. Likewise the utilitarian philosopher Jeremy Bentham was the "spiritual founder" of the entirely secular University College London (1826) the "godless college" that ended the hitherto Anglican religious monopoly of university education in England. UCL unsurprisingly was the first to admit students regardless of their religion and the first to admit women on equal terms with men.

Unfortunately, the inability of secularists and secular organizations to assert themselves as the guardians of high culture and of the heritage of civic cultural institutions also has linkages to their paucity of language and failure to create a uniquely secular vocabulary:

When an atheist feels "awe" when considering the majesty of nature, at present they have just one term to describe that – a "spiritual" experience. And that term is owned by the religious. Humanists need new terminology (e.g., a "human" experience) to describe phenomena like this that are secular in orientation else they will cede this ground to the religious. (Cragun & Kosmin 2011).

5 Future Prospects

Opening up a new field like the study of secularism, which lacks a common terminology and tools of analysis, is a learning process. Analyzing the relationship of secular identity to boundaries and group membership is a challenge due to this lack of conceptual clarity. Nevertheless, we have to study secularism not as the mirror image of religion nor using a theological paradigm. As the contributions to this volume suggest, secularism requires a new conceptual armory so it can be understood as an intellectual and social force in its own right.

On a practical level, organized secularism tries to keep up and remain relevant to a society and culture that is constantly evolving. Yet alongside new issues, old questions return and this volume highlights the challenges secular organizations face working out their values and policies on a whole range of issues. Organized secularism, reflecting the range of agendas of polysecularism (Shook, this volume), should have an advantage going forward because of its ability to rationally answer society's growing bio-medical, environmental and climate change challenges and the ethical issues created by accelerating scientific and technological advances. Also on the individual level, despite their differences of style and approach (Fazzino & Cragun, this volume) secularist organizations do have a firm consensus about personal issues such as gender, abortion, and dignity in death. This agreement or common purpose provides a firm basis for alliances among secularist organizations and has the potential to make them more relevant and influential in the future. Their growing coherence could be accelerated if organized secularism could overcome its main structural weaknesses, lack of resources due to poor recruitment and fund-raising (Fazzino & Cragun, this volume). Here secularism stands in marked contrast to the highly mobilized and remarkably well-funded (often by tithing) Religious Right. This weakness can be viewed as the secular free rider problem. Here I should declare an interest not only as the founding director of the first and still only existing academic research institute on secularism only but also as a member of the Board of Directors of the Center for Inquiry. Organized secularism cannot flourish without adequate resources. As with any start-up the solution is an injection of substantial funds. Somehow, progressive populations such as the young, wealthy, socially progressive tech elite of places like Silicon Valley need to be persuaded that their social, economic, political and personal career interests lie with support for the secular cause.

Bibliography

Baggini, Julian. 2007. Toward a more mannerly secularism. *Free Inquiry*, 27(2): 41–44.
Beckford, James A. 2003. *Social theory & religion*. Cambridge, U. K.: Cambridge University Press.
Bevis, Charlie. 2003. *Sunday Baseball: The Major Leagues' Struggle to Play Baseball on the Lord's Day, 1876–1934*. Jefferson, NC: Mcfarland.
Bruce, Steve. 2002. *God is Dead: Secularization in the West*, Malden, MA: Blackwell.
Flynn, Tom. 2016. "Politically Speaking," *Secular Humanist Bulletin*, Vol.32 (2), 1.
Budd, S. 1977. *Varieties of unbelief: Atheists and agnostics in English society: 1850–1960*. London: Heinemann.
Bullivant, S. 2010. "The new atheism and sociology: Why here? Why now? What next?" In Amarnath Amarasingam (Ed.), *Religion and the New Atheism: A critical appraisal*, 109–124. Leiden, Belgium: Brill.
Chalom, Rabbi Adam. 2010. *Introduction to Secular Humanistic Judaism*, Lincolnshire, IL: International Institute for Secular Humanistic Judaism.
Campbell, C. 1971. *Toward a sociology of irreligion*. New York: Herder and Herder.
Cimino, R. and Smith, C. 2011. "The New Atheism and the formation of the imagined secularist community." *Journal of Media and Religion*, 10(1): 24–38.
Cragun, Ryan T., Kosmin, B., Keysar, A., Hammer, J. H., and Nielsen, M. 2012. "On the receiving end: Discrimination toward the non-religious in the United States." *Journal of Contemporary Religion*, 27(1): 105–127.
Cragun, Ryan and Barry A. Kosmin. 2011. "Repackaging Humanism as 'Spirituality': Religion's New Wedge Strategy for Higher Education," *Free Inquiry*, 31(4),30–33.
Demerath, N. J. III and Thiessen, V. (1966). On spitting against the wind: Organizational precariousness and American irreligion. *American Journal of Sociology*, 71: 674-687.
Dewey, John. 1916. *Democracy and Education*, New York: The Macmillan Company.
Grossman, C. L. (2009). "An inaugural first: Obama acknowledges non-believers." *USA Today*, 22 January.
Ellison, Christopher G. and Darren E. Sherkat. 1993. "Obedience and Autonomy: Religion and Parental Values Reconsidered." Journal for the Scientific Study of Religion 32(4):313–29.
Hout, Michael, and Claude S. Fischer. 2002. "Why more Americans have no religious preference: Politics and generations." *American Sociological Review*, 67: 165–190.
Keysar, Ariela. 2007. "Who are America's atheists and agnostics?" In Barry A. Kosmin and Ariela Keysar, (Eds.), *Secularism and Secularity: Contemporary International Perspectives,* 33–39. Hartford, CT: Institute for the Study of Secularism in Society and Culture (ISSSC), Trinity College.
Kosmin, Barry A. and Ariela Keysar. 2006. *Religion in a Free Market,* Ithaca, NY: Paramount Market Publishing, Hartford, CT: ISSSC, Trinity College.

Kosmin, Barry A. and Ariela Keysar. 2009a. *American Nones: A profile of the no religion population*. Hartford, CT: ISSSC, Trinity College.

Kosmin, Barry A. and Ariela Keysar. 2009b. *American Religious Identification Survey (ARIS 2008)*. Hartford, CT: ISSSC, Trinity College.

Kosmin, Barry A. and Juhem Navarro-Rivera. 2012. *The Transformation of Generation X: Shifts in Religious and Political Self-Identification 1990–2008*. Hartford, CT: ISSSC, Trinity College.

Kosmin, Barry A. 2007. Contemporary secularity and secularism. In Barry A. Kosmin and Ariela Keysar (Eds.), *Secularity and secularism: Contemporary international perspectives*, 1–13.

Kosmin, Barry A. 2013. "The Unexpected Rise of Secularity in the United States 1990–2008," *Ethique, Politique, Religions*, Garnier, Paris, 2013, 1, No.2, 143–162

Kosmin, Barry A. 2014a. "Secular Republic or Christian Nation? The Battlefields of the American Culture War" In Christopher Hartney, ed. *Secularisation: New Historical Perspectives*, Newcastle-upon-Tyne, U.K.: Cambridge Scholars Publishing, pp.151–172.

Kosmin, Barry A. 2014b. "The Vitality of Soft Secularism in the United States and the Challenge Posed by the Growth of the Nones," in Jacques Berlinerblau, *Sarah Fainberg and Aurora Nou*, Eds., *Secularism on the Edge: Rethinking Church-State Relations in the United States, France and Israel*. New York: Palgrave MacMillan, pp.35–50.

Kosmin, Barry A. 2014c. "American Secular Identity, Twenty-First Century Style: Secular College Students in 2013," *Free Inquiry*, Vol. 34, (2014), No. 3, 1–11.

Kosmin, Barry A. 2014d. "The Secular Are Skeptics: The Worldviews of Today's University Students," *Skeptical Inquirer*, Vol.38, (2014), No. 4, 38–41.

Kosmin, Barry A. 2016. "An evidence-based strategy or sustaining the growth of unbelief," *Free Inquiry*, 36 (3), 2016, 38–43.

MacCambridge, M. (2004) *America's Game: The Epic Story of How Pro Football Captured a Nation* (New York: Random House).

McGraw Stef. 2016. "Campus Update," *Secular Humanist Bulletin*, Vol.32 (2),.8.

Manning, Christel. 2015. *Losing our religion*. New York: New York UniversityPress.

Navarro-Rivera, Juhem, Barry A. Kosmin and Ariela Keysar. 2010. *U.S. Latino Religious Identification 1990–2008: Growth, Diversity & Transformation*, Hartford, CT: ISSSC, Trinity College,

Pasquale, Frank L. 2007. "The 'Nonreligious' in the American Northwest." In Barry A. Kosmin and Ariela Keysar, (Eds.), *Secularism and Secularity: Contemporary International Perspectives, 33–39*. Hartford, CT: ISSSC, Trinity College.

Pasquale, Frank L. 2010. A Portrait of secular Group Affiliates. In *Atheism and Secularity*, edited by Phil Zuckerman, vol I, 43–88. Santa Barbara, CA, Praeger.

Putnam, Robert. D. 2000. *Bowling Alone: The Collapse and Revival of American Community*. New York: Simon & Schuster.

Putnam, Robert .D. and Campbell, D.E. 2010. *American grace: How religion divides and unites us*. New York: Simon & Schuster.

Radest, Howard. 1969. *Toward Common Ground: The Story of the Ethical Societies in the United States*. Ungar, New York

Rowens, Marilyn. 2004. *A Life of Courage: Sherwin Wine and Humanistic Judaism*. Lincolnshire, IL: IISHJ.

Smith, C. and Cimino, R. (2012). "Atheisms unbound: The role of the new media in the formation of a secularist identity." *Secularism and Nonreligion*, 1(1): 17–34.
Stark, R. 1999. "Secularization, R.I.P." *Sociology of Religion*, 60(3): 249–273.
Stark, R. and Bainbridge, W.S. 1985. *The future of religion: Secularization, revival, and cult formation*. Berkeley, CA: University of California Press
Uhl, S. (2011). "Secular humanism is atheism." *Free Inquiry*, 31(2): 28–29.
Warren, S. (1943). *American freethought: 1860–1914*. New York: Columbia University Press.
Weber, Max and S. Kalberg. 2009 [1905]. *The Protestant Ethic and the Spirit of Capitalism, With other writings on the Rise of the West*. New York, Oxford University Press.

Index

Abington School District v. Schempp   3, 22, 67, 126
accommodation   36, 105, 167 f., 178 f., 181, 183, 186, 188, 191–194, 202, 205, 207, 215, 217, 247
Adler, Felix   310
African American   154, 308 f.
American Association for the Advancement of Atheism   16–19, 27, 67
American Atheists   4, 19, 22 f., 59 f., 63 f., 66–69, 76–79, 81, 106, 165 f., 177, 224, 232, 235, 246, 263, 293, 301, 303, 308
American Civil Liberties Union   1, 224
American Ethical Union   64, 81, 310
American Humanist Association   15, 23, 28, 63–73, 76–79, 81, 107, 261, 301, 303, 308
American Religious Identification Survey   216, 301, 311
American Secular Census   196, 209–214, 216
apatheism   97, 303
Arisian, Khoren   274
Asian American   309
Atheist Alliance International   224
Atheist Alliance of America   64, 102 f., 105, 107 f., 224
Atlanta Freethought Society   225, 230, 232, 242, 246

Barker, Dan   63, 69
Bentham, Jeremy   313
boundary   92, 137, 142, 147 f., 159, 172, 176, 179, 184, 188 f., 255, 305
Brights   78, 228
Budd, Susan   191, 215, 302, 312
Bund für Geistesfreiheit Bayern   225
Bush, George W.   231

Campbell, Colin   4, 32, 61, 114, 191 f., 302 f., 312
Camp Quest   63, 81, 224
celebrant   65 f., 179, 253, 259, 261 f., 275, 296, 311

Center for Inquiry   59, 69, 71 f., 75, 78 f., 107, 165, 261 f., 273, 301, 307 f., 314
Chambers, Bette   63, 70, 73 f.
Christianity   3, 14 f., 18, 20–22, 24, 27 f., 32, 35, 51, 53, 96, 193, 217, 240 f., 263, 287, 309 f.
church and state   69, 99, 103, 107 f., 119 f., 126, 166, 180, 194, 202, 221, 224, 229, 263, 303, 308, 312
churches   8, 16, 24, 28, 40, 74, 104, 107, 120, 123 f., 127, 157, 228, 230, 257, 260, 265 f., 268, 309, 312
Comte, Auguste   36 f., 43, 311
confrontation   50, 103, 105 f., 143, 167, 179, 183, 247
congregations   8, 28, 66, 124, 128, 152–160, 162–164, 168, 171, 173, 192, 263, 309–312
Council for Secular Humanism   59 f., 63 f., 69, 71 f., 76–79, 81, 303, 308

Darwin Day   242
deism   106
democracy   16, 105, 282
De Tocqueville, Alexis   307
Dewey, John   22, 24, 66, 303, 312
diversity   7 f., 48, 62, 82, 89, 97, 99, 109, 118, 129, 167 f., 204, 215, 226 f., 233, 255, 265, 279, 303, 308, 313
Doer, Edd   63, 81
donations   69, 80, 124
DuBois, W.E.B.   66
Dunak, Karen   255, 259

Edgell, Penny   1, 113, 115, 125, 129, 145, 147, 166, 284
Edwords, Fred   63, 70, 73
elimination   17, 32, 50, 78, 192–194, 202, 205, 207, 215–217, 303
Ethical Culture Society   19, 104, 152, 192, 262, 274, 310 f.
ethics   1, 20 f., 25, 32, 36, 40, 42, 44, 50 f., 97, 100, 102, 105–107, 124, 151, 166, 199

frame bridging 229
Freedom From Religion Foundation 1, 59f., 64, 68f., 76–79, 81, 177, 301, 303, 308, 311
Free Inquiry 36, 43, 45, 59, 63, 71, 167, 308
Freeman, George 257, 265, 295

Gaylor, Annie Laurie 59, 69, 77
gender 61, 78, 146, 154, 195f., 206f., 209f., 215, 226, 308, 310, 314
German Democratic Republic 240
Germany 5, 9, 174f., 221f., 224f., 230, 240, 248
goals 61f., 81, 91f., 98f., 103, 114–116, 130, 137, 164–166, 168, 176, 179, 192, 194f., 198, 200, 202f., 205f., 208f., 224, 229, 235f., 238, 244, 246f., 303
Grimes, Ronald 271, 274
group identity 8, 101

humanism 3, 13–16, 18–26, 28, 60, 65, 72, 78, 98, 103–105, 107, 137, 167, 179, 234, 254, 274, 302, 310, 313
Humanistische Union 224
Humanist Society 27
HUUmanists 66

ideal types 9, 121, 223, 227, 236
Ingersoll, Robert G. 66
Institute for the Study of Secularism in Society and Culture 308f.
Internal Revenue Service 263, 265, 311
irreligion 13–15, 20, 26f., 61, 77, 88f., 100, 191, 302f.

Jefferson, Thomas 106, 303, 313
Johnson, James Hervey 67, 78
justice 13, 45, 97, 164, 199, 204, 209, 258, 274, 281, 283

Kettell, Steven 62, 108, 173, 177–180, 188, 191, 193f., 204, 208, 217, 223
Kirschenbaum, Howard 258
Knott, Kim 274
Kurtz, Paul 14f., 22, 24, 57, 59–61, 66, 69–73, 75–78, 80, 82, 289, 304

labels 113f., 117, 138, 167, 179, 195, 197f., 208f., 236, 267, 272f., 279, 285, 306
Lamont, Corliss 70f., 78, 139, 141, 274
Latino 154, 308f.
LeDrew, Stephen 57, 61, 106, 108, 113, 116, 135, 173, 177f., 193, 222, 228, 234
Lee, Lois 6, 92, 114, 116, 157, 173f., 177, 189, 222, 231, 242, 273, 275, 286
liberalism 90, 107, 193, 308

Mead, Rebecca 255, 258
meditation 118, 120, 128f., 266f.
Military Association of Atheists and Freethinkers 81, 301
Minnesota Atheists 225, 231f., 242
modernity 89f., 279f., 313

naturalism 41, 104, 157, 302
Naylor, Sharon 259
New Atheism 27, 61, 87, 108f., 113, 137, 165, 168, 173, 177–179, 192–194, 221, 247, 303f.
Newman, Carol 37f., 47, 259
non-overlapping magisteria 105f., 108
non-profit organizations 121, 311

Obama, Barack 302
O'Hair, Madalyn Murray 3f., 19, 22, 28, 57, 59f., 67–69, 71–77, 80, 82, 215, 232, 263
Olympic Movement 312
online communities 28, 140, 146f.
Openly Secular 64, 76, 296, 308
organizational identity 116, 120f., 130
organization theory 114f.

Paine, Thomas 31, 66
personality 67, 71–76, 101, 244, 246, 306
Pinn, Anthony 125
pluralism 15f., 20, 89, 109
psychologist's fallacy 92, 94, 96
psychology 94

rationalism 51, 105f., 199, 302, 313
Reason Rally 60f., 63f.
Religious Right 26, 80f., 162, 231, 314
religious studies 7, 15, 61, 88, 92, 222, 272

Index — 321

ritual   7f., 19, 103f., 151, 156f., 159–162, 164f., 168, 172–174, 176, 178f., 181, 184–186, 188, 238, 243, 253, 255f., 258–260, 263f., 270f., 273f., 281, 294, 296, 309–311

San Francisco Atheists   224, 232, 238f.
science   13, 32, 36f., 41–43, 50f., 61, 75, 78, 87, 100, 103–106, 108, 122, 124, 136, 145, 161, 168, 175, 177f., 193f., 199, 201, 205, 242, 266, 279, 289f., 296, 301, 312f.
– science and religion   105, 191, 205, 207
Secular Coalition for America   64, 81
secularism   1–10, 13–16, 20f., 25, 31–33, 36–44, 47–53, 57–59, 61f., 64, 71–73, 76f., 80, 88–91, 93, 98–101, 109, 126, 145, 151, 156, 162, 165, 168, 178, 191, 212, 224, 234, 237, 253, 272–274, 301–311, 313f.
– polysecularism   7, 87, 89, 98–102, 106, 108f., 304, 314
secularity   31, 33, 36, 42, 51–53, 87–93, 95–101, 104, 108f., 117, 138, 144, 147, 151, 155f., 158, 160, 162–168, 172–223, 254, 275, 279f., 303f., 308
– polysecularity   7, 87, 89, 97, 101f., 105, 108f., 167
secularization   15, 19, 51–53, 61, 89f., 95f., 99, 104, 255, 258, 262, 279f., 301–303, 305f., 312
Secular Student Alliance   63f., 72, 224, 301, 307
Secular Studies   7, 88, 90, 92, 98
Seligson, Marcia   259
Silicon Valley   315
skepticism   33, 97, 102, 106, 114, 118, 120f., 125, 197, 224, 302
socializing   120, 213, 222, 224f., 248
social media   117, 135–138, 147, 153, 162f., 290, 307
social movement organization   5, 57–60, 80, 82
Society for Humanistic Judaism   63f., 81
sociologist's fallacy   92, 94, 96
Speckhardt, Roy   63, 66, 79–81
spiritual but not religious   255, 260, 273f.

spirituality   128f., 147, 161, 165, 172, 178, 184f., 187f., 258f., 262, 266, 272–274
status   9, 19f., 23, 28, 50, 67, 90, 107, 121, 141f., 151–153, 167, 179, 191, 193, 216, 263, 268, 284f., 292, 311
Stensrud, Rockwell   258
stereotypes   88, 93, 116, 239, 309
Stigma   33, 77, 115, 129, 146, 166, 200f., 214f., 248, 296
Sunday Assembly   8, 27f., 102, 104f., 118, 151–168, 171f., 174–176, 178–189, 192, 285, 303, 309f.
Supreme Court   13f., 19–22, 25, 67, 126, 230, 264

tax-exempt   67, 263
Texas   21, 68, 114, 117, 126f., 140, 195, 231, 234, 263
The Humanist   27, 63, 65f., 69–71, 73, 107, 118, 130, 167, 261, 273, 285
theology   7, 17f., 36, 41, 43f., 47f., 50, 53, 88–91, 93, 103, 162, 164, 191, 229, 281
The Truthseeker   67
typology   9, 102, 113f., 117, 120f., 221–223, 227f., 232, 236, 305

Unitarian Universalism   20, 28, 37, 65f., 104, 128, 157, 192, 230, 261f., 310
United States of America   222
Universal Life Church   9, 28, 253–258, 261–265, 267–275, 310
Universal Life Church Monastery   256f., 265
University College London   313
University of Virginia   313

volunteering   8, 120, 127, 175, 183
– charity   127, 152, 164, 183, 198f., 208, 310

Weber, Max   158, 279, 312f.
Wilson, Edwin   44, 65f., 258, 260, 296
Wine, Sherwin   310
Wolf, Gary   221
Women in Secularism Conference   308

Zindler, Frank   59, 64, 68, 74
Zuckerman, Phil   9, 88, 113, 116, 125, 127, 129, 145, 147, 163, 222, 274, 287

www.ingramcontent.com/pod-product-compliance
Lightning Source LLC
Chambersburg PA
CBHW031723230426
43669CB00007B/216